Contemporary
Developments in
Indonesian Islam

The **Institute of Southeast Asian Studies (ISEAS)** was established as an autonomous organization in 1968. It is a regional centre dedicated to the study of socio-political, security and economic trends and developments in Southeast Asia and its wider geostrategic and economic environment. The Institute's research programmes are the Regional Economic Studies (RES, including ASEAN and APEC), Regional Strategic and Political Studies (RSPS), and Regional Social and Cultural Studies (RSCS).

ISEAS Publishing, an established academic press, has issued more than 2,000 books and journals. It is the largest scholarly publisher of research about Southeast Asia from within the region. ISEAS Publishing works with many other academic and trade publishers and distributors to disseminate important research and analyses from and about Southeast Asia to the rest of the world.

Contemporary Developments in
Indonesian Islam

Explaining the "Conservative Turn"

EDITED BY

MARTIN VAN BRUINESSEN

ISEAS

INSTITUTE OF SOUTHEAST ASIAN STUDIES

Singapore

First published in Singapore in 2013 by
ISEAS Publishing
Institute of Southeast Asian Studies
30 Heng Mui Keng Terrace, Pasir Panjang
Singapore 119614

E-mail: publish@iseas.edu.sg • Website: bookshop.iseas.edu.sg

The responsibility for facts and opinions in this publication rests exclusively with the authors and their interpretations do not necessarily reflect the views or the policy of the publisher or its supporters.

ISEAS Library Cataloguing-in-Publication Data

Contemporary developments in Indonesian Islam: explaining the "conservative turn" / edited by Martin van Bruinessen.
1. Islam—Indonesia—20th century.
2. Radicalism—Religious aspects—Islam—Indonesia.
3. Islam and politics—Indonesia.
4. Muslim—Indonesia.
5. Majelis Ulama Indonesia.
6. Muhammadiyah (Organization).
7. Komite Persiapan Penegakan Syariat Islam.
I. Bruinessen, Martin van.
BP63 15C761   2013

ISBN   978-981-4414-56-2 (soft cover)
ISBN   978-981-4414-57-9 (E-book PDF)

Cover Photo Credit:
Placard carried along in an FPI demonstation against liberal Islam. Photographed by Ahmad Najib Burhani.

Typeset by International Typesetters Pte Ltd
Printed in Singapore by Mainland Press Pte Ltd

CONTENTS

List of Indonesian Muslim Organizations and Institutions   vii

Acknowledgements   xxv

Glossary   xxvii

About the Contributors   xxxiii

1. Introduction: Contemporary Developments in Indonesian   1
    Islam and the "Conservative Turn" of the Early
    Twenty-first Century
    Martin van Bruinessen

2. Overview of Muslim Organizations, Associations and   21
    Movements in Indonesia
    Martin van Bruinessen

3. Towards a Puritanical Moderate Islam: The Majelis Ulama   60
    Indonesia and the Politics of Religious Orthodoxy
    Moch Nur Ichwan

4. Liberal and Conservative Discourses in the Muhammadiyah: 105
    The Struggle for the Face of Reformist Islam in Indonesia
    Ahmad Najib Burhani

5. The Politics of Shariah: The Struggle of the KPPSI in   145
    South Sulawesi
    Mujiburrahman

6. Mapping Radical Islam: A Study of the Proliferation of   190
    Radical Islam in Solo, Central Java
    Muhammad Wildan

7. Postscript: The Survival of Liberal and Progressive Muslim   224
    Thought in Indonesia
    Martin van Bruinessen

Index   233

LIST OF INDONESIAN MUSLIM ORGANIZATIONS AND INSTITUTIONS

Aisyiah   Muhammadiyah's women's association (named after the prophet Muhammad's beloved wife, Aysha).

Al Irsyad   Muslim reformist association, exclusively active among Indonesia's Arab community.

Baitul Muslimin Indonesia   (Indonesian House of Muslims) Muslim "wing" of the nationalist political party PDI-P, established in 2007 under the patronage of Megawati Sukarnoputri and leading personalities from Muhammadiyah and NU.

Bakom-PKB   Badan Komunikasi Penghayatan Kesatuan Bangsa (Contact Organ for Awareness of the Unity of the Nation), a body aiming at the integration of Indonesian Chinese into the Indonesian nation through conversion to Islam. Established in 1974 by the (Chinese Indonesian) economist Junus Jahja as the successor to a similar body (LPKB, Lembaga Pembina Kesatuan Bangsa) that he had established under the Old Order and that was dissolved in 1967.

Bakor Pakem	Badan Kordinasi Pengawasan Aliran Kepercayaan Masyarakat (Coordinating Body for the Surveillance of Spiritual Movements in Society), an official body (affiliated with the Attorney General's office) charged with the surveillance of religious sects and movements. Unlike the MUI, which can only declare certain teachings and practices deviant and un-Islamic, Pakem can recommend banning them.
BAZ	Badan Amil Zakat (Office for Collecting the Alms Tax).
BKPRMI	Badan Kontak Pemuda dan Remaja Masjid Indonesia (Contact Organ of Indonesian Mosque Youth), a semi-official association, with central offices in Jakarta's Istiqlal mosque, the state mosque.
BKSPP	Badan Kerjasama Pondok Pesantren (Association for Cooperation between Pesantrens), a West Java-based association of ulama, mostly with former Masyumi affiliations.
BMI (1)	Bank Muamalat Indonesia, Indonesia's first Islamic bank, opened by Soeharto in 1991. Considered as one of the first achievements of ICMI and an indication of the "Islamic turn" in the late New Order.
BMI (2)	Baitul Muslimin Indonesia, Muslim wing of PDI-P.
Brigade Hizbullah	Currently a militia affiliated with the Partai Bulan Bintang. In 1998 it was a large and broad coalition of militant youth groups, the major component of Pam Swakarsa.
Darul Arqam (1)	Lit. "The House of Arqam" (Arqam was one of the Prophet's companions, in whose house the first Muslims used to gather). Religious movement of Sufi inspiration and strong millenarian beliefs, originally established in Malaysia and also active in Indonesia since the 1980s. Banned in Malaysia; declared a "deviant sect" by the MUI in Indonesia and formally dissolved in 1994. The Malaysian Darul Arqam used its extensive network to transform itself into a successful trading corporation, the Rufaqa' Corporation.

Darul Arqam (2)   The same name is used for a religious training programme within Muhammadiyah and the staff and members co-operating in it. Hence several Muhammadiyah pesantrens have adopted this name. There is no connection with the above movement.

Darul Islam   The movement for establishing an Islamic state that controlled parts of West Java, South Sulawesi and Aceh until 1962 or 1963 and that has maintained an underground existence ever since. Also known as DI and NII/TII (q.v.).

DDI   Darud Dakwah wal Irsyad (House of Predication and Guidance), Muslim educational association, established by the Buginese scholar Haji Abd. Rahman Ambo Dalle (d.1996), whose school in Sengkang in South Sulawesi produced many graduates who became leading scholars, and spawned a network of secondary schools among Buginese communities all over Indonesia.

DDII   Dewan Dakwah Islamiyah Indonesia (Indonesian Council for Islamic Propagation), a body established by Mohamad Natsir and other former Masyumi leaders in 1967, with the aim of making Indonesian Muslims more Islamic.

Depag   Departemen Agama (Ministry of Religious Affairs). Recently renamed Kementerian Agama.

DI   *see* Darul Islam

DKM   Dewan Kesejahteraan Masjid (Mosque Welfare Council). Many mosques have a DKM that occupies itself with the social welfare of the mosque's congregation (jama`ah), e.g. in the form of a funeral fund.

DMI   Dewan Masjid Indonesia (Council of Indonesian Mosques), the umbrella organization of mosque committees.

èLSAD   Lembaga Studi Agama dan Demokrasi (Institute for the Study of Religion and Democracy), Surabaya-based NGO active among the NU constituency.

Fahmina Institute	Cirebon-based NGO, active in the pesantren world and focusing on gender issues. Led by Kyai Haji Husein Muhammad.
Fatayat NU	Nahdlatul Ulama's young women's association.
FKAWJ	Forum Komunikasi Ahlussunnah Wal Jama'ah (Forum of Communication of the People of the Prophet's Path and his Congregation), one of two wings of the Indonesian "purist" Salafi movement, established and led by Ja'far Umar Thalib. It gave rise to the armed militia, Laskar Jihad.
FPI	Front Pembela Islam (Front for the Defence of Islam), Jakarta-based vigilante group, led by "Habib" Rizieq Syihab, known for raids on bars and nightclubs and demonstrations against enemies of Islam and "deviant" groups.
FPIS	Front Pemuda Islam Surakarta (Muslim Youth Front of Surakarta), a radical vigilante group in Solo that gained notoriety in the first post-Soeharto years for raids on bars, nightclubs and hotels with foreign guests.
FSPP	Forum Silaturrahim Pondok Pesantren (Forum for Friendly Relations between Pondok Pesantrens), a Banten-based association of pesantren ulama that has been actively agitating for implementation of the Shariah.
FUI	Forum Ukhuwah Islamiyah (Forum for Islamic Brotherhood), a front organization of the MUI for mass mobilization, with representatives of various Muslim organizations. First emerged during Abdurrahman Wahid's presidency, and organized demonstrations to influence the political process. Not to be confused with the Front Umat Islam.
FUI	Front Umat Islam (Front of the Muslim Community), a loose coalition of radical groups brought together by HTI leader Al-Khatthath in the early 2000s. A similar coalition with the same name had earlier been established in South Sulawesi in 1999.

Furkon   Youth group affiliated with ICMI in the period of transition from the Soeharto to the post-Soeharto period.

FUUI   Forum Ulama Umat Islam (Forum of Scholars of the Islamic Nation), a small, West-Java based group that issues statements showing sympathy for radical groups such as Ba'asyir's MMI. Gained national notoriety by issuing a fatwa declaring Ulil Abshar-Abdalla of the Liberal Islam Network an apostate who deserves to be killed. Its chairman, 'Athian Ali M. Da'i, and secretary-general, "Ustadz" Hedi Muhamad, gained some renown for their radical statements, but have not impressed anyone with the level of their religious learning.

GAI   Gerakan Ahmadiyah (Lahore) Indonesia, the national-level organization of the Indonesian branch of the Lahore Ahmadiyah.

GPI   Gerakan Pemuda Islam (Islamic Youth Movement), established in 1967 to take the place of the banned GPII.

GPII   Gerakan Pemuda Islam Indonesia (Indonesian Islamic Youth Movement), youth movement of Masyumi, established in 1945 and dissolved in 1963 by Sukarno. Although the organization does not officially exist anymore, its network of solidarity still appears to be largely intact.

GPK   Gerakan Pemuda Ka'bah (Youth of the Ka'bah Movement), paramilitary youth movement affiliated with the PPP. The Ka'bah (the huge black cube in Mecca's holy mosque) had been an electoral symbol of the PPP, until the New Order regime ordered the party to replace it with a less overtly Islamic symbol.

GUPPI   Gabungan Usaha Perbaikan Pendidikan Islam (Consortium for the Improvement of Islamic Education), a Golkar-affiliated association of ulama. Several former Darul Islam activists were re-integrated into society through GUPPI.

Hidayatullah	The name of a pesantren established in 1973 in Balik-papan (East Kalimantan) by Abdullah Said, a former adjutant of Kahar Muzakkar, the leader of the Darul Islam of South Sulawesi. This school became the centre of an Indonesia-wide network of local associations. The journal *Suara Hidayatullah*, associated with this network and published since 1988, is one of Indonesia's most successful and prominent radical Islamic publications.
HIPMI	Himpunan Pengusaha Muslim Indonesia (Association of Indonesian Muslim Businessmen).
Hizbut Tahrir	*see* HTI
HMI	Himpunan Mahasiswa Indonesia (Indonesian Students' Association), moderately reformist students' union, in the 1950s and 1960s ideologically close to Masyumi though formally independent of it. In the 1970s, it became associated with the modernist thought of Nurcholish Madjid. In 1986, a group that resisted the HMI board's acceptance of Soeharto's "sole ideology" policy and established the unofficial HMI-MPO (Majelis Penyelamatan Organisasi, Council for Saving the Organization).
HTI	Hizbut Tahrir wilayah Indonesia (Liberation Party, region Indonesia), the Indonesian branch of this transnational movement that aims to establish a new caliphate and unite the entire Muslim world under its banner. The party rejects democracy and opposes taking part in Indonesian elections.
IAIN	Institut Agama Islam Negeri (State Institute for Islamic Studies).
ICIP	International Center for Islam and Pluralism, an NGO that was established at the initiative of, and with generous support from, The Asia Foundation. Organizes seminars, has introduced many foreign Muslim thinkers of liberal persuasion to the Indonesian public.

ICMI   Ikatan Cendekiawan Muslim Indonesia (Alliance of Indonesian Muslim Intellectuals), an association of educated Muslims (mostly civil servants), formally established by B.J. Habibie in December 1990, with Soeharto's explicit endorsement.

IJABI   Ikatan Jama'ah Ahlul Bait Indonesia (Indonesian Assembly of Ahl al-Bait Associations), organization of converts to Shi'ism, led by Jalaluddin Rachmat. (<www.jalal-center.com>).

IMM   Ikatan Mahasiswa Muhammadiyah (Muhammadiyah Students' Association).

IMMIM   Ikatan Masjid dan Mushalla Muttahidah (United Association of Mosques and Prayer Houses), based in South Sulawesi.

INSISTS   Institute for the Study of Islamic Thought and Civilization. Conservative think-tank established by graduates of ISTAC in Malaysia (the Institute for Islamic Thought and Civilization). Focus is on the Islamization of knowledge. [Initially named INSIST, but since there is also a left-leaning development NGO of that name, a final "S" was added to represent the first consonant of "civilization".]

Islam Jama'ah   Sectarian movement emerging in the 1950s, under the leadership of the charismatic teacher Nurhasan Ubaidah of Kediri (also known as Amir Nurhasan Lubis). The first Indonesian Islamic movement with a *jama'a* structure and strong authoritarian leadership. Repeatedly declared a deviant sect, but surviving under different names (Lemkari, LDII) under the patronage of various Golkar personalities.

JAI   Jama'ah Ahmadiyah Indonesia, the national-level organization of the Indonesian branch of the Qadian Ahmadiyah.

Jama'ah Islamiyah	"Islamic Congregation", an Islamist network or organization established by Abdullah Sungkar and Abu Bakar Ba'asyir. The name is mentioned several times in the late 1970s and appears synonymous with the Usroh movement led by these men. In the mid-1990s, when Sungkar broke with the Darul Islam movement, his network again became called Jama'ah Islamiyah or JI. Documents later captured by security forces suggest that JI had a well-developed regional structure covering all of Southeast Asia and Australia.
Jama'ah Tabligh	Transnational piety movement with a strong missionary character, of South Asian origin. Active in Indonesia from the 1980s onwards (and perhaps even earlier). Internationally known as Tablighi Jama'at.
Jamiat Chair (al-Jam`iyya al-Khayriyya)	Benevolent and educational association of "traditionalist" Arabs, established in 1905.
JAT	Jamaah Ansharut Tauhid (Jama`ah Ansar al-Tawhid, Congregation of the Helpers of Belief in the One God), association established by Abu Bakar Ba'asyir after his break with the MMI in 2008.
JATMI	Jam'iyah Ahlith Thoriqah al-Mu'tabarah Indonesia (Indonesian Association of Respectable Sufi Orders), umbrella organization of "orthodox" Sufi orders that joined forces to distinguish themselves from heterodox mystical movements. After a political conflict within the organization in the late 1970s, the orders whose leaders were loyal to the NU massively left this association and established the JATMN.
JATMN	Jam'iyah Ahlith Thoriqah al-Mu'tabarah Nahdliyyin (Association of Respectable Sufi Orders Affiliated with Nahdlatul Ulama).
JI	*see* Jama'ah Islamiyah
JIL	Jaringan Islam Liberal (Liberal Islam Network)

JIMM   Jaringan Intelektual Muda Muhammadiyah (Muhammadiyah Young Intellectuals Network), a loose group of progressive young thinkers of Muhammadiyah background, not formally part of the Muhammadiyah organization (as Pemuda Muhammadiyah and IMM are).

KAHMI   Korps Alumni Himpunan Mahasiswa Indonesia, the association of former HMI members. A powerful and influential network due to the strategic positions many members have in business, bureaucracy and politics.

KAMI   Kesatuan Aksi Mahasiswa Indonesia (Action Committee of Indonesian Muslim Students), action front of anti-communist and anti-Sukarno students whose demonstrations in 1965–66, closely coordinated with the military, played a role in ushering in the New Order.

KAMMI   Kesatuan Aksi Mahasiswa Muslim Indonesia (Action Committee of Indonesian Muslim Students), students' association affiliated with the Tarbiyah movement, established in March 1998. Ideologically close to the PKS though officially independent. (<http://kammi.or.id/last>)

KISDI   Komite Indonesia untuk Solidaritas Dunia Islam (Indonesian Committee for Solidarity with the Muslim World), action committee closely associated with the DDII, that during the 1990s carried out increasingly aggressive street demonstrations against foreign embassies and against media it considered to have insulted Islam in their reporting.

KOMPAK   Komite Aksi Penanggulangan Akibat Krisis (Action Committee for Crisis Management). Relief organization established by DDII at the time of inter-religious conflicts. KOMPAK sent humanitarian and, allegedly, military help to embattled Muslim communities.

KPPSI   Komite Persiapan Penegakan Syari'ah Islam (Preparatory Committee for the Implementation of the Islamic Shari'a), a pressure group in South Sulawesi agitating for shari'a legislation in the province. Many members have family connections with the Darul Islam movement in this province.

KUA   Kantor Urusan Agama (Office for Religious Affairs), the local office of the Department, in charge of performing and registering marriages, offering services to pilgrims departing for Mecca, etc.

KUII   Kongres Umat Islam Indonesia (Indonesian Congress of the Muslim Umma). The first congress of this name, in which all major Muslim associations took part, took place in November 1945; here Masyumi was constituted as a political party. A Fourth Congress, again attended by all major organizations, including some of the more radical ones, was held in April 2005 at the initiative of the MUI.

KW IX   Komando Wilayah IX (9th Regional Command), regional structure of the underground Darul Islam movement (NII) covering the region Jakarta-Banten.

Lakpesdam   Lembaga Kajian dan Pengembangan Sumber Daya Manusia (Institute for Research and Development of Human Resources), NU-affiliated NGO (<http://www.lakpesdam.or.id>). Besides the central, Jakarta-based NGO, there are several such NGOs at the provincial level, usually going by the same name (abbreviated as LKPSDM).

LAPAR   Lembaga Advokasi dan Pendidikan Anak Rakyat (People's Institute for Advocacy and Education), a Makassar-based NGO whose members are mostly former PMII activists. It took a clear position against the formalization of shari'a in South Sulawesi.

LDII   Lembaga Dakwah Islam Indonesia (Indonesian Institute for Islamic Predication), one of several names adopted by the sectarian movement Islam Jama'ah in an attempt to evade a ban. Other names included LKI or Lemkari,

	Lembaga Karyawan Indonesia (Institute of Indonesian Employees).
LDK	Lembaga Dakwah Kampus (Campus Institute for Religious Propagation), association based in the campus mosque that is in charge of religious activities.
Lemkari	*see* LKI
LIPIA	Lembaga Ilmu Pengetahuan Islam dan Arab (Institute of Islamic and Arabic Sciences), an institute in Jakarta for teaching Arabic and the Salafi/Wahhabi version of Islam, established and funded by Saudi Arabia.
LKI	Lembaga Karyawan Indonesia (also Lemkari, Institute of Indonesian Employees), one of several names adopted by the sectarian movement Islam Jama'ah. *See* LDII.
LKiS	Lembaga Kajian Islam dan Sosial (Institute for Islamic and Social Studies), Yogyakarta-based NGO active among the NU constituency.
LKPSDM	*see* Lakpesdam
LPPI	Lembaga Penelitian dan Pengkajian Islam (Institute for Islamic Study and Research). Led by M. Amin Djamaluddin and with IAIN and Azhar graduate Hartono Ahmad Jaiz as its most vocal publicist, this institute has been in the forefront of the struggle against what it considers to be deviant teachings, in writing as well as in the form of violent action.
LPPOM-MUI	Lembaga Pengkajian Pangan, Obat-Obatan dan Kosmetika Majelis Ulama Indonesia (Institute for Food, Drugs and Cosmetics Assessment of the Indonesian Ulama Council).
LP3ES	Lembaga Penelitian, Pendidikan dan Penerangen Ekonomi dan Sosial (Institute for Economic and Social Research, Education and Information), trendsetting research institute and development NGO, established in 1971 by former student activists affiliated with Masyumi and the Indonesian Socialist Party.

LP3SyI	Lembaga Pengkajian Penegakan Penerapan Syariat Islam (Institute for the Study of the Establishment and Implementation of Islamic Shariah), an action committee in Garut (West Java) striving for the adoption of Shariah-based regional regulations.
LSAF	Lembaga Studi Agama dan Filsafat (Institute for the Study of Religion and Philosophy), established in the mid-1980s by liberal Muslims of Masyumi background. Led by M. Dawam Rahardjo. Published the journal *Ulumul Qur'an*, which introduced many new concepts into the intellectual debates of the period and contained serious, appreciative articles on other religions as well.
Maarif Institute	Think-tank established by Syafi'i Maarif prior to his resignation as Muhammadiyah's chairman (2004), in order to provide an institutional setting to "liberal" Muhammadiyah activists.
MAN	Madrasah Aliyah Negeri, state school of upper secondary level offering a curriculum of 30 per cent religious and 70 per cent general subjects.
Masyumi	Majelis Syura Muslimin Indonesia (Consultative Council of Indonesian Muslims), established as an umbrella of all Indonesian Muslim organizations towards the end of the Japanese occupation; became a political party upon Independence, and was dissolved in 1960 after a grave conflict with Sukarno. Although there has been no organization of this name for almost half a century now, it still appeals to the loyalties of a significant segment of the Muslim community.
MER-C	Medical Emergency Rescue Committee, a Muslim NGO established in 1999 to bring medical relief to conflict zones.
MMI	Majelis Mujahidin Indonesia (Council of Indonesian Holy Warriors), an association established in 2000 to provide a legal framework for various groups striving to turn Indonesia into an Islamic state, most of them originating in the Darul Islam movement. Until 2008,

	Abu Bakar Ba'asyir was the amir or commander of this organization; Irfan S. Awwas was and remains its chief organizer.
MTA	Majelis Tafsir Alqur'an (Council for Exegesis of the Qur'an), a reformist association originating in Solo that directs its dakwah activities especially towards a lower-class following with little education and syncretistic (abangan) background.
Muhammadiyah	Muslim reformist association, established in 1912. The second largest organization of Indonesia.
MUI	Majelis Ulama Indonesia (Indonesian Ulama Council), established in 1975 as an official interface between the government and the Muslim umma, advising the government and explaining (i.e. legitimizing) government policy to the nation. After the demise of the New Order, MUI took greater distance from the government (although still partially funded by it) and has acted like a pressure group.
Muslimat NU	Nahdlatul Ulama's women's association.
Nahdlatul Ulama (NU)	Muslim traditionalist association, established in 1926. The largest organization in the country, and arguably the largest Muslim association in the world.
Nasyiatul Aisyiah	Muhammadiyah's young women's association.
NII/TII	Negara Islam Indonesia/Tentara Islam Indonesia (Indonesian Islamic State/Army).
NU	*see* Nahdlatul Ulama
PAKEM	*see* Bakor Pakem
Pam Swakarsa	Voluntary Security Force, recruited by the military (more specifically by General Wiranto) among Muslim youth groups, at the time of the special session of the People's Legislative Assembly in November 1998 (following Soeharto's abdication). This is the origin of all later

Muslim militias. Major components were the Brigade Hizbullah, then a 100,000 to 125,000 strong coalition of various factions, and Furkon, a youth group affiliated with ICMI.

PAN

Partai Amanah Nasional (National Mandate Party), a secular party established in the Reformation period by Amien Rais and a rainbow coalition of intellectuals. Considered to be close to Muhammadiyah because this organization is strongly represented in it.

Paramadina

Institute established in 1986 as a "klub kajian agama" (religious study club) to disseminate sophisticated religious ideas among Indonesia's rising Muslim middle class. Strongly associated with alumni of the student movement HMI. During his lifetime, Nurcholish Madjid (d. 2005) was the figurehead and contributed strongly to its liberal and pluralistic discourse. A university of the same name was established towards 2000.

Parmusi

Partai Muslimin Indonesia (Party of Indonesian Muslims), political party established in 1968 to take the place of the banned Masyumi party and appeal to the reformist Muslim vote.

PBB

Partai Bulan Bintang (Crescent and Star Party), political party with an Islamic (pro-shari'a) programme, targeting the Masyumi constituency but representing only a tiny fraction of it (crescent and star were the symbol of Masyumi).

PDII

Pusat Dakwah Islam Indonesia (Indonesian Centre for Islamic Propagation), a body established by the Ministry of Religious Affairs in 1969, as a pro-government alternative to DDII.

Persis

Persatuan Islam (Islamic Union), puritan reformist Muslim association with centres in Bandung and Bangil.

Perti

Persatuan Tarbiyah Islamiyah (Union for Islamic Education), an originally West Sumatra-based association of traditionalist religious schools; became a political party in 1948. Part of Perti merged in 1973 with other Muslim parties into PPP, another part joined Golkar (within which it remained a distinct entity named Tarbiyah Islamiyah).

PII   Pelajar Islam Indonesia (Indonesian Muslim Students), association of Muslim students (secondary school and higher), affiliated with Masyumi. Though officially dissolved, it remained active for most of the New Order period.

PITI   Persatuan Islam Tionghoa Indonesia (Indonesian Union of Chinese Muslims).

PK   Partai Keadilan (Justice Party), political party established by activists of the Tarbiyah movement, the Indonesian version of the Muslim Brotherhood, in 1998. For technical reasons dissolved in 2003 and re-established as PKS.

PKB   Partai Kebangkitan Bangsa (National Awakening Party), Muslim political party, established by Abdurrahman Wahid and leading NU kyais in 1998, and appealing to the traditionalist segment of Indonesian Muslims.

PKS   Partai Keadilan Sejahtera (Prosperous Justice Party), successor to the PK.

PMB   Partai Matahari Bangsa (Sun of the Nation Party), established in 2006 by young Muhammadiyah activists as a Muhammadiyah-based political party, but not recognized as such by Muhammadiyah.

PMI   Partai Muslimin Indonesia, Parmusi (Party of Indonesian Muslims), political party established in 1968 to take the place of the banned Masyumi party and appealing to the reformist Muslim vote.

PMII   Pergerakan Mahasiswa Islam Indonesia (Indonesian Muslim Students' Movement), NU-affiliated students' association.

PPIM   Pusat Pengkajian Islam dan Masyarakat (Centre for Islamic and Social Studies), a research institute at the

	UIN (formerly IAIN) Syarif Hidayatullah, Ciputat, Jakarta.
PPP	Partai Persatuan Pembangunan (Unity for Development Party), political party established in 1973 through the forced merger of the various Muslim political parties, notably the NU and the PMI.
P3M	Perhimpunan Pengembangan Pesantren dan Masyarakat (Association for the Development of Pesantren and Society), NGO carrying out pesantren-based development projects and various forms of training. Both the NU and the Masyumi network are represented in its board; since its establishment in 1986, the director has been Masdar F. Mas'udi.
PPTI	Partai Politik Tharikat Islam (Political Party of Muslim Sufi Orders), later renamed Persatuan Pengamal Tarekat Islam (Union of Muslim Sufi Order Devotees), a political party established in the late 1940s by a Minangkabau teacher of the Naqshbandi order. Under Guided Democracy it was transformed into a "functional group" and joined the corporatist functional group (golongan karya, Golkar) joint secretariat.
PSII	Partai Syarikat Islam Indonesia, political party emerging from the Sarekat Islam movement. Merged into PPP in 1973. Contested the 1999 elections as an independent party, but won no seat.
PTDI	Pendidikan Tinggi Dakwah Islam ([Institute for] Higher Education in Islamic Predication), established and led by the firebrand preacher Usman al-Hafidy in Jakarta.
PUI	Persatuan Umat Islam (Union of the Muslim Umma), West Java-based educational association, politically affiliated with Masyumi.
Rabithah Alawiyah	Contact organ of Alawis, i.e. sayyids or descendants of the Prophet, established in the 1920s to defend the common interests of this elite among the Arab community.
Rahima	Muslim NGO focusing on gender issues.

RMI

Rabithah Ma'ahid Indonesia (Indonesian League of Institutes [of Islamic Education]), association of pesantrens affiliated with Nahdlatul Ulama.

SI

Sarekat Islam

Syarikat

NU-based NGO focusing on reconciliation between families of victims and perpetrators of the 1965–66 mass killings.

Tablighi Jama'at   *see* Jama'ah Tabligh

Tarbiyah

Lit. "educating, disciplining", an Islamic movement based on the method and ideology of the Egyptian Muslim Brotherhood, that became influential on university campuses from the 1980s onwards. Gave rise to the students' association KAMMI, which played a part in the protest demonstrations of the late New Order, and to the political party PK(S).

TII

Tentara Islam Indonesia (Islamic Army of Indonesia), the military wing of the Darul Islam movement.

UIN

Universitas Islam Negeri (State Islamic University). The IAINs of Ciputat (Jakarta), Bandung, Yogyakarta, Malang and Makassar were upgraded to full universities with the addition of a number of non-religious faculties.

Wahdah
Islamiyah

(Islamic Unity), a Muslim association of Salafi orientation, based in South Sulawesi with branches in various other provinces. Focuses on education and social work, according to its website. (<www.wahdah.or.id>)

Wahid Institute

Think-tank established by people loyal to Abdurrahman Wahid and focusing especially on issues of religious pluralism. (<www.wahidinstitute.org>)

YAPI

Yayasan Pesantren Islam (Islamic Pesantren Foundation), a Shi'i centre based in Bangil, established in 1976 by Ustadz Husein bin Abu Bakar Al-Habsyi, i.e. before the Iranian revolution and the subsequent wave of conversions to Shi'ism. (<http://www.yapibangil.org>)

ACKNOWLEDGEMENTS

The research on which this book is based was supported by the International Institute for the Study of Islam in the Modern World (ISIM) and the Netherlands Ministry of Foreign Affairs. Numerous persons and institutions provided valuable help and feedback during the original fieldwork in 2007–08 and subsequent field trips, as well at seminars where the findings were first presented.

Moch Nur Ichwan wishes in addition to acknowledge support from the Royal Netherlands Academy of Arts and Sciences (KNAW) in the form of a Rubicon postdoctoral grant, that allowed him to continue his research on the MUI. He also thanks Abdul Wasik and Dr Asrorun Niam Shaleh for their kind help during his research at the MUI headquarters in Jakarta.

Ahmad Najib Burhani thanks Raja Juli Antoni, Fajar Riza Ul Haq, and the staff of the Maarif Institute for their assistance in conducting a survey and interviews during the Muhammadiyah *Tanwir* in Yogyakarta on 26–29 April 2007, and for providing him with an office during his visits to Indonesia.

Mujiburrahman thanks Andi Ali Amiruddin, Hamdan Juhanis, Nurman Said, Sabir Maidin of the UIN Alauddin, and Arsyad, Syamsurijal, Mubarak and Subair of LAPAR, for their kind help during his fieldwork in the city of Makassar. An earlier version of his contribution to this volume appeared in *Asia Pacific Forum*, no. 43 (March 2009).

Muhammad Wildan thanks Sudharmono and M. Fajar Sodik for their kind help during his research at Solo.

GLOSSARY

abangan (Jav)	nominal Muslim
ahl al-halli wa al-ʿaqd (Ar)	"those who loosen and bind": an elite that takes decisions on behalf of the entire community (or organization)
Ahlus Sunnah wal Jamaʾah (Ind) [*ahl al-sunnah wa-l-jamaʿah* (Ar)]	"followers of the Prophet's tradition and congregation": the orthodox mainstream, to which all non-sectarian Muslims claim to belong
aliran (Ind)	(religious) movement
aliran sesat (Ind)	deviant sect
amir (Ar)	commander
ansar (Ar)	"helpers": the men who joined Muhammad during the Medina period
ʿaqidah (Ind/Ar)	creed, belief
bidʿah (Ind/Ar)	"innovation": beliefs and practices that cannot be shown to have been present at the time of the Prophet and his immediate successors
bupati (Ind)	regent, governor of a regency of *kabupaten*, the administrative unit below the level of the province

cabang (Ind)	branch (of an organization, at the regency level)
da`i (Ar)	Islamic preacher, proselytizer
dakwah (Ind), *da`wa* (Ar)	preaching, proselytization
darurah (Ar)	emergency
dewan (Ind, <Pers/Ar *diwan*)	council
dluhur (Jav, <Ar *zuhr*)	noon prayer
fatwa (Ar)	authoritative opinion, issued in response to a question
fiqh (Ar)	Islamic jurisprudence
ghazwul fikri (Ar: *al-ghazw al-fikri*)	"war of thought", cultural invasion
Golongan Karya, Golkar (Ind)	Functional Groups
hadits (Ind), *hadith* (Ar)	report on sayings or deeds of the Prophet, handed down orally for the first three centuries by a chain of transmitters (*rawi*)
halal (Ar)	licit, allowed by Islam
haram (Ar)	illicit, forbidden
harakah (Ind, Ar)	movement; more specifically: Islamist movement
hijab (Ar)	Islamic covering of head and shoulders (for women)
hijrah (Ind, Ar)	emigration; esp. the Prophet's emigration from Mecca to Medina
`ibadah (Ind/Ar)	worship

`Id al-Adha (Ar)	Feast of Sacrifice
ijtima` (Ar)	meeting, convention
al-Ikhwan al-Muslimun	Muslim Brothers
infaq (Ar)	spending (for a charitable purpose)
inlander (Dutch)	indigenous Indonesian
islah (Ar)	reform (of Islam)
jama`ah (Ind/Ar)	"congregation": Islamic group
jihad (Ar)	effort, "holy war"
kejawen (Ind/Jav)	Javanese syncretistic mysticism
khaul (Jav, <Ar *hawl*)	death anniversary of a saintly person
khurafat (Ar)	superstition
kiai (Jav)	religious teacher heading a traditional *pesantren*
laskar, lasykar (Ind)	militia, paramilitary group
ma`had `ali (Ar)	institute for higher education; more specifically college-level Islamic school
madrasah diniyah (Ind, Ar)	Islamic school
madzhab (Ind), *madhhab* (Ar)	school of Islamic jurisprudence
majelis (Ind), *majlis* (Ar)	council, gathering
majelis taklim (Ind)	religious study group
maksiat (Ind), *ma`siyya* (Ar)	immoral practices

manhaj (Ar)	method, approach
masjid (Ar)	mosque
mu`amalat (Ar)	conduct, behaviour; the part of Islamic jurisprudence that concerns human interactions
mujahidin (Ar)	"holy warriors"
munkarat (Ar)	reprehensible acts
murtad (Ar)	apostate
mushalla (Ind/Ar)	prayer room
pemuda (Ind)	youth
pemurtadan (Ind/Ar)	apostasy, luring Muslims away from Islam
penghulu (Ind)	religious official, appointed by a local court or the colonial administration
perwakilan (Ind)	representation: provincial branch of an organization
pesantren (Jav, Ind)	traditional Islamic boarding school
pondok (Jav)	(1) dormitory in a *pesantren*; (2) *pesantren*
priyayi (Jav)	bureaucratic upper class
sadaqah (Ar)	voluntary charitable gift
santri (Jav)	(1) student in a *pesantren*; (2) pious, practicing Muslim
sayyid (Ind/Ar)	descendant of the Prophet Muhammad
syahadah (Ind/Ar)	Muslim confession of faith (the proclamation that there is one God and that Muhammad is His Prophet)

tajdid (Ar)	"renewal": revitalization of Islam
tafsir (Ar)	Qur'anic exegesis
takhayul (Ind/Ar)	beliefs based on fantasies and hallucinations
taklim (Ind), *ta`lim* (Ar)	religious instruction. See also *majelis taklim*
tarbiyah (Ind, Ar)	intensive Islamic education, disciplining
tarjih (Ar)	preference: establishing the best of various opinions
tausiyah (Ind), *tawsiyya* (Ar)	advice, counsel
ukhuwah (Ind), *ukhuwwa* (Ar)	brotherhood
ulama (Ar)	scholars of Islamic learning
ummah (Ind/Ar)	the community of all Muslims
usrah (Ind/Ar)	"nuclear family": small and tightly-knit study groups in Muslim Brotherhood-influenced movements
ustadz (Ind), *ustadh* (Ar)	religious teacher
zakat (Ar)	obligatory Islamic alms-giving
ziyarah (Ind/Ar)	pilgrimage, grave visitation

ABOUT THE CONTRIBUTORS

Ahmad Najib Burhani is a researcher in theology and philosophy of religion at the Indonesian Institute of Sciences (LIPI) and a Ph.D. candidate in Religious Studies, with emphasis on minority religions with Islamic origins, at the University of California in Santa Barbara. He published several books, including *Sufisme Kota: Berpikir Jernih, Menemukan Spiritualitas Positif* (2001), *Islam Dinamis: Menggugat Peran Agama, Membongkar Doktrin yang Membatu* (2001) and *Muhammadiyah Jawa* (2010), and numerous articles, including "Revealing the Neglected Missions: Some Comments on the Javanese Elements of Muhammadiyah Reformism", *Studia Islamika* 12, no. 1 (2005) and "*Lakum dinukum wa-liya dini*: The Muhammadiyah's stance towards interfaith relations", *Islam and Christian-Muslim Relations* 22 (2011). Najib can be contacted at najib27@yahoo.com.

Moch Nur Ichwan is a lecturer of Islamic politics at the State Islamic University (UIN) Sunan Kalijaga in Yogyakarta and the director of the research institute CIS-Form at that university. He obtained his Ph.D. degree from the University of Tilburg in 2006, with a dissertation titled "Official Reform of Islam: State Islam and the Ministry of Religious Affairs in Contemporary Indonesia, 1966–2004". A Rubicon grant from Royal Netherlands Academy of Arts and Sciences (KNAW) enabled him to carry out postdoctoral research on the Majelis Ulama Indonesia (2008–09). His current research concerns various forms of resistance to the imposition of Shariah in Aceh. Ichwan's recent publications include "The Making of a Pancasila State: Political Debates on Secularism, Islam and the State in Indonesia", SOIAS Research Paper Series No. 6, Sophia Organization for Islamic Area Studies, Sophia University (February 2012); "Official Ulema and the Politics of Re-Islamization: The Majelis Permusyawaratan Ulama, Shari'atization and Contested Authority in Post-New Order Aceh", *Journal of Islamic Studies* 22 (2011). Ichwan can be contacted at ichwanmoe@ yahoo.com.

Mujiburrahman is a lecturer at the State Institute for Islamic Studies (IAIN) Antasari in Banjarmasin, South Kalimantan, where he also obtained his undergraduate degree. He pursued postgraduate studies at McGill University, Montreal, was a Ph.D. fellow at the International Institute for the Study of Islam in the Modern World (ISIM) and obtained his doctorate from Utrecht University. His dissertation was published as *Feeling Threatened: Muslim-Christian Relations in Indonesia's New Order* (2006). His other publications include *Mengindonesiakan Islam* (2008), *Polisi Tidur, Kekuasaan Membela Yang Bayar* (2010), *Badingsanak Banjar-Dayak: Identitas Agama dan Ekonomi Etnisitas di Kalimantan Selatan* (2011) and numerous articles, most recently "Religion and dialogue in Indonesia: from the Soeharto period to the present", *Studia Islamika* 17, no. 3 (2010). Mujiburrahman can be contacted at mujib71@hotmail.com.

Muhammad Wildan is a lecturer at the State Islamic University (UIN) Sunan Kalijaga in Yogyakarta, where he also did his undergraduate studies. He received an MA in Islamic Studies at Leiden University in 1999 and pursued doctoral studies at the Universiti Kebangsaan Malaysia (UKM) in Kuala Lumpur, where he submitted his dissertation "Radical Islamism in Solo: A Quest of Muslims' Identity in a Town of Central Java" (2009). A graduate of Pondok Ngruki himself, he is engaged in efforts to exert a moderating influence in this and related *pesantren* in the region of Solo. Wildan can be contacted at wildan71@yahoo.com.

Martin van Bruinessen is Emeritus Professor of Comparative Studies of Contemporary Muslim Societies at Utrecht University and was one of the chairs at the International Institute for the Study of Islam in the Modern World (ISIM). His most recent publications include the edited volumes *The Madrasa in Asia: Political Activism and Transnational Linkages* (with Farish A. Noor and Yoginder Sikand (2008), *Islam and Modernity: Key Issues and Debates* (with Khalid Masud and Armando Salvatore, 2009), and *Producing Islamic Knowledge: Transmission and Dissemination in Western Europe* (with Stefano Allievi, 2011), and a collection of articles on traditionalist Islam in Indonesia, *Kitab Kuning, Pesantren dan Tarekat* (2012). Martin can be contacted at m.vanbruinessen@uu.nl.

1

INTRODUCTION: CONTEMPORARY DEVELOPMENTS IN INDONESIAN ISLAM AND THE "CONSERVATIVE TURN" OF THE EARLY TWENTY-FIRST CENTURY

Martin van Bruinessen

Developments in Indonesia since the fall of Soeharto in 1998 have greatly changed the image of Indonesian Islam and the existing perception of Indonesian Muslims as tolerant and inclined to compromise. In the heyday of the New Order, the 1970s and 1980s, Indonesian Islam had presented a smiling face — perhaps appropriately so, under an authoritarian ruler who was known as "the smiling general". The dominant discourse was modernist and broadly supportive of the government's development programme. It embraced the essentially secular state ideology of Pancasila, favoured harmonious relations (and equal rights) with the country's non-Muslim minorities, and rejected the idea of an Islamic state as inappropriate for Indonesia. Some key representatives spoke of "cultural Islam" as their alternative to political Islam and emphasized that Indonesia's Muslim cultures were as authentically Muslim as Middle Eastern varieties of Islam.

Like Soeharto's smile, the friendly face of the most visible Muslim spokespersons hid from view some less pleasant realities, notably the mass killings of alleged communists during 1965–66, which had been orchestrated by Soeharto's military but largely carried out by killing squads recruited from the main Muslim organizations.[1] There was also an undercurrent of more fundamentalist Islamic thought and activism, and a broad fear in Muslim circles — not entirely unjustified — of Christian efforts to subvert Islam.[2] However, the liberal, tolerant and open-minded discourse of the likes of Nurcholish Madjid and Abdurrahman Wahid was almost hegemonic. It was widely covered in the press and was influential in the universities, in the Ministry of Religious Affairs and other major Muslim institutions, and among the emerging middle class.

The post-Soeharto years have presented a very different face of Indonesian Islam. For several years, there were violent inter-religious conflicts all over the country. Jihad movements (supported by factions of the military and local interest groups) carried the banner of Islam to local conflicts, turning them into battlefields in a struggle that appeared to divide the entire nation.[3] Terrorist groups with apparent transnational connections carried out spectacular attacks, including a series of simultaneous bombings of churches all over the country on Christmas eve of 2000 and the Bali bombings of October 2002, which killed around two hundred people and wounded hundreds more, many of them foreign tourists.[4] Opinion surveys in the early 2000s indicated surprisingly high levels of professed sympathy for radical Muslim groups among the population at large and unprecedented support for the idea of an Islamic state.[5] Efforts to insert a reference to the Shariah — the so-called Jakarta Charter — into the Constitution were rejected by the People's Consultative Assembly (MPR) in its 2001 and 2002 sessions, but in the following years numerous regions and districts adopted regulations that at least symbolically enshrined elements of the Shariah.[6]

Most of these developments, however, appear to have been temporary responses to the tremors of the political landscape rather than indications of a pervasive change of attitude of Indonesia's Muslim majority. Meanwhile, both communal and terrorist violence have abated and it has become clear that much of the violence was directly related with struggles for the redistribution of economic and political resources in post-Soeharto Indonesia.[7] In most of the conflict-ridden regions a new balance of power has been established, although in some cases only after the relocation of considerable numbers of people, and the need for good neighbourly relations between the communities is widely affirmed. The terrorist networks have been largely uncovered and rounded up by the police, many of their activists being killed or arrested; the popular acceptance of violence in the name of Islam has been considerably reduced. The issuance of new regional Shariah regulations has by and large stopped — Aceh being the main exception where implementation of the Shariah remains on the agenda. The Muslim political parties, which in the general elections of 1999 and 2004 had recovered the high yield of around 40 per cent they had obtained in 1955, recorded significant losses in 2009, falling back to just over 25 per cent.[8]

A more lasting development, however, appears to be the emergence of dynamic transnational Islamic movements that compete for influence with the older established Indonesian mainstream organizations, Muhammadiyah and Nahdlatul Ulama (NU), and make major contributions to setting the terms of the debate in Indonesia. Most significant among them are the Prosperous Welfare Party (PKS) and its affiliated associations, which constitute the Indonesian version of the Muslim Brotherhood, the Indonesian chapter of the Hizb ut-Tahrir (HTI), and the apolitical Tablighi Jama`at and Salafi movements. Within Muhammadiyah and NU, moreover, the balance between liberals and progressives on the one hand and conservative and fundamentalist forces on the other has shifted towards the latter.

THE CONSERVATIVE TURN

By 2005 it appeared that a conservative turn had taken place in mainstream Islam, and that the modernist and liberal views that had until recently found relatively broad support within Muhammadiyah and NU were increasingly rejected. Both organizations held their five-yearly congresses in 2004, and on both occasions the boards were purged of leaders considered as "liberals", including persons who had rendered great service to their organizations. Many ulama and other Muslim leaders appear preoccupied with the struggle against "deviant" sects and ideas.

The clearest expression of the conservative turn was perhaps given by a number of controversial *fatwa*, authoritative opinions, issued by the Majelis Ulama Indonesia (MUI, Indonesian Council of Islamic Scholars) in 2005. One of the *fatwa* declared secularism, pluralism and religious liberalism — SiPiLis, in a suggestive acronym coined by fundamentalist opponents — to be incompatible with Islam. This *fatwa*, believed to be inspired by radical Islamists who had recently joined the MUI but supported by many conservatives from the mainstream, was ostensibly a frontal attack on the small group of self-defined "liberal" Muslims of Jaringan Islam Liberal (JIL, Liberal Islam Network) but attempted to delegitimize a much broader category of Muslim intellectuals and NGO activists, including some of the most respected Muslim personalities of the previous decades.[9] Other *fatwa* condemned the practice of inter-religious prayer meetings (which had emerged in the days of political strife and inter-religious conflict, when representatives of different faiths joined each other in praying for well-being and peace) and declared inter-religious marriage *haram*, even in the case of a Muslim man marrying a non-Muslim woman. A fatwa on the Ahmadiyah not only declared this sect to be outside the boundaries of Islam and Muslims who joined it to be apostates, but it also called upon the government to effectively ban all its activities.[10]

The MUI had been established in 1975 as an adviser to the government on policy matters concerning Islam and as a channel of communication between the government and the Muslim *umma*. For a quarter century its voice had predominantly been one of moderation and compromise, if not political expedience; but it also saw itself as the watchdog of religious orthodoxy and repeatedly made statements condemning deviant movements and sects. (It had already condemned the Qadiyani branch of the Ahmadiyah as early as 1980, but without any effect on government policy.) Critics of the Soeharto regime had heaped scorn on the MUI for its subservience to the wishes of the government, but the existence of a body that could represent the viewpoint of the *umma* to the government was generally appreciated (see also Bruinessen 1996). After Soeharto's fall, the MUI declared itself independent from the government, and it has since been setting its own agenda. At least one analyst interprets its current more assertive (and conservative) positioning as "an attempt to demarcate a role more aligned with the *umma*", suggesting that the majority of Indonesian Muslims may have held such conservative views all along (Gillespie 2007, p. 202).

The conservative turn does not mean that the liberal and progressive voices of the past have suddenly been silenced. There were in fact many who did protest. The former chairmen of Muhammadiyah and NU, Ahmad Syafi'i Ma'arif and Abdurrahman Wahid, who had been genuinely popular among their constituencies, spoke out loud and clearly, and so did several other prominent members of these organizations, as well as larger numbers of young activists. But they had lost the power to define the terms of debate and had to leave the initiative to the conservatives and fundamentalists.

WHAT HAPPENED?

These developments call for an explanation. It is tempting to see a direct connection between Indonesia's democratization and the declining influence of liberal and progressive views, but the assumption that the majority are inherently conservative or inclined to fundamentalist views is not a priori convincing. This would suggest that liberal Islamic thought could only flourish when it was patronized by an authoritarian regime. A related argument is that political democratization has drawn many of those who were previously involved in organizations or institutions supporting intellectual debate towards careers in political parties or institutions, thereby weakening the social basis of liberal and progressive Islamic discourse.

Another explanation (repeatedly proffered by embattled liberals) concerns influences emanating from the Middle East and more specifically the Arabian Peninsula, in the form of returning graduates from Saudi universities, Saudi-owned and Saudi or Kuwaiti-funded educational institutions in Indonesia, sponsored translations of numerous simple "fundamentalist" texts, and ideological as well as financial support for transnational Islamic movements. The high visibility of Indonesian Arabs holding leading positions in radical movements seemed to point to their role as middlemen in a process of Arabization of Indonesian Islam. The increased presence of Arab actors and Arab funding is undeniable, but, as I have argued elsewhere, their influence does not exclusively work in an anti-liberal or fundamentalist direction.[11]

The public presence of the new transnational Islamic movements is an important phenomenon that has definitely changed the landscape of Indonesian Islam, reducing the central importance of Muhammadiyah and Nahdlatul Ulama in defining the moderate mainstream. It is too early to say whether the slide of the latter organizations towards more conservative views was temporary; my observations at the most recent NU congress in March 2010 suggest that the anti-liberal trend has subsided and may even be reversed (Bruinessen 2010).

The four detailed studies that make up the main body of this volume constitute, in my view, major contributions towards understanding the developments in Indonesian Islam in the post-Soeharto period and provide, on the basis of original field research, new insights into major aspects of what may be called the "conservative turn" in Indonesian Islam. In order to place these developments in a broader social and historical context, these chapters are preceded by a broad overview of Indonesian Muslim organizations and movements.

THE MAJELIS ULAMA INDONESIA (INDONESIAN COUNCIL OF ISLAMIC SCHOLARS)

Moch Nur Ichwan's contribution focuses on the new roles the Majelis Ulama Indonesia has been trying to carve out for itself since it redefined itself as the servant of the *ummah* (the Muslim community) rather than of the government. Rather than a simple pendulum swing away from liberal towards conservative views, Ichwan perceives a consistent and pervasive effort to purify Indonesian Muslims' beliefs and practices, harmonizing them with an idealized orthodoxy.

One important function of the Council has been, from the start, the issuance of *fatwa* (authoritative opinions on matters of religious importance) and counsels (*tausiah*) to the government as well as the public. The members of the Council were chosen by the government to reflect the various strands of mainstream Islam; although most were affiliated with one Muslim association or another, they did not represent these associations but were accountable to the government only. There was no place for regime critics in the Council, but at least some members believed they could through the Council persuade the government to carry out an Islamic agenda. Perceiving Habibie, Soeharto's first successor, to be sympathetic to this agenda, the Council gave his government its wholehearted support and cooperated closely with other Habibie supporters including the "Muslim intellectuals" association ICMI and the youth groups from which volunteer security forces, PAM Swakarsa, were recruited.

When the 1999 elections brought the Habibie regime to an end, the MUI began distancing itself from the government (neither Abdurrahman Wahid nor Megawati Sukarnoputri were sympathetic to it). It restyled itself as a civil society institution — without, however, giving up the financial contributions from the government. Like all large voluntary associations, the Council organized national conferences and congresses (the first congresses in 2000 and 2005), where the national leadership was elected and major policy decisions taken. Membership, and participation in the congresses, however, appear to be based on co-optation. The Council expanded its membership, that originally consisted of New Order supporters, with persons of Islamist persuasion, including activists of the Dewan Dakwah Islamiyah Indonesia and Hizbut Tahrir Indonesia. No liberal Muslims were admitted, nor Shiah or Ahmadiyah Muslims.

The MUI remained formally a deliberative council but was intent on more active participation in the political process. It became indirectly involved in street politics through a front organization, the Forum Ukhuwah

Islamiyah (FUI), which on several occasions organized mass demonstrations in support of Muslim demands. The mobilization of mass support corresponds with the Council's self-image of representing the interests of the Muslim community (*ummah*) rather than those of the government. Backed up by an FUI demonstration, the Council played a part in drafting the law on national education and ensuring Muslim demands were met. It also appointed itself as the guardian of public morality and, among other things, campaigned for legislation against pornography and "porno-action", its counsels addressed to the authorities being supported again by street demonstrations. (In this case, success was limited; legislation was long stalled, and the law that was issued in 2008 failed to incorporate all the MUI's demands.)

The Council's clearest intervention in Indonesia's religious politics was in the form of its 2005 *fatwa* against the Ahmadiyah and against liberalism, secularism and pluralism. Although both caused considerable opposition from prominent individuals and several of these put the legitimacy of the MUI into doubt, the opposition never managed to unite itself into an organized force and remained ineffective. Vigilante groups meanwhile have viewed the Council's *fatwa* as legitimating violence against the targets of these *fatwa*.

MUHAMMADIYAH: WAS THERE A CONSERVATIVE TURN?

The Muhammadiyah, studied here by Ahmad Najib Burhani, is one of the oldest Muslim associations and the second largest after the Nahdlatul Ulama. It is reformist, in the sense of being intent on purging local religious practices and beliefs that find no basis in the Qur'an and *hadith*, and it considers education and social work as its most central activities. The Muhammadiyah has established a vast network of schools all over the country, and a dozen universities, as well as hospitals and orphanages. Unlike the NU, the Muhammadiyah can pride itself in an enormous pool of highly educated members who are employed in all modern sectors of society. A very high proportion of Muhammadiyah members, however, including virtually all members of the board, appear to be civil servants — many of them university teachers. Within the organization, observers distinguish a "progressive" and a "puritan" or "conservative" wing. In the view of the "puritans", the organization should first and foremost defend an orthodox and rigid Islam against syncretism and laxness, insisting on a literal reading of scripture, whereas "progressives" are open to contextual and metaphorical readings of the text, tend to emphasize the element of social justice in Islam, and to endorse religious pluralism. For a brief period, the "progressives" seemed to have the upper hand in the Muhammadiyah, revitalizing religious and societal debate in the organization with thought-provoking new ideas. This caused a backlash and a temporary reversal, as the organization veered to the right.

Like other large associations, the Muhammadiyah has five-yearly congresses, where a new board is elected and major policy decisions are taken. At the 2005 congress, the "progressives" suffered a severe blow, for none of them was re-elected into the board. It is important to realize that decisions at the congress are taken by majority vote by the delegates, who represent local branches and are close to the grassroots. Jakarta and Yogyakarta, where most of the "progressive" thinkers as well as organization officers are based, have only a minor voice in the congress. There has therefore often been a disjunction between the discourse of leading thinkers and the decisions of the congresses. The 1995 and 2000 congresses had brought a new generation of intellectuals at the helm of the organization, who represented various shades of "progressive" thought and revived critical thought in the organization. Hermeneutics replaced Islamic legal thought as the dominant mode of discourse. Dialogue with other religions received more emphasis, as well as a more positive appreciation of local culture and art, to which the Muhammadiyah had always had an ambivalent attitude.

The internal opposition to the rise of the "progressives" from the side of the "puritans" was also fed by the growing opposition to liberal and pluralist religious thought within the Muslim community in general, where these new intellectual trends were perceived as part of a broader military and ideological assault of the West on an embattled Islam. The "progressives" had little support in the regions away from Java and were defeated at the 2005 congress. The new board consisted largely of non-ideological organization bureaucrats and a few outspoken "puritans". The new chairman, Din Syamsuddin, was widely seen as embodying the conservative backlash. He had in previous years acquired the image of a hardliner, often speaking out against the West on behalf of embattled Muslims. As the secretary general of the MUI he had made his mark as a spokesman for conservative causes, in defence of radical movements, and against the rights of religious minorities. Nothing is, however, exactly as it seems from outside, and within the organization Din is widely perceived as a person who can bridge the gap between the "puritans" and the "conservatives". Significantly, he has been patronizing some prominent young progressives and as the chairman has kept the Muhammadiyah on a middle course.

In Burhani's analysis, the victory of the "puritans" and "conservatives" was less absolute and more ephemeral than many outside observers thought. Whatever the differences between the "conservatives" and the "progressives", when the organization itself appears under threat they tend to unite in its defence. A case in point was the recent threat to the very identity of the Muhammadiyah from the side of radical Muslim groups, notably the Tarbiyah movement (out of which the political party PKS emerged). In the last few years, both the NU and Muhammadiyah discovered that they were vulnerable to infiltration and takeover of assets by radical Islamist movements that to some extent shared their discourse. In the case of the NU, this was especially the Hizb ut-Tahrir, several of whose leading activists have a NU family and educational background; in Muhammadiyah, Tarbiyah activists appeared most successful. Several mosques that had been the bases of local Muhammadiyah or NU communities were gradually taken over by members of one of the radical movements, who created an entirely different atmosphere and monopolized the pulpit for their own preachers. More seriously, a Muhammadiyah school was taken over by Tarbiyah activists, who changed the curriculum and renamed the school. The Muhammadiyah's authority in religious matters was threatened when the PKS announced another date for the Feast of Sacrifice in 2005 than the one determined by the Muhammadiyah, and some Muhammadiyah members followed the PKS rather than their own organization.

These incidents caused grave concern among committed Muhammadiyah members. In 2007 the Muhammadiyah organized a *Tanwir* (a national conference of smaller scope than a congress, held between two consecutive congresses), which was completely dominated by the issue of how to defend the organization against further takeovers and to define its identity *vis-à-vis* the PKS and other radical groups. "Conservatives" and "progressives" were largely in agreement on the need to keep the Muhammadiyah and PKS strictly separate, even though the conservatives may have held many ideas in common with the latter. There are in fact numerous people who are members of both the Muhammadiyah and the PKS. Perceiving that this could cause conflicts of loyalty, the *Tanwir* ended with a decision demanding strict loyalty to the organization from its members, especially those employed at Muhammadiyah-owned institutions. (The demand of unambiguous loyalty, incidentally, was not only meant to counter the threat of infiltration and takeover by the PKS or other radical movements, but also that of tying the Muhammadiyah to any specific political party, and more specifically the efforts of some young people to establish a Muhammadiyah-based political party, PMB.)

In taking the first, modest, steps against the growing influence of PKS and other radical movements within the organization, the Muhammadiyah may start moving back towards a position "in the middle" as favoured in words if not always in practice. It does not mean, however, that the position of the progressives has improved; they remain marginalized within the organization. The Muhammadiyah has not been very supportive of some of the MUI's pet projects, such as the anti-pornography legislation and local Shariah regulations, but the organization consented with the *fatwa* against the Ahmadiyah (although in the past the relations between the Muhammadiyah and Ahmadiyah had been quite good) and against Islamic liberalism.

SHARIAH AND POLITICS IN SOUTH SULAWESI

South Sulawesi is a province with a strong tradition of Islamic radicalism, and it is perhaps not surprising that after the fall of the Soeharto regime the region was home to one of the most vocal movements for the enforcement of the Shariah in the country, KPPSI (Preparatory Committee for the Implementation of Shariah). This Shariah movement, the Muslim opposition to it, and its impact on Muslim-Christian relations in the province in the early twenty-first century are the subjects of Mujiburrahman's contribution.

Along with West Java and Aceh, South Sulawesi had been, between 1952 and 1962, one of the regional bases of the Darul Islam rebellion, with which several later radical movements appear to have had historical connections. The South Sulawesi Darul Islam, led by Kahar Muzakkar, had combined a strong regionalist aspect with Islamic Puritanism. Unlike its West Javanese counterpart, it had strongly opposed syncretistic religious practices as well as Sufism, and it had also been oppressive towards the significant Christian minority in the province. This had limited the popularity of the movement even among pious Muslims.

Many leading personalities preferred to accommodate themselves with the government, and both traditionalists and reformist Muslims massively joined Golkar during the New Order, turning this political machine into a vehicle for representing regional as well as personal career interests. South Sulawesi became the province where Golkar received the highest percentage of votes. Two famous and successful sons of the region, B.J. Habibie and Jusuf Kalla, established strong patronage networks in the worlds of education and trade, and helped strengthen the voice of the province at the centre. Several other persons from the region became influential and powerful at the national level while remaining strongly attached to their region, making South Sulawesi probably the most influential part of Indonesia's outer islands.

After the demise of the New Order, various groups and networks with personal or ideological links to the Darul Islam resurfaced, as did the regionalist and Islamist demands associated with the movement. One important network is that of the *pesantren* Hidayatullah, established in Balikpapan (East Kalimantan) in the early 1970s by an adjutant of Kahar Muzakkar. It became the centre of a nationwide network of *pesantren* (most of them linked with the Bugis diaspora) of an internationalist Islamist orientation and published a journal, *Suara Hidayatullah*, that took up major international issues from an Islamist standpoint and after the fall of Soeharto openly supported radical movements. The Hidayatullah *pesantren* in Makassar, the capital of South Sulawesi, is led by a son of Kahar Muzakkar, Aziz Kahar, who came to play a prominent role in Islamic activism in the post-Soeharto years, becoming the chief leader of the pro-Shariah committee KPPSI.

The KPPSI grew out of a broad coalition of Muslim groups of different ideological persuasion, similar to such committees set up elsewhere in the country, the Front Umat Islam. Besides persons with a Darul Islam background, it included well-known activists of the Muslim students movement of the 1980s and 1990s (HMI-MPO and PII), representatives of the Dewan Dakwah (DDII), and members of Wahdah Islamiyah (Islamic Unity), a group originally affiliated with a wing of the Muhammadiyah that was sympathetic to the Darul Islam and that had come under Salafi influence. Several activists of the FUI took part in the convention in Yogyakarta in 2000 at which the Majelis Mujahidin Indonesia (MMI) was established, and officers of the MMI were present at the meeting in Makassar where the KPPSI was formally launched. A paramilitary group, Jundullah, that had earlier been established by people from South Sulawesi in Solo, joined the KPPSI as its military arm, strengthening the perception that this was just a reincarnation of the Darul Islam. The arrest of several members of Jundullah in connection with bombings in Makassar in 2002 damaged the reputation of the KPPSI in the public eye.

The KPPSI was vocal in its demand of the enforcement of Shariah in the province but not very explicit about what this should mean nor very successful in achieving even symbolic successes. Politicians, up to the provincial governor, paid some lip service to the idea of enacting regional Shariah legislation but since a broad range of public personalities with solid Islamic credentials opposed it, the issue was shelved — except in the district of Bulukumba, in the southernmost part of the province. Bulukumba was a strong basis of the Darul Islam rebellion; its population is almost without exception Muslim, and the district has a high degree of organization, with numerous mosques and Islamic study clubs and Muslim associations. The regent (*bupati*) of this district issued in 2002 and 2003 a number of "Shariah regulations", ranging from a ban of alcohol and the imposition of the Islamic alms tax (*zakat*) on civil servants to an Islamic dress code and some aspects of Islamic criminal law. Significantly, this *bupati* was a Golkar politician and had no connections with the KPPSI but believed the regulations would be popular with his constituency.

The KPPSI has an ambivalent attitude towards democracy — it does not think highly of a system in which a majority vote carries more weight than the divine command — but its members do take part in elections, and several were elected into the provincial parliament. Aziz Kahar himself was elected as one of the province's four deputies in the Regional Representative Council (DPD) in the centre, and in 2007 he stood as a candidate in the elections for provincial governor. He had the support of the Islamic parties PPP and PBB as well as what remained of the Darul Islam network but had to compete with two candidates who had the support of Golkar and of PAN and PDIP respectively. His poor showing in the contest (just over 20 per cent of the vote) indicated that the people of the province have other priorities than the formalization of the Shariah.

THE STRUGGLE FOR TRUE ISLAM IN SOLO

The Central Javanese city of Solo, the site of Muhammad Wildan's contribution, is home to various radical Islamic movements, which have manifested themselves quite conspicuously since 1998. Yet there has not even been an attempt to have local Shariah regulations enacted here. This paradox is easily explained: strict, practising Muslims are a minority in the city and even more so in the surrounding district; syncretistic Muslims (*abangan*) constitute the majority here. Solo is a centre of refined Javanese court culture but also has a history of political radicalism, of the left as well as Islamic, and including such unlikely phenomena as the Muslim Communism of Haji Misbach in the 1920s and the "Mega-Bintang" (i.e., PDI-P and PPP) coalition of nationalist and Islamic opponents of the Soeharto regime in the mid-1990s. The city has sizable Chinese and Arab communities, both involved in trade and still strongly concentrated in distinct neighbourhoods, Jebres and Pasar Kliwon, respectively. Two other neighbourhoods are known as concentrations of Javanese pious Muslims, the Kauman next to the court mosque, where court and mosque officials live, and Laweyan, home to Javanese small entrepreneurs, mostly in the batik industry. The other neighbourhoods are predominantly *abangan*.

Contrary to the widely held view that opposes the syncretistic culture of the Javanese courts to scriptural Islam, the first institutions of Islamic education in Solo were established at the initiative of the court. Surprisingly, neither the Muhammadiyah nor the NU had much influence here until much later, and these associations that dominate Islamic education elsewhere in Java have remained rather weak in Solo. The school Manba' al-'Ulum, established a century ago for the education of the courtly elite, was opened to the general public at Independence and has remained a major centre of religious learning since. It was only during the New Order period that it received serious competitors.

Solo was one of the places where the Indonesian Dakwah Council (DDII) concentrated its efforts at improving the quality of Indonesian Muslims. The DDII was established by former Masyumi politicians who were no longer allowed to participate actively in politics and who saw *dakwah*, Islamic propagation, as the most needed and appropriate method of changing social norms and social behaviour. Strongly supported by the national leadership, the Central Javanese branch based in Solo established an Islamic radio station, an Islamic hospital, and a *pesantren* dedicated to training committed preachers for carrying out the *dakwah* mission. The *pesantren*, Al-Mukmin, later became widely known by the name of the village where it moved after a few years, Ngruki. Its chief leader, Abdullah Sungkar, was born into Solo's Arab community, had in his youth been active in Masyumi's youth league and was a board member of the Central Javanese DDII. His closest collaborator, Abu Bakar Ba'asyir, also of Arab descent, hailed from Jombang in East Java, was educated in the "modern" *pesantren* of Gontor (which was strongly oriented towards the Arab world) and at an Al Irsyad college (also strongly Arabic-oriented).

In Sungkar's view, the ultimate aim of *dakwah* should be the establishment of an Islamic state. Increasingly influenced by the ideas and strategies of the Egyptian Muslim Brotherhood, he joined the underground Darul Islam network when this was being revived and used the pesantren for recruiting committed cadres of an Islamic movement. The recruits were trained in small groups (*usrah*) that constituted cells of a clandestine movement. In 1985 Sungkar and Ba'asyir, who had already spent three years in detention for their opposition to New Order policies, fled to Malaysia with some loyal followers to avoid renewed arrest. Much of the *usrah* network remained in place, however, and several other teachers in Ngruki were deeply involved, as well as a part of the students. This gave rise to an internal conflict in the *pesantren* between these "*haraki*" ("activist") elements and the managing foundation, that wanted to put the school on a more solid financial footing and get rid of the radical stigma in order to attract more students. In a major clash between the two factions in 1995, some of the radical teachers were expelled from Ngruki and established a new *pesantren* or joined an existing one in the Solo region. Several former students of these two "radical" *pesantren* were later involved in violent actions.

Possibly the conflict in Ngruki was also related to another rupture that emerged around the same time. In Malaysia Sungkar had come increasingly under the influence of global Salafi jihadism. After a clash with Masduki, the leader of the branch of the Darul Islam (NII) to which he adhered, Sungkar broke away and set himself up as the *amir* (commander) of his own network, henceforth known as Jamaah Islamiyah. The NII underground in Central Java thus split into two separate groups, with different command structures, JI and the part of NII that remained loyal to Masduki. Both appear to have been present in Ngruki, but NII predominated.

For understandable reasons, Ngruki has received a lot of attention, but it is not the most influential *dakwah* initiative of the early New Order. The Majelis Tafsir Al-Qur'an (MTA) started as the adult education equivalent of a *pesantren*, led by some of the men who also started the Islamic radio station, and it developed into a local, informal variant of Muhammadiyah with numerous Islamic study classes, focussing especially on the purification of Islamic belief and practice. Adapting its style to local culture and specifically addressing *abangan* audiences while spreading a message critical of that culture and worldview, this movement reaches a much wider public than any other. Its constituency is mostly the social and geographical periphery of Solo; no Arabs are active in it, and only a small number of university educated people.

In the first years after the demise of the New Order, Solo witnessed the emergence of a large number of Islamic vigilante groups, similar to those in the Jakarta region but larger in number and even more active. Most of these groups were ephemeral, emerging and dissolving in response to specific events in Indonesia or the world outside (the civil war in the Moluccas, the American attack of Iraq). Perhaps the most conspicuous and the most stable of the vigilante groups is the FPIS (Front Pemuda Islam Surakarta, Muslim Youth Front of Surakarta). Besides the occasional anti-

Western demonstration, its main activity seemed to consist of "sweepings" of bars, nightclubs, brothels and other places of immoral behaviour, as well as hotels with foreign guests. (One is tempted to say that they did not waste energy on demanding local Shariah regulations but directly imposed their own version of Shariah rule instead.)

FPIS (not to be confused with Jakarta's FPI or Front Pembela Islam, Front of Defenders of Islam) has close links with another Solo-based Islamic group, known as the Jamaah (congregation) of Gumuk, after the location of the mosque where the group is based. This is a rather closed community or sect, whose members distinguish themselves by dress style similar to that of the Salafis but who have no relation to the broader Salafi movement. Most of the group's members hail from poor families in peripheral districts of Solo and must have *abangan* backgrounds.

There has been a general shift in religious orientation towards Salafism, the extremely puritan brand of Islam that is the official doctrine in Saudi Arabia, which appears to have affected almost all radical movements and organizations in Solo. Both wings of the Salafi movement that was established by young graduates from Saudi universities in the 1990s — the activist wing led by Ja'far Umar Thalib, which became Laskar Jihad, as well as Ja'far's apolitical rivals — have a certain presence in Solo. Sungkar and Ba'asyir, and following them their disciples in Solo, shifted from Muslim Brotherhood ideology towards Salafism, and even within those branches of the NII that had not followed Sungkar in his conflict with Masduki, Salafism gained influence.

There seems to be a paradox in the fact that the Salafi movement is making its advances especially in parts of the country where syncretistic varieties of Islam, the opposite extreme to Salafism, are predominant, such as Solo. Salafism appears to be attractive precisely to people of *abangan* background because it is simple and rigid, and has clear rules; its transnational character gives it the additional attraction of cosmopolitanism. More generally, one may conclude that radical movements were relatively successful in Solo because the large national mainstream Muslim organizations such as Muhammadiyah and NU were only marginally present there. To an important segment of society that had long felt marginalized, the radical movements offered a more "modern" form of religious involvement and integration into larger society. In spite of their relative successes, however, the radical movements remained minorities among a majority that still holds strongly to *abangan* views and values.

A BRIEF NOTE ON THE TERMS
"LIBERAL", "PROGRESSIVE", "CONSERVATIVE",
"FUNDAMENTALIST", AND "ISLAMIST"

I have, in the preceding, hesitantly used the term "liberal", for lack of a better and less controversial one, but I am aware that this term carries connotations that many of the thinkers to whom it is applied reject. The founders of the Liberal Islam Network (JIL) adopted this name from an influential anthology of texts by modern Muslim thinkers that represented a broad range of intellectual positions (Kurzman 1998). They have also defended political and economic liberalism, which some of them see as inseparable from religious liberalism. Others, who may share many of the religious views of JIL, object to the term "liberal Islam" precisely because of the association with neo-liberalism. Conservatives have tended to employ the term "liberal" as a stigmatizing label against a wide range of critical religious thought, equating it with rationalism and irreligiosity.

The term "neo-modernist", used by the Australian scholar Greg Barton to describe the thought of Nurcholish Madjid and friends (Barton 1995, 1997), does not carry the same connotations of economic and political policy, and it is in fact appropriate for those who, like Nurcholish, are influenced by Fazlur Rahman, but does not really fit the thinkers, such as Abdurrahman Wahid, whose intellectual roots lie on the traditionalist rather than the reformist side of the spectrum. Some of those who reject the label of "liberal" prefer to call their views, because of the emphasis on human rights (especially women's and minority rights) and on empowerment of the weak and oppressed, and because of their generally left orientation, "progressive" or "emancipatory Islam".[12] Several other terms have been suggested but none has gained general acceptance. I shall be speaking of "liberals and progressives" to refer to the entire range of thinkers and activists offering non-literal reinterpretations of Islamic concepts.

The term "conservative" refers to the various currents that reject modernist, liberal or progressive re-interpretations of Islamic teachings and adhere to established doctrines and social order. Conservatives notably object to the idea of gender equality and challenges to established authority, as well as to modern hermeneutical approaches to scripture. There are conservatives among traditionalist as well as reformist Muslims (i.e., in Nahdlatul Ulama as well as Muhammadiyah), just as there are liberals and progressives in both camps.

By "fundamentalist", I mean those currents that focus on the key scriptural sources of Islam, i.e. Qur'an and *hadith*, and adhere to a literal and strict reading thereof. They obviously share some views with most conservatives, such as the rejection of hermeneutics and of rights-based discourses, but may clash with conservatives over established practices lacking strong scriptural foundations. The term "Islamist" finally refers to those movements that have a conception of Islam as a political system and strive to establish an Islamic state.

Notes

[1] Judicious studies and analyses of these events can be found in Cribb (1990), especially in Cribb's own contribution. On the role in these massacres of a major Muslim youth organization, affiliated with Nahdlatul Ulama, see Bruinessen (2007).

[2] The fear of "Christianization" (*Kristenisasi*) is the subject of the excellent dissertation by Mujiburrahman (2006).

[3] Probably the best study of these movements so far is Noorhaidi Hasan's dissertation on Laskar Jihad (Hasan 2006).

[4] The events have spawned a considerable industry of terrorism and security studies, most of the products of which are of dubious quality. The best analyses of Indonesia's Muslim terrorist networks are those written by Sidney Jones for the International Crisis Group, available at <www.crisisgroup.org/>.

[5] The stated sympathy with Islamist issues was not translated, however, in corresponding voting behaviour. See the survey carried out by Saiful Mujani and the Jakarta-based research institute PPIM, reported in Mujani and Liddle (2004), and the critical comments in Bruinessen (2004).

[6] Most of these regional regulations (*perda Syariah*) concern the prescription of modest dress codes, limitations of women's freedom of movement, bans of gambling and the sale and consumption of alcohol, and such like. A good overview of these regulations is given in Bush (2008); see also Mujiburrahman's contribution to this volume.

[7] A persuasive case for this analysis is made by Gerry van Klinken (2005, 2007).

[8] This includes such parties as PAN and PKB, that appeal to pious Muslim voters affiliated with Muhammadiyah and Nahdlatul Ulama, respectively, but do not call for implementation of the Shariah by the state. The Islamist parties (PKS, PBB and PPP) jointly gained less than 15 per cent.

[9] The Indonesian text of these *fatwa*, which were adopted by the MUI's fatwa commission at the Majelis' Seventh Conference (July 2005), as well as an explanation of the reasoning behind the fatwa against secularism, pluralism and liberalism, can be found at the MUI's website, <www.mui.or.id/> (accessed

June 2010). The concepts of "pluralism" and "religious liberalism" were defined in a restrictive sense as "proclaiming the equal validity of all religions" and "the purely rational interpretation of religious texts and the acceptance of only those religious doctrines that are compatible with reason". The fatwa clearly targeted, however, various groups that adhered to less radical views of liberalism and pluralism and that will be discussed below.

[10] The Ahmadiyah had been the target of physical attacks by vigilante squads only weeks before the MUI conference. Significantly, the MUI made no statement condemning the violence against Ahmadiyah members and appeared to consider the Ahmadiyah as the offending party. See Crouch (2009).

[11] Ethnic Arab leaders of radical Islamic movements in Indonesia included Ja'far Umar Thalib of Laskar Jihad, Abdullah Sungkar and Abu Bakar Ba'asyir of Jama'ah Islamiyah, "Habib" Rizieq Syihab of Front Pembela Islam, and Abdurrahman al-Baghdadi of Hizbut Tahrir Indonesia. The "Arabization thesis" is discussed more extensively in Dutch in Bruinessen (2006), and in English in a forthcoming article by the present author.

[12] A range of such approaches, mostly written by Muslim intellectuals living in the West, is presented in the programmatic volume edited by Omid Safi (2003). A collection of articles by one of the contributors to that volume, Ebrahim Moosa, were published in Indonesian translation by the Jakarta-based Center for Islam and Pluralism; see Moosa (2004).

References

Barton, Greg. "Indonesia's Nurcholish Madjid and Abdurrahman Wahid as Intellectual ʿUlamâ: The Meeting of Islamic Traditionalism and Modernism in Neo-Modernist Thought". *Studia Islamika* 4, no. 1 (1997): 29–81.

Barton, Gregory James. "The Emergence of Neo-Modernism: A Progressive, Liberal Movement of Islamic Thought in Indonesia. A Textual Study Examining the Writings of Nurcholish Madjid, Djohan Effendi, Ahmad Wahib and Abdurrahman Wahid, 1968–1980". Ph.D. thesis. Clayton: Monash University, 1995.

Bruinessen, Martin van. "Islamic State or State Islam? Fifty Years of State-Islam Relations in Indonesia". In *Indonesien am Ende des 20. Jahrhunderts*, edited by Ingrid Wessel. Hamburg: Abera-Verlag, 1996. Available online at <http://www.hum.uu.nl/medewerkers/m.vanbruinessen/publications/Bruinessen_State_Islam_or_Islamic_State.pdf>.

———. "Post-Soeharto Muslim Engagements with Civil Society and Democratization". In *Indonesia in Transition: Rethinking "Civil Society", "Region" and "Crisis"*, edited by Hanneman Samuel and Henk Schulte Nordholt. Yogyakarta: Pustaka Pelajar, 2004.

————. "Arabisering van de Indonesische Islam?" *ZemZem, Tijdschrift over het Midden-Oosten, Noord-Afrika en Islam* 2, no. 1 (2006): 73–84.

————. "Ansor". *Encyclopaedia of Islam*, 3rd ed., Part 2. Leiden: Brill, 2007.

————. "New Leadership, New Policies? The Nahdlatul Ulama Congress in Makassar". *Inside Indonesia* 101, July–September 2010. Online at <www. insideindonesia.org/>.

————. "What Happened to the Smiling Face of Indonesian Islam? Muslim Intellectualism and the Conservative Turn in Post-Suharto Indonesia". Working paper. Singapore: S. Rajaratnam School of International Studies, 2011.

————. "*Ghazwul Fikri* or Arabization? Indonesian Muslim Responses to Globalisation". In *Muslim Responses to Globalization in Southeast Asia*, edited by Ken Miichi and Omar Farouk Bajunid. Forthcoming.

Bush, Robin. "Regional Sharia Regulations in Indonesia: Anomaly or Symptom?" In *Expressing Islam: Religious Life and Politics in Indonesia*, edited by Greg Fealy and Sally White. Singapore: Institute of Southeast Asian Studies, 2008.

Cribb, Robert, ed. *The Indonesian Killings 1965–1966: Studies from Java and Bali*. Clayton: Centre of Southeast Asian Studies Monash University, 1990.

Crouch, Melissa. "Indonesia, Militant Islam and Ahmadiyah: Origins and Implications". Islam, Syari'ah and Governance Background Paper Series. Melbourne: Centre for Islamic Law and Society, University of Melbourne, 2009.

Gillespie, Piers. "Current Issues in Indonesian Islam: Analysing the 2005 Council of Indonesian Ulama *Fatwa* No. 7 Opposing Pluralism, Liberalism and Secularism". *Journal of Islamic Studies* 18, no. 2 (2007): 202–40.

Hasan, Noorhaidi. *Laskar Jihad: Islam, Militancy and the Quest for Identity in Post-New Order Indonesia*. Ithaca, NY: Cornell Southeast Asia Program, 2006.

Klinken, Gerry van. "New Actors, New Identities: Post-Suharto Ethnic Violence in Indonesia". In *Violent Internal Conflicts in Asia Pacific: Histories, Political Economies, and Policies*, edited by Dewi Fortuna Anwar. Jakarta: Yayasan Obor Indonesia, 2005.

————. *Communal Violence and Democratization in Indonesia: Small Town Wars*. London: Routledge, 2007.

Kurzman, Charles, ed. *Liberal Islam: A Source Book*. New York: Oxford University Press, 1998. Translated into Indonesian as *Wacana Islam Liberal*. Jakarta: Paramadina, 2001.

Moosa, Ebrahim. *Islam Progresif: Refleksi Dilematis tentang HAM, Modernitas dan Hak-hak Perempuan di dalam Hukum Islam* [Progressive Islam, Reflections on the Dilemmas of Human Rights, Modernity and Women's Rights in Islamic Law]. Jakarta: International Center for Islam and Pluralism (ICIP), 2004.

Mujani, Saiful and R. William Liddle. "Indonesia's Approaching Elections: Politics, Islam, and Public Opinion". *Journal of Democracy* 15, no. 1 (2004): 109–23.

Mujiburrahman. *Feeling Threatened: Muslim-Christian Relations in Indonesia's New Order.* Amsterdam: Amsterdam University Press, 2006. Available online at <http://igitur-archive.library.uu.nl/dissertations/2006-0915-201013/index.htm>.

Safi, Omid, ed. *Progressive Muslims: On Justice, Gender and Pluralism.* Oxford: Oneworld, 2003.

2

OVERVIEW OF MUSLIM ORGANIZATIONS, ASSOCIATIONS AND MOVEMENTS IN INDONESIA

Martin van Bruinessen

REFORMIST AND TRADITIONALIST ISLAM AND THE MAJOR ORGANIZATIONS REPRESENTING THEM

Indonesian Islam is characterized by an unusually high degree of organization. The two largest Muslim associations, **Muhammadiyah** and **Nahdlatul Ulama (NU)**, which have long dominated Muslim social life and educational activities in Indonesia, are probably the largest and most complex organizations of the entire Muslim world. Their claims of representing tens of millions of Indonesian Muslims were supported by a recent survey, according to which 12 and 42 per cent of Indonesia's Muslims identified themselves to some extent with the Muhammadiyah and NU, respectively. Those expressing a strong identification with these associations amounted to 4 and 17 per cent, which would amount to 9 and 38 million followers, respectively (Mujani and Liddle 2004). Card-carrying, dues-paying membership is no doubt considerably lower, but these two associations have reached a degree of societal penetration that is unparalleled in the Muslim world. They are administered by elected boards at the national, provincial, regency and district levels, and they have separate women's, youth and students' wings with parallel structures. The organizations provide a wide range of services to their constituencies, from education, health care and charity to answering religious questions and determining beginning and end of the fasting month.

It has long been common to distinguish two main streams in Indonesian Islam, dubbed "Modernists" (or "Reformists") and "Traditionalists". The Muhammadiyah and NU are the most conspicuous, though by no means the only representatives of these two streams. The Modernist/Reformist stream consists of a range of movements that strive to reform religious life by purging it of superstition, blind imitation of earlier generations, and beliefs and practices that are not supported by strong and authentic scriptural references. This includes especially relations with the spirit world, intercession by saints, and various forms of magic. The reformists' worship tends to be more austere, without the recitations of pious formulas and supererogatory prayers that characterize the worship of the traditionalists. As the most authoritative texts they refer, at least in theory, to the Qur'an and *hadith* (sayings and acts attributed to the Prophet) rather than to the classical texts of Islamic jurisprudence (*fiqh*) or mysticism (*tasawwuf*) studied by traditionalist ulama. Rejecting the scholastic tradition of pre-modern Islam, Indonesian Muslim modernists have not only called for a return to the Qur'an and *hadith* but insisted on rational interpretation of these sources, in the light of the needs of the time and in accordance with modern science. Most contemporary reformists, however, are wary of too much rationalism and contextualization, and one aspect of the developments discussed in this volume is the shift away from rationalistic modernism to more literal readings of scripture and puritanical reform.[1] In education, reformists generally favour modern, Western-type schools for their children, rather than the traditional Islamic *pesantren* education (reflecting the fact that Reformism has been largely an urban middle class phenomenon).

Traditionalists value rituals such as the commemoration of the Prophet's birth (*Mulud*), communal recitations of prayer formulas or of devotional poetry in praise of the Prophet, celebrations of the death anniversaries (*khaul*) of respected religious teachers and other saintly persons, visitations of saints' shrines and other graves (*ziyarah*), etc. They tend to be tolerant of the incorporation of local cultural forms of expression in their religious life. The scholars of Islam, ulama, are highly respected, and it is considered better to follow great ulama of the past rather than reason independently. The favourite form of education is the *pesantren* curriculum, in which the study of classical Arabic texts, with a strong emphasis on *fiqh*, Islamic jurisprudence, is central. The preferred self-designation is *Ahlus Sunnah wal Jama`ah* ("Followers of the Prophet's Tradition and Congregation").[2]

In the 1950s, there appeared to be a close correlation between religious and political affiliation, and Indonesia's Muslims could apparently be neatly divided into "modernist" and "traditionalist" blocs, besides an even larger bloc of "nominal" or "syncretistic" Muslims (*abangan*). The fierce competition between the major political parties of those years made this division appear as more pervasive and meaningful than it probably was in daily life: the NU was from 1952 until 1973 one of the two major Muslim political parties, and the other Muslim party, **Masyumi**, was dominated by "modernist" Muslims. The two large secular parties, **PNI (Partai Nasionalis Indonesia)** and **PKI (Partai Komunis Indonesia)** drew on different segments of the "nominal" Muslim and non-Muslim population. In practice, "traditionalist" Islam shaded into the syncretistic beliefs and practices of the nominal Muslims, and the difference between "modernist" and "traditionalist" Islam was not always all that sharp either. Masyumi, moreover, was a front of different Muslim associations, several of which were in fact "traditionalist" in religious orientation.

After the highly politicized Sukarno years, the New Order was a period of depoliticization and economic growth. The differences between the "modernist" and "traditionalist" associations became less rigid, and the dividing line between nominal and more strictly practising Muslims more fluid, as increasing numbers of "traditionalist" and *abangan* Muslims urbanized and gained access to modern education.

The major reformist associations

The **Muhammadiyah** was the first reformist (or modernist) association of Indonesia, established in Yogyakarta in 1912. The Muhammadiyah's most conspicuous activities have been in education and social work: it has established numerous schools, hospitals and orphanages, emulating the work of Christian missions. Muhammadiyah schools teach primarily modern subjects; religious instruction takes only a modest place and uses Indonesian textbooks, no Arabic texts.

Within the Muhammadiyah, the regions of Yogyakarta and West Sumatra have long been seen as competing poles, representing different styles of reformism. The founder of the Muhammadiyah, Ahmad Dahlan, was a religious official at the Sultan's court in Yogyakarta, and the central board of the organization long steered a course between the reform of the strictly religious practices and accommodation of Javanese cultural practices. West Sumatra had a strong reformist tradition even before the emergence of the Muhammadiyah, and the Sumatran Muhammadiyah branches have tended to be more puritan (i.e. placing more emphasis on purging Islam of practices not supported by Qur'an and *hadith*) than the Javanese branches.[3]

In colonial times, there was a certain correlation between the Muhammadiyah and Muslim entrepreneurship: the *batik* producers and traders of Yogyakarta and of Pekalongan were strong supporters of the Muhammadiyah. After independence, the Muhammadiyah became increasingly an association of Muslim civil servants, and presently the organization is pervaded by a civil servant ethos. The Muhammadiyah's concern with education has remained: it controls a vast network of primary, middle (SMP) and secondary (SMA) schools and even universities. The Muhammadiyah is strongly represented in the higher echelons of the Ministry of Education, and in the post-Soeharto period it has successfully attempted to gain control of the Ministry and have its views on education enshrined in legislation.[4]

Other reformist associations that were established around the same time as the Muhammadiyah include **Al Irsyad** and **Persis**. All three are reformist in religious doctrine (in the sense of rejecting beliefs and practices that were not present in original Islam) as well in method of education. Besides, there are a number of reformist associations of regional importance, about which more below.

Al Irsyad emerged in 1913 within Indonesia's Arab community, from a conflict between the *sayyids*, the putative descendants of the Prophet, who on the basis of their inherited charisma claimed special privileges, and progressive thinkers who proclaimed the equality of all men. The conflict split the Arab educational and welfare association **Jamiat Chair** (**al-Jam'iyya al-Khayriyya**), which had been established as early as 1905. Al Irsyad was to remain an ethnic association of exclusively non-*sayyid* Arabs, strongly influenced by Egyptian reformism (and Arab nationalism). It established Arabic-medium schools, using textbooks from Egypt. The Jamiat Chair henceforth remained firmly in the hands of the *sayyid* faction.[5] Al Irsyad was initially progressive in orientation but later became increasingly puritanical and conservative, drawing closer to the Saudi version of Salafi Islam.

Persis (an abbreviation of **Persatuan Islam**, Islamic Union) was established in 1923 by a group of reformist-minded Sumatrans living in the West Javanese city of Bandung, with a modest self-educated man of Indian descent, A. Hassan, as the leading religious thinker. Of all Indonesia's reformist movements, it was the least political and the most puritan, concentrating its attention on the purification of ritual and belief, to the virtual exclusion of social and economic concerns. Bandung has remained the centre of this organization, with its first major educational institution, a modernist *pesantren*. A secondary centre emerged later in

Bangil in East Java, when A. Hassan's son Abdul Qadir settled there. He established another religious school there and began publishing the influential journal *Al-Muslimun*, which found an audience well beyond the membership of Persis.[6]

Persis represents a home-grown version of Salafism, emphasizing a strict adherence to the Qur'an and *hadith* and perpetually struggling against beliefs and practices that were considered later accretions (*bid'ah*, "innovation"). Though a small organization, it has been quite influential, because its leading thinkers were highly respected by other reformists. Its most famous, and most influential, member was Mohamad Natsir, who in the struggle for independence joined the Masyumi party and became its most prominent leader.

A very different type of association, much more explicitly political than the others, was the **Sarekat Islam** ("Islamic League", **SI**). Established in 1912 as an association of indigenous traders to protect common interests against Chinese competition, it very soon turned into a Muslim nationalist association that drew its following from a broad cross-section of the indigenous population. Around 1920, some branches had a working class (Semarang) or peasant following (Solo) and drifted to a form of Muslim communism, causing a rift in the organization between the "Red S.I." and the "White S.I." — the latter patronized by the colonial government, the former suppressed.[7] The Sarekat Islam was not a Muslim reformist movement properly speaking, but it was Indonesia's first modern mass movement and became one of the first political parties (Partai Sarekat Islam, and from 1929 onwards Partai Sarekat Islam Indonesia, PSII). The PSII had a lasting influence on the social and political agendas of other movements. It lost its dramatic impact in the 1930s but survived into Independence, until it was forced to merge with the other Muslim parties into the PPP in 1973.

Traditionalist Islam and the Nahdlatul Ulama association

The **Nahdlatul Ulama** (**NU**) was established in 1926, i.e. a decade and a half after the reformist associations, and largely in response to the perceived threat to traditional religious practices such as the visiting of saints' graves and various other devotional practices that reformist movements represented. The abolition of the Caliphate by Mustafa Kemal (Ataturk) in 1924 and the conquest of Mecca by Abd al-Aziz ibn Saud in the same year were important triggers: the founders of the NU had spent years pursuing traditional Islamic studies in Mecca, and they were very much focused on developments in the Middle East. In Kemalist Turkey, the traditional Islamic schools (*medrese*) were abolished, Sufi orders banned and saints' shrines closed; in Saudi-dominated Arabia, holy graves were razed and traditional devotional practices banned. There were serious concerns that such purges of traditional Islamic practices as well as the traditional *pesantren* curriculum might also occur in Indonesia.

The establishment of a formal association was in itself a modern response, which did not at all come naturally to traditional Muslims, because of its association with the non-Muslim colonizing power. It involved drawing up by-laws in accordance with Dutch legislation, which had to be signed in front of a notary public. Only after the most senior Javanese Muslim scholar of those days, Hasyim Asy'ari, had reached the conclusion that under the circumstances such an innovation was religiously legitimate, did his colleagues dare to take this step. The name chosen for the association — Nahdlatul Ulama is Arabic for "Awakening of the Scholars" and brings to mind the modernizing cultural movement in Arab countries known as al-Nahda — indicates an awareness on the part of its founders that the times were changing.

The founders of the NU were religious scholars and traders (many in fact combined those roles), and the association has from the beginning been closely associated with the traditional religious schools (*pesantren*) and the charismatic teachers (*kiai*) ruling these institutions. It is especially the large *pesantren* of East and Central Java, the rural populations that they serve, and the local businessmen with whom the *kiai* entertain mutually beneficial relations who constitute the NU's main constituency. The NU defines its religious identity by the core elements of the traditional *pesantren* curriculum: Islamic jurisprudence (*fiqh*) of one of the four Sunni schools, Ash'ari theology, and the orthodox mysticism of Ghazali — the elements that puritanical reformers would replace by reliance on the Qur'an and *hadith* alone.[8] The relationship between the NU and the *pesantren* is, however, a very different one from that between Muhammadiyah and its schools. Whereas the latter organization controls its own modern schools, NU has no equivalent authority over the *pesantren*, which belong to individual *kiai*.[9] The *kiai* have a degree of control over the NU that would be unthinkable for school directors in the Muhammadiyah.

The NU was originally established as an association of *kiai*, and when it developed into an organization with a mass following, the *kiai* remained a special elite within the organization. This is reflected in the structure of the board, in which at all levels the executive (named *Tanfidziyah*) is at least nominally subordinate to a religious council (named *Syuriah*), of which only *kiai* are members. The *Tanfidziyah*, not surprisingly, tends to be more pragmatic than the *Syuriah* and more directly involved in politics and relations with other social and political actors, but *kiai* have often exerted considerable pressure on the *Tanfidziyah*. Major policy decisions were taken at congresses, at which the *kiai* retained a disproportionate influence, even when they were far outnumbered by other members.

After Indonesia had gained independence, the NU was transformed into a political party. In the 1955 parliamentary elections, it ended up as the third largest party, with 18.5 per cent of the vote. The pliability of its leaders helped it to survive the years of Guided Democracy under Sukarno and the transition to Soeharto's New Order. In 1973, the Soeharto regime forced all Muslim parties to merge into a single one, PPP (Partai Persatuan Pembangunan, United Development Party), and the NU disappeared as an independent political party (although its members remained a recognizable group within the PPP). The merger did not, however, affect the NU's existence as a religious and educational association. A decade later, at its 1984 congress, the NU decided to withdraw completely from party politics, to sever its special relationship with the PPP, and not to allow members to hold simultaneously positions in the NU and a political party. These decisions coincided with the rise of Abdurrahman Wahid as the chairman of the Tanfidziyah; he held that position for three periods (1984–99), during which he grew into one of the country's most influential civilians, an opponent of Soeharto's authoritarianism as well as political Islam. Soon after the fall of the Soeharto regime, it was Abdurrahman Wahid himself who established a political party that he intended to be the political vehicle of the NU and his own ambitions, the **PKB** (Partai Kebangkitan Bangsa, Party of National Awakening). The formal separation between the NU and political parties has remained, however.

The NU is a truly national organization, with active branches in all provinces (including even Papua), but it is significantly stronger in some provinces than in others. Its true heartland is still East Java, and Central Java comes second. North Sumatra (more precisely, the Mandailing Batak ethnic group) and South Kalimantan (the Banjarese) are two other regions where the NU is strongest.[10]

Regionally based Muslim associations

Besides these large, national associations, there are a number of associations whose impact has largely remained restricted to specific regions or ethnic groups.

Perti (**Persatuan Tarbiyah Islamiyah**, Union for Islamic Education) is strongly associated with the Minangkabau ethnic group of West Sumatra. It was established by teachers of traditional Islamic schools (*surau* and *madrasah*, corresponding to the Javanese *pesantren*). The Minangkabau have migrated all over the Archipelago, and one finds branches of Perti wherever there are significant Minangkabau communities. In matters of religious orthodoxy, Perti is perhaps even more conservative than NU.

At Independence, Perti declared itself a political party (it was the first group to leave the umbrella organization Masyumi). In the early 1960s, Perti was considered somewhat "leftist"; its leadership cooperated willingly in Sukarno's Guided Democracy and entertained cordial relations with the Communist Party. For this reason, the organization had some difficulties in the early Soeharto period. When all Muslim parties were ordered to merge into the PPP, one faction of Perti did so; another faction decided to join Golkar instead, in which it remained a distinct component under the name of **Tarbiyah Islamiyah**.

Three other traditionalist regional associations deserve mention: **al-Washliyah** in North Sumatra, strongly associated with the Mandailing Batak ethnic group; **al-Khairat** in Central Sulawesi; and **Persatuan Umat Islam** (**PUI**) in West Java. These associations introduced reforms in the method of education but remained traditionalist in terms of doctrine and ritual.

The one region with a strong regional association that is reformist in its religious views (besides West Java's Persis, which is not exclusively associated with that province nor with the Sundanese ethnic group) is Aceh, where **PUSA** (**Persatuan Ulama Seluruh Aceh**, All-Aceh Union of Islamic Scholars), which was deeply involved in efforts to purge Islam of local accretions, was long the most influential association. In the 1950s, PUSA also provided the core leadership of the Acehnese Darul Islam movement (Siegel 1969). The traditionalist association Perti also had a distinct following in Aceh, but this appeared to be restricted to regions with a strong Minangkabau influence.

A different but significant ethnic Muslim association is the Union of Indonesian Chinese Muslims, **PITI** (**Persatuan Islam Tionghwa Indonesia**). Since the demise of the New Order regime, PITI has adopted a higher profile and organized Muslim festivities with a Chinese cultural flavour. An earlier association, **BAKOM-PKB** (**Badan Komunikasi Penghayatan Kesatuan Bangsa**, Contact Organ for Awareness of the Unity of the Nation), had propagated the conversion of Indonesian Chinese as a means of being accepted as fully Indonesian citizens and had favoured cultural assimilation.[11]

Beyond modernism and traditionalism

The modernist-traditionalist dichotomy, though still frequently used as a shorthand by Indonesian Muslim actors, does not take account of a number of important developments of the past decades. On the one hand, traditionalists have come to adopt much of the discourse of earlier generations of reformists; on the other, reformist associations such as the Muhammadiyah have lost some of their modernist and innovating character and become more conservative. In the 1980s and 1990s, there was arguably more intellectual ferment in the NU, more critical reflection on the tradition, than there was reflection on reform in the Muhammadiyah.

More importantly, there were new intellectual trends that could not be assigned to the reformist or the traditionalist mainstreams but appeared to transcend both. The most significant of these, during the 1980s and 1990s, was the movement for renewal of Islamic thought, of which former student leader Nurcholish Madjid was the main protagonist and to which Abdurrahman Wahid later came to make major contributions. This movement took inspiration from early twentieth-century modernism but was critical of established Indonesian reformism as well as conservative traditionalist thought, and it showed great appreciation of intellectual dimensions of the Islamic tradition that had been rejected by earlier modernists. This movement will be discussed below, in the section focusing on Muslim intellectuals.

University campuses were also the breeding ground for an entirely new type of Islamic movement, organized as semi-clandestine Islamic study groups in the 1980s and 1990s, and emerging in public after the fall of the Soeharto regime as the Indonesian chapters of transnational Islamic movements. One of these networks of Islamic study groups, sometimes dubbed the **Tarbiyah** (disciplining, education) movement, appeared to be the Indonesian chapter of the Muslim Brotherhood and was later to establish the political party **PK** (**Partai Keadilan**, Justice Party) and its successor **PKS** (**Partai Keadilan Sejahtera**, Prosperous Justice Party). Another network made up the Indonesian chapter of the **Hizb ut-Tahrir** (Liberation Party). A movement that was slightly different in character, and notably less organized, was the **Salafi** movement. These three movements have, in different ways, become major challenges for the NU and Muhammadiyah. They have made significant inroads among the constituency of these large associations and have challenged their control over mosques, schools and other institutions.

The major distinction between these three movements and all earlier movements and organizations is their transnational character. The Muhammadiyah and NU are national organizations, in the sense of being organized nationwide but also of having been part of the movement for national independence and being dedicated to the idea of Indonesia as a nation. The Hizb ut-Tahrir and the Salafi movement reject the very idea of the nation as a legitimate entity. They follow authorities who are based outside Indonesia. The Tarbiyah movement also owed allegiance to authorities based in the Middle East; the PKS may now take its strategic decisions itself, but it regularly communicates with other national chapters of the Muslim Brotherhood.

Official Islam: The Majelis Ulama Indonesia

The **Majelis Ulama Indonesia** (Indonesian Council of Muslim Scholars, MUI) was established in 1975 by the Soeharto government to serve as an interface between the government and the Muslim community, advising the former on sensitive matters and explaining its policies in terms acceptable to the believers. Its members were drawn from the various Muslim organizations to represent the entire range of mainstream views, but they were government-appointed and not answerable to their organizations. After the demise of the New Order, the MUI attempted to transform itself from a semi-governmental to a civil society organization, with regular congresses at which leaders are elected and broad policies discussed. It moreover co-opted representatives of various strands of political Islam, that had been beyond the pale during the Soeharto period. The Council took various initiatives designed to give it a more active role in the Islamicization of society (see Ichwan's contribution to this volume).

MUSLIM POLITICAL PARTIES

After a period during which all legal Muslim political representation had been reduced to a single political party that was not even overtly Islamic, the United Development Party (Partai Persatuan Pembangunan, PPP), the fall of the Soeharto regime enabled the emergence of various new parties that appealed specifically to segments of the Muslim electorate. To some extent, the situation of the 2000s reminded of the political landscape of the period of liberal democracy in the 1950s, although there were also some entirely new phenomena, most significantly the Islamist party PKS with its highly trained cadres and explicitly Islamist ideology.

In the 1950s, there had been four main Muslim political parties. **Masyumi** and **NU**, which polled 21 and 18.5 per cent of the national vote in the 1955 elections, were the largest; the **PSII (Partai Syarikat Islam Indonesia)**, with 2.9 per cent, and **Perti (Persatuan Tarbiyah Islamiyah)**, with 1.3 per cent, were considerably smaller. Besides these legal parties, there was also the insurgent **Darul Islam** movement, which did not recognize the secular Republic of Indonesia and had proclaimed the Islamic State of Indonesia (**NII, Negara Islam Indonesia**), with its armed wing, the Islamic Army of Indonesia (**TII, Tentara Islam Indonesia**). The Darul Islam persisted as an underground movement throughout the Soeharto period and resurfaced in various forms in the 2000s.

Masyumi

The Masyumi party owed its existence to the Japanese occupying forces, which made an effort to bring all Muslim groups and associations together in a single anti-imperialist front of that name.[12] During the struggle for Independence, Masyumi was perhaps the strongest political party. In the early 1950s, the traditionalist associations Perti and NU broke away from Masyumi to become political parties in their own right. From then on, Masyumi was more strongly associated with reformist Islam, although some traditionalist groups preferred to remain politically affiliated with Masyumi. In the debates on Indonesia's Constitution, Masyumi politicians strongly supported the "Jakarta Charter", the formula that was meant to enshrine the *shari`a* in the Preamble to the Constitution (but which was always rejected by a majority in parliament).[13] Otherwise, however, the party embraced Western liberal democratic values and liberal economic policies. It was precisely over these issues that the party repeatedly clashed with Sukarno. Masyumi and the small secular elite party PSI (Indonesian Socialist Party) were united in their opposition to Sukarno's Guided Democracy, and leading members took part in a regional rebellion against Sukarno.

Both parties were formally dissolved in 1960 and could never be officially resuscitated. In 1965, students and intellectuals associated with these two parties played leading roles in the ousting of the Old Order; the PSI provided the technocrats who carried out the New Order's liberal economic policies. Soeharto never trusted the leading Masyumi politicians, however; the party remained banned, and he made sure its leaders played no part in any new political formation. The most prominent leaders, headed by Mohamad Natsir, turned from party politics to *dakwah*, Islamic predication, in an effort to change society and the political system from below. They established the Indonesian Council for Islamic Predication (**Dewan Dakwah Islamiyah Indonesia, DDII**), which was to have a great impact on changing Islamic discourse in Indonesia.

Some middle-ranking Masyumi politicians were allowed to continue playing a part in politics under the New Order. Some joined a new party that was established to appeal to Masyumi's old constituency (but never gained the legitimacy that Masyumi had enjoyed), the **Partai Muslimin Indonesia** or **Parmusi**. Others decided to join the government political machine, Golkar. During the 1960s and 1970s, strict Islam remained a minority current in Golkar, which was widely perceived to be an expression of Javanese syncretism, but gradually the members of Masyumi background succeeded in "greening" the party, to the extent where currently it is pervaded by a strict Muslim ethos.

Towards the end of the New Order and after Soeharto's resignation, there were various attempt to re-establish the Masyumi as a political party. The most credible of these was the Crescent and Star Party (**Partai Bulan Bintang, PBB**), named after the symbol of the Masyumi and affiliated institutions. The PBB appealed to those who remained most loyal to the Masyumi heritage; it performed very poorly in the elections, however, obtaining 1.9 per cent in 1999, rising to 2.6 per cent in 2004 and falling back to 1.8 per cent in 2009.

Nahdlatul Ulama

Originally an association of Islamic scholars and teachers (*ulama*), NU separated from Masyumi in 1952 and became a political party. It surprised itself by its success in the 1955 elections, and had to recruit competent persons outside its own circles to be able to fill all seats in parliament it had gained. Unlike Masyumi, it cooperated willingly in Sukarno's Guided Democracy (though some leaders dissented and, together with representatives from other parties and some military established the oppositional League for Democracy, which was soon banned by Sukarno). For most of the Old Order period, NU controlled the Ministry of Religious Affairs. It lost this control in the first New Order government (1972) and never regained it during the New Order.

In 1973, NU was forced to merge with the other Muslim parties (**Parmusi**, **PSII** and **Perti**) into the United Development Party (**PPP**). In

1985, NU's five-yearly national congress decided to break with PPP and withdraw from formal politics altogether, returning to its initial status as a non-political religious association. Individual members were free to be active in any political party of their choice but could not hold functions in a party as well as the NU organization.

Partai Persatuan Pembangunan (PPP)

The **United Development Party**, **PPP**, established by heavy-handed intervention of the New Order regime, was nonetheless the closest thing to an established opposition party and the military went to great length to weaken its performance in elections. PPP had a limited political agenda but fought for what it considered core Muslim interests: recognition of Islamic educational institutions, upgrading of the status of Islamic courts, no interference with Muslim family law, and such like. After the demise of the New Order, many members left PPP and joined one or the other of the new Islamic parties, but the party has, in spite of internal conflicts, managed to maintain a core of loyal supporters. In 1999 it still obtained 10.7 per cent of the vote, and its leader Hamzah Haz became vice-president under Megawati. Under his successor, Suryadharma Ali (who currently is the Minister of Religious Affairs), the party's vote dropped from 8.2 per cent in 2004 to 5.3 per cent in 2009.

Partai Kebangkitan Bangsa (PKB) and other NU-based parties

Soon after the fall of Soeharto, Abdurahman Wahid established a new political party to cater for the political ambitions of the NU constituency, the National Awakening Party (**Partai Kebangkitan Bangsa, PKB**). The PKB explicitly does not wish to be an Islamic party but one that represents the entire nation — but its personnel is almost exclusively of NU background. The party has been split over rivalries between Abdurrahman Wahid and various former allies, and rapidly declined in popularity, from 12.6 per cent of the vote in 1999 to less than 5 per cent in 2009. The PKB is not the only party claiming to represent the NU constituency, although definitely the largest one. The **Partai Kebangkitan Umat (PKU)**, established by Wahid's more conservative uncle, Jusuf Hasjim) and the **PNU (Partai Nahdlatul Ummah)**, established by the equally conservative Madurese kiai Syukron Ma'mun, polled poorly in the elections.

Partai Amanat Nasional (PAN) and Partai Matahari Bangsa (PMB)

Closely identified with the Reformation movement that challenged Soeharto is the National Mandate Party (**Partai Amanat Nasional, PAN**) led by Amien Rais. Because Amien was the chairman of Muhammadiyah until he resigned to lead this new party, PAN is often seen as a Muhammadiyah-affiliated party, but in fact it represented from the beginning a rainbow coalition also including non-Muslims, like the informal action committee from which it emerged, the Majelis Amanat Rakyat (MARA). The PAN does not have an Islamic programme, though in the course of the years its social base gradually narrowed to a largely Muslim constituency.

The latest addition to the Muslim party landscape is the Sun of the Nation Party (**Partai Matahari Bangsa**), established in 2006 by young men with a Muhammadiyah background (including former chairmen of Pemuda Muhammadiyah and Ikatan Mahasiswa Muhammadiyah). Their aim was to create a political vehicle more representative of Muhammadiyah than PAN. The Muhammadiyah board, however, has refused to recognize any specific connection between this party and the Muhammadiyah, and insists that the Muhammadiyah is non-political and does not endorse any party.

Partai Keadilan/Partai Keadilan Sejahtera (PK/PKS)

Probably the most significant Islamic party, since the restrictions on political parties were lifted, is the Justice Party (**Partai Keadilan**), which was established by activists of a formerly semi-underground Islamic students' movement strongly influenced by the Muslim Brotherhood (known as the *Tarbiyah* movement). Along with the PAN, the PK was the party with the most sophisticated party programme and most transparent structure among those contesting the first post-Soeharto elections. It won 1.3 per cent of the vote and 7 seats in the 1999; in 2004, after having been reconstituted, for legal-technical reasons, as a new party with a modified name (**Partai Keadilan Sejahtera**, Prosperous Justice Party), it garnered over 7 per cent of the vote and gained 45 seats, giving it a significant presence in parliament. Encouraged by this success, the leadership targeted even more significant growth during the following period, apparently at the expense of its former standards of admission of members and the quality of cadre training. This resulted in increasing tensions between the "pragmatic" leadership and critics who insisted the PKS should remain an Islamic vanguard party.

The PK(S) is an Islamist party but has embraced liberal democracy, and it is also generally favouring economic liberalism. Women are conspicuously active in the party; in the 2004 elections, it fielded a larger proportion of women candidates than most other parties. It appealed especially to those sections of the educated middle class that were ideologically committed to political Islam, but more generally to all those who were disaffected with the corruption and inefficacy rampant in other parties. The party has organized effective social welfare and disaster relief activities, which have won it much goodwill. The rapid growth has stalled, however. In the 2009 elections it obtained 7.9 per cent of the vote, only marginally more than in 2004, although this made it the largest of the Muslim parties and the only one that had not actually *lost* votes.[14]

POLITICAL MOVEMENTS OPERATING OUTSIDE THE LEGAL PARTY SYSTEM: DARUL ISLAM AND ITS OFFSHOOTS, OTHER RADICAL MOVEMENTS

Darul Islam — NII/TII

Most radical Islamic movements in Indonesia have a historical connection with the **Darul Islam** movement (alias **NII/TII**, the Islamic State/ Army of Indonesia). The Darul Islam movement emerged in the independence struggle from resistance groups in West Java that rejected concessions made to the Dutch by the Republican government. The leader and chief ideologist of the Darul Islam, S.M. Kartosoewirjo, had been an active member of the Sarekat Islam and a leading Masyumi politician in the early years of the Independence struggle, before he proclaimed the Islamic State of Indonesia. Similar movements in South Sulawesi (led by Kahar Muzakkar) and Aceh (led by Daud Beureueh) joined the West Java-based movement when they were frustrated with the central government. This was a political alliance; in terms of religious views the movements were rather different from one another. Kahar's movement was the most strictly puritanical (he was an active Muhammadiyah member) and it actually banned Sufi practices and syncretistic rituals in the region it controlled. The Acehnese DI leaders were affiliated with PUSA, the Muslim reformist association. The rank and file of the West Javanese DI, on the other hand, were largely traditionalist Muslims (which in the mid-1990s was to be the reason of a split in the underground movements).[15]

Until 1962–65, when these regional movements were finally subdued and their leaders killed or captured, the Darul Islam existed as an alternative government that actually controlled considerable stretches of territory. After that date, it survived as an underground movement, partly controlled and manipulated by intelligence operatives, and occasionally coming into the limelight with a series of terrorist actions. This underground network went by various names in the Indonesian press (besides the name **NII/TII**, which appears to have been the preferred self-designation). In the 1970s, when several waves of bombings of night clubs, cinemas and churches — as well as robberies of banks and gas stations to finance the movement — swept the country, it was generally labelled **Komando Jihad**, and one section of it **Kelompok Teror Warman** ("Warman's terror group", after the name of one leading activist). The movement appeared to be divided in a number of rival groups, of different degrees of sophistication.

One of these groups, the regional network of the larger Jakarta region (including the entire north coast of West Java), became later known as **KW IX** or Ninth Regional Command and was accused by other Islamic activists of being involved in robbery and a wide range of other criminal activities for fund-raising. The alleged leader of this NII wing, Panji Gumilang, established a huge and lavishly furnished *pesantren*, named Al-Zaytun, that drew much attention for its spectacular architecture and the patronage it appeared to receive from powerful politicians during the late Soeharto years as well as in the post-Soeharto period.[16]

Another influential group is associated with the names of Abdullah Sungkar and his helper Abu Bakar Ba'asyir, who were well-known Islamic activists in Solo — the former a leading member of the DDII, the latter a graduate of the reformist *pesantren* of Gontor. They were the founders, among other things, of the reformist *pesantren* of Ngruki, after which their network was later sometimes named, and they were familiar with contemporary Middle Eastern Islamist thought. They appear to have joined NII in the 1970s and infused the movement with new ideas and methods of cadre training derived from the Muslim Brotherhood. Sungkar and Ba'asyir established an underground network of youth, organized in study groups or cells (named *usrah*, Arabic for "nuclear family"), whom they trained in Islamist ideology and prepared for the struggle to establish an Islamic state. Following the arrests of several followers, and later of Sungkar and Ba'asyir in the early 1980s, this network became known as the **Usrah movement**; the network as a whole appears to have been integrated into the NII/TII structure. In the mid-1980s, having served some years in prison, Sungkar and Ba'asyir fled to Malaysia and settled there as refugees. Around the same time, they began to send small numbers of activists (altogether perhaps a few hundred) to Pakistan and Afghanistan, to join the Afghan jihad and gain useful military training.[17]

In the mid-1990s, Sungkar broke with the nominal leader of the NII/TII, Ajengan Masduki, and it appears that from then on he used the name **Jama'ah Islamiyah (JI)** for his own network. JI was involved in a series of violent incidents in Indonesia and neighbouring countries; in fact, most of the terrorists of the 2000s have been connected with JI or breakaway sections of it. Sungkar died in 1999, and Ba'asyir, who by then had resettled in Indonesia, replaced him as the nominal leader of the network. Analysts' opinions differ on the degree to which Ba'asyir exercised actual authority over the returned jihadis. There are indications that the group responsible for many of the terrorist actions from 2000 onwards operated under its own military leaders, without instructions from Ba'asyir. While remaining a figure of moral authority for many radicals, Ba'asyir chose to work with those activists who left the underground and established a public, legal organization through which to continue the struggle for an Islamic state in Indonesia, the **Majelis Mujahidin** (see below).

Very significant sections of the NII remained active underground (including those parts of Sungkar's old network that had not followed him into JI), and appear to have been rejuvenating themselves, recruiting new members in certain university campuses and especially in secondary schools. Anecdotal evidence suggests that NII has successfully recruited teenagers in various parts of Java, persuading them to leave their families and become full-time activists.[18]

Majelis Mujahidin Indonesia and Jama'ah Ansharut Tauhid

The **Majelis Mujahidin Indonesia** (Indonesian Council of Jihad Warriors, **MMI**), established at a congress in Yogyakarta on 8 August 2000, the date at which Kartosuwiryo had declared the Islamic State of Indonesia, appears to be an umbrella of various Islamist groups, most of them Darul Islam related, that shared the ideal of an Islamic state but opted for operating in legality. The MMI, like the PKS, looks to the Muslim Brotherhood for inspiration but criticizes the PKS for its participation in the existing political system and its acceptance of liberal democracy. The founding congress appointed Abu Bakar Ba'asyir, the alleged leader of the underground JI, as its chief religious authority (*amir al-mujahidin*, "Commander of the Warriors") and a number of respected intellectuals without JI connections as its council of advisers (*ahlul halli wal aqdi*). Day-to-day affairs were run by a small executive board, based in Yogyakarta.

In 2008, after the executive board had announced that MMI's third congress was to elect a new *amir*, Ba'asyir protested this un-Islamic procedure and broke with MMI, establishing his own association, **Jama'ah Ansharut Tauhid** (JAT), consisting of activists loyal to him personally and, allegedly, more inclined towards violent jihad. JAT has been accused of running an armed training camp in Aceh, and several leading activists, including Ba'asyir himself, have been under arrest since (International Crisis Group 2010).

Hizbut Tahrir Indonesia, Front Pembela Islam, and LPPI

Hizbut Tahrir Indonesia (**HTI**) is the Indonesian chapter of the transnational Hizb ut-Tahrir (Liberation Party) and faithfully follows the line set out by the Hizb's leadership abroad. It emerged in university surroundings, at Bogor's Institute for Agriculture in the early 1980s, and remained underground until 1998. It has a network stretching across the country and showed in August 2007 that it can mobilize at least 100,000 people. HTI also rejects liberal democracy and boycotts elections, and it aggressively proselytizes, especially in NU circles. Its ultimate aim is the establishment of a caliphate uniting the entire Muslim world but it has no clear strategy on how to achieve this objective. As long as there is not a Caliph to lead the *jihad* against the enemies of Islam, it rejects all political violence.

Front Pembela Islam (**FPI**, Front of Defenders of Islam) is part movement to impose Islamic moral norms, part protection racket. It is led by "Habib" Rizieq Syihab and other Jakarta Arabs, who appear to have close connections to politicians, sections of the police force as well as underworld bosses. The FPI made a name for itself with vigilante raids on nightclubs, bars and other dens of inequity. Most of the "muscle" in these raids appeared to consist of hired street toughs, some brought in from Banten or even Lampung for the occasion. More recently the FPI has been targeting "deviant" Muslim groups. Rizieq Syihab studied religion in Saudi Arabia and has a public discourse influenced by Salafism, but his organization is not taken seriously as a religious movement by most other committed Muslims.

Another movement that aggressively fights what it considers as deviant forms of Islam, and that is taken more seriously (though not necessarily respected) is the **Lembaga Pengkajian dan Penelitian Islam** (**LPPI**, Institute for Islamic Studies and Investigations), led by Amin Djamaluddin. LPPI has published various books and booklets about such deviants, from

Sufi orders to the Ahmadiyah. In 2005 it turned to street politics and joined the FPI in a physical attack on an Ahmadiyah compound in Parung, Bogor, where the Qadian Ahmadiyah was then having its annual national meeting. Earlier, in 2002, LPPI had organized a "seminar" on the Ahmadiyah in Jakarta's Istiqlal mosque, where inflammatory language was used.

MUSLIM YOUTH AND STUDENTS' ASSOCIATIONS

Prior to the depoliticization under Soeharto, most political parties had their own youth and students' associations, that provided cadre training and a channel of entry into the "parent" organization. Friendships formed in these associations often lasted a lifetime and very strong "old boys" networks exist.

PII (Pelajar Islam Indonesia) was the high school students' association affiliated with Masyumi. When Masyumi was formally dissolved (1960), PII also came under pressure but it maintained a semi-legal existence until 1985, when it rejected the regime's *azas tunggal* ("single ideological foundation") policy (which obliged all associations to be based on Pancasila and nothing else), and was formally closed down. PII networks are still strong, allegedly also in the armed forces and the bureaucracy.

HMI (Himpunan Mahasiswa Islam, Muslim Students' Association) was for a long time perhaps the most important organization of university students. It was ideologically close to Masyumi but formally independent and therefore did not suffer when Masyumi was banned. In 1965, HMI leaders joined the students' action committee **KAMI** that — encouraged by the military — organized the demonstrations against communism and Soeharto that ushered in the New Order. The most famous HMI leader ever was Nurcholish Madjid, who led the organization for two crucial periods, from 1967 to 1971, and became the country's most prominent liberal Muslim intellectual (Kull 2005). Not all members of the organization accepted his ideas, however; others tended towards more conservative or Islamist viewpoints. Numerous HMI members made successful careers in the bureaucracy, in education, in business, or in politics. After the 1999 elections, about half of all delegates, nicely distributed over all parties, were former HMI members.

In 1985, HMI's national congress adopted the regime's *azas tunggal* policy (which meant that HMI, which had both Islam and Pancasila in its statutes, had to strike out Islam). A group of dissidents who rejected this policy organized a rival HMI, named **HMI-MPO (Majelis Penyelamat Organisasi**, Council for Saving the Organization). Although HMI-MPO was not legally recognized, it was not seriously repressed either, and in various localities it had as many members as the "official" HMI, sometimes called **HMI-Dipo** after the address of its headquarters on Jl. Diponegoro in Jakarta (Karim 1997).

The NU also has an affiliated students' association, **PMII (Pergerakan Mahasiswa Islam Indonesia**, Indonesian Muslim Students' Movement). Because for a long time children of NU families studied in *pesantren* and not in general schools, PMII was primarily active at the State Institutes for Islamic Studies (IAIN), that were open to graduates of a *pesantren* with a *madrasah aliyah* diploma. From the 1980s on, PMII branches flourished at general universities as well. In the 1990s, many PMII members became politically involved and active in NGOs. Such NGOs as LKiS, eLSAD, LAPAR, Syarikat were established by leading PMII activists.

Muhammadiyah similarly has its own students' association, **Ikatan Mahasiswa Muhammadiyah (IMM)**.

The said organizations are so-called "off-campus", nationwide organizations, not allowed to be active at university campuses since the government banned students' political activities in 1978. The most influential "on-campus" organization is the **LDK (Lembaga Dakwah Kampus**, Institute for Predication on Campus), based in the campus mosque. Most of the LDK were initially under the influence of the DDII; in the 1990s, and especially since the fall of the Soeharto regime, various ideological currents have vied for control of the LDK: Hizbut Tahrir, NII, and Tarbiyah.

The most important of the campus-based student movements was the **Tarbiyah** movement. Inspired by the Egyptian Muslim Brotherhood, the Tarbiyah movement, which emerged in the course of the 1980s, organized religious discussion and mental training sessions. In March 1998, Tarbiyah members established the students' action committee **KAMMI (Kesatuan Aksi Mahasiswa Muslim Indonesia**, a deliberate reference to student action front KAMI, which had organized the 1965–66 demonstrations). KAMMI constituted the Islamic wing of the Reformation (anti-Soeharto) student movement, recruiting a broader constitution than Tarbiyah students only. The political party PK(S) was established by former Tarbiyah activists. KAMMI remains active on campuses, and is closely affiliated with the PKS.

An important network of non-university Muslim activists was the **BKPRMI (Badan Kontak Pemuda dan Remaja Masjid Indonesia**, Contact Organ of Indonesian Mosque-Affilated Young People and

Youth), a semi-official nationwide organization that existed during the New Order period. **Remaja Masjid** and **Pemuda Masjid** were teenage and youth groups active in major (non-university) mosques. Although BKPRMI was officially recognized and had offices in Jakarta's Istiqlal mosque, the state mosque, this body always attracted numerous young people who were disaffected with New Order policies. Numerous later radicals as well as moderates share a history of activism in this network in the 1970s or 1980s.

DAKWAH (PREDICATION) ORGANIZATIONS

The most prominent of all Indonesian *dakwah* organizations, to which numerous later movements and institutions are endebted, is the **Dewan Dakwah Islamiyah Indonesia (DDII)** or Indonesian Council for Islamic Predication, which was established by Mohamad Natsir and other former Masyumi leaders in 1967. It came to function as the Indonesian counterpart of the Muslim World League (Rabitat al-'Alam al-Islami) and was a major channel of transmission of Islamist ideas from the Middle East to Indonesia. Throughout the New Order period it remained critical of Soeharto's policies, though not all DDII officers were as critical as Natsir. The DDII kept the Masyumi network alive through various media ventures and had an ambitious programme of training preachers. The magazine *Media Dakwah* has been its most prominent print medium; besides, various regional chapters of the DDII established radio stations broadcasting religious sermons, such as RADIS (Radio Dakwah Islamiyah) in Solo, an initiative of the early 1970s. The DDII also established, or inspired the establishment of, various reformist-oriented *pesantren*, such as the "agriculture *pesantren*" Darul Fallah in Bogor and the more radically inclined Al-Mukmin in Ngruki, Solo. Furthermore, several major traditionalist *pesantren* in the Jakarta region (most prominently Asy-Syafi'iyah) and West Java remained closely allied with the DDII. (Unlike most Central and East Javanese *pesantren*, these had remained loyal to Masyumi after the conflict that caused NU to leave the party.) These *pesantren* are united in a loose alliance called **BKSPP (Badan Kerjasama Pondok Pesantren)**.

Members of DDII established the action committee **KISDI (Komite Indonesia untuk Solidaritas Dunia Islam**, Indonesian Committee for Solidarity with the Muslim World), which in the 1990s drew much attention with assertive demonstrations against Israeli policies towards Palestine, Serb aggression in Bosnia, and such issues. KISDI's anger was especially directed against Indonesian media and institutions (most of which were Christian-owned) which it accused of insulting Islam or being insufficiently sensitive to Muslim viewpoints.

A related *dakwah* organization, which in the mid-1980s adopted a radical stand against the New Order's policies of imposing Pancasila as the single acceptable ideological foundation, was the **PTDI (Pendidikan Tinggi Dakwah Islam**, Institute for Higher Dakwah Education), led by Usman al-Hafidy, an Arab scholar from Aceh. Al-Hafidy and at least one of his co-workers had prior Darul Islam connections in Aceh, and in Jakarta they appear to have been connected to the underground NII. Al-Hafidy was arrested in the wake of the Tanjung Priok riots of 1984 and attracted wide attention nationally and internationally due to his fearless and outspoken criticism of New Order policies during his defence in the courtroom.

A "moderate" and government-friendly *dakwah* organization was the **Pusat Dakwah Islam Indonesia (PDII)**, which appears to have been established by the Soeharto regime with the explicit purpose of constituting an alternative to the DDII. Like the latter, it provided preachers in the provinces with standardized sermons.

The Muhammadiyah considers itself as an organization for *dakwah*; but within the Muhammadiyah there is a special organization for predication, the **Majelis Tabligh** (Council for Dissemination), which is considered as the most conservative body within the Muhammadiyah organization. The NU also has its own organization for preachers, the **Ittihadul Muballighin** (Union of Preachers). This used to be one of the most conservative bodies within the NU, and the one that has had the most direct connections with Saudi Arabia and the Muslim World League.

The secular nationalist political party PDI-P established in 2007 a special Muslim wing, **Baitul Muslimin Indonesia** (Indonesian House of Muslims), which carries out *dakwah* among the Muslim sections of its constituency. Allegedly established at the initiative of Hasyim Muzadi and Din Syamsuddin, the chairmen of the NU and Muhammadiyah respectively, and under the direct patronage of Megawati, it serves to raise the party's Islamic legitimacy while at the same time bringing syncretistic *abangan* into the orthodox Muslim mainstream.

The transnational *dakwah* movement **Tablighi Jama'at**, which has become more visible and prominent in Indonesia in the 2000s, will be discussed below under "non-mainstream organizations".

MUSLIM INTELLECTUALS AND THEIR ORGANIZATIONS

A small number of young HMI activists who emerged in the public sphere in the late 1960s and early 1970s made a great impact on liberal Muslim discourse during the New Order. Nurcholish Madjid was hailed as the innovative thinker, who distanced himself from stagnant Islamic politics of the Old Order period and looked forward instead, preaching a message of tolerance and pluralism. M. Dawam Rahardjo was the organizer, active in a series of NGOs; and several friends provided support in the background. Together they were referred to as the Islamic Renewal (**pembaruan Islam** or **pembaruan pemikiran Islam**) movement.

There were various attempts to consolidate the mobilization of students and graduates of the years 1965–66 by establishing a Muslim intellectuals' organization, but the regime never permitted such an association — until much later, in 1990. Dawam Rahardjo and other activists of Masyumi-HMI background joined forces with young PSI (Socialist Party) intellectuals in establishing (in 1971) Indonesia's first and most influential development-oriented NGO, **LP3ES (Lembaga Penelitian, Pendidikan dan Penerangan Ekonomi dan Sosial**, Institute for Social and Economic Research, Education and Information), which was primarily focusing on social and economic development but also provided a forum for discussions on Islam and development.

Fifteen years later (1986), after Nurcholish Madjid had returned from Ph.D. studies in Chicago, it was Rahardjo who organized with and for him the "religious studies club" **Paramadina**, which provided Madjid and numerous invited speakers with a platform to address an increasingly affluent Muslim middle class audience. In the 1990s, Paramadina expanded its activities beyond the monthly seminar-style public lectures and debates in posh surroundings to include various courses and publications, in which the focus was increasingly on pluralism and respect for other religious traditions.

Another initiative of Dawam Rahardjo was the **Lembaga Studi Agama dan Filsafat** (**LSAF**, Institute for the Study of Religion and Philosophy), a venture that strongly stimulated Muslim intellectual debate, especially through its quarterly journal, *Ulumul Qur'an*, which was published from 1989 to the mid-1990s. Most non-fundamentalist Muslim intellectuals of the period were at one time or another associated with LSAF. Some of its staff later joined Paramadina.

In 1990, Soeharto suddenly allowed the establishment of a formal association of Muslim intellectuals, to be headed by his trusted minister of technology and later vice-president, B.J. Habibie. **ICMI (Ikatan Cendekiawan Muslim Indonesia)** inspired hopes and expectations both among the "liberal" intellectuals who had been active in the organizations mentioned so far and among their Islamist critics, who had been marginalized during the 1970s and 1980s. Analysts differed on whether ICMI represented a strengthening of Muslim civil society and a genuine intellectual forum or was a ploy of Soeharto to co-opt some of his former critics at a moment when he was facing challenges from the armed forces.

The most outspoken early critic of ICMI was Abdurrahman Wahid. As a counter move he established the **Forum Demokrasi**, in which he cooperated with intellectuals of various (mostly Christian) backgrounds. ICMI survived into the post-Soeharto period but has become insignificant. Forum Demokrasi simply faded away — but some of its core members later became assistants to Wahid when he was Indonesia's fourth President (1999–2001).

In the post-Soeharto years, **Paramadina** retained a highly visible presence, contributing to debates on the re-interpretation of received Islamic teachings. The most remarkable newcomer on the scene, however, was **Jaringan Islam Liberal** (**JIL**, Liberal Islam Network), which received appropriately liberal funding from The Asia Foundation until it ran into too much opposition from conservative Muslim circles. JIL is in many respects the successor to the *pembaruan Islam* movement, but it lacks the protection that Nurcholish Madjid and his colleagues enjoyed from the New Order regime.

A Yogyakarta-based group of young intellectuals of NU background, **LKiS (Lembaga Kajian Islam dan Sosial**, Institute for Islamic and Social Studies), has since the mid-1990s contributed much to the enrichment of Muslim intellectual discourse. LKiS has consistently positioned itself as more left-wing and committed to social and economic justice, whereas JIL embraced economic liberalism. Young Muhammadiyah intellectuals established a similar though smaller network, named **JIMM (Jaringan Intelektual Muda Muhammadiyah**, Network of Young Muhammadiyah Intellectuals).

Besides LKiS and JIL, progressive Muslim intellectuals of NU background have found a home in the **Wahid Institute** (<http://www.wahidinstitute.org>), a minor think-tank established by Abdurrahman Wahid after his presidency, and their Muhammadiyah peers have a similar modest outfit, the **Maarif Institute** (<http://www.maarifinstitute.org>), established by former Muhammadiyah chairman Ahmad Syafii Maarif before his resignation in 2004. Both institutes aim to keep the ideas of their founders alive and offer a protective umbrella to younger activists.

A "conservative" counterpart to these "liberal" and "progressive" Muslim intellectual groups is **INSISTS (Institute for the Study of Islamic Thought and Civilization**), a small think-tank established by graduates of Malaysia's Institute for Islamic Thought and Civilization (ISTAC).[19] Leading lights include Hamid Fahmi Zarkasyi and Adian Husaini. Like the mother institute, INSISTS has an avid interest in the "Islamization of Sciences" and is firmly opposed to "Orientalism" and other alleged Western conspiracies (<www.insistnet.com>). [INSISTS should not be confused with the left-leaning development and advocacy NGO, INSIST, Indonesian Society for Social Transformation.]

MUSLIM NGOS FOR SOCIAL ACTIVISM

The 1990s were a period of rapid growth of foreign-funded NGOs, which proliferated even further during the period of transition after the Soeharto years. Only a small proportion of these NGOs has an explicitly Islamic identity or character. Indonesian NGO activists often distinguish three types of (Muslim) NGOs, which represent distinct phases in the history of NGO activism, although they now coexist beside each other: development NGOs, advocacy NGOs, and discourse NGOs. The history of NGO activities begins with two influential national-level NGOs that became active in the 1970s: **LP3ES** (Institute for Economic and Social Research, Education and Information) and **LSP** (Institute for Development Studies). LP3ES, as mentioned in the previous section, was established by former student activists affiliated with the banned Masyumi and Indonesian Socialist Party (PSI), and it played an important role in introducing discourses of development from below, complementing the New Order's top-down development policies. LSP was a smaller NGO, also involved in both research and small grassroots development projects. Unlike LP3ES, LSP had a single leader, Adi Sasono, who had a strong Masyumi background and appeared to represent more left-leaning views of development and more explicit criticism of the role of the military. The leading Muslim development activist in LP3ES was M. Dawam Rahardjo. Towards the middle of the decade, Sasono and Rahardjo teamed up with Abdurrahman Wahid, scion of the most prominent NU family, for a programme of community development projects to be carried out in and around *pesantren*, the traditional Islamic boarding schools. The three men were to play parts in numerous later NGO ventures.[20]

Neither LP3ES nor LSP were explicitly Muslim NGOs, and most of their national and international contacts were with secular organizations. The *pesantren* and development programme was LP3ES' chief activity directed towards a specifically Islamic constituency. Because neither Sasono nor Rahardjo, with their urban Masyumi backgrounds, had easy access in the *pesantren* world, they needed the cooperation of Abdurrahman Wahid, and through the latter recruited a number of other young men of NU background, who were trained in the management of development programmes. These men (there were no women activists among them as yet) later laid the foundations of NGO activism in NU circles.

The first specifically Muslim NGO that took over some of LP3ES' *pesantren*-based activities was **P3M** (Association for the Development of Pesantren and Society), established in 1986, in which persons of NU and Masyumi background (the latter including Sasono) took part. The director was, and remains until today, Masdar F. Mas'udi, a young NU intellectual known for his original and provocative ideas. The foreign sponsor, initially Germany's Friedrich Naumann Stiftung (a foundation affiliated with the Liberal Party FDP), which had also supported LP3ES's *pesantren* programme for a decade, wanted P3M to continue carrying out development-related projects, but Mas'udi was more interested in "discourse", i.e. in using his NGO to stimulate new discussions on socially and politically relevant issues in the *pesantren* world. Other sponsors proposed different programmes, and P3M, like many other NGOs, has always had to find a balance between its own ideals and the changing global NGO agenda as mediated by such sponsors as the Ford Foundation.

One remarkable phenomenon in Indonesia's Muslim NGO world is the development of a broadly supported Muslim feminism. It was P3M that, initially at the insistence of sponsors, carried out several gender-related programmes (including discussion on women's rights in Islam, gender awareness training, and a programme on women's reproductive health). In the early 1990s, activists who had previously worked with P3M established a separate NGO exclusively focusing on gender-related issues, named **Rahima**. Just like P3M, Rahima has both Masyumi- and NU-affiliated activists; however, it focuses less specifically on the *pesantren* world. Several other NGOs that were closer to the *pesantren* world followed suit: **Puan Amal Hayati** (established in 2000 under the patronage of Abdurrahman Wahid's wife Sinta Nuriyah) as well as **Fahmina** (based in Cirebon, and led by the feminist Kiai Husein Muhammad) aimed at the empowerment of women and protection of children in the *pesantren* environment, striving to reform established practices and critically analysing established religious discourse on women's rights and duties.

Several of the other Muslim NGOs have had a close connection with NU and have been active among the NU's constituency of "traditionalist" Muslims. At the 1984 NU Congress, Abdurrahman Wahid was chosen to lead the organization, and a number of other men with experience in NGO work also took up leading positions. This was the year when the NU withdrew from "practical politics" and decided to become more involved in grassroots work in society. To this end, the NU established its own NGO, called **Lakpesdam** (Institute for Research and Development of Human Resources), that was to carry out a wide range of developmental and educational activities in segments of society where NU was strongly represented. Lakpesdam was based in the capital and active nationally; at the provincial level, similar NGOs with similar programmes were established.

NU's young women's association **Fatayat** also restyled itself as a sort of NGO and began carrying out similar programmes as Lakpesdam (gender awareness and health-related), besides continuing to function as a meeting place for young women. Quite a few active Fatayat members were previously or concurrently involved in Rahima, Lakpesdam or other NGOs; Fatayat provided one of the main channels through which Muslim feminist ideas reached the grassroots.

Another type of Muslim NGOs emerged out of discussion groups among students and young graduates of the IAINs of Yogyakarta and Surabaya, which gradually consolidated themselves as "discourse" NGOs and occasionally "advocacy" NGOs. The most interesting of these has perhaps been **LKiS** (Institute for Islamic and Social Studies) in Yogyakarta, which became a formal NGO in the mid-1990s. Its members were all alumni of PMII, NU's student association, and they combined an interest in liberation theology, Marxism and human rights discourse with modern Islamic thought and Western sociology. Through its own publishing house, LKiS introduced many new and thought-provoking authors to the Indonesian public. A programme of human rights training it carried out among *pesantren* youth throughout the country in the 1990s gave this NGO the reputation of being the most progressive Muslim institution. A similar NGO, that existed for only a few years, however, was Surabaya's **èLSAD** (Institute for the Study of Religion and Democracy).

LKiS has spawned a number of other, more specialized NGOs that became active after the end of the New Order. Each represents a specific strain within the progressive discourse often associated with Abdurrahman Wahid. **Syarikat**, based in Yogyakarta, carried out oral history research on the mass killings of 1965–66, in which many of the perpetrators were NU youth; it organized various activities to bring about reconciliation between the relatives of victims and perpetrators; and it was involved in advocacy on behalf of the victims of the New Order. **Desantara** is an advocacy NGO for religious practices with a strong local colour and for the protection of "syncretistic" religious minorities, which are threatened by the dominant trend towards puritan orthodoxy.

The most visible "discourse" NGO is probably **ICIP** (International Center for Islam and Pluralism), established (and initially lavishly funded) by The Asia Foundation. ICIP's staff originate from various other NGOs, and it has a board of advisers in which most of the movements discussed in this and the preceding section are represented. It has organized numerous seminars and introduced many liberal-minded foreign Muslim thinkers to the Indonesian public.

It is somewhat surprising that there are no serious Muhammadiyah-based counterparts to these NU-based progressive NGOs. JIMM, discussed above among the Muslim intellectual associations, comes closest to them, but its range of activities is very limited. Perhaps the most significant NGO-like organizations among reformist Muslims are the charities **Dompet Dhuafa** ("Relief fund for the weak") and **Rumah Zakat**, both of which became active nationwide in the period of crisis and transition at the turn of the millennium. Dompet Dhuafa was established by the daily *Republika*, initially (in 1994) only as a fund holding contributions deduced from its staff's salaries, to be spent on charitable projects. Since the end of the New Order, Dompet Dhuafa has been collecting charitable gifts (*zakat* and *sadaqa*) from the general public, with which it has supported various projects involving productive activities in needy communities. Rumah Zakat emerged out of a similar initiative by persons close to the Tarbiyah movement. It runs an impressive nationwide network of centres offering various services to the poor, including maternity clinics, and has also been active in relief aid to disaster-stricken regions.[21]

The DDII established its own, more interventionist, charitable NGO, **KOMPAK** (**Komite Aksi Penanggulangan Akibat Krisis**, Action Committee for Crisis Management) at the time of the conflict in the Moluccas and later inter-religious conflicts. It sent relief goods but allegedly also fighters (Afghanistan veterans) to support the Muslim communities in the conflict zones. Two other medical relief associations that emerged around the same time and have gained a stable core of support among reformist Muslims are **MER-C** (Medical Emergency Rescue Committee), established by medical students at Universitas Indonesia in 1999, and

Bulan Sabit Merah Indonesia (Indonesian Red Crescent), established in 2002 by persons closer to the Islamist end of the spectrum. Besides disaster relief in various parts of Indonesia, both organizations also pride themselves on participation in relief actions abroad, notably in Palestine in the wake of Israel's 2008–09 Gaza offensive.

NON-MAINSTREAM ISLAMIC MOVEMENTS

Ahmadiyah

The **Ahmadiyah**, a reformist movement that emerged in British India in the late nineteenth century, first arrived in Indonesia in the 1920s and found a following among the Dutch-educated indigenous elite. Both the Qadian branch and the Lahore branch of the Ahmadiyah are represented in Indonesia (the Qadian branch being the more controversial because they consider their founder Ghulam Ahmad as a prophet, whereas the Lahore branch calls him a "renewer" of Islam). The **Jama'ah Ahmadiyah Indonesia** (**JAI**), the Indonesian chapter of the Qadian Ahmadiyah, is the larger of the two Ahmadiyah associations; the **Gerakan Ahmadiyah Indonesia** represents the Lahore wing. Both wings have been victim to increasingly aggressive actions and physical attacks by radical Muslim groups, spearheaded by FPI and LPPI (see pp. 38–39).

Islam Jama'ah/Lemkari/LDII

Islam Jama'ah is a sectarian movement that emerged in the 1950s, under the leadership of the charismatic teacher Nurhasan Ubaidah of Kediri (also known as Amir Nurhasan Lubis — Lubis in this case not referring to the Batak clan of that name but being an abbreviation of Luar Biasa, "extraordinary"). Members pledged an oath of loyalty and obedience (*bay'ah*) to the leader and studied a body of *hadith* (sayings of the Prophet) that constituted the core of belief and practice in the movement. Although no heterodox teachings could be pinpointed, the movement aroused suspicion among the mainstream for their refusal to pray together with other Muslims. It was repeatedly declared a deviant sect by the Majelis Ulama Indonesia but enjoyed the protection of powerful Golkar personalities. In an effort to become less conspicuous, it changed its name several times: into **Lemkari** (Lembaga Karyawan Islam, Institute of Muslim Workers) and later **LDII** (Lembaga Dakwah Islam Indonesia, Indonesian Institute of Muslim Predication).

Shi`a movements

The Arab community of Indonesia is by and large of Hadrami descent and Sunni, strictly following the Shafi`i school. The considerable number of *sayyid* families (descendants of the Prophet Muhammad) among them are also Sunnis but because of their cultivation of devotional attitudes towards the *ahl al-bayt*, the family of the Prophet, they share at least some devotional practices with the Shi`a. A few Arab religious teachers were in fact already covertly spreading Shi`i ideas in the 1970s, before the Islamic revolution in Iran drew many young people towards the Shi`a. The most prominent of these was Ustadz Husein bin Abu Bakar Al-Habsyi of Bangil. The *pesantren* he established there in 1976 (**YAPI, Yayasan Pesantren Islam**) became the major centre of Shi`a religious education in Indonesia, and in the following decade he became the most trusted counterpart of the Iranian religious establishment (Zulkifli 2004).

In the mid-1980s, the works of the Iranian revolutionary religious thinker Ali Shariati and the philosopher Murtaza Mutahhari became very popular on university campuses, and Bandung especially became a centre of a movement for self-conversion to Shi`ism. The publishing house Mizan, which published numerous Shi`i works (besides many others), and the highly popular preacher and university lecturer Jalaluddin Rachmat played a major role in the emergence and growth of an Indonesian Shi`a movement. Later, tensions developed between the Shi`i groups around Arab sayyids and those entirely indigenous Indonesian, and between the first generation of self-made Shi`i preachers and the more "orthodox" teachers that in the 1990s started returning from study in Iran. The association **IJABI** (**Ikatan Jama'ah Ahlul Bait Indonesia**, Indonesian Assembly of Ahl al-Bait Associations), established and led by Jalaluddin Rachmat, represents the more "indigenous" wing of the Shi`i movement. It claims tens of thousands of adherents (Zulkifli 2004, 2009).

Tablighi Jama'at/Jama'ah Tabligh

The Tablighi Jama'at is a Muslim piety movement that originated in India in the early twentieth century, and it is currently probably the largest transnational Muslim movement in the world. It found its first basis in Indonesia in the "Indian" mosque of Kebon Jeruk, in the Kota area of Jakarta, and from there gradually spread to various parts of the country. Tablighis are apolitical and attempt to model their lives on that of the Prophet. Members are expected to regularly take part in missionary tours (*khuruj*), during which they live in mosques and attempt to persuade the communities around the mosque to participate more actively in prayer. The men wear long "Arab" robes and turbans or white skullcaps (at least when they are on *khuruj*), and the women are heavily veiled. This may cause confusion with two other movements whose members adopt similar (though not identical) dress codes, the Darul Arqam and the Salafi movement.[22]

Darul Arqam

Darul Arqam is a movement of Sufi inspiration, established in Malaysia by Ustaz Ashaari Muhammad. In the 1980s it spread to Indonesia (as well as Singapore and Southern Thailand). The movement stresses a combination of active participation in society and a lifestyle emulating the life of the Prophet. Many of its members are professionals. Core followers lived in a utopian community in the village of Sungai Penchala. (In Indonesia, a similar community was established in Depok.) The movement was characterized by strong millenarian expectations; Ashaari Muhammad several times announced the end of the world. The movement was banned in Malaysia in 1994, and has since then transformed itself into a successful trading corporation, the Rufaqa ("Friends") Corporation. In Indonesia, Darul Arqam has not suffered similar suppression. The Indonesian branch also uses the name Rufaqa; it has made sure not to appear too exclusive and has moved closer to the mainstream.

The Salafi movement

Studies of Salafism in the Middle East (e.g., Wiktorowicz 2006, Meijer 2009) commonly distinguish between three varieties: "purist" (or quietist) Salafism, which is the apolitical variety endorsed by the Saudi authorities; the "political" or activist (*haraki*) variety, which emerged as a result of the encounter of the Saudi Salafi tradition with Muslim Brotherhood ideas and has been critical of established political authority; and Salafi jihadism, of which Al Qaeda is the chief representative.

In the early 1990s, a handful of Indonesians who had studied Islam in Saudi Arabia, under Saudi and Yemeni teachers, began spreading the puritan Salafi message in Indonesia, through study circles targeting students and a few *madrasah* offering basic Islamic education to children. In the early post-Soeharto period, two competing wings emerged within the Salafi movement, led by Ja'far Umar Thalib and Abu Nida, respectively. The latter had the stronger financial support from rich Kuwaiti sponsors, leading the former to seek Indonesian allies. Ja'far named his wing of the movement **Forum Komunikasi Ahlussunnah Wal Jama'ah** (**FKAWJ**); Ahlus Sunnah wal Jama'ah, "People of the Prophet's Path and Congregation" is the name claimed by the traditionalist Sunni mainstream but also by the Salafis. In 2000, he transformed this organization, with covert military support, into the **Laskar Jihad**, which took part in inter-religious conflicts in the Moluccas and elsewhere. At the time of the first Bali bombing, in October 2002, Laskar Jihad was disbanded, and Ja'far and his remaining followers returned to apolitical Salafi preaching and teaching. The Abu Nida group has always stayed aloof from politics (Hasan 2006, 2010). In spite of differences among them, both groups follow quietist Salafi teachers in the Arabian peninsula.

Independent of these two Javanese groups, the movement **Wahdah Islamiyah** (Islamic Unity) in South Sulawesi is also of Salafi inspiration, at least in its theology. This movement has connections with Arabian "political" Salafis. Various other groups, such as the Jama'ah Gumuk in Solo, are to various degrees influenced by Salafi thought and practice, although they may not be Salafis in all respects. They have no connections with the more strictly Salafi groups. The only Indonesian groups that may be considered as Salafi jihadis are probably Jama'ah Islamiyah and Jama'ah Ansharut Tauhid. The Majelis Mujahidin Indonesia belongs, in spite of its name, to the "activist" (*haraki*) rather than the jihadist type of Salafis. These various groups have very little in common with the quietist Salafis.

SUFI ORGANIZATIONS

A large number of Sufi orders (*tarekat, tharikat*) are present in Indonesia, most prominently the Naqshbandiyya, Qadiriyya, Tijaniyya, Khalwatiyya, Sammaniyya, Shattariyya and Shadhiliyya. All of these are branches of "classical" international orders. Besides, there are also a number of Sufi orders of local origin and doubtful (in the eyes of non-members) orthodoxy, and various syncretistic mystical movements (*aliran kebatinan*). A number of formal umbrella organizations of Sufi orders were established to represent common interest and to demarcate "orthodox" orders from "heterodox" ones.

The first such umbrella organization was the **Partai Politik Tharikat Islam** (**PPTI**), originally a local West Sumatran association of Naqshbandi teachers, led by the politically astute Haji Jalaluddin, which during the 1950s developed into a nationwide association in which teachers of various other orders also took part. Haji Jalaluddin enjoyed Sukarno's patronage, which no doubt was a major factor in strengthening this organization. When Sukarno developed the "functional group" concept as an alternative to the party system, PPTI was transformed into a functional group (and its name appropriately changed into **Persatuan Pengamal Tharikat Islam**). It became a component of the Joint Secretariat of Functional Groups, Sekretariat Bersama Golongan Karya (Sekber Golkar), and has remained the only tarekat organization recognized by Golkar throughout the New Order. Since Jalaluddin's death in 1976, the organization has been run by colourless Sufi bureaucrats and been divided by factional struggles (Bruinessen 2007*a*).

The **Jam'iyah Ahlith Thariqah Mu'tabarah**, Association of Followers of Respected (i.e., "Orthodox") Sufi Orders, became nationally prominent in the 1970s (but its leaders then claimed it had existed since the late 1950s). Its charismatic leader was Kiai Musta'in Romly of Rejoso, Jombang in East Java, a teacher of the Qadiriyya wa-Naqshbandiyya order, and teachers of various other orders were members. Most if not all of the teachers were at least nominally affiliated with the Nahdlatul Ulama, and a conflict arose in the organization when Kiai Musta'in Romly openly deserted the NU and affiliated himself with Golkar instead (for which he was royally awarded). Teachers loyal to the NU took over most of the organization, including the majority of Musta'in's own deputies. There have since then been two Jam'iyah, one explicitly affiliated with NU (**Jam'iyah Ahlith Thariqah Mu'tabarah An-Nahdliyah, JATMN**) and a smaller one consisting of Musta'in's and his descendants' loyal followers (**Jam'iyah Ahlith Thariqah Mu'tabarah Indonesia, JATMI**). JATMN is recognized by NU as an affiliate, but JATMI never received that degree of recognition from Golkar, which recognized only PPTI as its affiliated *tarekat* organization.

Not all major Sufi orders joined JATMN or JATMI; the most significant exception is the branch of the Qadiriyah wa-Naqshbandiyya led by the charismatic Sundanese teacher Abah Anom (who died in 2011). This order, known by the acronym **TQN** (**Thariqah Qadiriyah wan Naqsyabandiyah**) has established a dense network of local branches all over Indonesia as well as in neighbouring Singapore and Malaysia.

Notes

[1]   The terms "Islamic Modernism" or "Modernist Islam" usually refer to those movements that expressly seek an accommodation of Islam and modernity, with an emphasis on rationality and compatibility with modern science (see Kurzman 2002, Masud 2009). In Indonesia the terms have been commonly used to refer to a much broader range of reformist movements, including

those that reject major aspects of modernity in favour of more literal readings of the sacred texts. Alternatively, the term *pembaruan*, "renewal", has been used. The pioneering overview of Indonesian Muslim reformist movements is Deliar Noer's dissertation (1973), which emphasizes the modern and modernist aspects. Pijper (1977) wrote a very perceptive study, with sympathetic portraits of leading reformists (whom the author knew personally) as modern and reasonable men. Peacock (1978*a*, 1978*b*) emphasizes the puritanical dimension, and Atjeh (1970) focuses on the effort to return to the pure Islam of the first generations of believers (the *Salaf*).

2   For reflections on what constitutes the traditionalists' tradition and to what extent it can accommodate change, see Bruinessen (1996).

3   On Muhammadiyah's reformism, see Federspiel (1970), Nakamura (1980), Peacock (1978*b*); on Muhammadiyah and Javanese culture: Burhani (2005), Nakamura (1983); on the Sumatran reformist style and Muhammadiyah: Hamka (1974).

4   In the second term of Susilo Bambang Yudhoyono as President, however, Muhammadiyah lost the position of Minister of Education. The incumbent minister, Prof. Muhammad Nuh, is closer to the NU.

5   The conflict dividing the Indonesian Arab community and its repercussions in Hadramaut itself are discussed in Mobini-Kesheh (1999).

6   The best study of Persis is Federspiel (2001). Pijper (1977) gives a sympathetic portrait of A. Hassan. See also Anshari and Mughni (1985).

7   On the turbulent early years of the Sarekat Islam, see Shiraishi (1990) and Elson (2009); on the "Red" Sarekat Islam and a Muslim communist uprising in Banten, see Williams (1990).

8   Of the four Sunni schools of jurisprudence (Hanafi, Maliki, Shafi`i and Hanbali), only the Shafi`i school has traditionally been present in Indonesia. Recognition of the other three schools allows in theory for greater flexibility. Ash`ari theology steers a middle course between philosophical rationalism and literal interpretation of revealed scripture, both of which it rejects. The adoption of Ghazali's mysticism amounts to a rejection of those mystical movements that proclaim an essential unity of God and human being.

9   On the *pesantren*, see Bruinessen (2008).

10   Significant studies of the NU are: Feillard (1995), Barton and Fealy (1996), Kadir (2000), Bush (2009), Bruinessen (1994).

11   On Chinese Muslims in Indonesia and the role of PITI and other associations, see Chiou (2012).

12   Masyumi is an abbreviation of Majelis Syura Muslimin Indonesia, Consultative Council of Indonesian Muslims. On the origins of Masyumi, see Benda (1958), pp. 150–68.

13   The other Muslim parties also unanimously endorsed the Jakarta Charter, but together they remained a minority in parliament. On the debates, see Boland (1971).

[14] On the various Muslim parties during the post-Soeharto period, see Platzdasch (2009); on the emergence of PK(S) from the Islamic students movement, see Rahmat (2008), Machmudi (2007).

[15] Major studies of the Darul Islam: Dijk (1981) and Dengel (1986). Formichi (2009) provides an interesting additional perspective on the basis of interviews with current sympathizers.

[16] Abduh (2001); Bruinessen (2008), pp. 236–38.

[17] Abdul Syukur (2003); Bruinessen (2002, 2008), pp. 231–34; International Crisis Group (2005); Ridwan (2008); Temby (2010). See also Wildan's contribution in this volume.

[18] Such is the claim of the film *Mata Tertutup* ("With Eyes Closed") by renowned filmmaker Garin Nugroho, which is based on research carried out by the Maarif Institute (a think-tank affiliated with Muhammadiyah) in 2011.

[19] On ISTAC and its founder Syed Naquib Al-Attas, see Abaza (2002), pp. 88–105.

[20] The story of the pesantren and development programme and later pesantren-based NGO activities is told in Bruinessen and Wajidi (2006).

[21] On Dompet Dhuafa, Rumah Zakat and other charitable associations and foundations, which have mushroomed in the first decade of the twenty-first century, see Latief (2012).

[22] On the Tablighi Jama'ah in Southeast Asia, there is now a major study by Noor (2012).

References

Abaza, Mona. *Debates on Islam and Knowledge in Malaysia and Egypt: Shifting Worlds*. London: RoutledgeCurzon, 2002.

Abduh, Umar. *Membongkar Gerakan Sesat NII di Balik Pesantren Mewah Al Zaytun*. Jakarta: Lembaga Penelitian & Pengkajian Islam, 2001.

Abdul Syukur. *Gerakan Usroh di Indonesia: Peristiwa Lampung 1989*. Yogyakarta: Ombak, 2003.

Anshari, H. Endang Saifuddin and Syafiq A. Mughni. *A. Hassan: Wajah dan Wijhah Seorang Mujtahid*. Bandung: Al-Muslimun & Lembaga Studi Islam, 1985.

Atjeh, H. Aboebakar. *Salaf. Muhji Atsaris Salaf. Gerakan Salafijah di Indonesia*. Djakarta: Permata, 1970.

Barton, Greg. "Indonesia's Nurcholish Madjid and Abdurrahman Wahid as Intellectual Ulama: The Meeting of Islamic Traditionalism and Modernism in Neo-modernist Thought". *Islam and Christian-Muslim Relations* 8, no. 3 (1997): 323–50.

Barton, Greg and Fealy Greg, eds. *Nahdlatul Ulama, Traditional Islam and Modernity in Indonesia*. Clayton, VIC: Monash Asia Institute, 1996.

Benda, Harry J. *The Crescent and the Rising Sun: Indonesian Islam under the Japanese Occupation 1942–1945*. The Hague: W. van Hoeve, 1958.

Boland, B.J. *The Struggle of Islam in Modern Indonesia*. The Hague: Martinus Nijhoff, 1971.

Bruinessen, Martin van. *NU: Tradisi, Relasi-Relasi Kuasa, Pencarian Wacana Baru*. Yogyakarta: LKiS, 1994.

————. "Traditions for the Future: The Reconstruction of Traditionalist Discourse within NU". In *Nahdlatul Ulama, Traditional Islam and Modernity in Indonesia*, edited by Greg Barton and Greg Fealy. Clayton, VIC: Monash Asia Institute, 1996.

————. "Genealogies of Islamic Radicalism in Indonesia". *South East Asia Research* 10, no. 2 (2002): 117–54.

————. "Saints, Politicians and Sufi Bureaucrats: Mysticism and Politics in Indonesia's New Order". In *Sufism and the "Modern" in Islam*, edited by Martin van Bruinessen and Julia Day Howell. London: I.B. Tauris, 2007*a*.

————. "Ahmad Sanusi bin Abdurrahim of Sukabumi". *Encyclopaedia of Islam*. 3rd ed., Part 2 (2007*b*).

————. "Traditionalist and Islamist Pesantrens in Contemporary Indonesia". In *The Madrasa in Asia: Political Activism and Transnational Linkages*, edited by Farish A. Noor, Yoginder Sikand and Martin van Bruinessen. Amsterdam: Amsterdam University Press, 2008.

————. "What Happened to the Smiling Face of Indonesian Islam? Muslim Intellectualism and the Conservative Turn in Post-Suharto Indonesia". Working paper. Singapore: S. Rajaratnam School of International Studies, 2011.

Bruinessen, Martin van and Farid Wajidi. "Syu'un Ijtima'iyah and the *Kiai Rakyat*: Traditionalist Islam, Civil Society and Social Concerns". In *Indonesian Transitions*, edited by Henk Schulte Nordholt. Yogyakarta: Pustaka Pelajar, 2006.

Burhani, Ahmad Najib. "Revealing the Neglected Missions: Some Comments on the Javanese Elements of Muhammadiyah Reformism". *Studia Islamika* 12, no. 1 (2005): 101–30.

Bush, Robin. "Regional Sharia Regulations in Indonesia: Anomaly or Symptom?" In *Expressing Islam: Religious Life and Politics in Indonesia*, edited by Greg Fealy and Sally White. Singapore: Institute of Southeast Asian Studies, 2008.

————. *Nahdlatul Ulama and the Struggle for Power within Islam and Politics in Indonesia*. Singapore: Institute of Southeast Asian Studies, 2009.

Chiou, Syuan Yuan. "In Search of New Social and Spiritual Space: Heritage, Conversion, and Identity of Chinese-Indonesian Muslims". Ph.D. thesis. Utrecht: Utrecht University, 2012.

Dengel, Holk H. *Darul-Islam. Kartosuwirjos Kampf um Einen Islamischen Staat in Indonesien*. Wiesbaden: Franz Steiner Verlag, 1986.

Dijk, C. van. *Rebellion under the Banner of Islam: The Darul Islam in Indonesia*. The Hague: Martinus Nijhoff, 1981.

Elson, Robert E. "Disunity, Distance, Disregard: The Political Failure of Islamism in Late Colonial Indonesia". *Studia Islamika* 16, no. 1 (2009): 1–50.

Federspiel, Howard M. "The Muhammadiyah: A Study of An Orthodox Islamic Movement in Indonesia". *Indonesia* 10 (1970): 57–79.

———. *Islam and Ideology in the Emerging Indonesian State: The Persatuan Islam (PERSIS), 1923 to 1957*. Leiden: Brill, 2001.

Feillard, Andrée. *Islam et Armée dans l'Indonésie Contemporaine: Les Pionniers de la Tradition*. Paris: L'Harmattan, 1995.

Feillard, Andrée and Rémy Madinier. *The End of Innocence? Indonesian Islam and the Temptations of Radicalism*. Leiden: KITLV Press, 2011.

Formichi, Chiara. *Islam and the Making of the Nation: Kartosuwiryo and Political Islam in Twentieth-Century Indonesia*. Leiden: KITLV Press, 2012.

Furkon, Aay Muhamad. *Partai Keadilan Sejahtera: Ideologi dan Praksis Politik Kaum muda Muslim Indonesia Kontemporer*. Jakarta: Teraju, 2004.

Hamka. *Muhammadiyah di Minangkabau*. Jakarta: Yayasan Nurul Islam, 1974.

Hasan, Noorhaidi. *Laskar Jihad: Islam, Militancy and the Quest for Identity in Post-New Order Indonesia*. Ithaca, NY: Cornell Southeast Asia Program, 2006.

———. "From Apolitical Quietism to Jihadist Activism: 'Salafis', Political Mobilization, and Drama of Jihad in Indonesia". In *Varieties of Religious Authority, Changes and Challenges in 20th Century Indonesian Islam*. Singapore: Institute of Southeast Asian Studies, 2010.

International Crisis Group. "Recycling Militants in Indonesia: Darul Islam and the Australian Embassy Bombing". Asia Report No. 92. Singapore/Brussels: International Crisis Group, 2005.

———. "Indonesia: The Dark Side of Jama'ah Ansharut Tauhid (JAT)". Asia Briefing N°107. Jakarta/Brussels: International Crisis Group, 2010.

Kadir, Suzaina. "Contested Visions of State and Society in Indonesian Islam: The Nahdlatul Ulama in Perspective". In *Indonesia in Transition: Social Aspects of Reformasi and Crisis*. London: Zed Books, 2000.

Karim, M. Rusli. *HMI MPO dalam Kemelut Modernisasi Politik di Indonesia*. Bandung: Mizan, 1997.

Kull, Ann. *Piety and Politics: Nurcholish Madjid and His Interpretation of Islam in Modern Indonesia*. Lund: Department of Anthropology and History of Religions, 2005.

Kurzman, Charles, ed. *Modernist Islam, 1840–1940: A Sourcebook*. Oxford: Oxford University Press, 2002.

Latief, Hilman. "Islamic Charities and Social Activism: Welfare, *Dakwah* and Politics". Ph.D. thesis. Utrecht: Utrecht University, 2012.

Machmudi, Yon. *Partai Keadilan Sejahtera: Wajah Baru Islam Politik Indonesia.* Jakarta: Harakatuna, 2007.

Madinier, Rémy. *L'Indonésie, Entre Démocratie Musulmane et Islam Intégral. Histoire du Parti Masjumi (1945–1960).* Paris: Karthala/IISMM, 2007.

Masud, M. Khalid. "Islamic Modernism". In *Islam and Modernity: Key Issues and Debates,* edited by M. Khalid Masud, Armando Salvatore and Martin van Bruinessen. Edinburgh: Edinburg University Press, 2009.

Meijer, Roel, ed. *Global Salafism: Islam's New Religious Movement.* London: Hurst & Company, 2009.

Mobini-Kesheh, Natalie. *The Hadrami Awakening: Community and Identity in the Netherlands East Indies, 1900–1942.* Ithaca, NY: Cornell University Southeast Asia Program, 1999.

Mujani, Saiful and R. William Liddle. "Indonesia's Approaching Elections: Politics, Islam, and Public Opinion". *Journal of Democracy* 15, no. 1 (2004): 109–23.

Mujiburrahman. *Feeling Threatened: Muslim-Christian Relations in Indonesia's New Order.* Amsterdam: Amsterdam University Press, 2006.

Nakamura, Mitsuo. "The Reformist Ideology of the Muhammadiyah". In *Indonesia: The Making of a Culture,* edited by J.J. Fox. Canberra: Research School of Pacific Studies The Australian National University, 1980.

———. *The Crescent Rises over the Banyan Tree.* Yogyakarta: Gadjah Mada University Press, 1983.

Noer, Deliar. *The Modernist Muslim Movement in Indonesia 1900–1940.* Kuala Lumpur, etc.: Oxford University Press, 1973.

Noor, Farish A. *Islam on the Move: The Tablighi Jama'at in Southeast Asia.* Amsterdam: Amsterdam University Press, 2012.

Peacock, James L. *Muslim Puritans: Reformist Psychology in Southeast Asian Islam.* Berkeley, etc.: University of California Press, 1978a.

———. *Purifying the Faith: The Muhammadiyah Movement in Indonesian Islam.* Menlo Park, Cal.: Benjamin/Cummings, 1978b.

Pijper, G.F. "Het Reformisme in de Indonesische Islam". In *Studiën over de Geschiedenis van de Islam in Indonesia 1900–1950,* edited by G.F. Pijper. Leiden: Brill, 1977.

Platzdasch, Bernhard. *Islamism in Indonesia: Politics in the Emerging Democracy.* Singapore: Institute of Southeast Asian Studies, 2009.

Rahmat, M. Imdadun. *Ideologi Politik PKS. Dari Masjid Kampus ke Gedung Parlemen.* Yogyakarta: LKiS, 2008.

Ridwan, Nur Khaliq. *Regenerasi NII: Membedah Jaringan Islam Jihadi di Indonesia.* Jakarta: Erlangga, 2008.

Shiraishi, Takashi. *An Age in Motion: Popular Radicalism in Java, 1912–1926.* Ithaca, NY: Cornell University Press, 1990.

Siegel, James T. *The Rope of God.* Berkeley: University of California Press, 1969.

Temby, Quinton. "Imagining an Islamic State in Indonesia: From Darul Islam to Jemaah Islamiyah". *Indonesia* 89 (2010): 1–37.

Wiktorowicz, Quintan. "Anatomy of the Salafi Movement". *Studies in Conflict and Terrorism* 29 (2006): 207–39.

Williams, Michael Charles. *Communism, Religion, and Revolt in Banten*. Athens, Ohio: Ohio University Center for International Studies, 1990.

Zulkifli. "Being a Shî'ite among the Sunnî Majority in Indonesia: A Preliminary Study of Ustadz Husein al-Habsyi (1921–1994)". *Studia Islamika* 11, no. 2 (2004): 275–308.

———. "The Struggle of the Shi'is in Indonesia". Ph.D. thesis. Leiden University, 2009.

3

TOWARDS A PURITANICAL MODERATE ISLAM: THE MAJELIS ULAMA INDONESIA AND THE POLITICS OF RELIGIOUS ORTHODOXY

Moch Nur Ichwan

INTRODUCTION

The collapse of the Soeharto regime in 1998 led to the opening up of previously unimaginable political opportunities and transformations in Indonesian society. The Reformasi (reformation) movement demanded democratization, good governance, and the empowerment of civil society. Most existing Muslim organizations redefined their orientation and political platforms, as did most other associations; and many new Muslim organizations, movements, and political parties emerged, armed with new nationalist, liberal or Islamist paradigms. They have endeavoured to present their own concepts of Reformasi, and to avoid the stigma of being anti-Reformasi.

The Majelis Ulama Indonesia (Indonesian Council of Ulama, or MUI),[1] a semi-official institution of Indonesian *ulama* established by Soeharto in 1975, is no exception.[2] At the beginning of the Reformasi era, the MUI seemed disoriented and struggled to come to terms with the changes. During the Habibie era, it focused not on issuing fatwas, but on producing *tausiyah*s to legitimize a number of Habibie's policies, and, in the period in which Habibie was confronted with political moves to discredit him, by visiting the president at the palace.[3] It was only at the 2000 National Congress, during the Abdurrahman Wahid era, that the MUI proclaimed its ambition to change its role from being the *"khadim al-hukumah"* (servant of the government) to serving as the *"khadim al-ummah"* (servant of the *ummah*). This resonated with the central Reformasi concept of empowering society *vis-à-vis* the state, besides expressing the MUI's vision of its own agenda-setting role in the Reformasi process. Since that time, the MUI has endeavoured to reposition itself in Indonesia's transitional politics by defending more conservative Muslim interests and aspirations. This can be seen from various fatwas, *tausiyah*s, and other statements produced by the MUI, and in the way in which it has dealt with social, political, economic and cultural issues.

In the present study, I shall focus on the MUI's endeavours to redefine its role in the post-Soeharto era, analyse its transformation from a government-oriented to an *ummah*-oriented body, and explore the implications of this transformation.[4] Particular emphasis will be given to the way in which the MUI has exercised its power as the "semi-official religious authority" in the country and the way it has defined "moderate Islam", which is in fact "puritanical moderate Islam" based on Sunni orthodoxy, in the context of ideologically and organizationally pluralistic Indonesian Islam. Below we will examine a number of issues that best reflect the MUI's changing role in post-New Order Indonesia, as well as its newly developed position in national politics. These issues range from the certification of *halal* foods and Islamic banking services to the "purification" of public morality (action against pornography and "porno-action"), education (the polemic on the Draft Law on the National Education System), the image of Islam (*jihad* and terrorism), Islamic thought (religious pluralism, liberalism and secularism), and Islamic faith (deviant belief and the Ahmadiyah movement).

"SOFTENING THE HARDLINERS, HARDENING THE SOFT-MINDED": THE MUI'S PURITANICAL MODERATION

The post-New Order MUI has introduced a new approach to the *ummah*, that is, in KH. Ma'ruf Amin's words, "softening the hardliners, hardening the soft-minded". However, the current state of the MUI's world-view is no longer characterized by moderate Islam *per se*, but rather by "puritanical moderate Islam".[5] The Council has always represented a moderate interpretation of

Islamic orthodoxy, and its orientation continues to be a moderate one, but it has undergone a shift towards more puritanical and strictly literalist interpretations of the faith during the last decade. This is part of what Van Bruinessen has called the "conservative turn" (Bruinessen 2011). The MUI puts forward puritanical moderate Islam, not puritanical radical Islam, as the ideal version for Indonesia, although it would not be impossible for the organization to turn to the latter type in the future. The MUI has retained its original concerns in the field of Islamic law, faith, morality and interest, but in these fields it has increasingly tended towards more puritan and conservative positions. In the past, the ideological struggle within the MUI was between Islamic traditionalism of Nahdlatul Ulama (NU) and Islamic modernism of Muhammadiyah, with the latter achieving victory (even when NU-affiliated ulama presided over the MUI). Presently, traditionalists, modernists, puritans and radicals vie for influence in the Council, and it is the reformist and puritanical voices that are victorious. The fact that the most senior positions in the Council have been held by ulama affiliated with the Nahdlatul Ulama has not made a difference, because these ulama happen to be closer to puritanical reformism than to mainstream traditionalism. There are very few radicals in the Council, but they have a significant voice, especially in influencing the *tausiyah*s or fatwas that are formulated not only by the Fatwa Commission and leadership board, but also by the forums that invite representatives from other Islamic organizations or movements, such as the Forum Ukhuwah Islamiyah (FUI), the Kongres Umat Islam Indonesia (KUII), and the Ijtima' Ulama. It is in these forums that the radicals have the opportunity to express their strict and rigid views, rhetorically accusing all those who have different opinions of hypocrisy (*nifaq*), sinfulness (*fisq*) or infidelity (*kufr*).

As a puritanical moderate Islamic organization, the MUI is characterized by a number of key tendencies. First, its normative orientation towards issues of *halal* and *haram* (licit and illicit) has become more legalistic in the sense of going beyond the boundaries of the traditional schools of Islamic law. It deals not only with purely religious issues, but also with the certification of *halal* food, cosmetics, drugs, banking, insurance, and other financial and economic issues, as well as political leadership — although it does not question the extent to which the state is Islamic. Second, its theological orientation has been basically conservative since its establishment, and has become more puritanical with the recruitment of some new and more radical members. The shift to a more puritanical position first became apparent at the 2000 National Congress, when the issue of Christianization through education emerged, and even more puritanical since the 2005

National Congress, when the fatwas on religious liberalism, secularism and pluralism, the Ahmadiyah, interreligious prayer, interreligious inheritance, and interreligious marriage were issued.[6] Third, its moralistic orientation has become more puritanical and interventionist in public affairs, not only through fatwas and *tausiyahs* and other public statements, but also through legal and political processes in parliament and mass demonstrations. Fourth, its ideological orientation has become more exclusive, protecting the interests of the Muslim *ummah* rather than inclusive national interests. However, despite these puritanical orientations, the MUI has tried to be moderate. Its moderation is indicated by, among other things, its rejection of radicalism and terrorism, its (admittedly selective) acceptance of modernity, and its acceptance of the Indonesian nation-state based on Pancasila and modern democracy, and not on Islam.

As mentioned above, there were already moves towards a more puritanical stance by the time of the 2000 National Congress, at which the MUI announced its new orientation towards becoming the *khadim al-ummah* (the servant of the Muslim community). Incontrovertibly, the biggest question raised by the slogan *khadim al-ummah* is: who is the *ummah*? When I asked MUI leaders in Jakarta and in local MUI offices for clarification on this matter, their answers varied. Some replied that *ummah* in this sense includes "all Muslims" in Indonesia, regardless of their ideological and political preferences, radical or liberal. Referring to the current MUI fatwas against religious liberalism, secularism and pluralism, others prefer to exclude liberal Muslims and those with "deviant beliefs" (*aliran sesat*), since they may pose a danger to the *ummah*. This second group has gone so far as to suggest that the MUI should not offer liberal Muslims MUI membership, and should instead be tolerant of so-called "puritan" and "radical" Muslims (such as Dewan Dakwah Islamiyah Indonesia [DDII], Hizbut Tahrir Indonesia [HTI] and Majelis Mujahidin Indonesia [MMI]) instead. Despite these differences, the general policy of the MUI is reflected in the phrase: *melunakkan yang terlalu keras, mengeraskan yang terlalu lunak* (which literally means: "softening those who are too hard, and hardening those who are too soft").[7] This implies that the MUI is playing the politics of "mediation",[8] as most MUI leaders believe, in the hope that both extremes will be persuaded to embrace "moderation". Despite this, it is clear that there has also been a change of course within the MUI towards a more conservative stance, reflected in the various fatwas and *tausiyah*s that it has issued since 2000.

In a move that would have been inconceivable under the New Order, a number of Muslim hardliners have been recruited, such as Adian Husaini,

Cholil Ridwan and Amin Djamaluddin.[9] Although more inclusion has been evident since the 2000 National Conference, until 2005 this had not resulted in the representation of radical organizations in the MUI. At the 2005 National Conference, members of such Islamist movements as the HTI and Front Umat Islam (FUI) were recruited to occupy certain positions in the central MUI and in some provincial and district offices, depending on the respective local politics inside and outside the MUI.[10] This strategy is the simplest way of implementing the MUI's supposedly new identity as the "*khadim al-ummah*".

This generosity of spirit has not been extended to "liberal Muslims", whether directly involved in Jaringan Islam Liberal (the Liberal Islam Network, or JIL) or otherwise associated with liberal interpretations of Islam.[11] A few intellectuals considered as "liberal", including Masdar F. Mas'udi and Siti Musdah Mulia, had been members of the MUI's central board up to 2005, although they were never involved in decision-making. From 2005 on, however, when the MUI issued its notorious anti-liberal fatwas, the Council has made efforts to protect itself from dangerous ideological influences by excluding all liberal Muslims from its ranks.[12] This policy has been implemented not only in the central MUI, but also in most provincial and district MUI offices.

There are indications that it will not be easy for the MUI to pursue its "moderation" strategy. Some extreme radical Muslim circles blame the MUI for being too soft, and, more specifically, too slow to endorse the implementation of Islamic Shariah.[13] Conversely, according to liberal Muslims, the MUI has gone too far in its interference in both the public and private dimensions of religious life. The latter also realize that a number of MUI fatwas and *tausiyah*s have been blatantly counter-productive, as they have hampered the progress of democratization in the country. They believe that some MUI fatwas threaten interreligious harmony and, indeed, the future of democracy (Munawar-Rachman 2010, pp. 26–38). Despite their disappointment in the MUI, however, radical groups have not rejected the organization and, instead, some of them have decided on positive action and have tried to penetrate the MUI by becoming members. They have proclaimed that they will try to change the MUI from within. The liberals, on the other hand, show no such tendencies. Instead, they have attempted to deconstruct the authority of the *ulama* council from outside, by developing discourses that undermine the MUI's authority and authoritativeness. Some have even called for the MUI's dissolution.

The MUI's negative reaction to liberal Muslims has been a logical response in such circumstances. The issuance of the fatwa on religious pluralism, liberalism and secularism, as we will see below, indicates the absence of liberal scholars within the MUI, and the failure of the liberals to win the MUI's sympathy. There have also been efforts, as a consequence of the fatwa on religious liberalism, to cleanse the MUI of all liberal ideas and of the scholars who support them. This may explain why there has been a "conservativization", in the sense of theological, legal, and moral puritanization, if not "radicalization", process visible in MUI discourses, and why the "moderating" efforts have resulted in "puritanical moderate" Islam, as we shall see from the cases discussed below.

BECOMING A "SERVANT OF THE MUSLIM COMMUNITY": THE PURITANICAL TURN

After the collapse of the Soeharto regime in May 1998, the MUI tried unsuccessfully to shake off its association with the New Order regime. During the B.J. Habibie era, the MUI adopted a position of unambiguous support for the Habibie regime. The relationship between the MUI and Habibie had been built up over many years during the New Order period, and had grown closer since the establishment of the Ikatan Cendekiawan Muslim Indonesia (Association of Indonesian Muslim Intellectuals, or ICMI), of which Habibie was the founding chairman, in late 1990. The ICMI and the MUI also cooperated assiduously in many religious activities, including the establishment of the first Islamic bank, Bank Mu'amalat Indonesia (BMI) (Porter 2002). Most Muslims had long considered Habibie to be the ideal Muslim intellectual, claiming that he had a "German brain but a Ka'ba heart" (*otak Jerman tapi berhati Ka'bah*).[14] At that time, Habibie was regarded as one of the most important Muslim figures, implying that, were political forces to oppose him, this could have a deleterious impact on Muslim society. Therefore, the MUI was placed in the position of defending Habibie against his opponents and supporting him in his bid to be elected as the next president. Before the general election, MUI issued three *tausiyah*s (on 29 April, 20 May and 1 June 1999). Respectively, these *tausiyah*s called for Muslims to participate in the election peacefully; for the choices of other Muslim political parties to be respected; and for the Qur'anic prohibition of non-Muslims standing as Muslim leaders (*auliya'*) to be respected (Ichwan 2005, pp. 55–58). It is clear that here, the MUI promoted Muslim political interests against those of nationalists and non-Muslims.

In 1998, the MUI revived the Kongres Umat Islam Indonesia (Indonesian Islamic Ummah Congress, or KUII), which was held between

3 and 7 November that year. This Congress was considered to be the continuation of Muktamar Islam Indonesia (known as the first KUII), held on 7–8 November 1945.[15] Organized after the collapse of Soeharto's New Order, this congress was politically significant in that it demonstrated the emergence of Islam as a political force. However, the Congress included some liberal thinkers, such as Nurcholish Madjid, Abdurrahman Wahid, Dawam Rahardjo, Azyumardi Azra, and Syafii Anwar, who were later excluded from the consecutive congresses. The KUII became a forum for discussing political, social, economic and religious issues. These issues would then be taken up by the MUI National Congress, which could not be held until after the 1999 general election. Later, the KUII became one of the most important forums for Islamic organizations and movements to voice their views and interests and to attempt to influence MUI fatwas and policies.

It is worthwhile to consider the MUI's role in the general elections, held on 7 June 1999. These were the first democratic elections since 1955, and no fewer than forty-eight parties with various ideological positions took part. The results were surprising: the secular nationalist parties won more votes than the Muslim-based nationalist parties and the Islamic parties together.[16] The results were as follows: PDI-P (Partai Demokrasi Indonesia-Perjuangan, or Indonesian Democracy Party-Struggle), with 34 per cent of the vote and 153 seats in parliament; Golkar (Golongan Karya, or the Party of the Functional Groups), with 22 per cent of the vote and 120 seats; PKB (Partai Kebangkitan Bangsa, or the National Awakening Party), with 12 per cent and 51 seats; PPP (Partai Persatuan Pembangunan, or the Development Unity Party), with 10 per cent and 58 seats; and PAN (Partai Amanat Nasional, or the National Mandate Party), with 7 per cent and 34 seats.[17]

In 1999, the president was not yet directly elected; the elections were only for parliament, and parliament, in turn, decided on the president.[18] Given the majority obtained by the secular parties, it appeared impossible that an individual who was strongly associated with Islam would be chosen as president, unless Muslim politicians in secular parties supported him and no politicians from Islamic or Muslim-based parties allied with secular politicians. At first glance, this appeared unlikely. Muslims politicians, both within parliament and beyond, found themselves facing a struggle.[19] In addition to expecting support from other Islamic organizations and movements, it was hoped that the MUI would assist them. Less than two months after the elections, the MUI held a national working conference, from 23–26 July 1999. There was a rumour that the MUI would produce a fatwa against the appointment of a female president or leader (aimed at Megawati). In fact, this never happened. It seems that the MUI trod very carefully when dealing with the delicate political situation. Nevertheless, it finally issued a *tadzkirah* statement on 25 September 1999, defending Habibie's position regarding the controversy surrounding the Bank Bali scandal, interreligious conflict in Ambon and the East Timor referendum[20] — thus broadcasting a clear message about the MUI's political position *vis-à-vis* the presidential election (Ichwan 2005, pp. 58–59).

Having the MUI's support, however, was of little help to Habibie, who was attempting to defend his position. His "state of the nation" address was rejected by most Members of Parliament, and although this did not actually prevent him from running in the presidential election, he decided to withdraw his candidacy. Habibie's withdrawal put the MUI in an even more difficult position, because this signified that it had lost its strongest patron in the government. It was, in fact, not only a defeat for Habibie, but also for the MUI.

The era of President Abdurrahman Wahid brought momentum for change. From the beginning of his presidential term of office, Wahid's political statements and attitudes on Islamic issues were seen as controversial in certain Muslim circles, including those of the MUI. Sometimes Wahid was even perceived as being hostile to Islamic interests, from his standpoints on Communism and Israel to those on the Muslim-Christian civil war in the Moluccas, and his open rejection of a fatwa by the MUI on a food additive it declared *haram*. Perhaps this was not surprising: Wahid had been a well-known and controversial intellectual figure since the 1970s. He had also been a fierce critic of the MUI, demanding that the organization become independent of the government and that it leave the Istiqlal Mosque, a state-funded mosque built during the Sukarno era.[21] These criticisms and the controversial nature of Wahid's approach left the MUI in a propitious position to declare its new vision. Having previously been seen as the "servant of the government" (*khadim al-hukumah*), from now on, it would strive to be the "servant of *ummah*" (*khadim al-ummah*). The proclamation was made at the MUI National Congress in 2000. In short, therefore, the period from the collapse of the Soeharto regime in May 1998 to the National Congress in 2000 can be regarded as a period of reorientation and loosening of the ties with the state.

The years between the national congresses of 2000 and 2005 constitute the second distinct phase of developments in the MUI of the post-Soeharto period. The 2000 National Congress was an important moment in the reconstitution of the MUI, marked by the revision of the organization's statutes.[22] In an important break with the recent past, the MUI declared that Islam was again its guiding principle, instead of the state ideology, Pancasila.[23] The transformation of the MUI is even more apparent in the document in which the Council presents itself, the "Outlook of the Indonesian Council of Ulama" (*Wawasan Majelis Ulama Indonesia*). This text lists its five major roles: (1) to act as heir of the Prophets (*warathat al-anbiya'*, a traditional description of the task of the ulama); (2) to issue fatwas; (3) to act as guide and servant of the Muslim community (*khadim al-ummah*); (4) reform and revival of Islam (*islah wa tajdid*); and (5) to enjoin good and forbid evil (*al-amr bi-l-ma'ruf wa al-nahy 'an al-munkar*) (Majelis Ulama Indonesia 2000, pp. 12–15). The three last points, not present in the earlier statutes, indicate clearly the MUI's new orientation. The concept of *khadim al-ummah*, as observed above, marked the shift from providing religious legitimacy to the regime and supporting its development agenda to representing Muslim interests — which are not purely religious but also economic and political. *Islah* and *tajdid* are terms from the agenda of religious reform associated with the puritan Persatuan Islam (Persis) and Dewan Dakwah Islamiyah Indonesia (DDII) as well as the modernist Muhammadiyah (but much less so with the NU). Enjoining good and forbidding evil, finally, is a core concept of Islamic social morality and is in principle embraced by most, if not all, Muslim organizations. However, it has connotations of enforcing the Shari'ah not by legislation but through various forms of persuasion, including vigilante action.

The 2000 National Congress also discussed other issues that reflected more conservative views of Islam and an awareness of the Muslim community's interests. It put forward reflections on how an ulama council should be organized, and how its newly adopted slogan, *khadim al-ummah*, should be put into action. The MUI declared that it was an "independent" organization. The President and the Minister of Religious Affairs were no longer the organization's official patron (*pelindung*) and chief adviser, respectively. Having become more "independent", the MUI was able to distance itself from the ruling party and from the hurly-burly of national politics during the 2004 general election.[24]

Claims of independence from the government notwithstanding, the MUI did not achieve (and probably never sought) a full separation of the ties connecting it with the government, and it remains quite unlike other non-governmental organizations (NGOs). It retains close links with the government, especially (but not exclusively) with the Ministry of Religious Affairs. It moved out of the Istiqlal Mosque, but currently uses an office building owned by the Ministry of Religious Affairs that has been lent to the MUI free of cost for an "indeterminate period of time".[25] Moreover, all post-New Order Ministers of Religious Affairs (KH Tholchah Hasan, Maftuh Basyuni and Suryadharma Ali) have been members of the MUI's Advisory Board. The MUI has also received donations from the Ministry of Religious Affairs.[26] A number of MUI activities were organized in cooperation with various government bodies, such as the Ministries of Religious Affairs, Communication and Information, National Education, Culture and Tourism, Defence and Security, Interior Affairs, Foreign Affairs, Employment, and Social Affairs.

The MUI also reorganized the way of discussing religious questions and issuing fatwas, which it continues to see as one of its main tasks. In 2003 a new forum was established, called *Ijtima' Ulama* (Ulama Assembly), in which members of the MUI's Fatwa Commission from all over Indonesia (including Majelis Permusyawaratan Ulama of Aceh) were invited to participate. Meeting every three years, the Ijtima' discusses three important clusters of issues: (1) *masa'il asasiyah wataniyah* (fundamental national issues); (2) *masa'il waqi'iyah mu'ashirah* (contemporary issues); and (3) *masa'il qanuniyah* (legal issues).[27] With this forum, the MUI has established its political moderation with the first cluster, responds to contemporary issues with the second cluster, and with the third, criticizes existing laws and draft laws being discussed in parliament. With this greater degree of flexibility, the MUI has become more active in directly responding to political issues, both national and international, by handing down fatwas and *tausiyah*s. It can also be effective in less direct ways. For example, it takes part in organizing street demonstrations through a body known as the Forum Ukhuwah Islamiyah (FUI).[28] However, it should be underlined that the MUI is not opposed to Pancasila as many radical Muslim groups are, and has even justified the existence of Pancasila as a "national philosophy" and part of a national consensus "to protect religious glory and regulate the welfare of shared life".[29] This support for Pancasila differentiates the organization from other puritanical radical Islamic groups.

This shift in the MUI's discourse and activities needs to be seen against the background of an upsurge of Islamic radical activism in the wake of Soeharto's resignation. The Front Pembela Islam (Islamic Defenders Front, or FPI), formally established on 17 August 1998, pioneered vigilante activism directed against nightclubs and other places of sin, and became involved in numerous violent demonstrations. The militia Laskar Jihad, emerging from a Salafi group naming itself Forum Komunikasi Ahlus Sunnah wal

Jamaah (FKAWJ, established on 14 February 1998), sent its members to take part in Muslim-Christian conflicts that broke out in various regions. The Hizbut Tahrir Indonesia, which had long been present underground, emerged from clandestinity and openly declared its existence in 2000. In the same year, various Islamist groups and individuals of a radical persuasion who shared the ideal of an Islamic state established the Majelis Mujahidin Indonesia (Indonesian Council of Holy Warriors), which openly proclaimed its allegiance to the historical Darul Islam movement. A paramilitary group that appeared affiliated with the MMI, Laskar Mujahidin, also took part in fighting in the Moluccas.[30] The prominent presence of these movements has influenced the MUI's perception of issues of concern to the *ummah* and thereby contributed, as we shall see below, to a shift in its discourse and the tone of its fatwas.

The MUI's National Congress of July 2005 marked the beginning of a third phase, continuing at the time of writing, in which the Council positioned itself as a firm defender of a conservative conception of orthodoxy. It took issue with, and strongly condemned: inter-faith prayer, inter-faith marriage, and inter-faith inheritance; religious pluralism, liberalism and secularism; so-called deviant beliefs, including the Ahmadiyah sect; dealings with the spirit world (*kahanah*) and fortune-telling (*irafah*); and any form of conversion of Muslims away from conservative orthodoxy (*pemurtadan*, "apostasy"). Most of these concerns were reflected in the fatwas issued during the 2005 conference.[31]

The struggle against "deviant beliefs", of which the Ahmadiyah and a local prophetic cult, al-Qiyadah al-Islamiyah, were the first main targets, was put on a more systematic footing with the publication of the MUI's "Guide for Identifying Deviant Beliefs" in 2007, which contains ten criteria of "deviant belief".[32] The Council's response to alleged apostasy concerned especially Christianization, an issue with which notably the DDII had long been obsessed.[33] In November 2006, the MUI established a Komite Nasional Penanggulangan Bahaya Pemurtadan (National Committee for Overcoming the Threat of Apostasy), which soon took position alongside various radical Islamist groups in actions against the building of (new) churches and against missionary activity. In this issue the MUI clearly adopted the radical Islamist agenda of challenging the development of Christian communities. Key roles were played by some of MUI leaders recruited after 2000, such as KH Cholil Ridwan (chairman of the committee), Amin Djamaluddin and Abu Deedat, who had previously been actively engaged in anti-Christianization and anti-apostasy movements.

PURIFYING FOODS AND OTHER CONSUMABLE PRODUCTS: *HALAL* CERTIFICATION

In Indonesia, *halal* certification has been managed by the MUI through its Institute for Foods, Drugs and Cosmetics Assessment (LPPOM-MUI). Established on 6 January 1989,[34] it took until 1994 before it issued its first *halal* certificate. The institute comprises two interrelated sub-institutions, one consisting of food scientists who deal with the laboratory assessment of foods, drinks, drugs, cosmetics and other products (located in Bogor and established in cooperation with the Bogor Institute of Agriculture (IPB) in 1994), the other consisting of Shariah experts (Fatwa Commission). It is the latter who decide whether or not the products are *halal* and issue a corresponding fatwa. The fatwa is then translated into a "*halal* certificate". Therefore, according to the MUI, a *halal* certificate is a written fatwa on the *halal*-ness of a product. To ensure the continued *halal* quality, the MUI formulated the so-called Halal Assurance System (HAS) in 2005 (not implemented until 2008), by which the factories of *halal* products recognized by the LPPOM-MUI are held to maintain independently the *halal* quality of these products. For this purpose, the factories should have their own internal *halal* auditor (for small factories) or institution (for big factories) (LPPOM-MUI 2008*a*). The MUI believes it needs a monopoly of the (financially very lucrative) *halal* certification in order to protect Muslim consumers from products that are of doubtful quality.

Halal certification became a major issue in the early Reformasi era in the context of the trend towards re-Islamization of the public sphere. Habibie endorsed it during his presidency by issuing Governmental Regulation No 69/1999 on Food Labelling and Advertisement, which regulated *halal* labelling. In the Abdurrahman Wahid era, the question of *halal* and *haram* food substances had become important enough to be capable of mobilizing opposition to the president. The LPPOM-MUI issued a fatwa declaring the popular food additive Ajinomoto (monosodium glutamate) *haram* because a pig enzyme was used in its production.[35] Wahid, a Muslim scholar himself, challenged the fatwa, arguing that although the enzyme was used in the production process, none of it remained present in the final product, and offering analogies with other cases where mere contact with a *haram* substance does not automatically make other substances *haram* too. To this he added the argument that a boycott of this product had a negative impact on the economy and on employment. He failed to convince most Muslim politicians, who sided with the MUI in this case and took up positions against him. This case probably strengthened the MUI's claims and gave it the political support to continue supervising *halal* foods and other consumable products.

Despite the MUI's monopoly, there is actually no strong legal basis for an NGO to deal with *halal* certification, because there is only a Letter of Cooperation, signed by the Ministry of Religious Affairs, the Ministry of Health, and the MUI on 21 June 1996. This was a compromise between these institutions, reached after long negotiations as to which institution should be in charge of managing *halal* certification.[36] The MUI considers the other existing laws and regulations as insufficient to protect the Muslim right to *halal* products, and as a justification for recognizing the LPPOM-MUI as the only institution for *halal* certification.[37] Therefore it called for a special law on *halal* product assurance, which should recognize and confirm the existence of LPPOM-MUI. However, the government, notably the Ministry of Religious Affairs, has its own agenda and appears interested in keeping the lucrative *halal* labelling business in its own hands.[38]

Halal food and non-food products are not merely matters of religious normativity, but represent a considerable economic business potential. The *halal* market has expanded significantly in the last decade, and the Indonesian Ministry of Trade perceives great potential for Indonesian exporters. In 2005 it estimated that the European Union alone, with 20 million Muslims, might import $195 million worth of *halal* products. At that time, Indonesia's non-oil, non-gas exports to Europe amounted to approximately $10 billion. This did not yet include *halal* products, a market segment that remained unexplored but that the Ministry was determined to capture.[39] At the third World Islamic Economic Forum (WIEF 2007), held in Kuala Lumpur, Malaysia, on 28 May 2007, President Susilo Bambang Yudhoyono said in his Special Keynote Address: "We would be remiss if we did not take advantage of the *halal* market" (Yudhoyono 2007).

The MUI is aware not only of the increasing volume of the *halal* market worldwide, but also of the importance of international recognition as an authoritative institution for *halal* certification. The drive behind its efforts to gain such recognition is ideological as well as economic in nature. Western capitalist states have procedures of quality assurance based on health and sometimes political considerations (such as human rights concerns), which has made it difficult for some Muslim countries to export their products to the U.S. or Europe. Muslim countries, the MUI argues, should implement not only health quality assurance, but also *halal* assurance, so that the producers in the West are also obliged to meet Muslim consumers' demands for *halal* quality.[40] At the same time, the MUI has been acutely aware of the potential earnings of *halal* certification, which may considerably reduce its dependence on government funding. In the past decade, *halal* certification has been one of the chief sources of income for the MUI (along with certification of Shariah banking, on which more below). It has therefore valiantly defended its de facto monopoly and expanded its activities throughout the country. As the demand for *halal* products continued to grow, the MUI established branches of the LPPOM-MUI in more than twenty provinces and cities (LPPOM-MUI 2008*b*). Despite criticisms, the LPPOM-MUI remains the sole institution of *halal* certification in Indonesia.

PURIFYING THE MARKET: SUPPORTING ISLAMIC BANKING AND FINANCE

The government's support for Shariah banking cannot be disassociated from the economic and political crises that hit Indonesia in 1997 and were followed by the fall of Soeharto in 1998. It is true that the country's first Islamic bank, Bank Muamalat Indonesia (BMI), was founded in 1991 with direct backing from Soeharto (Hefner 1996), but this was not followed by the establishment of any other Shariah banks until 1999, when several conventional banks adopted Shariah-compliant banking as part of their operations. The government at that time needed to revive economic development and trust in conventional banking was undermined. Some of the conventional banks were not managed well so that they collapsed, deepening the economic crisis. Owners of other conventional banks left the country and set up businesses abroad. The government needed alternative economic institutions that it hoped could stimulate national economic development. In this context, Islamic or Shariah-based economic institutions appeared to provide that alternative.

To endorse the development of Islamic banks, in 2003, the MUI issued a fatwa declaring conventional interest-based banking *haram*. As recently as 2000, the MUI had still considered conventional banking permissible on the basis of the consideration that a situation of *darurah* (emergency) prevailed. By 2003, however, there existed a reasonable number of Shariah banks, and the MUI decided that there was no more need for conventional banking. KH Ma'ruf Amin, the main actor behind the fatwa, told a journalist that the number of bank branches offering Shariah-compliant services had at that moment reached 210, and that certain banking practitioners had assured him that this was sufficient to declare conventional banking *haram* henceforth.[41] However, a fatwa is not binding, and thus far only a few Muslims have been persuaded to move their money from conventional banks to Islamic banks. Many conventional banks were, however, persuaded to prevent future losses by opening "Shariah windows" or establishing semi-independent Shariah branches. Most Islamic banks as well as conventional banks with "Shariah windows" have a Shariah Advisory Board (Dewan Pengawas Syariah), in which they prudently appointed prominent members of the MUI.[42]

The MUI has established a special body for dealing with banking and related matters (such as insurance), the National Shariah Council (Dewan Syariah Nasional, DSN). This body inspects all financial products individually and issues a fatwa for each one. This has resulted in a considerable output in fatwas on Shariah-compliant financial products, on which the central bank (Bank Indonesia) and the Ministry of Finance have come to rely. These two institutions do not issue permits for new "Islamic" financial products unless there is a corresponding fatwa from the DSN. In this sense, the MUI has obtained real influence over the government's policies concerning Islamic economics.

Nonetheless, in practice, the laws of economics prevail over those of state and religion. The introduction of new "Islamic" financial products require both a fatwa and a regulation from the state's financial institutions. When the market does not follow, the fatwas and regulations remain irrelevant. However, unlike other markets, the Shariah market responds to the degree of Shariah-mindedness of its participants, and not just to economic considerations. Compliance with Shariah principles and values becomes important in the banking system to the extent that the customer considers it to be important. For the MUI, persuading Muslims of the obligation to shift to more "Islamic" economic transactions is as important as ensuring that the proper financial products are available. The MUI's active interventions in support of Shariah-compliant banking may be considered a component of what some have termed "market Islam". This term refers to "how Islamic practices are mobilized to facilitate the transition from an authoritarian regime of state-fostered development to organizing labour and commercial activity according to market principles" (Rudnyckyj 2009a, p. 185). As a concept, it is similar to that of "civil Islam", which refers to the potential role of Islamic institutions in the democratic transition (Hefner 2000). Market Islam, however, is designed to merge Muslim religious practice and capitalist ethics, rather than to create commensurability between Islam and democracy. It aims to purify the economic market.

PURIFYING PUBLIC MORALITY: COUNTERING PORNOGRAPHY AND "PORNO-ACTION"

One of the roles that the MUI has assumed is that of the protector of public morality. It justifies this on the grounds that, because most Indonesians are Muslims, the MUI — as the representative of the ulama — is legally obliged to offer them guidance on public morality. The 1998 KUII, organized by the MUI, and the 2000 National Congress of the MUI recommended that the MUI tackle thirteen kinds of *munkarat* ("reprehensible acts"): deviant beliefs, corruption and bribery, adultery, abortion, pornography and "porno-action" (*pornoaksi*),[43] narcotics, gambling, alcohol, intellectual copyright, criminality, destruction of the environment, violence, and enmity. Among other suggestions, the KUII recommended that the MUI issue a fatwa and draw up a draft law on pornography and "porno-action". This proposal was motivated by the growing number of explicit programmes on TV channels, CDs, DVDs and Internet sites, as well pornographic books and magazines.

The MUI duly issued a fatwa on Pornography and Porno-action (no. 287/2001) and drew up its own version of the Draft Law on Anti-Pornography and "Porno-action", which has elicited numerous public debates and controversies since it was first proposed in 2002. It would be correct to say that the Draft Law that was debated in parliament was a product of the MUI, although it was formally submitted by the Ministry of Religious Affairs. The Draft Law was in fact a response to recommendations made in the MUI fatwa, especially Point 2.1, which demands all state apparatuses "create a legal statute which pays genuine attention to the content and is reinforced by the sanctions which function as *zawajir* and *mawani'*" [i.e., making evil-doers repent and preventing others from committing the same sin] (Majelis Ulama Indonesia 2003, p. 304).

Amidst the controversy on the Draft Law on Anti-Pornography and "Porno-action", the international "men's magazine", *Playboy*, published its first edition in Indonesia in April 2006, despite strong protests lodged before its publication. A group of FPI members attacked the building in which the *Playboy* office was situated. Not surprisingly, the MUI was among the bodies supporting the protest movements against *Playboy*. In its *Ma'lumat* (public statement), the Team for Securing the Draft Law on Pornography and "Porno-action", which included the MUI and representatives of other Islamic organizations, expressed the view that the publication of *Playboy*, an icon of pornography, was "tantamount to a declaration of war on the moral health of the nation" and that no response was possible other than "a declaration of war against all kinds of pornography and porno-action which they considered undermining the nation's morality" (quoted in Abdullah 2006, pp. 6–7). They raised the slogan "eradicate pornography, protect the nation's morality, make Indonesia dignified" (*Berantas pornografi, lindungi akhlak bangsa, wujudkan Indonesia bermartabat*).

The Team for Securing the Draft Law on Pornography and "Porno-action" symbolized the close relation between MUI and Islamist movements, especially those coordinated by the FUI, in facing the pornography — although this does not mean that they had similarly close relations in other cases. The said *Ma'lumat* was signed by the head of the MUI's Fatwa Commission, KH. Ma'ruf Amin, and the coordinator of the protest actions, Muhammad al-Khatthath, the prominent leader of the FUI and HTI. The MUI and the Islamists were in this case in complete ideological agreement on the importance of challenging pornography and "porno-action". This was followed by legal proceedings against the editor of *Playboy* and the artists whose pornographic artwork appeared in it. *Playboy* paid no heed to their protests, and the magazine continued to be published in Indonesia.[44] However, its editor, Erwin Arnada, was finally brought to court in 2009, found guilty under Articles 281–82 of the Penal Code (on public morality) and sentenced to two years imprisonment. After this, publication of Indonesian *Playboy* was discontinued.

The Draft Law underwent a number of changes as attempts were made to satisfy opposing groups, before it was finally approved by parliament on 30 October 2008. Although not all of the MUI's demands were incorporated, including use of the term "porno-action", the spirit of the law is line with the MUI rather than with "secular" forces. Undoubtedly, seen from the MUI's viewpoint, the imprisonment of the editor of Indonesian *Playboy* and the discontinuation of this magazine, as well as the enactment of the Pornography Law were great successes.

PURIFYING THE SCHOOLS: PREVENTING APOSTASY THROUGH THE NATIONAL EDUCATION SYSTEM

Through the Ministry of Education, the government proposed a Draft Law on the National Education System to parliament on 2 May 2003. The draft law suffered a stormy passage through parliament, however, because a number of legislators thought that it displayed a heavy Muslim bias. The same draft was proposed again on 20 May 2003, but again failed to achieve a consensus. This caused controversy between proponents and opponents of the draft law. The latter, both inside and beyond parliament, argued that it did not do justice to the religiously pluralistic nature of Indonesian society, and that it was therefore undemocratic. Among its provisions, the draft law would have obliged schools to provide all their students with teaching of religious subjects by teachers of their own religion. This would disproportionately affect Christian schools, which are generally considered the best, so that many Muslim parents send their children there, whereas few if any Christian parents would send their children to a Muslim school. Concerned Muslim puritans have long deplored this situation as rife with the danger of Christianization, and therefore felt that the new law might finally restore the balance. The opponents of the draft law believed that this provision would be difficult to implement, as certain religiously plural private schools would find it difficult to provide teachers based on the religious orientation of their students. The proponents of the draft law, the majority of whom were Muslims, believed that the law was "pluralistic" and "democratic", on the grounds that it reflected the rights of believers to be given religious instruction.

The MUI played an important role in the promulgation of the draft law. The MUI was consulted from the outset, having been requested to read and give feedback on the first draft. Although the same task was also required of other, non-Muslim, representative religious organizations, the draft law was in line with Muslim views on education. Several organizations representing other religions later joined the protests against the draft law. The MUI appears to have played a significant role in adding an Islamic touch to the Draft Law — quite apart from the fact that the Minister of National Education at the time, Professor Malik Fadjar, was a prominent Muhammadiyah leader and a former Minister of Religious Affairs. The MUI was also active in organizing support at both the national and local levels. Various large demonstrations were organized by the Forum Ukhuwah Islamiyah, the MUI's vehicle for mobilizing grassroots support, in which representatives of almost all Islamic organizations in Indonesia took part. The national demonstrations in Jakarta were also supported by a number of MUI branches around Jakarta, including those from the provinces of Banten and West Java, and other more remote branches, such as Yogyakarta and South Sulawesi.[45]

On 1 June 2003, the FUI and the MUI organized a demonstration they called "Aksi Sejuta Ummat" (Action of One Million Muslims) in front of the Al-Azhar Mosque in Jakarta's middle-class district of Kebayoran Baru. The demonstration was attended by thousands of Muslims from various backgrounds and such disparate organizations as the Muhammadiyah,

Nahdlatul Ulama, the DDII, Partai Keadilan Sejahtera (PKS), the HTI, and the MUI. The MUI was likewise an important supporter of other Muslim demonstrations in various regions. This was a moment when the MUI was deeply involved in the fine details of the political struggle, no longer confining itself to a "behind-a-desk" style of politics (consultation, issuing fatwas and *tausiyah*s and the like), but instead throwing itself into street politics. This was a palpable sign that the issue of education had become very important to the MUI. Most MUI leaders consider education to be the first line of defence in protecting the religious beliefs of Muslim children (*aqidah*). In their perception, education can easily be used as a means of luring Muslim students away from Islam (*riddah* or *pemurtadan*, apostasy) or, at the very least, to introduce them to un-Islamic teachings. The MUI's leaders were afraid of attempts to convert Muslim students to Christianity, their fears fed by the alleged conversion of many Muslim students who attended Roman Catholic or Protestant schools, which were generally (perceived to be) of much higher quality than state schools or Muslim private schools.[46]

Muslims were not the only group to be roused into action by the proposed law. Counter-demonstrations were arranged by the Masyarakat Prihatin Pendidikan Nasional (Society Concerned with National Education, or MPPN), a coalition of mostly Roman Catholic schools in Jakarta, Bogor, Tangerang and Bekasi. One large demonstration was staged in front of the parliament building on 5 June 2003. Similar demonstrations were also held in Medan, Palembang, Yogyakarta, North Sulawesi, Denpasar, Kupang, and Flores. They demanded that the draft law should take Indonesian plurality into consideration (*Tempo Interaktif*, 5 June 2003).

Towards the final session of parliament, the MUI general secretary, Din Syamsuddin, personally campaigned in some regions to drum up Muslim support for parliamentary approval of the draft law. At the Tabligh Akbar in Sidoarjo, Syamsuddin said that the MUI would ensure that legislators approved the draft law, and that the organization would back them up; and he called on Muslims to join the "Aksi Sejuta Ummat" demonstration to be held in front of parliament on 10 June 2003 (*Kompas*, 10 June 2003). Huge numbers of Muslim demonstrators poured in from neighbouring regions. The Banten MUI organized the demonstrators who descended on Jakarta in more than 380 buses, while others came on their own initiative. Professor KH. Wahab Afif, the chairperson of the Banten MUI, estimated that, in all, about 40,000 Bantenese Muslims joined the demonstration in Jakarta.[47]

The draft law was approved by parliament on 11 June 2003.[48] This elicited protests and demonstrations in many regions, but these remained without further effect. The Muslim groups had achieved a real victory, but the victory was particularly sweet for the MUI, which, from the initial drafting process onwards, had helped to ensure that the law did not run counter to Muslim aspirations and interests.

PURIFYING THE IMAGE OF ISLAM: REJECTING TERRORISM, DEFENDING *JIHAD*

In the aftermath of the 11 September 2001 terrorist attacks, and in response to the U.S. war in Afghanistan, the MUI organized a meeting of the FUI that was attended by thirty-two representatives of Islamic organizations. The then MUI secretary general, Professor Din Syamsuddin, read out an MUI statement which condemned the terrorist attacks, but also felt compelled to call upon Muslims to prepare for *jihad* should the U.S. and its allies commit any act of aggression against Afghanistan in their search for Osama bin Laden, who was alleged to have masterminded the attacks. The MUI later clarified that it meant *jihad* in its generic sense as a struggle for good, and not in the sense of *jihad* as war.

In its Fatwa on Terrorism (fatwa no. 3/2004), which was the result of the *Ijtima' Ulama* (ulama meeting) of 16 December 2003 and issued on 24 January 2004, the MUI also made a distinction between *jihad* and terrorism (Majelis Ulama Indonesia 2010, pp. 725–29). The fatwa declared that *jihad* encompasses two meanings: first, *jihad* pertains to every difficult endeavour, or readiness to shoulder difficulties in combating and defending against any manifestation of enemy aggression; and second, *jihad* pertains to all difficult and continuing endeavours to protect and honour Allah's word (*li i'lai kalimatillah*). Moreover, in both its senses, *jihad* should be undertaken for the sake of reform (*islah*), if necessary by war; and it is intended to establish Allah's religion and/or to protect the rights of the oppressed (*terzalimi*). Lastly, it should be pursued according to the Shariah by targeting clearly defined enemies. Despite these nuances, the fatwa's notion of *jihad* is still based on conflict, and ultimately entails war (*qital* or *harb*). It did not refer to the classical distinction between the "smaller *jihad*" (*jihad asghar*), which is a physical struggle, and the "greater *jihad*" (*jihad akbar*) or spiritual struggle against weakness and evil in one's self. The latter sense is entirely absent from the fatwa.

The MUI's fatwa did, however, explicitly take issue with terrorism. It states unequivocally that, "terrorism is a crime against humanity and civilization, a serious threat to state authority, security, world peace and the prosperity of society. Terrorism is a form of organized transnational crime; it can be defined as an extraordinary form of criminal violence with indiscriminate targets." Terrorism is described as destructive (*ifsad*) and anarchical or chaotic action (*fauda*), which is perpetrated for the purpose of creating fear and/or annihilating other groups; it is committed without regard to rules; and its targets are unlimited. The fatwa states that committing terrorism is *haram* (forbidden), but that pursuing *jihad* is an obligation. The fatwa also declares suicide bombings *haram*, like any other form of suicide, but it permits warlike struggle for the sake of Islam, even when this may claim the lives of innocent victims. Its message is clear: *jihad* should not be equated with terrorism, and vice versa.

The formulation of this fatwa reflects the MUI's problematic position regarding the issues of *jihad* and terrorism. The MUI did its best to respond to international terrorism, but in doing so, it also had to take the orthodox view of *jihad* into consideration. In other words, while the MUI wanted its fatwa on terrorism to gain international acceptance, it simultaneously justified it according to Islamic law. By adopting this moderate position, the MUI circumvented the liability of being charged by the international community with having a pro-terrorist attitude, and from being accused of harbouring anti-*jihad* sentiments by Islamist groups. In doing so, it was vulnerable to being misunderstood by both sides. Some Islamists criticized the MUI for being afraid of the West,[49] but it also came under fire from "secular" activists who claimed that the MUI was dancing to the tune of radical movements (*Jakarta Post*, 1 August 2005). It was an object lesson for the MUI on how to survive: while it should stand firm on the grounds of Sunni orthodoxy in order to maintain its credibility as the most authoritative religious institution in Indonesia, at the same time, it should also never lose sight of the political context, either locally or globally.

PURIFYING ISLAMIC THOUGHT: AGAINST RELIGIOUS PLURALISM, LIBERALISM AND SECULARISM

Since the 1970s, Indonesia has seen the development of various strands of critical religious thought that differed considerably from mainstream reformist thought, and that aroused deep suspicions among conservatives and puritans both in the Muhammadiyah and NU. In response to the increasing presence of radical Islamic voices in the public sphere after the fall of Soeharto, the critical trends manifested themselves in various organized forms and platforms. They described themselves and their religious thought by a range of different names, including post-traditionalist Islam, emancipatory Islam, progressive Islam, and liberal Islam.[50] Perhaps the most unusual example of this phenomenon was the establishment of Jaringan Islam Liberal (the Liberal Islam Network, or JIL) in 2001. The activities and thinking of this organization, which promotes critical thinking and the adoption of a liberal and rational attitude to religious teachings, have been a source of anxiety to most Islamists and ulama in the region. A host of articles and books attacking their projects have been published. On 30 November 2002, Forum Ulama Umat Islam (FUUI) — a "private" organization of ulama, led by Athian Ali M. Da'i — issued a fatwa stating that it is considered *halal* (lawful) to shed the blood of anyone who dishonours Allah, the Prophet Muhammad, Islam, and the Islamic *ummah* (*Pikiran Rakyat*, 26 December 2002). This fatwa was particularly controversial, as it appeared to be a direct response to a programmatic statement by former JIL coordinator Ulil Abshar-Abdalla, in which he expressed his liberal views (Abshar-Abdalla 2002). It was the first fatwa in modern Indonesian history to condemn a person for blasphemy and consequently to sanction the perpetration of violence against him.[51] In response, the FUUI claimed that the fatwa did not mention any particular name, but that all persons who entertain such (liberal) understandings of Islam are blasphemers.

Despite the strength of their reaction, the ulama felt that they had not done enough to put a stop to the JIL's activities and those of other liberal Islamic movements. They needed stronger legitimacy, which could only be accorded by an MUI fatwa. The Fourth Kongres Umat Islam Indonesia, held in Jakarta in April 2005, recommended that the MUI issue a fatwa denouncing liberal Islam, specifically mentioning the JIL, because it disseminated heterodox, "deviant" (*sesat*) thoughts or teachings which could "mislead the *ummah*". The head of the DDII, Husein Umar, said that the seeds of thought developed by the JIL should be included under the category of "reprehensible actions" (*munkarat, kemungkaran*). He also considered that the JIL presented a challenge to Islamic *da'wa*. Some months beforehand, similar demands had also been voiced at the MUI Regional Coordination Meeting (Rakorda) for the MUI chapters of East Java, Bali, West Nusa Tenggara (NTB) and East Nusa Tenggara (NTT). The head of the organizing committee of the KUII, Din Syamsuddin, believed that this sentiment reflected the aspirations of mainstream Islamic organizations in the country, and that these could not simply be disregarded. Although he did not name specific organizations, he described the forces of secularism and liberalism as menacing challenges to *da'wah*, saying that they could engender "shallowness of faith" (*pendangkalan akidah*).[52] The issue of liberal Islam had been anticipated prior to the congress, because it was mentioned in a booklet, *Materi IV Masalah Aktual Keumatan dan Kebangsaan*, that was circulated among the participants (Majelis Ulama Indonesia 2005c, pp. 40–41, 47–50).

In response, the 2005 National Congress of the MUI issued *fatwa* no. 7/2005 on Religious Pluralism, Liberalism and Secularism. This fatwa soon caused controversy, because it not only had implications for liberal thought in Islam, but was also bound to impinge on inter-religious relations in such a religiously plural society. Because the terms "pluralism", "liberalism" and "secularism" are not fully clarified within the text of the fatwa, their meanings can be interpreted differently. Some scholars simply omit the word "religious" so that the fatwa opposes all forms of pluralism, liberalism and secularism; others argue that it stands against religious pluralism in particular, and not other kinds of pluralism, as well as against secularism and all varieties of liberalism, whether religious or not.[53] In its explanation of the fatwa, which was written later after the controversy had emerged, the MUI clarified that the text should be read as "religious pluralism", "religious liberalism", and "religious secularism", implying that only pluralism, liberalism and secularism within religious belief are rejected. The MUI fatwa does in fact promote this final reading, but the problem is that neither the MUI nor, for that matter, anyone else, is able to exercise control over the different interpretations that emerged.

The most severe criticism of the fatwa came from liberal-progressive Muslims, including Abdurrahman Wahid, Azyumardi Azra (UIN Syarif Hidayatullah), Ulil Abshar-Abdalla (JIL), Djohan Effendi (International Centre for Religious Pluralism), Syafi'i Anwar (International Centre for Islam and Pluralism, or ICIP) and Dawam Rahadjo (Lembaga Studi Agama dan Filsafat, or LSAF). Their principal contention was that either the MUI's leaders did not fully understand the terms "pluralism", "liberalism" and "secularism", or that their understanding deviated from the academic definition of these terms. Azyumardi Azra, for instance, criticized the fact that they had taken the Qur'an and *hadith* literally, without applying reason to their interpretations. He believes that the Qur'an teaches tolerance of other religions. In his view, the Qur'an and Prophet accept differences not only as reality but also as Allah's grace. He interpreted the MUI's rejection of liberalism as an indication that the MUI thought liberals no longer believed in the Qur'an, the Prophet Muhammad or true Islamic teachings, and did not even bother to perform the daily prayers (*salat*). He suggested that the MUI should evaluate its own methodology of *ijtihad* (*Tempo Interaktif*, 2 August 2005). Syafii Anwar, meanwhile, asserted that the MUI's fatwa was a serious violation of religious freedom. Ulil Abshar-Abdalla said that it reflected the "stupidity" (*tolol*) of the MUI ulama.[54] Moeslim Abdurahman considered that it was the MUI, rather than the liberals, who had deviated from the true faith (*Tempo Interaktif*, 4 August 2005). Dawam Rahardjo even said that in issuing an unreasonable fatwa the MUI had in fact itself committed blasphemy. Generally speaking, they considered the MUI's fatwa to be in breach of freedom of expression and human rights.[55]

This criticism of the fatwa by liberal Muslims was challenged by the hardliner Adian Husaini in his book, *Pluralisme Agama: Haram*, published a couple of months after the issuance of the fatwa (Husaini 2005). As with the MUI fatwa, Adian Husaini understood religious pluralism to be an ideology which considers all religions to be equally true. In another book, the head of the MUI in East Java, KH. Abdusshomad Buchori, accused JIL of being part of the so-called "religious pluralism sect" (*sekte pluralisme agama*) (Buchori 2006). However, unlike Adian, Abdusshomad demonstrated a better understanding of the JIL and of the discourse on religious pluralism. Published by the MUI of Surabaya, the book reflects the official MUI position on the issue, and endorses the fatwa.[56]

The issuance of the fatwa has elicited some concerned responses from non-Muslim leaders, because, as religious minorities, they expect tolerance and wisdom from the Muslim majority. They are apprehensive that the fatwa will spark intolerance and hostility towards them. They are also convinced that lay Muslims will interpret the fatwa as meaning that cordial relations and cooperation with non-Muslims are prohibited.[57] If this were indeed to happen, it would deal a considerable blow to decades-long attempts to build inter-religious dialogue. It does not help that Adian Husaini, one of the radicals who were recruited into the MUI in the early 2000s, was made a member of the MUI's Commission for Harmonious Relations amongst Religious Communities. The fatwa as well as Husaini's fierce rejection of pluralism indicate that the views on religious harmony prevailing in the MUI are superficial and full of prejudice.

The impact of the fatwa, especially as it relates to "religious pluralism", has been cause for concern. Most preachers on TV have been careful to avoid the word "pluralism" and have instead spoken of "plurality" when discussing inter-religious relations. Hence, they talk about "plurality" without "pluralism". Anti-pluralism speeches have frequently been made in mosques, especially those with conservative and radical inclinations. Most Islamist magazines, such as *Sabili*, *Hidayatullah*, *Al-Wa'ie*, and *Risalah Mujahidin*, have been actively engaged in the campaign against "religious pluralism". What is surprising is that the government, and in particular the Ministry of Religious Affairs, has failed to recognize the precariousness of the country's future inter-religious relations.

PURIFYING THE ISLAMIC FAITH: EXCLUDING THE AHMADIYAH MOVEMENT FROM ISLAM

On 15 July 2005, in the run-up to the 2005 MUI's National Congress (which was to be held two weeks later), a hostile crowd of between 5,000 and 10,000 people, led by activists of the FPI and the Lembaga Penelitian dan Pengkajian Islam (Islamic Research and Study Institute, or LPPI), attacked the campus of the Jamaah Ahmadiyah Indonesia (Indonesian Ahmadiyah Congregation, or JAI) in Parung, near Bogor in West Java, demanding the dissolution of this organization. In the view of at least some analysts, the attack appeared to be intended as a message to the MUI National Congress that it should tackle the problem of the Ahmadiyah. As leaders of the crowd claimed, the Ahmadiyah movement had deviated from the Islamic religion and should be banned.[58] Made uneasy by this attack, more than 1,000 Ahmadiyah followers sought police protection in Bandung, the capital of the province of West Java, to ensure that the security of their two mosques in Cikutra and Bojongloa was safeguarded.

The Ahmadiyah movement worldwide is divided into the Qadian branch, led by the *khalifat al-masih*, the successors of Mirza Ghulam Ahmad, and the Lahore branch, led by Muhammad Ali, who has striven to bring the Ahmadiyah closer to the Sunni tradition. The JAI is Indonesia's Qadiani organization, while the Lahore branch has formed its own organization, Gerakan Ahmadiyah Lahore Indonesia (GAI).[59] From the orthodox point of view, the Qadian branch is particularly deviant, notably because of their conviction that Mirza Ghulam Ahmad was divinely inspired and therefore a prophet. As early as 1980, the MUI had already issued a fatwa on the Ahmadiyah, in which it declared only the Qadiani branch to be incompatible with Islam. Among the general public there is considerable confusion as to the nature of the beliefs of the Ahmadiyah and the difference between its two branches, and the Islamist activists of the 2000s were equally upset by both branches. Estimates of the numbers of Ahmadiyah followers diverge widely: Ahmadiyah spokespersons claim 300,000 to 400,000 followers, whereas the Ministry of Religious Affairs speaks of 50,000 to 80,000 (Crouch 2009, p. 5). The Qadian branch appears to be considerably larger than the Lahore branch.

The 1980 MUI fatwa on Ahmadiyah was used to legitimize the "Parung violence" of 2005; indeed, the attackers publicly claimed that they were inspired by the 1980 fatwa. But why did such a violent attack not occur under the New Order, under which the fatwa had been issued? Why did it take twenty-five years to unleash violence? There must have been other factors at work than the fatwa itself, and this was indeed the case. First and foremost, there has been a significant shift in Islamist political attitudes since the collapse of the Soeharto regime, induced mainly by the Reformasi spirit of democratization. This has allowed critics to articulate their views more openly and even to resort to violence, unheard of during the Soeharto era. Their views on the Ahmadiyah and other "deviant beliefs" were overwhelmingly negative, and they were convinced that the Ahmadiyah had strayed beyond the boundaries of Islam. In their view, the Ahmadiyah movement is no longer a part of Islam, and its followers are "non-Muslims".

Such views have recently been fuelled by a number of books and pamphlets condemning the Ahmadiyah movement's "deviation" from Islamic teachings in a more provocative way. Some books condemning the Ahmadiyyah had been published before the Reformasi, but they portrayed the Ahmadiyah as part of Islam, although not part of Sunni orthodoxy.[60] Starting some years before the 2005 violence, a new series of books on the subject, especially those published by the LPPI, argued that Ahmadiyah was not part of Islam and accused the movement of being hostile to Islam.[61] Amin Djamaluddin, the director of LPPI, is a frequent critic of Ahmadiyah. His aim is either to eliminate Ahmadiyah, both Qadian and Lahore, from the country, or to make it an independent religion outside Islam, as in Pakistan.[62] Besides accusing Mirza Ghulam Ahmad of being a "false prophet", Djamaluddin also accused the Ahmadiyah movement of "having its own scripture" (meaning the *Tadhkirah*, the most substantial of Ghulam Ahmad's books), of "plagiarizing the Qur'an", "changing the Qur'an", "counterfeiting the Qur'an", "hijacking the Qur'an", and "changing the words of the *syahadah* (confession of faith)".[63] Such terms were not used in previous publications on the subject. The LPPI books present the evidence in detail, pointing at the numerous similarities between the *Tadhkirah* and the Qur'an, as well as additions to or alterations of the Qur'anic narrative. Moreover, unlike other publishers, the LPPI is not content with simply publishing books attacking the Ahmadiyah and other "deviant beliefs". It has also mounted actual campaigns against the sect, which have undoubtedly fanned hatred and prejudice against the Ahmadiyah.

Five years earlier, in its National Congress of 2000, the MUI had indicated that "*aliran sesat*" (deviant sects) constitute a danger for the mainstream *ummah*. Although it did not specify which sects it considered deviant, the statement reflected the MUI's desire to deal with this issue. This was then reinforced in the Fourth KUII, coordinated by the MUI and held in April 2005, three months prior to the attack in Parung. Indeed, the KUII gave higher priority to the issue of deviant and heterodox sects than to other major social problems such as corruption, bribery, adultery, abortion, pornography, porno-action, narcotics, gambling, alcohol, intellectual copyright, criminality, destruction of the environment, violence and enmity (Olle 2006, p. 2).

The attack at Parung, as mentioned earlier, appeared to be intended as a strong message to the MUI urging it to be much more stringent in its handling of the Ahmadiyah movement at the upcoming congress. It also expressed the Islamists' frustration that in spite of the 1980 fatwa, the Ahmadiyah had been able to continue its activities, and signalled their conviction that action was needed. At the MUI congress, it became clear that the views of the MUI had shifted towards those of the anti-Ahmadiyah activists. In the new Ahmadiyah fatwa, issued at the congress, the MUI no longer restricted its censure of the Ahmadiyah to the Qadian group but declared both branches to be equally deviant and outside Islam. It moreover lobbied the government in order to have the fatwa followed up by a legal ban of the Ahmadiyah.

This shift in the MUI's position on the Ahmadiyah was no doubt in part due to the overall shift towards more puritanical and conservative positions on the part of leading members of the MUI. More specifically, the most vocal critic of the Ahmadiyah and other "deviant sects", Amin Djamaluddin, whose LPPI was one of the organizers of the attack in Parung, appears to have had a considerable influence on the MUI's thinking on the issue; the various accusations of replacing, plagiarizing and abrogating the Qur'an, which he directed at the Ahmadiyah (see above), however incoherent, became part of the MUI's own discourse. To further buttress its condemnation of the Ahmadiyah, the MUI formulated in 2007 ten explicit criteria of "deviant belief", in order to systematically exclude non-mainstream Islamic groups from the "right" belief, and even from Islam.[64] Seen from this perspective, Ahmadiyah fits almost all of the criteria.

The JAI and GAI each responded differently to the fatwa. The JAI chairman Abdul Basit, accompanied by the well-known Muhammadiyah intellectual M. Dawam Rahardjo, asked the Indonesian Legal Aid Foundation (YLBHI) to help it to prepare legal measures against the MUI and the attackers.[65] Their agitation was understandable, because the demonstrators had used both psychological and physical violence against the JAI. The GAI took a different course and published a book criticizing the fatwa, written by Ali Yasir, former chairperson of GAI. Ali Yasir claimed that most of the fatwas referring to the Ahmadiyah movement are directed against the

Qadian and not against the Lahore Ahmadiyah, but that the MUI fatwa had deliberately selected some foreign fatwas (especially from Saudi Arabia and Pakistan) that had been directed against them. Yasir even suspected that the fatwa was issued to satisfy demands made by the Rabitat al-ʿAlam al-Islami (Muslim World League) and its Saudi sponsors.[66]

The MUI denied that it was responsible for the violence against Ahmadiyah. During the public hearing held before parliament, the head of the Fatwa Commission, KH. Ma'ruf Amin, explained that the MUI had never enforced its fatwas violently, and that it had no control over the interpretation of those who might have understood the fatwa differently. The MUI also circulated a letter ordering local MUI branches to respond peacefully to MUI fatwas, including that concerning Ahmadiyah.[67] In the second published edition of the controversial fatwas (Majelis Ulama Indonesia 2005*b*), the Fatwa Commission included explanations of the fatwas, and it also offered some guidance to "avoid misunderstanding and abuse" of the fatwas. Here we need only quote point four, as it is most relevant to the present discussion: "… *the MUI cannot justify* any acts leading to the destruction of others, let alone anarchical attacks against groups, affairs or activities which are not in step with the MUI fatwas; because such acts are not tolerated by Islamic teachings".[68]

Despite the MUI's explanations, violence against the Ahmadiyah movement did not cease and it continued to use the MUI fatwa as its justification. On 4 February 2006, the houses of Ahmadiyah followers in Gegerung and Lingsar villages, West Lombok, were attacked and set on fire. The fatwas were unquestionably used or abused by Islamist groups to attack the houses of followers of the movement. More than 130 harassed Ahmadiyah believers asked for political asylum in Australia, but this was not forthcoming. Until quite recently they had been accommodated in the Transito Majeluk dormitory; afraid of attacks, they did not dare to return to their homes.[69] Unfortunately, both central and local government were unable or unwilling to guarantee their right to live peacefully. Rather, both shared the attackers' view that Ahmadiyah was not part of Islam. The central government had no clear solution as to how to protect Ahmadiyah believers' civil rights.

A survey conducted by the Pusat Pengkajian Islam dan Masyarakat (Centre for Islamic and Social Studies, or PPIM) in 2006 showed some surprising results. About 47 per cent of the respondents supported the MUI fatwa on the Ahmadiyah sect; 28.7 per cent of the respondents agreed with the expulsion of Ahmadiyah followers from their current residences; but only 0.6 per cent had ever actually themselves expelled

Ahmadiyah followers. The survey indicates that there is strong support for the MUI fatwa among Muslim communities. Although no such survey was undertaken during the New Order, we can safely assume that there was less support for the MUI fatwa of 1980, even though it was a less sweeping condemnation of the Ahmadiyah. Despite the fatwa, the Qadian continues to survive, and almost no violent attacks have been reported. Although only 0.6 per cent of people surveyed had actually driven Ahmadiyah members away from their homes, those who supported the expulsion of the Ahmadiyah followers were also numerous; about a half of those who support the fatwa (Jahroni 2006). The figure of 0.6 per cent only covers those who took part in such action in the past, and it is impossible to predict how many of those agreeing with the expulsion might actually put their views into practice in the future.[70]

The bloodiest action against the Ahmadiyah community following the issuance of the MUI fatwa of 2005 was the attack on the Ahmadiyah community in Cikeusik, in Pandeglang, Banten, that took place on 6 February 2011. Three Ahmadiyah members were killed and a number of others were injured. Some attackers brought blades and swords, and police officers on the spot did nothing to prevent the violence. What is surprising is that the Minister for Religious Affairs, Suryadharma Ali, who is also the chairman of the PPP, has strongly endorsed the idea of a legal ban of the Ahmadiyah unless it accepts the status of an independent religion (i.e., different from Islam). He personally believes that the Ahmadiyah movement has violated Islam and should be excluded from Islam. He explicitly refers to MUI fatwas on the Ahmadiyah, and not to the existing state constitution and legal statutes. He was quoted as saying, "It is in the competence of the MUI to observe whether or not the Ahmadiyah is part of Islam; the MUI has confirmed that the Ahmadiyah has deviated [from Islam] and therefore it should be dissolved as soon as possible" (*Republika*, 20 March 2011).

It is undisputable that the MUI's fatwas of 1980 and 2005 on the Ahmadiyah were used by certain Islamist movements to commit violence and crimes against other citizens who were members of the Ahmadiyah movement. Mosques, offices, educational campuses and even houses were burnt as a result. These members lost their rights to freedom of thought, conscience and religion, to freedom of peaceful assembly and association, to live peacefully, to social security, to education, to possess property, and to equality before the law. In short, the state has discriminated against Ahmadiyah members and has treated them like second-class citizens.

CONCLUSION

The MUI has been trying to re-establish its authority and gain fresh recognition as the "true" defender of the Islamic *ummah*. It wants to shed its burdensome image as the "servant of the government". The initial period after the fall of the Soeharto regime was a difficult time for the council. It had to adapt to the Reformasi agenda, while at the same time formulating its own concept of reform. Before long, it began to use the slogan, "the servant of the Muslim community" (*khadim al-ummah*). The MUI has done its utmost to prove itself the main protector of the Islamic *aqidah* (faith) and Muslim interests in Indonesia. This fits the internal logic of the MUI, which reasons that other religions have their own councils of scholars, such as the WALUBI for Buddhism, to protect their respective adherents' faith and interests.

By and large, the MUI has shifted from a moderate to a "puritanical moderate" path to protect Sunni orthodoxy; ideologically, this path is tinged with puritanism and conservatism. This stems largely from the involvement of Muslim hardliners in various regional and national MUI congresses, which address problems that require an MUI response, and from the membership of the MUI, both central and regional. The rhetorical slogan, "softening the hardliners, hardening the soft-minded", has proved useful to the MUI in its efforts to build a moderate image in the face of opposing radicalizing and liberalizing forces. As a body that has been portrayed as one of the "soft", or indeed the "softest", of the New Order Muslim institutions, the MUI is now trying to "harden" itself, and it has been quite successful in presenting this new image through various discourses. Yet, the degree to which it will become harder depends very much on the struggle between the moderate and conservative wings within the MUI — there being no liberal wing, liberals having been gradually excluded from the organization since the 2000 National Congress, and drastically since the issuance of the fatwa on religious liberalism, secularism and pluralism. The result has been puritanical moderate Islam. The MUI has concerned itself not only with Islamic law, but also with the Islamization of public morality, education, thought and faith.

The issue of Shariah implementation is not considered by all Indonesian regions to be equally strategic or relevant. Although the central MUI instructed local chapters to support the creation of Shariah-inspired bylaws, the response has been more sporadic than consistent, depending on the actions of Shariah-oriented pressure groups in the particular region, as well as the political will of local governments and parliaments. In this context, the MUI generally acts as a "channel" or "mediator" between the Shariah-oriented pressure groups, the government, and parliament. Despite this fact, both the central and the local MUIs have contributed to the success of the creation of Shariah-inspired bylaws in a number of regions. Nonetheless, only a limited number of local MUI chapters adopted the "formalization" paradigm, especially in those regions where Shariah-oriented pressure groups are actively articulating their ideological frameworks.

The most serious problem is that the MUI's puritanical moderate discursive products (fatwas or *tausiyah*s) have been used or abused by radical Islamists to enforce their ideological interests by interpreting them arbitrarily. Some of these efforts have led to the violation of human rights, such as in the cases of fatwas on religious pluralism, liberalism and secularism; of pornography and "porno-action"; and of the Ahmadiyah, as argued in this chapter. Today, despite the limited number of Muslim hardliners in the organization, the MUI has produced fatwas and other discourses which justify the practices of radical Muslims, and, to some extent, even defend them. Representatives of progressive or liberal Muslim movements have been systematically excluded from membership of the MUI. Many critics consider the MUI, because of the disproportionate influence of the relatively few radical members and the absence of balancing progressive voices, as a potential threat to human rights, freedom of thought, and freedom of religious practice and conscience in Indonesia.

However, we may perceive other trends in the MUI as well. As argued above, the organization has, through its efforts in *halal* certification of food and drugs as well as financial products, positioned itself as a central player in the field of "market Islam". This role is likely to strengthen the existing trends of moderation and conservatism rather than radical Islamist inclinations. The MUI's interventions in the economic sphere may even occasionally be "progressive", as in the case of a recent fatwa on environmentally safe mining (Fatwa no. 22 of 2011). In this fatwa, that was hailed by the Ministry of the Environment (which may have requested it), the MUI appears to be supporting the mining industry as well as the objective of environmental protection. In the sphere of market Islam, the MUI appears to have no difficulty adopting liberal positions. It appears unwilling, however, to adopt a more flexible position where freedom of religion is concerned. The MUI favours moderation, but only of the puritanical kind.

Notes

[1] Elsewhere (Ichwan 2005) I have discussed the MUI's transformation in the early Reformasi era through its political *fatwa*s and *tausiyah*s, produced during the B.J. Habibie and Abdurrahman Wahid eras. The present article offers a broader picture of the MUI's transformation, from the collapse of the New Order to Susilo Bambang Yudhoyono's first period, covering not only its discursive products (*fatwa*s and *tausiyah*s), but also its political attitudes.

[2] The MUI was established by Soeharto on 26 July 1975 (17 Rajab 1395 AH), at the Ulama Conference held by the Ministry of Religious Affairs. The official roles played by the MUI, as set out by Soeharto in his speech delivered at that conference, were: (1) to serve as the translator of concepts and activities of national or local development for the people; (2) to give advice and recommendations to the government concerning religious life; (3) to become a mediator between the government and the *ulama*; and (4) to provide a place where the *ulama* could discuss problems related to their duties (Majelis Ulama Indonesia 1995, pp. 18–20).

[3] Apart from producing *fatwa*s, the MUI also issues *tadzkirah* (admonitions), *amanah* (mandates/instructions), *pernyataan sikap* (position statements), *himbauan* (appeals/suggestions), *sumbangan pemikiran* (considered opinions), and *tausiyah* (recommendations/advice). The term *tausiyah* means admonition, mandate, instruction, advice, thought contribution, and suggestion. Therefore, it is logical to categorize these non-*fatwa* discourses as "tausiyah". This is also the way the *Mimbar Ulama*, the official MUI magazine, organizes its "tausiyah" rubric, which includes MUI non-*fatwa* discourses. See Ichwan (2005), pp. 50–53; Wehr (1973), p. 1075.

[4] I exclude Aceh here, because the MUI of Aceh transformed itself into the Majelis Permusyawaratan Ulama (Council of Ulama Deliberation, or MPU) in 2001. Unlike the MUI, the MPU is part of the local state apparatus. On the MPU, see Ichwan (2011).

[5] In this study, I define "puritanical moderate Islam" as basically moderate Islamic thought and practices that are imbued with some aspects of puritanical Islamic teachings emphasizing the purity of the faith from any polytheistic (*shirk*) beliefs and associated beliefs, including blasphemy, heresy, heterodoxy, and apostasy (*pemurtadan*) as well as religious liberalism, secularism and pluralism (usually in the sense of relativism); adopts a stricter legal orientation in *ibadah* (devotion); is more sensitive to morality issues, such as pornography and gambling, which it defines as "*munkarat*" (sinful actions); is more aware of the exclusive political interests of the Muslim ummah; but at the same time endorses Islamic economic development through a Shari'ah-based banking system and *halal* market, and recognizes and even supports an ideologically non-Islamic nation-state. I use the term "puritanical moderate Islam" for the MUI, because although it used to be less puritan, it has undergone

a process of theological, legal, and moral puritanization in the last decade, despite attempting to be moderate in its puritanical orientation. It puts forward "puritanical moderate Islam", not "puritanical radical Islam", as an ideal type of Indonesian Islam. It also implies that moderate Islam is pluralistic; there are other kinds of moderate Islam, such as traditionalist moderate Islam embraced by Nahdlatul Ulama (the NU) and modernist moderate Islam embraced by Muhammadiyah. Saeed defines puritanism merely in theological terms (Saeed 2007, pp. 397–98).

[6]   The text of these fatwas was published in Majelis Ulama Indonesia (2005a).

[7]   Interview with KH. Amin Ma'ruf, former head of the Fatwa Commission, 16 July 2008. Another formulation is sometimes used: "Mengerem yang terlalu cepat, mempercepat yang terlalu lambat" [slowing down the fastest, speeding up the slowest]. Interview with KH. A. Baijuri Khatib, secretary of the MUI of Kota Tangerang, April 2007.

[8]   By this, I mean that the MUI has tried to lead Muslims in certain directions that are idealized by the MUI; that is, "moderate" Islam, or to be precise, "puritanical moderate" Islam.

[9]   All three have been involved in agitation against "liberal" or "heterodox" groups. Adian Husaini, a young and radical DDII activist, currently is deputy head of the MUI's Commission for Harmony among Religious Believers, an important institution for dialogue with other religious communities; Cholil Ridwan is one of the chairmen (ketua) of the MUI; and Amin Djamaluddin, is a member of the Commission for Research and Development. Husaini was recruited before 2005, and Ridwan and Djamaluddin were recruited in 2005. It is surprising that Amin Djamaluddin's name is not mentioned as part of the MUI's boards for 2005–10 and 2010–15. However, he is mentioned as a "member" of the Commission for Research and Development in internal documents, e.g., Majelis Ulama Indonesia (2007), p. 7. Djamaluddin became known through a number of books fiercely criticizing various "deviant" sects, published by his own "research institute", the LPPI. We shall encounter him below as one of the leading anti-Ahmadiyah agitators.

[10] It has become conventional, as Halliday points out, to distinguish "Islamic" from "Islamist" movements, the former denoting any religiously oriented trend, the latter the specific Islamic variant of fundamentalism. Nikki Keddie has argued that the term "Islamist" is probably the most accurate, distinguishing belief ("Islamic") from "movements designed to increase the role of Islam in society and politics, usually with the goal of an Islamic state". See Halliday (1995), p. 399; Keddie (1986), p. 26.

[11] It has become common among Islamists to associate those who oppose the idea of Shari'a implementation with the JIL, even though these opponents might not be members of the JIL or might disagree with most of its standpoints.

[12] The "liberals" expelled from the MUI included the only prominent woman member, Siti Musdah Mulia, a feminist scholar and activist who promotes

gender equality and human rights. There was internal informal discussion in the central MUI on whether or not Musdah Mulia's husband, Prof. Dr Ahmad Thib Raya, who also was a member of central MUI, should also be removed, because of the liberal ideas of his wife. The final decision was that he should not be associated with his wife, because he does not share her liberal ideas. One of the administrative officials of MUI told me that he was also questioned via email by a member of MUI on some controversial issues which had been discussed in liberal Muslim circles. Although the questioner claimed that it was just for a discussion, the staff member who was questioned felt that this was a test to see whether he was a liberal.

[13] Interview with Ustadz Enting Ali Abdul Karim, Lc, Serang, 1 April 2007. Ustadz Enting later joined Abubakar Ba'asyir's Jama'ah Anshorut Tauhid (JAT). The same view was expressed by Shobbarin Syakur, the secretary of Majelis Mujahidin Indonesia (MMI), in my conversation with him during the third MMI Congress, 9 August 2008. MMI did not wish to join the MUI because of its different ideological stance.

[14] Thus Adian Husaini, in a eulogy of Habibie published under the New Order (Husaini 1995). Later, Adian Husaini joined the MUI, reportedly at the invitation of the then secretary general, Din Syamsuddin.

[15] During colonial times, there were actually thirteen Muslim Congress between 1922 and 1945. It is not entirely clear why the KUII of 1998 was called the "second KUII" — possibly referring to the 1945 Muslim Congress, which used exactly the same name, as its relevant predecessor. See Azra (1999), pp. iii–xiv.

[16] Secular nationalist parties include the PDI-P and Golkar; Muslim-based nationalist parties include the PKB and the PAN; and Islamic parties include the PPP, the PKS and the PBB (Partai Bulan Bintang, or the Moon and Crescent Party).

[17] Twenty-one parties obtained at least one of the 462 seats in parliament (out of a total of 500 contested seats). The remaining 38 seats were assigned to delegates from the armed forces. See Liddle (2000), pp. 33–34.

[18] Later, constitutional changes introduced direct presidential elections, and these took place for the first time in 2004.

[19] Facing such a problem, Amien Rais and other Muslim political leaders, especially those with a "modernist" religious orientation, created the so-called "Middle Axis" (*Poros Tengah*) coalition. This endeavoured to gain support from Muslim legislators from various parties, including secular parties. The problem was that the PKB, which is mostly NU-based and has a "traditionalist" religious orientation, had strong connections with the nationalist secular party, the PDI-P. If PKB legislators took sides with the PDI-P, Megawati would become president. The Middle Axis had no choice but to support Abdurrahman Wahid as president. The deal was made between the Middle Axis and the PKB, and the eventual outcome was obvious: Megawati was defeated, and

Abdurrahman Wahid was elected as the fourth president of Indonesia. See Platzdasch (2009), pp. 270, 273.

20 The Bank Bali scandal erupted after a payment by Bank Bali of more than $70 million to a firm run by Setya Novanto, a leading official in the ruling Golkar party, for the recovery of loans from the Indonesian Bank Restructuring Agency (IBRA). The central bank and IBRA approved repayment of the loans. However, an audit by PricewaterhouseCoopers questioned whether the loans were eligible for repayment. Most opposition parties claimed that the money had been plundered for Habibie's re-election, because the key figures in the scandal were on President Habibie's informal re-election committee (*Tim Sukses*). Soon after Soeharto's resignation, interreligious conflict in Ambon broke out between Muslims and Christians, during which many from both sides were killed or injured. Habibie had no clear vision on how to end the conflict. Moreover, Habibie's policy of supporting the East Timor referendum on 30 August 1999, one month before the parliamentary session, led to this province's independence (East Timor had been annexed in 1975). While this policy was praised by the international community, it was condemned by most political parties. It seems that the close and affectionate relationship between the MUI and Habibie was caused by the fact that most members of the MUI elite at that time were also members of the ICMI, and most of them viewed Habibie as someone who represented the hopes and interests of certain Muslim circles. Sharma (2003), p. 165; Symonds (1999).

21 Despite his severe criticism, Wahid had in fact allocated land in Jakarta for a MUI building and had granted it Rp 5 billion per year in a perpetual fund (*dana abadi*) from a promised total of Rp 25 billion, which would be given over five years. Due to Wahid's fall in 2001, the MUI only received one payment of Rp 5 billion, and the next president, President Megawati, did not continue Wahid's policy. Interview with Sholahuddin Al-Aiyub, assistant to the MUI chairperson, KH Sahal Mahfudz, Jakarta, 28 March 2007.

22 A revision of the statutes is essential for any organization that wishes to make reforms. This does not necessarily imply that all organizations should embark on reforms after revising their statutes. Statutes are merely an official requirement for any public organization. In some organizations, reform does not require any alterations to their statutes. However, if an organization does reformulate its statutes, naturally such reform will be reflected in this reformulation.

23 Article 2 of the MUI statutes reads: "This organization is based on Islam". Majelis Ulama Indonesia, *Wawasan dan PD/PRT Majelis Ulama Indonesia* (Jakarta: Majelis Ulama Indonesia, 2000), p. 21. Soon after the collapse of the New Order regime, the House of Representatives, under the leadership of Amien Rais, issued a decree stating that Pancasila would no longer be the "sole ideological foundation" (*asas tunggal*) of mass organizations, thereby complying with the demands of most Muslim organizations. In the previous statutes, the MUI had explicitly made Pancasila its ideological

foundation (*asas*) and Islam its religious foundation (*'aqidah*). Mentioning both Pancasila and Islam in one and the same breath was actually a survival tactic to circumvent the ban. Although it was unthinkable that the MUI would be banned under the New Order, it seems that the MUI did not want to take the risk. In its third National Congress in July 1985, the MUI revised its previous statutes and put Pancasila as its *asas* and Islam as its *aqidah*. It seems that in doing so, it was inspired by the NU, which was the first Muslim organization to adopt such a formulation.

24 On the 2004 general election, see Nakamura (2005).

25 Statement heard by the author during the inaugural speech given by the Minister for Religious Affairs, 23 July 2008.

26 In 2008, the MUI received IDR 3 billion. It was said that such an amount was "not enough", but would "suffice for maintaining the routine activities". See Majelis Ulama Indonesia (2008*b*), p. v.

27 The results of the 2003, 2006, and 2009 *Ijtima'* can be found in Majelis Ulama Indonesia (2010), pp. 713–845.

28 This should not be confused with Front Umat Islam (Front for Islamic *Ummah*), also abbreviated as the FUI. Forum Ukhuwah Islamiyah is part of the MUI's loose, *ad hoc* institutions under the Commission for Ukhuwwah Islamiyah, which is comprised of representatives of Muslim organizations. The Commission for Ukhuwah Islamiyah has existed since the establishment of the MUI in 1975. The idea of establishing a forum of *ukhuwah* (fraternity) between Muslim organizations and personalities first emerged at the MUI National Congress of 1980 and was reiterated at the 1984 National Working Conference (Majelis Ulama Indonesia 1995, pp. 47, 114, 124–25). The Forum Ukhuwah Islamiyah was finally established in 1989, by persons who represented the puritan side of the spectrum but including prominent critics of the New Order (Platzdasch 2009, pp. 38, 76). Not much was heard from it until it was revived by the MUI in the early 2000s. The Front Umat Islam, meanwhile, is an independent vehicle for Muslim activism in which various Muslim organizations, most of them of a radical orientation, are represented. Muhammad al-Khatthath, who was one of the important leaders of Hizbut Tahrir Indonesia (HTI), is also the secretary general of Front Umat Islam. The name and abbreviation (FUI) appear to have been deliberately chosen to create confusion with the MUI's Forum Ukhuwah Islamiyah and suggest MUI backing for the demonstrations and other actions Khatthath organized.

29 This is expressed, for instance, in the first consideration of the Decision of the *Ijtima' Ulama* of 2006 on "Masa'il Asasiyah Wathaniyah" (fundamental national issues). In the Decision of the Ijtima' Ulama of 2009, this stance is formulated more systematically, that "Pancasila as a national philosophy and the 1945 Constitution of the Republic of Indonesia constitute an endeavour to protect the religious glory and regulate the welfare of shared life" (Majelis Ulama Indonesia 2010, pp. 747, 783).

30 On these and various other radical groups that emerged, see Bruinessen (2002).

31 Other issues reflected in the fatwas issued in 2005 are criteria of *maslahah* (the common good); women as *salat* leaders; protection of intellectual property rights; relinquishing private property for public use; and the death penalty for certain crimes (Majelis Ulama Indonesia 2005*b*). I refer to the second edition of this book; the first edition did not contain any explanation of the *fatwas*. The second edition was published in response to public demand for such an explanation, because they had aroused much controversy.

32 Majelis Ulama Indonesia (2008*a*), pp. 7–8. The details of the ten criteria of "deviant belief" will be set out further below.

33 An excellent overview of the discourses on Christianization is presented in Mujiburrahman (2006).

34 Its establishment was based on MUI's own letter No. Kep-018/MUI/I/1989, not on a government decree.

35 More precisely, the fatwa concerned Ajinomoto produced between June 1999 and the end of November 2000, when it was manufactured using bacto soytone, a pig enzyme, instead of the usual polypeptone, a soybean-based enzyme (Kobayashi 2002). Ajinomoto is produced by a major Japanese transnational corporation, which gave the issue an international dimension, affecting relations with Japan.

36 Soeharto played an important role in making this possible. This policy should be read in the context of Soeharto's "Islamic turn" around 1989 or 1990, in which he supported the establishment of the All-Indonesian Muslim Intellectuals Association (ICMI) and Bank Muamalat Indonesia and endorsed other policies concerning Islam. On the Islamic turn, although the *halal* issue is not fully discussed, see Liddle (1996), pp. 613–34.

37 The relevant laws and regulations include Law No. 23/1992 on Health, Law No. 7/1996 on Foods, Law No. 8 on Consumer Protection, and Governmental Regulation No. 69/1999 on Food Labelling and Advertisement.

38 The Ministry's efforts to take over *halal* certification management date back to the Megawati era, when the then Minister for Religious Affairs, Said Agil Husin al-Munawar, issued Ministerial Decree No. 518/2001 on the Guidance and Procedure of Assessment and Decision for Halal Foods (2001) and drafted a special Government Regulation on Labelling of Halal Products (2003). This draft was rejected not only by other government institutions, such as the Ministry of Industry and Trade, but also by various associations of producers and traders. These supported, instead, MUI's *halal* certification, but not *halal* labelling as regulated by the draft regulation, which would lead to increased costs of production and thereby overburden consumers. The Indonesian Consumers Foundation (YLKI) perceived the commercial motive behind the draft regulation (*Kompas*, 11 July 2003; *Sinar Harapan*, 10 July 2003). Because of protest and criticism, the draft regulation was never issued by the State Secretariat. The Ministry of Religious Affairs drafted a Law on Halal Product Assurance in 2005, but did not see it pass until recently (2011).

39   These figures were cited in a newspaper article (Hakim 2005). One of the sources mentioned there as an expert of *halal* marketing, the French marketing consultant Antoine Bonnel, elsewhere gives the much larger estimate for the volume of the European *halal* market of EUR 15 billion (US$19.5 billion). See <http://www.saphirnews.com/Halal-C-est-au-consommateur-musulman-d-etre-arbitre_a3681.html>.

40   Interview with Ichwan Sam, secretary general of the MUI, Jakarta, 16 June 2009; and with Dr Amirsyah Tambunan, member of Commission of Research of MUI, Jakarta, 16 June 2009.

41   Atmanto (2003). Significantly, before issuing this fatwa, the MUI had consulted Indonesia's central bank not to request its consent but to ask whether the Shariah banking institutions were ready to be put into operation.

42   Thus as of 31 December 2006, the Shariah Supervisory Board of the Bank Muamalat Indonesia consisted of the following persons: KH. M.A. Sahal Mahfudh (Chairman), KH. Ma'ruf Amin, Prof. Dr H. Muardi Chatib, Prof. Dr H. Umar Shihab, and that of the Bank BNI consisted of KH. Ma'ruf Amin and Dr Hasanuddin. All of these figures belong to the MUI elite.

43   The term "porno-action" does not exist in the English dictionary. It is a local, Indonesian creation and functions as a translation of *pornoaksi*. Unlike pornography, "porno-action" means sensual behaviour that arouses sexual attraction in public or as a means of business.

44   The fact that an anti-porn Draft Law was no longer discussed in parliament, that the movements for and against the law are no longer heard for relatively long time, and the fact that *Playboy* continued to appear for several years led to rumours that large sums of money from the pornography business had effectively silenced the issue. Though obviously impossible to prove, this conspiracy theory would explain recent events.

45   Interview with Prof. Burhanuddin Daya, the former head of the MUI's Ukhuwah Islamiyah Committee of Yogyakarta, 29 December 2006; and Prof. Abdur Rahim Yunus, the former secretary of the MUI branch of South Sulawesi, 20 January 2007.

46   Interview with Prof. Umar Shihab, Jakarta, 27 March 2007; Prof. Burhanuddin Daja, Yogyakarta, 29 December 2006. See also Hutapea (2003), pp. 28–29.

47   Interview with Prof. KH. Wahab Afif, Serang, 3 April 2007, and Drs H. Sibli Sarjaya, LML, the general secretary of the Banten chapter of the MUI, 2 April 2007.

48   Most political factions approved the Draft Law, with the exception of the PDI-P, which did not attend the final session. The Christian-dominated parliamentary group Kesatuan Kebangsaan Indonesia (KKI) had previously disagreed with the draft law and considered that it was not ready for final agreement. As most factions did approve it, however, KKI eventually also agreed to accept it.

49   Interview with Ustaz Enting Ali Abdul Karim, Lc, Serang, 1 April 2007.
50   The terms "post-traditionalist" and "emancipatory Islam" are usually
      associated with young NU intellectuals involved in such NGOs as
      LAKPESDAM and P3M (Pusat Pengembangan Pesantren dan Masyarakat),
      Jakarta; "progressive Islam" with the ICIP (International Centre for Islam and
      Pluralism) and the Internet-based discussion forum, Islam Progresif; while
      "liberal Islam" primarily refers to the JIL (Jaringan Islam Liberal), whose
      activists are mostly NU young intellectuals, and the JIMM (Jaringan Intelektual
      Muda Muhammadiyah).
51   Prior to the twentieth century, there had been *fatwas* against the deviant Sufism
      of the legendary saints Shaikh Siti Jenar and Shaikh Ahmad Mutamakkin,
      who had claimed to be God incarnate and were sentenced to death.
52   Din Syamsuddin mentioned two examples of liberal thought: the view that
      religion is just like organism that develops continuously, and that the Qur'an
      is not the final revelation. The latter example seems to refer to the Ahmadiyah.
      Pikiran Rakyat, 20 April 2005.
53   Gillespie (2007) even translates the phrase in five different ways: (1) "pluralism,
      liberalism and secularism", omitting the word "religious" in the title of his
      article; (2) "secularism, pluralism and liberal Islamic movements"; (3) "religious
      pluralism, liberalism and secularism"; (4) "religious pluralism, liberalism and
      religious secularism"; (5) "pluralism, liberalism and religious secularism"
      (Gillespie 2007, pp. 202, 219).
54   Ulil Abshar-Abdalla later apologized for using these words.
55   "Religious Leaders Express Deep Concern over MUI Fatwa", <http://www.
      gusdur.net/english/ index.php?option=com_content&task=view&id=732&Ite
      mid=1> (accessed 7 June 2007) (this site is no longer functioning). Interview
      with Azyumardi Azra, "MUI's fatwa encourage use of violence", *Jakarta Post*,
      1 August 2005.
56   I call it the "official view" because there are a number of MUI members who
      do not fully agree with this MUI *fatwa*, and in fact several prominent members
      previously held different views. For instance, one of the most influential
      chairpersons of MUI, Amidhan, had written in 1999 that "pluralism is a fact"
      (Amidhan 1999).
57   Interview with Dr Zakariya Ngelow (lecturer at the State Christian College),
      Makassar, January 2007.
58   On the attack on the Ahmadiyah campus in Parung, see Hamdi (2007); on
      the broader issues, see Olle (2006) and Crouch (2009).
59   On the history of the Ahmadiyah in Indonesia, see Zulkarnain (2005).
60   These books, most of them inspired by the Muslim World League, include:
      al-Hadar (1977); Thaha (1981); al-Badry (1981); Hariadi (1988) and Daulay
      (1990).
61   Djamaluddin (2000, 2007, and 2010), Nashruddin (2002); Fathullah (2005).
62   Interview with Amin Djamaluddin, 14 July 2008.

63   Djamaluddin (2000). Indeed, the Qadiani Ahmadiyah (JAI) did respond to these allegations by publishing a book entitled *Penjelasan Jemaat Ahmadiyah Indonesia* (Jemaat Ahmadiyah Indonesia 2001). But such a book was not a means to win over most Sunni Muslim readers, who already harboured prejudices against the movement.

64   The ten criteria of "deviant belief" are: (1) rejecting the pillars of faith (*rukun iman*) and pillars of Islam (*rukun islam*); (2) believing and/or following a belief (*aqidah*) incompatible with *shariah* proofs; (3) believing that there is revelation (*wahy*) after the Qur'an; (4) rejecting the authenticity and/or the truth of the contents of the Qur'an; (5) interpreting the Qur'an without basing this interpretation on the (correct) principles of interpretation; (6) rejecting the prophetic tradition (*hadith*) as the source of Islamic teachings; (7) disrespecting, disgracing and/or downgrading the Prophets and Messengers (of Allah); (8) rejecting Muhammad as the final Prophet and Messenger; (9) changing the principles of devotion (*ibadah*) established by *shariah*; and (10) accusing other Muslims of being "unbelievers" (*kafir*) without the proper basis of *shariah* (Majelis Ulama Indonesia 2008*a*, pp. 7–8).

65   *Jakarta Post*, 19 July 2005, <http://www.thejakartapost.com/detailheadlines. asp?fileid=20050719. A06&irec=5> (accessed 5 June 2007).

66   Interview with Ali Yasir, former chairperson of the GAI, Yogyakarta, 23 April 2007. When the second edition of the MUI book was published, Ali Yasir also revised his book, commenting on the explanation of the MUI fatwa that condemned the Ahmadiyah Sect.

67   Interviews with Prof. Abdur Rahim Yunus, Makassar, January 2007, and Prof. KH. Wahab Afif, Serang, April 2007. Although there are no Ahmadiyah followers in Bulukumba, the local MUI also received the instruction from the provincial MUI. Interview with KH. Tjamiruddin, the general secretary of the MUI of Bulukumba, January 2007.

68   Majelis Ulama Indonesia (2005*b*), pp. v–vi. Emphasis in the original.

69   *Antara News*, 16 May 2007, <http://www.antara.co.id/en/arc/2007/5/16/ ahmadiyah followersin-w-nusa-tenggara-permited-to-seek-asylum> (accessed 6 June 2007).

70   The second half of 2007 witnessed the emergence of other "deviant beliefs". The first was known as al-Qiyadah al-Islamiyah, whose leader (Ahmad Musaddeq) declared himself to be a new prophet and the promised messiah (*al-masih al-mau'ud*); and the second, al-Qur'an Suci, which claims that Muslims need to rely only on the Qur'an and not the *hadith*. The MUI also issued a fatwa stating that the al-Qiyadah al-Islamiyah and the al-Qur'an Suci were deviant. Violence against the members and property of these movements had already erupted prior to the issuance of the fatwa, and this violence subsequently intensified. Despite the fact that the fatwa discourages the use of violence and insists on the peaceful treatment of the followers of these movements, some Muslim groups, such as Front Pembela Islam (FPI),

have simply ignored these prescriptions. They are convinced that "deviant" movements are a *munkarat* that should be eliminated, once and for all.

References

Abdullah. "Lindungi Akhlak Bangsa". *Mimbar Ulama* 27, no. 329 (April 2006): 6–7.

Abshar-Abdalla, Ulil. "Menyegarkan Kembali Pemikiran Islam". *Kompas*, 18 November 2002. Reprinted in Ulil Abshar-Abdalla, *Menjadi Muslim Liberal*. Jakarta: Nalar, 2005.

Amidhan. "Pluralisme Sebuah Kenyataan". *Pesan* 1, no. 21 (1999): 3–16.

Atmanto, Irwan Andri. "Fatwa Haram Setengah Hati". *Gatra*, Edisi 2, 17 November 2003. Online at <http://arsip.gatra.com/2003-11-18/artikel.php?id=32241>.

Azra, Azyumardi. "Kongres Umat Islam: Sebuah Pengantar". In *Kumpulan Hasil-hasil Kongres Umat Islam Indonesia, Jakarta, 3–7 Nopember 1998*, edited by Majelis Ulama Indonesia. Jakarta: Majelis Ulama Indonesia, 1999.

Al-Badry, Hamka Haq. *Koreksi Total terhadap Ahmadiyah*. Jakarta: Yayasan Nurul Islam, 1981.

Bruinessen, Martin van. "Indonesia's Ulama and Politics: Caught between Legitimising the Status Quo and Searching for Alternatives". *Prisma: The Indonesian Indicator* 49 (1990): 52–69.

––––––. "Genealogies of Islamic Radicalism in Indonesia". *South East Asia Research* 10, no. 2 (2002): 117–54.

––––––. "What Happened to the Smiling Face of Indonesian Islam? Explaining the Conservative Turn in Post-Suharto Indonesia". RSIS Working Paper No. 222. Singapore: RSIS, 2011.

Buchori, Abdusshomad. *Santri Menggugat JIL & Sekte Pluralisme Agama. Dilengkapi dengan Komentar Tokoh dan Ulama Serta Sikap Majelis Ulama Indonesia (MUI)*. Surabaya: MUI Propinsi Jatim, 2006.

Crouch, Melissa. "Indonesia, Militant Islam and Ahmadiyah: Origins and Implications". Islam, Syari'ah and Governance Background Paper Series. Melbourne: Centre for Islamic Law and Society, University of Melbourne, 2009.

Daulay, Pangadilan. *Aliran Ahmadiyah Ancaman Terhadap Dunia Islam*. Jakarta: Yayasan Pengkajian Islam dan Pengembangan Ilmu Pengetahuan Madani, 1990.

Dhofier, Zamakhsyari. *The Pesantren Tradition: The Role of the Kyai in the Maintenance of Traditional Islam in Java*. Ph.D. dissertation, ANU. Republished by State Arizona University, 1999.

Dijk, C. van. "Ulama and Politics". *Bijdragen tot de Taal-, Land-, en Volkenkunde* 152, no. 1 (1996): 109–43.

Djamaluddin, M. Amin. *Ahmadiyah dan Pembajakan al-Qur'an*, Jakarta: LPPI, 2000.

————. *Ahmadiyah menodai Islam: Kumpulan Fakta dan Data*. Jakarta: LPPI, 2007.

————. *Mirza Ghulam Ahmad Qadiani & Fakta Penghinaan Ahmadiyah Terhadap Agama: Jejak Hitam Sang Pendusta dan Pengkhianat Agama*. Jakarta: LPPI, 2010.

Fathullah, Ahmad Luthfi. *Menguak Kesesatan Aliran Ahmadiyah*. Jakarta: Al-Mughni Press, 2005.

Gillespie, Piers. "Current Issues in Indonesian Islam: Analysing the 2005 Council of Indonesian Ulama Fatwa No. 7 Opposing Pluralism, Liberalism and Secularism". *Journal of Islamic Studies* 18 no. 2 (2007): 202–40.

Habermas, Jürgen. "The Public Sphere: An Encyclopedia Article". In *Media and Cultural Studies: Keyworks*, edited by Meenakshi Gigi Durham and Douglas M. Kellner. Oxford: Blackwell, 2001.

Al-Hadar, Abdullah Hasan. *Ahmadiyah Telanjang Bulat di Panggung Sejarah*. Bandung: PT al-Maarif, 1977.

Hakim, Zakki P. "Indonesia Eyes European Halal Food Market". *Jakarta Post*, 5 February 2005. Online at <http://www.thejakartapost.com/news/2005/02/05/indonesia-eyes-european-halal-food-market.html>.

Halliday, Fred. "The Politics of 'Islam' — A Second Look". *British Journal of Political Science* 25 no. 3 (1995): 399–417.

Hamdi, Mujtaba. "Sang Liyan dan Kekerasan: Kasus Penyerangan Kampus Mubarak Jemaat Ahmadiyah Indonesia Kemang Bogor Jawa Barat". In *Politisasi Agama dan Konflik Komunal: Beberapa Isu Penting di Indonesia*, edited by Ahmad Suaedy et al. Jakarta: The Wahid Institute, 2007.

Hariadi, Ahmad. *Mengapa Saya Keluar dari Ahmadiyah*. Makkah: Rabithah 'Alam Islami, 1988.

Hefner, Robert W. "Islamizing Capitalism: On the Founding of Indonesia's First Islamic Bank". In *Toward A New Paradigm: Recent Developments in Indonesian Islamic Thought*. Tempe: Programme for Southeast Asian Studies, Arizona State University, 1996.

————. *Civil Islam: Muslims and Democratization in Indonesia*. Princeton: Princeton University Press, 2000.

Hosen, Nadirsyah. "Fatwa and Politics in Indonesia". In *Shari'a and Politics in Modern Indonesia*, edited by Arskal Salim and Azyumardi Azra. Singapore: Institute of Southeast Asian Studies, 2003.

————. "Behind the Scenes: Fatwas of Majelis Ulama Indonesia (1975–1998)". *Journal of Islamic Studies* 15, no. 2 (2004): 147–79.

Husaini, Adian. *Habibie, Soeharto, dan Islam*. Jakarta: Gema Insani Press, 1995.

————. *Pluralisme Agama Haram: Fatwa MUI yang Tegas dan Tidak Kontroversial*. Jakarta: Pustaka Al-Kautsar, 2005.

Hutapea, Rivai. "Dari Piagam Jakarta sampai RUU Sisdiknas Kaum Salibis Menjegal Islam". *Sabili* 10, no. 25 (2003): 28–29.

Ichwan, Moch Nur. "Ulama, State and Politics: Majelis Ulama Indonesia After Suharto". *Islamic Law and Society* 12, no. 1 (2005): 45–72.

——. "Official Ulema and the Politics of Re-Islamization: The Majelis Permusyawaratan Ulama, Shari'atization and Contested Authority in Post-New Order Aceh". *Journal of Islamic Studies* 22, no. 2 (2011): 1–32.

Jahroni, Jajang. "Tekstualisme, Islamisme, dan Kekerasan Agama". *Kalteng Pos*, 5 November 2006 (accessed 7 June 2007).

Jemaat Ahmadiyah Indonesia. *Penjelasan Jemaat Ahmadiyah Indonesia*. Bogor: Jemaat Ahmadiyah Indonesia, 2001.

Keddie, Nikki. "The Islamist Movement in Tunisia". *Maghreb Review* l, no. 1 (1986): 26–39.

Kobayashi, Yasuko. "Ajinomoto Indonesia: Halal or Haram?". *ISIM Newsletter* no. 9 (2002): 32.

Liddle, R. William. "The Islamic Turn in Indonesia: A Political Explanation". *Journal of Asian Studies* 55 (1996): 613–34.

——. "Indonesia in 1999: Democracy Restored". *Asian Survey* 40, no. 1 (2000): 32–42.

Lindsey, Tim and M.B. Hooker. "Shari'a Revival in Aceh". In *Islamic Law in Contemporary Indonesia: Ideas and Institutions*, edited by R. Michael Feener and Mark E. Cammack. Cambridge, Massachusetts: Islamic Legal Studies Programme, Harvard Law School & Harvard University Press, 2007.

LPPOM-MUI. *Panduan Umum Sistem Jaminan Halal LPPOM-MUI*. Jakarta: LPPOM-MUI, 2008*a*.

——. *Daftar Belanja Produk Halal*. Jakarta, Bogor: LPPOM-MUI and Pusat Pelatihan dan Informasi Halal (PPIH), 2008*b*.

Madjedie, Abdulghanie. "Menggalang Potensi Ummat Islam Dipelopori Alim Ulama Memenangkan Revolusi Indonesia". Paper presented at the Musjawarah Alim Ulama Islam se-Kalimantan Selatan, Banjarmasin, 26–29 April 1965.

Majelis Ulama Indonesia. *Majelis Ulama Indonesia*. Jakarta: Sekretariat MUI, 1976.

——. "Keputusan Rapat Kerja ke-III Majelis Ulama se-Indonesia tentang Mu'amalah, Dakwah, Kerukunan Organisasi dan Hubungan Luar Negeri". Jakarta, 18 October 1978. Reprinted in *Mimbar Ulama* 3, no. 24 (November 1978): 60–67.

——. *20 Tahun Majelis Ulama Indonesia*. Jakarta: Majelis Ulama Indonesia, 1995.

——. *Kumpulan Hasil-hasil Kongres Umat Islam Indonesia, Jakarta, 3–7 Nopember 1998*. Jakarta: Majelis Ulama Indonesia, 1998.

——. *Wawasan Majelis Ulama Indonesia*. Jakarta: Majelis Ulama Indonesia, 2000.

——. *Himpunan Fatwa Majelis Ulama Indonesia*. Jakarta: Departemen Agama, 2003.

——. *Himpunan Keputusan Musyawarah Nasional VII Majelis Ulama Indonesia tahun 2005*. Jakarta: Sekretariat Majelis Ulama Indonesia, 2005*a*.

————. *Fatwa Munas VII Majelis Ulama Indonesia: Disertai Lampiran Penjelasan Fatwa.* 2nd ed. Jakarta: Majelis Ulama Indonesia, 2005*b*.

————. *Materi IV Masalah Aktual Keumatan dan Kebangsaan.* Jakarta: Kongres Umat Islam Indonesia, 2005*c*.

————. *Laporan Kegiatan Majelis Ulama Indonesia tahun 2007, Bahan Rapat Kerja Nasional.* Jakarta: Majelis Ulama Indonesia, 2007.

————. *Mengenal Aqidah Umat: Fatwa MUI tentang Aliran-aliran Sesat di Indonesia.* Jakarta: Sekretariat Majelis Ulama Indonesia, 2008*a*.

————. *Laporan Kegiatan Dewan Pimpinan Majelis Ulama Indonesia Pusat Tahun 2008.* Jakarta: Majelis Ulama Indonesia, 2008*b*.

————. *Himpunan Fatwa Majelis Ulama.* Jakarta: Sekretariat Majelis Ulama Indonesia, 2010.

Masud, M. Khalid, Brinkley Messick and David S. Powers, eds. *Islamic Legal Interpretation: Muftis and their Fatwas.* Cambridge: Harvard University Press, 1996.

Mudzhar, M. Atho'. *Fatwas of the Indonesian Council of Ulama: A Study of Islamic Legal Thought in Indonesia, 1975–1988.* Ph.D. dissertation. Los Angeles, University of California, 1990.

————. "The Council of Indonesian Ulama on Muslims' Attendance at Christmas Celebration". In *Islamic Legal Interpretation: Muftis and their Fatwas*, edited by M. Khalid Masud, Brinkley Messick and David S. Powers. Cambridge: Harvard University Press, 1996.

————. "The Ulama, the Government, and Society in Modern Indonesia: The Indonesian Council of 'Ulama' Revisited". In *Islam in the Era of Globalization*, edited by Johan Meuleman. Jakarta: INIS, 2001.

Mujiburrahman. *Feeling Threatened: Muslim-Christian Relations in Indonesia's New Order.* Amsterdam: Amsterdam University Press, 2006.

Munawar-Rachman, Budhy. *Argumen Islam untuk Liberalisme.* Jakarta: Grasindo, 2010.

Nakamura, Mitsuo. "Islam and Democracy in Indonesia: Observations on the 2004 General and Presidential Elections". Occasional Publications 6. Harvard: Islamic Legal Studies Programme, Harvard Law School, 2005. Online at <http://www.law.harvard.edu/programs/ilsp/publications/nakamura.pdf>.

Nashruddin, Dede A. *Ahli Sunnah Menjawab Ahmadiyah dalam Masalah Kenabian.* Jakarta: LPPI, 2002.

Noer, Deliar. *Administration of Islam in Indonesia.* Monograph Series No. 58. Ithaca: Cornell Modern Indonesia Project, Southeast Asia Programme, Cornell University, 1978.

Olle, John. "The Campaign Against 'Heresy': State and Society in Negotiation in Indonesia". Paper presented to the 16th Biennial Conference of the Asian Studies Association of Australia in Wollongong, 26–29 June 2006.

Platzdasch, Bernhard. *Islamism in Indonesia: Politics in the Emerging Democracy.* Singapore: Institute of Southeast Asian Studies, 2009.

Porter, Donald J. "Citizen Participation through Mobilization and the Rise of Political Islam in Indonesia". *The Pacific Review* 15, no. 2 (May, 2002): 201–24.

Ridwan, Kafrawi. "Adanya MUI, Kehendak Pemerintah dan Ummat". *Mimbar Ulama* 263 (July 2000): 16–17.

Rudnyckyj, Daromir. "Market Islam in Indonesia". *Journal of the Royal Anthropological Institute* 15 (2009), special issue, pp. 183–201.

Saeed, Abdullah. "Trends in Contemporary Islam: A Preliminary Attempt at a Classification". *The Muslim World* 97, nos. 3 (July 2007): 395–404.

Schulze, Fritz. "Der islamische Diskurs im heutigen Indonesien und seine politische Relevanz". *Internationales Asien-Forum* 37, nos. 1–2 (2006): 37–58.

Sharma, Shalendra D. *The Asian Financial Crisis: Crisis, Reform and Recovery*. Manchester: Manchester University Press, 2003.

Skovgaard-Petersen, Jacob. *Defining Islam for the Egyptian State: Muftis and Fatwas of the Dar al-Ifta*. Leiden: Brill, 1997.

Sulaiman, Aberanie. "Pengintegrasian Pelaksanaan Keputusan-2 K.I.A.A.-I dengan Pembangunan Daerah". Paper presented at the Musjawarah Alim Ulama Islam se-Kalimantan Selatan, Banjarmasin, 26–29 April 1965.

Symonds, Peter. "Bank Bali Scandal Puts Pressure on Indonesian President Habibie". World Socialist Web Site, 24 August 1999. Online at <http://wsws.org/articles/1999/aug1999/ind-a24.shtml>.

Thaha, Fawzy Saied. *Ahmadiyah dalam Persoalan*. Bandung: Al-Maarif, 1981.

Wehr, Hans. *Dictionary of Modern Written Arabic*. 3rd ed. Ithaca: Spoken Language Services, 1973.

Willis, John Ralph. "The Fatwas of Condemnation". In *Islamic Legal Interpretation: Muftis and their Fatwas*, edited by M. Khalid Masud, Brinkley Messick, and David S. Powers. Cambridge, MA: Harvard University Press, 1996.

Yudhoyono, Susilo Bambang. "Special Keynote Address by the President of the Republic of Indonesia H.E. Dr Susilo Bambang Yudhoyono at the Opening Ceremony of the 3rd World Islamic Economic Forum". In *Islam and the Challenge of Modernization*. Kuala Lumpur, 2007. Online at <www.setneg.go.id> (accessed 18 August 2009).

Zulkarnain, Iskandar. *Gerakan Ahmadiyah di Indonesia*. Yogyakarta: LKiS, 2005.

4

LIBERAL AND CONSERVATIVE DISCOURSES IN THE MUHAMMADIYAH: THE STRUGGLE FOR THE FACE OF REFORMIST ISLAM IN INDONESIA

Ahmad Najib Burhani

INTRODUCTION

Since the conquest of Mecca by the Wahhabis in 1924, the Muhammadiyah has often been associated with the Wahhabi movement.[1] This perception is partly due to the similarities between the efforts made by the Wahhabi and Indonesian reformists to purify religious beliefs and practices through the eradication of elements considered external to Islam, opposition to Sufi practices,[2] and calls for a return to the Qur'an and Sunna to replace the practice of *taqlid*.[3] Recently, scholars and journalists such as Khaled Abou El Fadl (2005) and Stephen Schwartz (2003) have pointed to strong connections between Wahhabism, which is the official religious ideology of Saudi Arabia, and the upsurge of radical and fundamentalist movements throughout the Muslim world. This has raised the question whether the Muhammadiyah's ideology today can still be compared with the Salafism of Saudi Arabia, and whether it has similarly played a part in the emergence of radical movements.

The Muhammadiyah became even more strongly linked with Islamic radicalism when young people with Muhammadiyah family or school backgrounds were arrested for involvement in violent radicalism. Only a few days after the 45th Congress of the Muhammadiyah in Malang in 2005, for instance, an activist from this organization, Joni Achmad Fauzani, was arrested by the Indonesian police on charges of harbouring a terror suspect in Pacet district, Mojokerto regency, East Java (Nugroho 2005). Furthermore, a number of known convicted terrorists, including the Bali bomber Amrozi, were raised in Muhammadiyah families or educated in Muhammadiyah schools. This has added to the confusion, particularly in the West, about the religious stance of the Muhammadiyah: is it a fundamentalist group or a moderate Muslim group that leans towards conservatism?

In order to unravel these tangled perceptions of the Muhammadiyah, this chapter will analyse the development of the organization since 1995, a year that marked the beginning of a series of competing religious discourses in the Muhammadiyah. This study covers four *Muktamar*s or congresses: the 43rd Muktamar in Banda Aceh in 1995, the last Muktamar of the New Order regime; the 44th Muktamar in Jakarta in 2000; the 45th Muktamar in Malang in 2005; and the 46th Muktamar in Yogyakarta in 2010. Particular attention will be paid to the 45th Muktamar, where the movement's "conservative turn" was most visible.

This chapter will argue that the conservative leanings of the Muhammadiyah, that became particularly apparent in the 45th Muktamar, have not been characteristic of the organization in general and at all times. The conservatism that cropped up in the Muhammadiyah in the early years of the twenty-first century was mainly influenced by external factors, such as Indonesian national politics and the resurgence of new ideologies brought by transnational movements such as Hizbut Tahrir. In doing so, this chapter will address the following topics: first, the Muhammadiyah at a glance; second, the progressive and conservative groups in the Muhammadiyah; third, the 45th Muktamar in Malang; fourth, combating conservatism, and the response from within the Muhammadiyah; fifth, the religious attitude of the Muhammadiyah; and sixth, the dilemmas facing the Muhammadiyah.

THE MUHAMMADIYAH AT A GLANCE

The Muhammadiyah is the second largest Muslim movement in Indonesia. It claims to have approximately 30 million supporters and sympathizers. However, from an administrative perspective, the number of members who actually have Muhammadiyah ID cards is smaller than that. The organization was established in Yogyakarta in 1912 by Ahmad Dahlan (1868–1923), who was an entrepreneur, a religious official of the Sultanate of Yogyakarta, and an Islamic scholar or *ulama*. Some scholars have compared the Muhammadiyah to the Nahdlatul Ulama (NU), the largest Muslim movement in Indonesia, characterizing the two organizations in terms of their supporters, geography, cultural attachment, education, economy, political inclination, and religious attitudes. Traditionally, the Muhammadiyah has been categorized as representing Indonesia's urban middle and upper middle class Muslims; its members were educated in modern (European-style) schools, were reformist-modernist in matters of organization, culturally rooted in the Javanese variant of Islam, and puritan in religious orientation. Members of the NU, by contrast, used to be largely rural, *pesantren*-educated and traditionalist (Hefner 1995; Nakamura 1983; Noer 1973; Peacock 1978*a* and 1978*b*). Nowadays, the differences between the organizations' constituencies have become less pronounced than in previous decades. In spite of its persistence in preserving the traditional *pesantren* educational system, the NU has also been trying to emulate the Muhammadiyah in embracing modern education. Culturally, this organization has become even more associated with Javanese culture than the Muhammadiyah in past decades.

The Muhammadiyah has five levels of leadership: *pimpinan pusat* (nation), *pimpinan wilayah* (province), *pimpinan daerah* (county), *pimpinan cabang* (district), and *pimpinan ranting* (village or ward). Each is responsible for managing the organization's affairs at that particular level. Several councils are attached to each level of leadership, such as councils for education, social health, propagation or *tabligh*, and religious counsel or *tarjih* and *tajdid*. At the national level, besides these councils, there are several departments with special functions, such as the departments of international affairs, politics, the environment, and the arts and literature. Among other things, these councils are responsible for supervising and maintaining schools, hospitals, mosques, and orphanages owned by the Muhammadiyah. In 2003, there were 3,980 kindergartens, 6,728 elementary schools, 3,279 junior high schools, 2,776 senior high schools, and over 166 colleges and universities (Basri 2003; Tuhuleley 2003).

In the field of education, at least on paper, the Muhammadiyah has a hierarchical leadership structure. The provincial leaders are in charge of universities, while the lower levels of leadership are responsible for the lower educational levels. For example, the provincial leaders are responsible for selecting the rector of the Muhammadiyah university in their area. The Muhammadiyah also applies this structural managerial system when maintaining its other profit-oriented or entrepreneurial activities (*Amal Usaha Muhammadiyah*, or AUM), including hospitals; the organization runs over 300 health institutions (Basri 2003). A different system is applied to non-profit institutions, such as mosques and orphanages, which are normally assigned to the village level of leadership.

The movement also has a sister (women's) organization, known as Aisyiah; youth and young women's wings, which are often dubbed its son and daughter organizations (Pemuda Muhammadiyah and Nasyiatul Aisyiah); and associations for teenagers (the Association for High School Students of the Muhammadiyah, or IPM),[4] college students (*Ikatan Mahasiswa Muhammadiyah*, or IMM), scouts (Hizbul Wathan), and the martial arts or *pencak silat*. These organizations are managed autonomously, and have the same leadership structure as the Muhammadiyah.

The leaders of the Muhammadiyah are elected by its members at the national congress (Muktamar), which is held every five years and attended by representatives from all over the country, from the national to the *ranting* levels of leadership.[5] While electing new leaders is not the only purpose of the Muktamar, people often see this as the most important agenda item, because electing new leaders determines the kind of policies that will be implemented by the movement. In addition to the Muktamar, the Muhammadiyah also has a conference called the Tanwir, which is its second highest and largest national assembly. The Tanwir is held on a necessity basis, but it must be held at least twice during one period of leadership.[6] The status of a Tanwir is lower than that of the Muktamar, and only delegations from the national, provincial, and *kabupaten* levels take part.

Since the 43rd Muktamar in Banda Aceh in 1995, the Muhammadiyah has experienced a number of major shifts in policy, composition of leadership, and internal organization. A number of observers and activists have spoken of a struggle between two competing groups within the Muhammadiyah, using terms such as "progressives vs. conservatives", "liberals vs. anti-liberals", "liberals vs. moderates", "liberal Islam vs. Islam" (Boy 2007; Mulyadi 2005; *Tabligh* 2004a, 2004b, 2004c). There is no agreement between the opponents about the appropriate terms to describe their positions. This article will use the relatively neutral terms "liberal" and "conservative" to refer to them, although the author is aware that the groups in question might consider these terms as stigmatizing and prefer *Islam progresif* ("progressive Islam") and *Islam murni* ("pure" or "puritan Islam"), respectively. The liberals embrace modernist interpretations and tend to emphasize contextual reading and interpretation of scripture; the conservatives tend to stick more closely to established and more literal readings of the sources, and to consider liberal ideas as a threat to the very essence of Islam.

LIBERAL AND CONSERVATIVE GROUPS IN THE MUHAMMADIYAH

The 43rd Muktamar of the Muhammadiyah in Banda Aceh in 1995 marked the beginning of the quarrel between liberal and conservative factions in the Muhammadiyah. Initially, the liberal group took control. Muhammad Amien Rais, who holds a doctoral degree in Political Science from the University of Chicago and is a professor at Gadjah Mada University, was elected as the new president. During his leadership, new faces, particularly university professors, were appointed at the national level. A number of religious reforms were also introduced during this leadership. The transformation of the *Majelis Tarjih* (the Council for Religious Rulings) into the *Majelis Tarjih dan Pengembangan Pemikiran Islam* (the Council for Religious Rulings and the Furtherance of Islamic Thought, henceforth the MTPPI), the publication of *Tafsir tematik al-Qur'an tentang hubungan sosial antarumat beragama* (Thematic exegesis of the Qur'an on interfaith relations, henceforth *Tafsir tematik al-Qur'an*), and the decision to declare art *mubah* (permitted, allowed), thereby revising a previous decision which regarded works of art as *haram* (forbidden, prohibited), are all examples of how the organization accommodated progressive ideas.

The change in the Muhammadiyah was even more remarkable during the 44th Muktamar of the Muhammadiyah in Jakarta in 2000. The Muktamar elected Ahmad Syafii Maarif as the new president of the Muhammadiyah; a progressive scholar who holds a Ph.D. degree in Islamic Thought from the University of Chicago, who studied under the tutelage of the eminent scholar of Islam and neo-modernist Muslim, Fazlur Rahman. The Muktamar also elected and appointed a number of progressive thinkers, such as Amin Abdullah, Abdul Munir Mulkhan, and Dawan Rahardjo, to the national leadership of the Muhammadiyah.[7] These developments are thought to explain why the Muhammadiyah underwent a notable intellectual upheaval during Maarif's term. Under his leadership, progressive ideas dominated the movement and were gradually introduced into the Muhammadiyah's programmes. These included a programme for reforming religious thought, such as reinterpreting the theological stance on interfaith relations and *dakwah kultural* (religious propagation using cultural strategies), or indigenizing

Islam instead of Islamizing local culture. The programme of *dakwah kultural* obviously conflicts with a puritan paradigm that opposes any external elements of religion, such as local-syncretistic culture.

The rise of the liberal group provoked opposition from those with different religious views. At the beginning, these differences did not take the form of a power struggle, but instead stemmed from different interpretations of particularities (*furu'iyya*) of *fiqh* law, such as how the Muhammadiyah should perceive traditional dance, which sometimes features "erotic" body movements, or any traditional culture that does not fit with the spirit of modernism. However, people then moved from these small differences onto serious issues. Every possible effort was made to resist the religious reforms proposed by the liberal group, which, in their view, deviated too far from the puritan mission of the Muhammadiyah. This resulted in a tug of war for religious domination.

The clearest expression of this competition for influence between liberal and conservative groups was the conflict between the occupants of the third and the fourth floors of the *Gedung Pusat Dakwah Muhammadiyah*, or GPDM (which literally means House of Muhammadiyah's Propagation), the head office of the Muhammadiyah in Menteng, Jakarta. The third floor of the GPDM housed the *Majelis Tabligh* (Council of Islamic Propagation), while the fourth floor was home to the IPM, the IMM, the youth wing Pemuda Muhammadiyah and the *Pusat Studi Agama dan Peradaban* (the Centre for Religion and Civilization Studies, or PSAP).[8] These two vying groups competed in various arenas, such as seminars, discussions, publications, and other programmes. The groups usually had opposing programmes. For example, when the PSAP promoted pluralism and multiculturalism in its journal, *Jurnal Tanwir*, the Majelis Tabligh responded with opposing opinions in its magazine, *Majalah Tabligh*.[9] During the 45th Muktamar of the Muhammadiyah in Malang, the conservatives set up a shopping stand called the *Pojok Anti Liberal* (Anti-liberalist corner), which sold anti-liberal books, DVDs, t-shirts, magazines and other merchandise. Strikingly, some of the t-shirts featured the phrase "Muhammadiyah Anti-Liberal" (Anti-Liberal Muhammadiyan).

As reflected by *Tabligh*'s headlines, discussion topics and other materials produced by the two competing groups, each group employed a process of inversion to claim that they represented the truth, while simultaneously discrediting and denigrating their opponents. Pluralism and liberalism were among the issues used by both groups to deconstruct and reconstruct the movement. In this way, the liberal group tried to convince both members of the Muhammadiyah and people outside the organization that change was necessary within the movement. In the opposite camp, the conservative group suggested that the issues proposed by the liberal group, which in their eyes were deeply dangerous, would only take the Muhammadiyah towards ruin and damnation.

The conservatives condemned pluralism, liberalism, and the use of hermeneutics in interpreting the Qur'an as methods that aimed at nothing other than the crippling of Islam. A Western academic might find it strange that hermeneutics — a method for understanding holy books — was condemned by a conservative group. The conservatives, however, believe that hermeneutics is not a neutral method; rather, it is a Western (to be precise, Christian) approach that is incompatible with the Qur'an, and must therefore be rejected (Pasha 2004). Pluralism and liberalism are also contrary to Islamic doctrine. For the conservatives, the belief that all religions are equally valid violates the belief that Islam is the only true religion, whereas liberalism conflicts with the basic tenet of Islam that all Muslims must submit totally to God. In response to hermeneutics, pluralism, and liberalism, this group struggles to guard the continuity of classical methods of interpreting the Qur'an, such as using ancient *tafsir* and beliefs in the superiority of Islam and the central role of revelation in human activities.

In order to undermine the liberals and their programmes, the conservatives did not hesitate to describe the liberals as a "virus" or "poison". They frequently described the liberals as "destroyers", and sometimes accused them of being Jewish or American agents, driven by greed (Pasha 2004; *Tabligh* 2004*b*, 2004*c*; *Hidayatullah* 2005). These offensive labels were used to try to convince people of the potential danger posed by liberal thought: that such thought would act like a poison or virus, and that it would destroy the Muhammadiyah and Islam. For example, one of the author's respondents, a Yogyakarta regional leader of the Muhammadiyah, even suggested that religious liberalism was more dangerous than the radical *Tarbiyah* movement that was infiltrating the organization (see further below), claiming that liberalism undermined the fundaments of Islam:

> In the context of theology, liberalism is far more dangerous [than the *Tarbiyah* movement]. This ideology stabs at the heart of Islamic theology. This ideology believes in the relativity of truth and consequently it believes that all religions are equally valid. The Tarbiyah movement is not that dangerous. In term of beliefs and practices, the Tarbiyah does not depart too far from the Muhammadiyah. Even in religious teaching, the Tarbiyah has the same spirit as the Muhammadiyah, namely, taking everything back to the Qur'an and the Sunna. The conflict between the Muhammadiyah

and the Tarbiyah is more related to organizational issues and religious ethics.[10]

The liberal faction used the same method to ridicule its opponents. Besides calling the conservatives derogatory names, the liberal group also described the conservatives' actions as evil and harmful. On certain occasions, they exposed the destructive beliefs and the threat posed by the conservative group. In their view, the religious perspective that belongs to the conservatives is the main root of decadence, rigidity, uncreative, and stagnation (Qodir 2003; Baidhawy 2006). The liberals wanted to convince Muhammadiyah members of the need to adopt new perspectives and avoid the conservative mindset.

Sometimes, when the opposing factions felt threatened, they abandoned discourse and started employing force. The response of the conservative group to the publication of a book entitled *Tafsir tematik al-Qur'an* by the MTPPI (under the initiative and editorship of its chair, Amin Abdullah) is one example. After its launch, the book became the subject of controversy within the Muhammadiyah. The book expressed liberal thought clearly and systematically. It presented a new hermeneutic method for interpreting the Qur'an, new perspectives on pluralism, and a new method of understanding religion — all of which were condemned as "liberal thought" by the conservative group. The book argued that Muslims are permitted to marry not only Christians, but also Jews, Buddhists, Hindus, and others. The book even stated that in theory, Muslim girls could marry people from any religion, aside from polytheists (*al-mushrikun*). It also argued that salvation does not belong exclusively to the Muslim community, but that there is also salvation in other religions (MTPPI 2000).

The book elicited a surprising response. A group of Muhammadiyah members calling themselves *Warga Muhammadiyah Pembela Syariat* (Muhammadiyah members who defend Islamic Shari'a, or WMPS) attacked the book through various media, including the Friday sermon, a weekly mandatory congregation for Muslims (Latief 2003). They demanded that the Muhammadiyah take this book out of circulation and ban its members from reading it.

THE 45TH MUKTAMAR OF THE MUHAMMADIYAH AND THE RISE OF CONSERVATISM

The rise of conservatism in the Muhammadiyah began during Maarif's leadership term, between 2000 and 2005. As mentioned above, the response to *Tafsir tematik al-Qur'an*, the headlines of *Tabligh* magazine, and the quarrel in the Muhammadiyah headquarters in Jakarta are all examples of increasing conservatism during this period. However, it was only during the 45th Muktamar in Malang, East Java, in 2005, that this attitude became more visible. This was demonstrated by the conservative group's takeover of the leadership of the Muhammadiyah, the organization's response to women's issues and women's representation in the congresses, and the attack on the *Jaringan Intelektual Muda Muhammadiyah* (the Muhammadiyah Youth Intellectual Network, or JIMM).

The election of conservative representatives

At the 45th Muktamar of the Muhammadiyah, the conservatives successfully took over the leadership of the organization. Seven of the thirteen new national leaders were "newcomers" to the upper ranks of the leadership: the then minister of national education, Bambang Sudibyo; Sudibyo Markus, a convert from Christianity who had become a renowned civil society activist and anti-Christian polemicist; Dahlan Rais, the chairman of Muhammadiyah-Central Java and a younger brother of Amien Rais; Zamroni, one of the most important figures at the Ministry of Education; Fasich, chairman of Muhammadiyah-East Java and then chairman of the National Council of Islamic Students Association (KAHMI)-East Java; Yunahar Ilyas, a proponent of conservative Islam and a graduate of Ibn Saud Islamic University, Riyadh; and Goodwill Zubir, a key figure in the Muhammadiyah's missionary activities. The last two individuals were well known for their inclination towards the Islamic right wing. Examining the leadership structure in detail, it is interesting to note that individuals such as Ahmad Syafii Maarif, Amin Abdullah and Abdul Munir Mulkhan no longer sat on the executive board. Maarif decided not to run for office, whereas Abdullah and Mulkhan failed to get enough votes to become national leaders. Among many things, it is suspected that their failure to attract voters was closely related to their failure in the competitive discourse between progressivism and conservatism.

The election of Din Syamsuddin, who holds a Ph.D. degree in Islamic Studies from the University of California Los Angeles (UCLA) and who was at that time the secretary-general of the Indonesian Ulama Council (MUI), as the new president of the Muhammadiyah for the 2005–10 period, confirmed the widespread opinion that the Muhammadiyah was becoming more conservative. Indeed, at that time, Syamsuddin had links to the Islamic right, but his success could not be attributed solely to his religious connections. It is true that for some observers and civil society activists, Syamsuddin had previously been notorious as a mastermind of anti-Semitic, anti-Christian, anti-secular Muslim and anti-democratic discourse and action in Indonesia (Hefner 2002). According to some foreign researchers, Syamsuddin was regarded as a fundamentalist Muslim, an apostle of conservative Islam, and the "brain" behind militant Islam (Smith 2005; Hefner 2000 and 2002; Liddle 2005; Shiraishi 1999). However, Syamsuddin has a good reputation among the members of the Muhammadiyah. He is well-known for visiting Muhammadiyah branches and supporters, even in remote areas. He is also a popular figure at the national level and has a broad international network. His behaviour appears at odds with the accusations levelled at him by foreign observers. Furthermore, some Muhammadiyah members believed that Syamsuddin could mediate in the clash between the liberal and conservative elements of Islam in the Muhammadiyah.

The role played by the 45th Muktamar as an arena for the competition of ideas was paramount for both sides. The Muktamar was like the climax of a tiresome contest that had been dragging on for years, and the congress tended to be perceived as a barometer of the groups' fortunes. During the 43rd and 44th congresses, the liberal camp took the lead, only to be overtaken by the conservatives in the 45th Muktamar. Just like the liberal group before them, the conservatives also changed the names of some of the councils. New representatives were appointed at the national leadership level. Adian Husaini, an activist at the *Dewan Dakwah Islamiyah Indonesia* (the Indonesian Council for Islamic Propagation) and a proponent of anti-liberal movements, was one of new faces on the *Majelis Tabligh* (Council of Religious Propagation).

In relation to the feud with the liberals, the most obvious change was the renaming of the MTPPI as the *Majelis Tarjih dan Tajdid* (Council for the Law-Making and Renewal [of the understanding of Islam]). The A Commission, which was in charge of discussing general issues, demanded that *Majelis Tarjih* omit the words "*Pengembangan Pemikiran Islam*" (Furtherance of Islamic Thought) from its title; words that had been added under the previous leadership. The council was renamed the *Majelis Tarjih dan Tajdid*. The new name served primarily as a symbolic construct to signify change. It symbolized a new era and was used to inverse the council's paradigm, to set a new focus, and to "cover up" the influence of the liberals. Instead of focusing on progressive thought and issues, the *Majelis Tarjih dan Tajdid* was more concerned with classical Islamic sciences, such as *Ilmu Falak* (the astronomical system used for calculating the beginning and end of the fasting month).

The position of women: excluded from the leadership and deprived of representation

The inclusion of women on the executive board of the central or national leadership of the Muhammadiyah has been a contentious topic in recent years. During the leadership of Syafii Maarif in 2000–05, the Muhammadiyah had pursued a policy of affirmative action by introducing a special quota for women to be elected to the executive board. Every *pimpinan wilayah* (provincial leadership) that sent delegates to the Muktamar was required to have women in its team. Unfortunately, during the 45th Muktamar, only 8 of the 35 provincial leaderships of the Muhammadiyah included women in their delegations.[11]

This failure to include women in the provincial representatives of the Muktamar did not stimulate the organization to solve the problem of how to maximize the number of female representatives. Rather, the 45th Muktamar even displayed a rise in resistance to the inclusion of women in the organization. The C Commission, which was responsible for the organization's structure, for instance, rejected the idea of allowing female candidates for the thirteen positions of high-ranking official, as had been affirmed during the previous leadership.

Strong resistance to the idea of gender equality was also apparent when it came to nominating thirty-nine candidates for national leadership positions for the 2005–10 term, as no women appeared on the list. Siti Chamamah Suratno, then the chairwoman of Aisyiah, was almost nominated. Suratno was listed as the fortieth nominee, only one vote behind Professor Sjafri Sairin of Gadjah Mada University of Yogjakarta, who received the last nomination. Suratno's exclusion from the final list was a logical consequence of the fact that only a small number of women were present at the congress. Indeed, the conservative wing uses the existence of Aisyiah to justify its refusal to include women at the official level of Muhammadiyah's central organization. They argue, on the one hand, that if women want to lead Muhammadiyah, they would have to dump Aisyiah first, after which they could compete for positions in the Muhammadiyah leadership. However, on the other hand, the idea of merging the Aisyiyah and the Muhammadiyah is actually something unacceptable in their religious understanding.

The Aisyiyah was established in 1917 under a modernist paradigm. Unlike fundamentalist paradigms that confine women to a life of domesticity and childbearing, modernist Muslims support the empowerment of women and allow them to actively participate in social life. They believe that it is essential for women to play leadership roles in society (as doctors, lawyers or judges) and follow education (to pursue highest level of education and to play a role in the education system). Modernists thus rescue women from exclusion, but their social role is still segregated from men. In view of this, a key question relates to the status of women in the Muhammadiyah: do they have full membership? Culturally, they are members of the Muhammadiyah, and the organization certainly includes women when calculating its total number of followers. But when the question arises as to whether to adopt a special quota for women in the leadership of the Muhammadiyah, this idea is usually rejected on the grounds that these women already have their own organization, Aisyiyah; and if they want to run for leadership in the Muhammadiyah, they have to follow the normal process of election.

Resistance to liberal thought

In a similar vein, resistance to liberal thought was also shown during the 45th Muktamar. For instance, the D Commission, which was in charge of recommendations, sought to mitigate the spread of liberalism. One of the commission's members demanded that the organization disband the JIMM, or at least force the organization to drop "Muhammadiyah" from its name. Arguing that the name "Muhammadiyah" is part of the organization's property, which I think quite mistaken, Yunahar Ilyas stated that the name Muhammadiyah should not be used without permission. "A new institution could only use the name of Muhammadiyah after it is granted by the Tanwir to use that name or agreed by the Muktamar" (*Tabligh* 2004b). Some members of the Muhammadiyah believed that the JIMM had betrayed the Muhammadiyah's original mission and had promoted conflicting ideals that would bring this organization to different ends. For this reason, they demanded that the JIMM be disbanded, and expressed their contempt by labelling the JIMM "malevolent".

Antipathy towards liberal thought and its proponents, particularly the JIMM and its supporters, emerged even before the 45th Muktamar. Because of their promotion of a new method of interpreting the Qur'an, different ways of interacting with non-Muslims and new perspectives on Islam and the Muhammadiyah, proponents of the JIMM were often accused of being *anak durhaka* (prodigal sons). The very name JIMM was often translated as *Jaringan Iblis Muda Muhammadiyah* (network of young devils of the Muhammadiyah) (*Tabligh* 2004a). In short, the 45th Muktamar was merely an occasion for announcing the organization's final verdict.

The JIMM is often associated with the *Jaringan Islam Liberal* (Liberal Islam Network, JIL), which was established in 2001. Before the establishment of the JIL, however, progressive ideas had been proposed in the Muhammadiyah and implemented in its policies. The above-mentioned transformation of *Majelis Tarjih* into the MTPPI and the publication of *Tafsir tematik al-Qur'an* are two examples of how this organization accommodated progressive and liberal ideas. Furthermore, the appointment of liberal figures, such as Amin Abdullah and Munir Mulkhan, to the national leadership of the Muhammadiyah at the 44th Congress of Muhammadiyah in 2000, shows how progressive ideas were gradually fed into Muhammadiyah programmes.

This progress was indirectly obstructed when a number of young Muslim intellectuals, including Ulil Abshar Abdalla and Luthfi Assyaukanie, established the JIL. The name "liberal Islam" and the group's activities offended some Indonesian Muslims, and caused them to resist everything associated with liberalism (see El-Baroroh 2005; Latif 2003). Those promoting progressive and liberal ideas in the Muhammadiyah were accused of having links with the JIL. The establishment of the JIMM in 2003, with its similar-sounding abbreviation, strengthened these accusations. One of my respondents suggested that a more appropriate name for the JIL would be *Jaringan Iblis Laknatullah* (Satan's network, God curse them!). It is probably unfair to blame the JIL for inflaming the Islamist camp in the Muhammadiyah, because it had no connections with the organization. However, the establishment of the JIL elicited an unforgiving response from various Muslim groups in Indonesia, including some members of the Muhammadiyah, and these groups sought to lessen the JIL's influence in the organization.

COMBATING CONSERVATISM: THE RESPONSE FROM WITHIN THE MUHAMMADIYAH

The mass media concluded that the 45th Muktamar had been a triumph for the conservative group in the Muhammadiyah. With respect to the role of women, liberal thought and the national leadership elections, journalists and observers wrote that the Muhammadiyah had experienced a major setback (Mulyadi 2005; Diani 2006). However, the developments a few years after the Muktamar suggest that this conclusion needs to be reconsidered. The efforts taken by the Muhammadiyah to rid the organization of the conservative elements that had taken hold in 2006 suggests that the media's reports of a conservative triumph were unfounded. There was widespread belief within the Muhammadiyah that the organization's conservative inclinations had been influenced by the infiltration of an external movement. Haedar Nashir (2007), for instance, suspected the Tarbiyah movement (henceforth the Tarbiyah) of trying to influence the Muhammadiyah.

The Tarbiyah was initially an underground movement influenced by the thought of the Egyptian Hassan al-Banna and *al-Ikhwan al-Muslimun* (the Muslim Brotherhood, or MB). After the fall of the New Order in 1998, the Tarbiyah group reorganized into a political party, the Prosperous and Justice Party (PKS), currently one of the most successful parties in Indonesian politics. The religious views of this movement are similar to those of the conservative group within the Muhammadiyah, and it is therefore unsurprising that some proponents of this group, such as Yunahar Ilyas, have been treated with great respect by the Tarbiyah members. Instead of defending the Tarbiyah's influence on the Muhammadiyah, however, the conservatives joined the liberals in expelling the Tarbiyah from the Muhammadiyah. This appeared to end the split between the liberal and conservative camps; the Tarbiyah virtually reunited them. Nonetheless, at a deeper level, the disagreement between the two groups continued, and they took different lines on how to deal with the Tarbiyah. In order to understand the importance of this case in the framework of the conservative-liberal debate, we need to look more closely at the background to the rupture with the Tarbiyah and the PKS.

The coming of the Tarbiyah movement

At the end of 2005, some within the Muhammadiyah complained that a number of mosques that had previously been administered by the organization had been taken over by activists from the Tarbiyah religious movement, which had transformed itself into a political party, the PKS.[12] In fact, this issue was not only affecting the Muhammadiyah; the NU was experiencing the same problem. A Jakarta-based Islamic magazine, *Syir'ah*, for instance, reported:

> In Jatinegara [East Jakarta], there is a mosque named Al-Bahri. This mosque was built by *guru* Marzuki, the founder of the first *pesantren* in Betawi. This mosque has now been taken over by another

group of Muslims ... as a result, when certain Muslims perform
qasidahan [a type of Indonesian Islamic music], the new officials respond
by displaying a pamphlet saying, "a mosque is not a place for performing
Ondel-ondel" [a traditional Betawi musical performance].

(Fathuri 2007)

In the Muhammadiyah, the alleged annexation of mosques was
followed by a more bitter controversy. A provincial leader of the
Muhammadiyah in Central Java revealed that an attempt had been made
to take over one of Muhammadiyah's *sekolah dasar* (elementary schools)
in Boyolali, and that its leadership and ownership had shifted from the
Muhammadiyah to activists from another Muslim organization, namely
the PKS. Even more dramatic rumours were circulating: it was said that
the PKS was not only trying to take over the Muhammadiyah's mosques,
but also its schools, universities, and hospitals. This was logical, since most
of the Muhammadiyah mosques were located in these institutions. It was
also reported that a number of PKS supporters, some of whom were also
Muhammadiyah members who happened to work at Muhammadiyah
institutions, had failed to show loyalty to the Muhammadiyah, and had
even campaigned for the PKS and organized pro-PKS activities in these
institutions. Moreover, several Muhammadiyah schools had allegedly been
taken over by PKS activists and had their names changed to *sekolah Islam
terpadu* (integrated Islamic schools).

Similar developments were also reported by Muhammadiyah activists
at the University of Muhammadiyah Yogyakarta and the University of
Muhammadiyah Prof Dr Hamka in Jakarta. On these two campuses,
PKS activists initially participated in mosque activities, but then they
tried to transform the Islamic programmes at these mosques in line with
their agendas. After this, they allegedly tried to take over the mosques by
replacing existing *takmir*s (those who are responsible for Islamic activities
in a mosque) with new ones from their circle or individuals who shared
their ideas. In an article published by *Suara Muhammadiyah*, Abdul Munir
Mulkhan described the infiltration of Muhammadiyah activities in Sendang
Ayu, Lampung, by a political party.[13] Preachers from this party attacked
the Muhammadiyah activists who had been nurturing and developing the
organization in that area.

The most blatant challenge by the PKS occurred when this party-
cum-movement organized its own ʿId al-Adha prayer in 2005. At this
time, there were two different decisions about the dates for observing ʿId
al-Adha (the Feast of Sacrifice). The Indonesian government and the two

main Muslim organizations, the NU and the Muhammadiyah, decided that 'Id al-Adha would be celebrated on Friday, 21 January 2005, whereas the PKS and Hizb al-Tahrir of Indonesia decided that it would be held on Thursday, 20 January 2005. The latter's argument was based on the decision of the PKS party's *Dewan Syariah* (Shari'a Council), which itself faithfully followed the decision of the Kingdom of Saudi Arabia.[14] What is notable in this regard is that some members of the Muhammadiyah followed the PKS, ignorant or unaware of their own organization's decision.

These incidents and the gradual flow of Muhammadiyah members to the PKS contributed to fears in the Muhammadiyah leadership about the future of their organization. This was not simply a matter of changing the *takmir masjid* (committees controlling mosques), the names of Islamic schools or days of prayer for the two Islamic holidays; some liberal figures feared that this was the first step in changing the very face of Islam in Indonesia. "In some areas, Muhammadiyah members feel frustrated and get tricked by political parties, in this case the PKS, that come to mosques owned by the Muhammadiyah, and to the Muhammadiyah's communities and its enterprises", said one of the movement's national chairmen. "Once I asked a teacher from a Muhammadiyah school about the movement's statutes, and he knew nothing. Then I asked him about the beliefs of a certain religious party and he eagerly, spontaneously and fluently described them", said another national chairman.

The rationale behind the conflict will be addressed in more detail below. At this point, suffice it to say that the Muhammadiyah responded to the challenge seriously. The national leadership of the Muhammadiyah issued a *surat keputusan* or decree (SK) on 1 December 2006, popularly known as SK 149/2006, on organizational and entrepreneurial consolidation. In this decree, the Muhammadiyah obliged all of its members to disassociate themselves from any kind of external political activity, to show loyalty, integrity and commitment to the Muhammadiyah, to optimize the cadres' training and to uphold organizational discipline. The decree was implicitly intended as a response to the PKS, and at one point, it even explicitly mentioned that the PKS was the target of the policy.

The Muhammadiyah then took the further step of fortifying its organization and enterprises against infiltration by external forces, particularly the PKS. Four months after issuing SK 149/2006, the Muhammadiyah organized a Tanwir in Yogyakarta from 26–29 April 2007, with the theme *Peneguhan dan Pencerahan Gerakan untuk Kemajuan Bangsa* (revitalizing and enlightening the movement for national progress).[15]

The discussions mainly focused on organizational and ideological revitalization: how the Muhammadiyah should respond to and compete with new Islamist organizations, such as the PKS and the Hizb al-Tahrir (Ar. *hizb al-tahrir*); how the Muhammadiyah should respond to members who exploited the movement for the benefit of other organizations; and how the Muhammadiyah should avoid being directly involved in political parties. At the end of the Tanwir, the commission in charge of discussing ideology formulated policies commonly known as "organizational discipline". These required loyalty and commitment on the part of all Muhammadiyah members, particularly those employed within Muhammadiyah enterprises. If they could not demonstrate their loyalty, they would be asked to leave the organization.

The decisions of the Tanwir were further specified in decree no. 101/ 2007 issued by the central board of the Muhammadiyah, concerning the holding of dual offices. Board members of the Muhammadiyah at any level were forbidden from holding official positions in political parties or other mass organizations. Even within the Muhammadiyah itself, dual office-holding was no longer tolerated: a member of the national leadership, for instance, could not hold a leadership position at any other level of the organization. Moreover, in order to protect the Muhammadiyah and its enterprises from external influence, the decree also stated that every person who worked in one of the enterprises owned by the Muhammadiyah must sign a statement of commitment and loyalty to the Muhammadiyah. To strengthen their faithfulness to the organization, it became mandatory to attend activities held by the Muhammadiyah.

Based on that decision, the Muhammadiyah also maintained strict requirements for cooperation with other organizations. This contrasted with previous policies, in which the organization had endorsed cooperation with other Muslim organizations, including political parties such as the National Mandate Party (PAN) and the PKS, and Muslim movements in general. Furthermore, the Muhammadiyah began to scrutinize its preachers carefully. The organization also intends to stop giving financial assistance to preachers who are formally affiliated with the Muhammadiyah but in reality preach teachings that differ from those of the organization.

Although this decree intentionally targeted Islamic movements such as the Tarbiyah or the PKS and the Indonesian Hizb al-Tahrir, some political activists in the Muhammadiyah thought that there were also other targets, namely the proponents of the Partai Matahari Bangsa (Sun of the Nation Party, or PMB), a new political party that vied for the votes of Muhammadiyah members. Some of the younger members of the organization, such as Imam Ad-Daruquthi and Ahmad Rofiq, who believed that the PAN did not really represent the political aspirations of the Muhammadiyah (even when it was under the leadership of Amien Rais), had established a new political party, the PMB. One of the party's aims was to represent the Muhammadiyah in politics. The PMB's supporters believed that the decisions of the Tanwir and decree no. 101/2007 targeted their party specifically, precisely because they had claimed that the PMB would be the party of the Muhammadiyah. The proponents of this party were activists from and members of the Muhammadiyah, particularly from the youth wings. The PAN, meanwhile, a party that was also founded mostly by members of the Muhammadiyah, did not feel targeted by the decision, because its relationship with the Muhammadiyah had become looser. The decision was even felt to favour the PAN, since it would obstruct the establishment of the PMB and help the PAN retain the loyalty of some Muhammadiyah members.

A heated debate occurred after decision no. 101/2007 was issued. Some proponents of the Muhammadiyah, particularly from the youth movement (Pemuda Muhammadiyah), continuously challenged the decision. On the other hand, the Muhammadiyah was also hesitant to punish those members who had dual commitments (i.e. to the Muhammadiyah and to a political party). The decisions were only enforced in the case of people who held dual positions in the Muhammadiyah and other Islamic organizations, such as the Tarbiyah or the PKS. It is understandable that the decisions were not enforced in the context of the PMB and the PAN, as these organizations were not the target of the decree.

Two models of response: liberal and conservative

As we saw above, the liberals and the conservatives cooperated to protect the Muhammadiyah from the danger of dual loyalties on the part of its active members. This raises a number of questions: why did the conservatives, who were ideologically close to the Tarbiyah, cooperate with the liberals? What were the points of agreement and difference? The two factions in the Muhammadiyah had different motivations for opposing the Tarbiyah. According to the liberal group, the Tarbiyah (PKS) posed a threat to the Muhammadiyah, not only in terms of leadership and the ownership of certain enterprises, but also, more importantly, in terms of ideology. Haedar Nashir, one of the national leaders of the Muhammadiyah, explained:

> [Muhammadiyah and the PKS are] ideologically different. The
> Muhammadiyah is a moderate Islamic movement; it represents *Islam
> murni* [puritan Islam] and *berkemajuan* [progressive Islam]. It tries to
> preserve the purity of Islam, on the one hand, and always to be orientated
> towards the future, on the other hand. The striking feature of the
> Muhammadiyah is that this organization does not have an inclination
> towards any political parties, it is not a political party, and it does not
> struggle to achieve political power or hegemony. The PKS is based on
> Islamic political ideology. That is the difference. The Muhammadiyah
> is an Islamic social movement, not a political movement.[16]

The political orientation of the PKS and the non-political orientation
of the Muhammadiyah can be observed from the way the two organizations
perceive two Islamic holidays, `Id al-Adha (the Feast of Sacrifice) and `Id
al-Fitr (the feast ending the fasting month). In the Muhammadiyah, the
events of `Id al-Adha and `Id al-Fitr are interpreted in various ways: i)
`Id al-Adha and `Id al-Fitr are a medium of communication between all
elements of this organization, a means for bridging socio-economic divides
among its members; ii) they are a medium for displaying the strength of the
organization compared to that of others; iii) they are a way to gauge the
adherence of Muhammadiyah members to their organization's decisions (as
regards the decision of the *Majelis Tarjih*). Organizationally, disobeying the
central board's decisions means showing disloyalty to the organization. Thus
although the celebration of these two holidays has political elements, they
are mostly social and religious occasions. This is different from the PKS,
which is inclined to use them for political purposes, both nationally and
internationally. Nationally, the festivals form part of a religious programme
that can be utilized for political ends. Internationally, they are a symbol of
the unity, uniformity, and solidarity of all Muslims in all countries. The case
of `Id al-Adha also supposedly made Muhammadiyah leaders aware that
the PKS had a different *manhaj* (methodology) of *fiqh* or *tarjih* (Islamic
law in Muhammadiyah terminology) and its own shari`a council, which
offers practical religious guidance to its members, advice that occasionally
conflicts with the *Majelis Tarjih* of the Muhammadiyah.[17]

To explain the liberal group's fears regarding the challenge of the PKS,
which began with a struggle over mosques, it is useful to consider a similar
case in the United States, namely the coup by fundamentalist Muslims
led by Mahmoud Abu Halima at the Abou Bakr mosque in Brooklyn.
Jim Dwyer has shown how the leadership coup in the Abu Bakr mosque
was the first sign of the coming of Islamic fundamentalism in the United
States (Dwyer 1994). At this coup, radical expatriate Muslims overthrew

more moderate *imam*s and mosque officials. "Without warning, Abu Bakr
found itself the victim of a hostile takeover, the latest battlefront in a
global struggle over the future of Islam" (Dwyer 1994, p. 141). People
who had built, nurtured and organized the mosque for several decades,
such as Abdukalder Kallash, were fired from their positions. Preaching
on ethics and maintaining a peaceful relationship with non-Muslims was
replaced with preaching on global conflict. The mosque was transformed
from "a house of worship into a paramilitary safe house" (Dwyer 1994,
p. 153). Reflecting on the relationship between immigrant Muslims and
the American government, Kallash commented, "The Koran tells us you
must be kind to your neighbor ... Yet you have been invited into your
neighbor's home and now you are trying to takeover that home. How can
you say that is just?" (Dwyer 1994, p. 151). In the Indonesian context,
there appear to be parallels between the Tarbiyah movement (PKS) and
the group led by Mahmoud Abu Halima. The Tarbiyah was welcomed by
the Muhammadiyah, but then it tried to take over the organization and
launched a serious challenge that threatened to determine the future of
Islam in Indonesia.

For conservatives, the Tarbiyah was primarily a threat to the
Muhammadiyah as an organization, not as an Islamic movement. Yunahar
Ilyas, a Muhammadiyah national leader known for his sympathy with
Islamist groups, even said that the conflict was not related to ideological
issues, but that it was an organizational conflict. Explaining this, Ilyas
compared the Muhammadiyah's response to the PKS with how this
organization responded to the JIL and the Indonesian Ahmadiyah-
Qadiyani, followers of Mirza Ghulam Ahmad of India. First of all, he
made a distinction between religious (Islamic) ideology and organizational
(Muhammadiyah) ideology. He said:

> The Muhammadiyah is totally different from the JIL. The ideology
> of the JIL is liberalism. Therefore, the conflict with the JIL should
> be treated as a conflict in the area of religious ideology. It is different
> from the Tarbiyah [the PKS], which is more related to organizational
> strategy or organizational ideology. On the surface [of religious practices],
> there is no difference between the Muhammadiyah and the PKS. Both
> organizations fall under the same religious creed, namely, taking religious
> understanding directly from the Qur'an and the Sunna. Both of them
> also promote *ijtihad* [as a way to perceive religion]. The difference is
> only in political strategy; the Muhammadiyah chose a cultural strategy,
> while the PKS prefers a structural one ... [the conflict between
> Muhammadiyah and the PKS is] more related to technical issues [in

schools and hospitals], not about Islamic ideology. This is also different from the conflict with the Ahmadiyah, which is related to the heart of religious ideology.[18]

Ilyas' statement suggests that from a conservative perspective, the Muhammadiyah and the PKS have much in common. Therefore, on a theological basis, it is completely unacceptable to expel the Tarbiyah from the Muhammadiyah; the only reasons for expelling the Tarbiyah are organizational and political. If the Muhammadiyah allows the Tarbiyah to exist and grow within its body, sooner or later it will take over the organization. In anticipation of this, the Muhammadiyah must bind together to rid the organization of the Tarbiyah's influence.

Historical records also reveal that ideologically, there are no significant differences between the Muhammadiyah and the PKS. Previously, the Muhammadiyah had a close relationship with the PKS, particularly after the 1999 Indonesian election and during the 2004 election (Sulistiyanto 2006). The PAN (a party that was closely associated with the Muhammadiyah) and the PKS formed a single faction in the Indonesian parliament, the Reformation Faction. More generally, many people perceived that the Muhammadiyah and the PKS had similar religious views. It was therefore very common for people to have dual membership of the PKS and the Muhammadiyah.

The 46th Muktamar in Yogyakarta: a cultural congress

At first glance, there were significant differences between the 45th Muktamar in Malang in 2005 and the 46th Muktamar in Yogyakarta in 2010. The former seemed to reflect the modern orientation of the Muhammadiyah, while the latter showed the organization's cultural face. Malang, and more specifically the high-tech buildings of the University of Muhammadiyah Malang (UMM), is where the Muhammadiyah presented itself as a modern organization. The physical building of the UMM, which is held in high esteem and is a source of confidence and pride for the members of the Muhammadiyah, is, for the time being, this organization's greatest achievement in terms of its modern orientation. The 45th Muktamar was held at this university and it emphasized the modern aspect of the organization. The 46th Muktamar, by contrast, showed the symbiosis between the Muhammadiyah's conception of Islam and Indonesian, particularly Javanese, culture. The receptionists and usherettes wore full Javanese attire, with *kris* (daggers), *beskap*, *blangkon*, and batikked *kain*.

Traditional Javanese music was played to accompany the *muktamirin* (Ar. *mu'tamirin*; those attending the congress sessions). At night, there were cultural performances, including traditional Indonesian dances. Even the president of the Muhammadiyah, Din Syamsuddin, participated in a *ketoprak* (Javanese folk theatre) show entitled *Pleteking Surya Ndadari* (the large-bright-shining-rising sun), which is the symbol of the Muhammadiyah, with *ketoprak* costumes. Regardless of whether the contrast between the two occasions was deliberate, it still reveals the two very different faces of the organization.

What was the significance of the 46th Muktamar in the general discourse on conservatism in the Muhammadiyah? Unlike the earlier Muktamar in Malang, the 46th Muktamar showed that the Muhammadiyah was discriminating in its adoption of a strict conservative line. It showed that it could accommodate local culture, which was rejected and condemned by the conservatives, and that the conservatives had failed to dominate the organization. Although the conservatives again attempted to exploit fears of liberalism, pluralism, and secularism in the leadership elections, the Muktamirin were unconvinced. The main figure in the effort to eliminate the Tarbiyah from the Muhammadiyah, Haedar Nashir, was even almost elected as the new president of the Muhammadiyah — and he lost due to political issues, not religious ones.[19]

One of the important decisions taken by the new leadership of the Muhammadiyah in responding to conservatism was the appointment of Siti Noordjannah Djohantini as one of the national leaders of the Muhammadiyah. Djohantini, who had recently been elected as the chairwoman of the Aisyiyah, was given a leadership position in the Muhammadiyah, and made responsible for women's and children's issues. Although a few voices said that her position in the Muhammadiyah was only symbolic, in terms of affirmative action, this decision marked a significant improvement on past leaderships. The adoption of affirmative action was an opportunity for women to participate formally in directing the Muhammadiyah, including holding high-status positions.

The 46th Muktamar also revealed the fruit of the Muhammadiyah's efforts to eradicate the movement's conservative image. Unlike the 45th Muktamar in Malang, women were not subjected to abuse and hostility by the Muktimirin when they expressed their views. In Malang, people had often laughed and made cynical remarks when women spoke in a forum. In the same vein, there was no serious effort to attack people with liberal views.

THE MUHAMMADIYAH:
A MODERNIST OR CONSERVATIVE MOVEMENT?

Herman L. Beck has written an interesting article in which he asks whether the Muhammadiyah can be categorized as a modernist or fundamentalist movement. He concludes that, "the Muhammadiyah movement cannot be considered a religious fundamentalist movement, although it shares some aspects with what is commonly called Muslim fundamentalism" (Beck 2001, p. 280). The Muhammadiyah lacks the characteristics that are usually associated with fundamentalist movements, such as fanaticism, violence, intolerance, and exclusivism. However, according to Beck, like Muslim fundamentalists, the Muhammadiyah sees "the central position of Koran and Sunna as the fundamental sources of Islam" (Beck 2001, p. 291). Apparently, this aspect is one of the most important teachings in the Muhammadiyah and "one of the most significant characteristics of fundamentalism" (Beck 2001, p. 286).

Beck's conclusion can be reconsidered in the framework of the debate between conservatives and liberals. The quarrel between these groups centres on the issue of the Qur'an and the Sunna; how the Muhammadiyah members should approach them, and how the slogan of "return to the Qur'an and the Sunna" should be manifested. Going back to the sacred texts of Islam is the core religious principle of the Muhammadiyah, to the extent that this principle differentiates the organization from its traditional rival, the NU. Theoretically, the idea of *al-ruju`* (return) to the Qur'an and the Sunna can produce two contrasting religious views: regressive and progressive. For example, take the differences between Sayyid Qutb, the most important proponent of fundamentalist Islam, and Fazlur Rahman, a neo-modernist Muslim. Although both promote the idea of a return to the Qur'an and the Sunna, their proposed methods are quite different. The liberal-conservative debate is a discursive competition to decide who has the "true" and most "authentic" interpretation of the concept of *al-ruju`*. Both groups struggle with the same goal, for the sake of the glory of Islam. However, they are divided by the differences in their interpretation of Islam.

Al-Ruju` and the instrumentality of "beginning"

Since the early years of the organization, the concept of *al-ruju`* has played a vital role in the Muhammadiyah. The literal meaning of the Arabic word *al-ruju`* is "return", meaning a return to the pristine teaching of Islam as taught by the Qur'an and the prophetic traditions (the Sunna). The

Muhammadiyah adopted this idea from Muhammad ʿAbduh of Egypt, the most important proponent of Islamic modernism. ʿAbduh believes that the backwardness of the Muslim world is caused by the deviation of Muslims from the teachings of the Qurʾan and the Sunna. Islam has been polluted by innovations, superstitions, and foreign teachings. The only way to revive the religion is by returning to the teaching of the Qurʾan and the Sunna. The Muhammadiyah made this concept one of its reform strategies. By employing the concept of *al-rujuʿ*, the Muhammadiyah aims to purify Islam from any external religious elements. The conservative group believes that the Muhammadiyah should wage war on the heretical innovations and heterodox practices that flourish in Indonesian Islam. They believe that these innovations and practices are a source of weakness and trouble. Muslims have been left behind, particularly behind the West, because they are corrupting their own religion. To be successful in this world and hereafter, it is necessary for all Muslims to return to the "true", "authentic" Islam.

To understand the idea of "authentic" Islam in Muhammadiyah, it will be helpful to differentiate between the concepts of "origin" and "beginning". Muhammadiyah people consider the Qurʾan to be the main source of Islam. Whenever people from this movement talk about the origin of Islam, they refer to this text. Besides the concept of "origin", they also talk about the concept of a beginning. This concept refers to the belief that the initial years of Islam were an ideal time, and that perfect models of human behaviour and the way to be a good Muslim can be found in the deeds and words of the Prophet Muhammad. The Prophet Muhammad is also the faultless interpreter of the Qurʾan. From this follows that the history of early Islam and the life of Muhammad in particular have the status of a sacred story or myth; a story that has authority, credibility and a truth-claim (Lincoln 1989; Smith 1982).[20] Since the early years of the organization, *al-rujuʿ* has been the battle cry of the Muhammadiyah. Its supporters consider the Qurʾan and the Sunna to be the only proper bases of religious authority.

Currently, the concept of *al-rujuʿ* lies at the heart of disputes between conservatives and liberals. For the former, *al-rujuʿ* should be rendered as a literal repetition, in Mircea Eliade's conception (1968; 2005), of the origin and beginning, whereas the latter sees this literal re-enactment as no more than a way of imprisoning Muslims in a dead past. A literal imitation of the origin and beginning, instead of liberating Muslim people, will only subject them to the "terror of history" or distance them from contemporary time. For the liberals, *al-rujuʿ* should be interpreted as re-enactment of the spirit of the origin and beginning of Islam. In short, liberals aim to re-enact the origin and beginning contextually, whereas conservatives try to re-enact them as literally as possible.[21]

A few examples might help to further explain the nature of this dispute. The formalization of Islamic shari`a is a subject of enduring debate in the Muhammadiyah. Conceptually, the notion of the implementation of shari`a is similar to the Platonic dualistic conception of the world. For proponents of the formalization of shari`a, there are two laws: God's law and the law of human beings. Muslims should follow God's law written in the Qur'an, the main source of Islam. As a perfect law, human beings should gain perfection by implementing and following that law. Conservatives believe that shari`a is God's law and that it should therefore be re-enacted as accurately as possible. This, in turn, resembles Eliade's conception of double worlds. Everything in this world has an archetype in the ideal world, and human beings should try to follow this archetype. Eliade quotes Plato: "To become as like as possible to God" (Eliade 2005, p. 32). The liberals, in fact, also believe in the dualistic world, but they put human agency above the text. God's law must be understood in a human context. The spirit of God's law, for the liberal, liberates human beings. If its literal meaning contradicts the effort to liberate human beings, then it is necessary to use reason to find a correct interpretation of the text.

Polygamy is an example of the aforementioned debate. Although a survey of 128 respondents conducted in 2007 (Burhani 2007) suggested that only a few members of the Muhammadiyah practise polygamy, conservatives do not deny the legitimacy or lawfulness of this type of marriage. Liberals, on the other hand, interpret the text on polygamy as an indication of the unlawfulness of this practice, and as a step towards eradicating it completely. For liberals, polygamy is only permissible in exceptional cases. Relations with non-Muslims are another example. Based on the textual prophetic tradition and the origin (the Qur'an), the conservative group only applies the term *ahl al-kitab* (people of the Book) to Jews and Christians. Conservatives do not consider Buddhists, Hindus, or followers of indigenous religions to be *ahl al-kitab*. Therefore, male Muslims cannot marry them. For the liberals, by contrast, as mentioned in the *Tafsir tematik al-Qur'an* (2000), the meaning of *ahl al-kitab* covers all people with a holy book, and only the polytheists (*al-mushrikun*) are excluded from this concept. Conservatives also perceive the relationship between Muslims and their fellow Muslims as, using Avishai Margalit's terminology (2004), a "thick" relation, a relation that has a high level of caring. It is even thicker than the relationship between parents and children.

The liberal group wants to extend this notion of a thick relationship to include the relationship with non-Muslims.[22]

Discourse on the concept of beginning

As mentioned previously, both the liberal and conservative groups of the Muhammadiyah believe in the perfection of the origin, namely the Qur'an, and consider it mandatory for every Muslim to re-enact the beginning of Islam; namely, the deeds and words of the Prophet as the valid exemplum of the implementation of the Qur'an. However, liberals think that the conservative re-enactment of this beginning is too literal. The case of female leadership is an example of this difference. Based on the practice of the Prophet, conservatives consider female leadership to be unacceptable, or at the least, they are reluctant to acknowledge it.

As theorized by Lincoln, a number of methods can be used to change an existing social formation: modifying an existing myth, giving a new interpretation to a long-held myth, promoting a new myth, and elevating a narrative to the status of myth (Lincoln 1989). These techniques were used by the liberal faction in the Muhammadiyah when challenging conservative views on female leadership. The first step was to challenge the long-held myth on female leadership by modifying the very myths that underpinned it. Of course, neither group attempted to change the narration of the myth or insert new lines into it; such actions would only deprive them of authority and credibility. Historicity is central to the discourse on prophetic traditions or myths of beginning. Muslims believe that a hierarchical classification determines the level of authority of these traditions; this is part of the science of *hadith* that is commonly called `*ilm al-ahadith*. Because all prophetic traditions have been codified, any kind of change, deletion or insertion would be easily identifiable. In this context, modification is only possible by giving a new interpretation to the codes. This can be done by bringing the texts into contemporary contexts or by comparison: placing certain myths with other myths.

In the context of inheritance, for instance, liberal Muslims say that men and women lack equality due to the inferior status of women in Muhammad's day, in Arabia in the 6th century C.E. At that time, women were considered to be property that could be sold, inherited, and killed. Muhammad engaged in a revolutionary struggle by elevating the status of women and granting them the right to inherit. It is this spirit of liberation that should be preserved by Muslims, not the amount of inheritance specified in the text. Interpreting this in a contemporary context, liberals propose that women should be allowed the same inheritance rights as men. The issue of female leadership can be interpreted in the same way.

The second step in challenging the myth of beginning is to invent new myths or to elevate lesser narrations to the status of myth. The new myths developed by the liberal group are based on the beginning of the Muhammadiyah and the stories of its founding father, Ahmad Dahlan. Recalling his endeavours is a way to re-enact the origin and beginning of Islam in the Indonesian context. Dahlan was one of many interpreters of the Qur'an and the Sunna in Indonesia. For the liberal group, the re-enactment of the origin and beginning of Islam in Indonesia serves as a model for contemporary times. At the same time, the same model challenges the conservative approach to the origin and beginning of Islam. In the liberal view, by agreeing to be a member of the Muhammadiyah, one is also required to follow the example of the founder, or at least to take his spirit as a model of behaviour.

Currently, there is no consensus among Muhammadiyah members on the interpretation of the beginning and origin, or how to re-enact it. Although all members of the Muhammadiyah still refer to the same two main source texts (the books of prophetic traditions and the Qur'an), they interpret these sources differently. Each group has its own interpretation and believes in the truth of its reading, and makes truth-claims. The question of relations with non-Muslims is among the examples. Based on their interpretation of the Qur'an and the prophetic tradition, as elaborated in *Tafsir tematik al-Qur'an* (2000), the liberal believes that he or she is allowed to greet non-Muslims on their religious days, to join them in celebrating their religious days, and to offer a place for non-Islamic religious rituals. On these issues, the conservative holds opposite views.

The history of Islam suggests that these debates may never end; it is hard to imagine agreement on a single, united interpretation of the Qur'an and the Sunna. To overcome the multiple interpretations within the Muhammadiyah and to bring the movement back to its original mission, the liberals promote new myths by exploring the beginning of the movement. In this context, Dahlan's tolerant stance toward non-Muslims is used by the liberals as a model of how contemporary members of the Muhammadiyah should behave towards people from different religions.

The effort to create new myths is motivated by the hope that members of the Muhammadiyah can develop alternative models for their behaviour, in addition to the models supplied by early Islam. These new models, in the liberal view, are more appropriate to the contemporary Indonesian socio-cultural context, while they do not actually contradict the origin and beginning of Islam. By developing a narrative about the beginning of the movement, liberals want to make the Muhammadiyah more progressive and modern, which was the original goal of the movement. Liberals intend to convince people that they are walking in the footsteps of the movement's founders, and that they are therefore the legitimate heirs of the Muhammadiyah.

Abdul Munir Mulkhan and Sukidi Mulyadi are among the proponents of such liberal views. They have often referred to the beginning of Muhammadiyah as a prototype for contemporary practices within the movement. They mention, for instance, that Dahlan was both a pluralist and a liberal and a Muslim par excellence (Mulyadi 2005). Furthermore, in his article on "Max Weber's Remarks on Islam" (Sukidi 2006), Mulyadi describes the early years of the Muhammadiyah as a beautiful and excellent time, which deserves to be replicated in the Muhammadiyah's present and future. The failure on the part of Muhammadiyah members to re-enact the examples from the beginning has made the movement lose its progressiveness. To solve contemporary problems progressively, members of the Muhammadiyah must inject this original spirit into the practical life of the movement (Sukidi 2006). Instead of applying the well-known motto "back to the Qur'an and the Sunna" as a battle-cry, the liberal group follow the slogan, "back to Ahmad Dahlan and his interpretation of the Qur'an and the Sunna", as the principal way to liberate people from the Muhammadiyah's current problems.

Of course, the effort to create new myths or modify long-held beliefs does not automatically succeed or win people's support. Many people oppose the liberal stance, adamantly protect the old myths and condemn the new myths and models of re-enactment. The conservative group in the Muhammadiyah, for instance, rejects the idea that the early years of the movement should be taken as the model for the present. In debates with the liberals, they rarely refer to the formative period of the movement to justify their reasoning. Although some proponents of this group are very familiar with the historical record of the founding fathers and their deeds, they rarely refer to them in their arguments. This group appears to reject the authority of the historical narrative of the Muhammadiyah, and considers it to be less authoritative than the origin of Islam. They even try to undermine the authority of these myths. One of the leaders of the conservative faction, Yunahar Ilyas, firmly expressed his indifference to the heritage of the founding fathers when he said "this is the Muhammadiyah, not the Dahlaniyah", (Muhammadiyah.or.id 2008).

The conservative group believes that the Muhammadiyah is merely an Islamic organization that works in various areas of life (society, economy, politics, religion). The teaching and doctrines of the Muhammadiyah are but one interpretation of Islam, and the main sources of the Muhammadiyah are the Qur'an and the Sunna. Therefore, the true model for the Muhammadiyah is not the life of Ahmad Dahlan, but the life of Muhammad. Conservatives believe that the examples and religious interpretation from Ahmad Dahlan can be set aside, if needs be; they do not have the status of myth. While they have credibility, they do not have authority. Therefore, they wish to return not to Ahmad Dahlan and the beginning of Muhammadiyah, but to Islam and the early time of this religion.

The myth of the beginning is employed by the liberal and conservative groups with the intention of persuading people that their ideas are correct, and winning their support for their programmes. By quoting Ahmad Dahlan on the importance of maintaining a good relationship with non-Muslims and engaging in peaceful dialogue with Christian priests, liberals want to implement these policies in present-day Indonesia. Conservatives, by contrast, find it difficult to employ the historical narratives of Ahmad Dahlan as a model for their imagined future of the Muhammadiyah. Therefore, they go far back to the origins of Islam as the exemplary model. By referring to the prophetic tradition, they attempt to convince members of the Muhammadiyah that their interpretation is sounder.

Name-calling as bid for support

In the context of the conflict between liberals and conservatives in the Muhammadiyah, name-calling is often employed to undermine the group's opponent. There is no grey area: each group identified itself as "good", whereas its opponent is "bad". When the liberals described themselves as "progressive" or "liberal", they created an imaginary picture of people who held the opposite values — the "bad" group. Calling themselves "defenders of shari`a" or "Muslim *kaffah*" (perfect Muslims) implied that their adversaries were offenders against shari`a and corrupt Muslims. In this section, we show how name-calling played a role in the clash between the liberal and conservative groups in the Muhammadiyah.

The most common names used by liberal group are "progressive", "liberal", "inclusive", "pluralist", and "moderate". With these terms, liberals want to show that they are forward-looking, and that they have a progressive view of history: this age is better than our father's age, our father's age was better than our grandfather's age, and so forth. Being liberal, they wish to show that they are able to free themselves from the oppression of certain dogmatic schools in interpreting the Qur'an, and that they are liberated from the prison of ideology. Being inclusive and pluralist means that they have friendly and peaceful relations with non-Muslims, and are eager to cooperate with them. By promoting moderate values, they want to show that they are not on the extreme right or extreme left, and neither blindly fanatical nor excessively liberal. On several occasions, this group has coined derogatory names for their rivals, including "literalist", "scripturalist", "conservative", "fundamentalist", and "purist".

In response, the conservative group has shown its discomfort with the names and labels employed by liberals. They are more comfortable calling themselves "Muslims", without any adjective, "Muslim *kaffah*" (perfect Muslims), "purist/puritan Muslim", or even "defenders of the *shari`a*". Just like the liberal group, they also engage in negative name-calling. An effective way of stigmatizing one's opponent is to adopt alternative explanations for well-known acronyms; thus JIMM became the *Jaringan Iblis Muda Muhammadiyah* (network of young devils in the Muhammadiyah). Nicknames recalling horrible diseases were also effective; the liberals were said to be tainted with "*Sipilis*" (syphilis), short for *Sekularisme, Pluralisme, Liberalisme*. This is reminiscent of the "TBC" label given to traditional believers by an earlier generation: *Takhayul, Bid'ah, Churafat* (irrational beliefs, heterodoxy and superstition).

By naming themselves and their opponents, each side classified society and created hierarchies. Of course, each group placed itself at the top of the hierarchy. The names given to opponents usually had insulting and derogatory meanings. By labelling their opponents conservatives, literalists, fundamentalists, or even purists, liberals have tried to portray their opponents as having retrograde characteristics, such as being backward-looking, overly literal in their understanding of the Qur'an, fanatical, and hostile towards non-Muslims.

Using names in this way has been a vehicle for winning support. By describing the JIMM as a network of young devils, the conservative group hopes that people will avoid it. The JIMM, it implies, is just like the devil in that it persuades human beings to leave the true path and take the path to hell. Likewise, in calling the liberal group "*Sipilis*", the conservatives try to convince people that the threat posed by the liberal group was like the threat of the chronic sexual disease syphilis. Like a disease, the liberals would torture Muhammadiyah and Islam and subject them to long suffering, just like syphilis does to the human body. The 45th Muktamar suggested that the members of the Muhammadiyah had bought the conservatives' arguments and abandoned the liberals; it seemed that their campaign had been effective.

THE DILEMMAS FACING THE MUHAMMADIYAH

In the wake of the attacks of 11 September 2001 on the World Trade Center and the Pentagon in the U.S., and the subsequent bomb blasts in Indonesia perpetrated by radical Muslims, some studies described the Muhammadiyah as a Wahhabi-influenced movement (Desker 2002; Michel 2003; Mansurnoor 2004). Wahhabism, often associated with the religious ideology of Osama bin Laden, has commonly been portrayed as a puritanical, fanatical, anti-modern, extreme, backward-looking, literal and scriptural movement, characterized by indoctrination and intolerance (Abou El Fadl 2005; Schwartz 2003; Rashid 2000, 2002).

Although the accusations of a connection between the Muhammadiyah and Wahhabism are not new, the events of 9/11 gave them new, more negative connotations. The success of the conservative group in taking over the leadership of the Muhammadiyah at the 45th Muktamar has often been perceived as a shift within this movement in a more conservative direction. The detention of a Muhammadiyah activist, Joni Achmad Fauzani, on charges of harbouring a terrorist suspect in the Pacet district of Mojokerto regency, East Java (Nugroho 2005), gave a further boost to allegations of close relations between the puritans and Islamist and conservative movements. The kinship relations between a number of Islamic hardliners, such as the Bali bomber, Amrozi, and Muhammadiyah families have sometimes been used to link fundamentalism with the Muhammadiyah's doctrines and teachings.

However, connecting the conservative group with fundamentalism is anachronistic in some respects. Historically, orthodoxy or puritanism, as pursued by both the conservative and liberal groups since the establishment of the Muhammadiyah, has not led to radical action. Puritanism is only one of the elements of Muhammadiyah's reformism. Another important element of the movement is modernism. The spirit of Ibn Abdul Wahhab and Ibn Taymiyyah has been blended with the rational and modernist spirit of the Egyptian scholar Muhammad 'Abduh (1849–1905), and brought together in an Indonesian context. 'Abduh's thought allowed the Muhammadiyah to rationalize and modernize religious beliefs through educational programmes and social activities (Ali 1989; Lubis 1993; Fuad 2004). Therefore, accusing the Muhammadiyah of turning into fundamentalist movement because some of its members have a conservative interpretation of the concept of al-ruju` is not convincing.

However, the conflict between conservatives and liberals reveals that this movement faces serious ideological dilemmas. Some of its members considered the Muhammadiyah to have been either too soft or too hard. Some Muhammadiyah members regarded the movement's attitude towards puritanism as inconsequential and superficial. They left the organization and joined more radical and fundamental movements, such as Hizb ut-Tahrir (HT), the Front for the Defense of Islam (FPI), the Council of Indonesian Holy Warriors (MMI), and the Lasykar Jihad (Jihad Troops). They felt that their interests no longer tallied with the Muhammadiyah's programmes. As a result, it is not surprising that many members of radical movements in Indonesia were originally members of the Muhammadiyah. The town of Lamongan in East Java, for example, is a strong base for both the Muhammadiyah and the Islamic radical movement (several of the Bali bombers lived there).

In the opposing camp are those Muhammadiyah members who believed that the movement showed extreme rightist tendencies, and that the Muhammadiyah had become too puritanical, rigid, and conservative. As such, the movement no longer reflected their interests and visions. They did not consider the Muhammadiyah to be a safe sanctuary for liberal thought. Even the JIMM, sometimes associated with the JIL by its opponents, was not considered to be sufficiently liberal. For this reason, some liberal activists with Muhammadiyah backgrounds, such as Lies Marcoes, a woman activist, and Hamid Basyaib, one of the founders of the JIL, prefer not to be associated with the Muhammadiyah.

The move by some of the members of the Muhammadiyah to the left or the right would, theoretically, free the movement of extremists. Those remaining would supposedly be moderate in religious orientation; people in the middle with limited appetite for ideological confrontation. On this basis, one might suppose that the movement is now on a steady, untroubled course. However, the current situation suggests that such a conclusion would be incorrect. The tug of war between two opposite groups, the conservatives and the liberals, is an indication that ideologically, the movement is unstable. The penetration of the Tarbiyah into the Muhammadiyah is a further example of the instability of the organization's ideology. The Muhammadiyah was unable to stand firm when challenged by an external ideology. What is normally called the moderate ideology of the Muhammadiyah is not absolutely moderate; it is perhaps more appropriate to call it "shakily moderate". In this context, Abu Bakar Ba'asyir, the former spiritual leader of the MMI, cynically called Muhammadiyah a *banci* (hermaphrodite) or "sexless" movement.

Indonesian Muslim scholars, such as Azyumardi Azra (2005), have attempted to trace the concept of moderate Islam from an Arabic term, *al-din al-wasat* ("the middle religion"), in the Quran (2, p. 143). The term *wasat* or "middle" has various connotations. In explaining this term, Syariati (1979) and Hamka (1994) state that Islam lies between Christian esoteric-extremism and Jewish exoteric-extremism. The majority of contemporary Muslim scholars believe that the true Islam lies at the mid-point between extreme liberalism and extreme Islamism or conservatism (Mazrui nd.; Azra 2005). A person or organization is considered moderate, as that term is commonly understood in Indonesia, if they remain in the mid-position between liberalism and conservatism.

The Muhammadiyah is among those Indonesian organizations that claim to be moderate Islamic organizations, occupying this median position between liberals and conservatives. This position is regarded by some within the organization as an ideal position (Syamsuddin 2005), yet it is probably this position that has made the movement susceptible to different orientations in recent years. For this movement, the meaning of moderate is close to the meaning of pragmatic.

The moderation of the Muhammadiyah often creates ambivalence towards religious belief, practice, and ethics. In terms of understanding the Quran and Islamic teaching, the Muhammadiyah has tended to adopt a scriptural and uncritical position, but when implementing that understanding, the Muhammadiyah has tended to use practical reason based on the sociological context. Polygamy is one of the striking instances of this moderate-in-practice-but-conservative-in-belief attitude. The leaders of the Muhammadiyah believe, for instance, that polygamous marriage is allowed by Islam, but, for practical reasons, they do not practise it.

The moderate religious stance of the Muhammadiyah might be related to its socio-historical context. The organization is renowned for its social activities, such as establishing and maintaining health, welfare and educational institutions. Because of its focus on real and practical activities, Muhammadiyah members are less interested in a sophisticated theological and philosophical discourse; instead, they want a simple, applicable approach that can be implemented in the present-day context. In this respect, a moderate position is more appealing. Furthermore, in terms of its socio-economic position, the majority of the Muhammadiyah leaders are civil servants (*Pegawai Negeri Sipil*) from the middle classes. And one of the characteristics of the middle classes is their preference for stability (also a characteristic of civil servants), and dislike of disorder and confusion (Jones 1984). As a result, they tend to adopt a safe — that is, a moderate — position.

CONCLUSION

Theoretically, both the conservative and the liberal groups in the Muhammadiyah accept the Qur'an and the Sunna as examples of perfect Muslim behaviour. However, they differ on the interpretation and implementation of the concept of *al-ruju`*. The conservatives render and re-enact the Qur'an and the Sunna as literally as possible, whereas the latter tend towards the spirit of these texts. Various issues, including pluralism, liberalism and Islamism, have become subject to competing interpretations. Using various methods, both groups try to win support for the argument that their interpretation is the "true", "authentic" Islam.

The conflict reveals two important issues in the Muhammadiyah: generation and ideology. Ideologically, this movement has been called upon to answer numerous contemporary problems that were never addressed by its founding fathers. Currently, the Muhammadiyah seems to lack a solid ideological basis to adequately and effectively answer the needs of its members. This failure to solve problems makes it easy for external actors to intervene in and influence this movement. In many instances, the organization has failed to communicate its philosophy and ideology to people. The old slogan of fighting TBC (*Takhayul, Bid'ah* and *Churafat*; irrational belief, unorthodoxy and superstition), for instance, has no relevance to contemporary society. The contemporary market does not accept the training and educational systems used by this organization. Consequently, this has created a further, generational problem. In view of this, it is telling to recall a metaphor used by one of its members: "The people want hamburgers, but Muhammadiyah always sells *gethuk* [Javanese traditional food made from a sweet, steamed loaf of pounded cassava]."

Notes

[1]   As an illustration of the pride some Muhammadiyah members took in the victory of Wahhabism, see for example, Hamka (1946), pp. 10 and 108. The Muhammadiyah regarded it as an honour to be known as the Indonesian version of Wahhabism. When the Muhammadiyah held its 25th Congress in Banjarmasin (South Kalimantan) in 1932, the welcoming call of the local people was "*Wahabi! Wahabi! Wahabi!*". See Gani (1932), p. 14.

2   Sufism, and the practices that are often associated with it, such as visits to saints' graves and prayers to invoke intercession or supernatural support, are considered *shirk*, a deviation from pure monotheism. Reformists also reject the asceticism and renunciation of the world that are often associated with Sufism.

3   *Taqlid*: following established rulings by schools of Islamic law, the *madhhab*.

4   Formerly known as the Association for Teenagers (*remaja*) of Muhammadiyah, or IRM. Since 2007, the IRM has been known by its original name, IPM.

5   First, the participants of the *Tanwir* elect 39 Muhammadiyah national leaders. Second, the participants of the Muktamar elect 13 of these 39 leaders, who work together as a team to lead the Muhammadiyah at the national level. They decide who will be the president of the Muhammadiyah. Although it is not automatic, normally this position is given to the person who has the most votes.

6   During the last term of leadership of the Muhammadiyah (2005–10), two *Tanwirs* were held. Under the previous leadership (2000–05), there was a *Tanwir* every year.

7   Abdullah is a professor of Islamic philosophy and currently the rector at the State Islamic University (UIN) of Yogyakarta. Mulkhan is also a professor of Islamic education at the UIN of Yogyakarta, specializing in the mystical and cultural dimensions of religion. Rahardjo is a professor of economics and a civil society activist.

8   Unlike the central office of the Muhammadiyah, in some areas, including East Java and Sulawesi, students and youth of the Muhammadiyah were inclined towards the conservative camp. During the emergence of the Tarbiyah movement, they were likewise more influenced by this movement and its ideology derived from the Muslim Brotherhood than by the Muhammadiyah's teachings.

9   Numerous issues of *Tabligh* magazine, the main publication used by puritans to oppose progressives, were dominated by articles that aggressively condemned progressive views. *Tabligh* 02/07/February 2004, *Tabligh* 02/08/March 2004, and *Tabligh* 02/09/April 2004 are examples of issues that were dedicated to attacking progressives. Among the headlines of *Tabligh* magazine were: "*Laisa Minna: Liberalisme, Pluralisme, Inklusivisme*" (No longer part of us [i.e., of Muhammadiyah and Islam]: liberalism, pluralism and inclusivism), "*Virus Liberal di Muhammadiyah*" (the virus of liberalism in Muhammadiyah), "*Islam Liberal Meracuni Kalangan Muda*" (the idea of liberal Islam poisons a young generation [of Muhammadiyah]) and "*Talbis Iblis Fiqih Pluralis*" (Devil's Deception: pluralist Islamic law). *Talbis Iblis* was initially the title of a book by al-Ghazali, and the same title was later used by Ibn al-Jawzi against al-Ghazali to express his hostility towards *tasawwuf*.

10   Personal communication, 27 April 2007.

11   As recorded by Abduh Hisyam, one of the participants.

12 Usually, old mosques in Indonesia were built by a prominent Muslim figure or a Muslim missionary, or there was at least a single person with a dominant idea or share in that mosque. This is different from newer mosques, which tend to be built by communities surrounding the mosques, and these communities have an equal share in them. In the Muhammadiyah, a mosque is considered the property of the organization if the land is formally endowed to the Muhammadiyah, or was built by Muhammadiyah members, or built at Muhammadiyah institutions.

13 Mulkhan does not mention the name of the political party to which he refers in his article, but it seems likely to be the PKS. The article was entitled "Sendang Ayu: Pergulatan Muhammadiyah di Kaki Bukit Barisan" (2006).

14 The argument that 'Id al-Adha should be on a Thursday was based on the fact that the ninth day of Dhu al-Hijja, the twelfth month of the Islamic lunar calendar, when pilgrims spend the afternoon in Arafah (*wuqf*) in Mecca, was on a Wednesday.

15 The author attended this Tanwir and conducted field research there, including interviews for this chapter.

16 Personal communication, 29 April 2007.

17 To defend the Muhammadiyah from the challenge of the Tarbiyah, Haedar Nashir, a religious scholar and one of the national leaders of the Muhammadiyah who holds a Ph.D. in sociology from Gadjah Mada University, devoted himself to write a number of books that explicate and reveal the ideological differences between the Muhammadiyah and the PKS. Among these books is his 2007 Ph.D. dissertation titled *Gerakan Islam Syariat: Reproduksi Salafiyah Ideologis di Indonesia* (Shari'a movements: the reproduction of Salafi ideology in Indonesia) (2007). This book and his other works on the Tarbiyah movement have been used by the Muhammadiyah in its cadre training, to empower them against the challenge of the PKS.

18 Personal communication, 30 April 2007.

19 The political issues which obstructed his chance for being elected as president for the 2010–15 leadership term were the alleged support from Amien Rais, who was out of favour with the Muktamirin, and rumours that the Indonesian government was also behind his challenge to Din Syamsuddin, who had been hostile to the Indonesian president, Susilo Bambang Yudhoyono, on several occasions. These two issues seemed counterproductive to his run for the presidency of the Muhammadiyah.

20 In this chapter, the word "myth" is used in this sense.

21 Using Muhammad 'Abid al-Jabiri's epistemological approach (2009) that consists of three categories: al-bayan (indication), al-'irfan (illumination), and al-burhan (demonstration), the system of knowledge that shapes and dominates the puritan mind can be classified in al-bayani framework that emphasizes the relation between lafz and ma'na (expression and meaning), while the progressives try to adopt al-burhan that relies on the use of reason.

22   This inclusive paradigm was introduced as a critique of puritan individuals who, in certain cases, do not care for non-Muslims simply because of their religion. For example, if a Muslim converts to another religion, he will not receive inheritance from his family and, in some cases, his kinship relationship with his family is cut off. The inclusive paradigm is very different from that governing radical Islam. Radical Muslims, such as Osama bin Laden, put a higher value on their relations with fellow Muslims than on those with relatives. When waging *jihad* in the sense of war, for instance, people do not need to ask their parents' permission. People can abandon their parents if they hinder a Muslim from waging *jihad.*

References

Abou El Fadl, Khaled. *The Great Theft: Wrestling Islam from the Extremists.* New York, NY: HarperSanFrancisco, 2005.

Ali, A. Mukti. *Ijtihad dalam Pandangan Muhammad Abduh, Ahmad Dakhlan, dan Muhammad Iqbal* [Ijtihad in the view of Muhammad Abduh, Ahmad Dakhlan, and Muhammad Iqbal]. Jakarta: Bulan Bintang, 1989.

Azra, Azyumardi. "Salafisme Wasathiyyah". *Republika,* 13 October 2005.

Baidhawy, Zakiyudin. "Intelektualisme Muhammadiyah: Masa Depan yang Terpasung" [Muhammadiyah's Intellectualism: The Imprisoned Future]. *Maarif* 1, no. 1 (2006): 20–23.

Basri, Agus. *Muhammadiyah, Facing the Global Era: Profile of Muhammadiyah.* Jakarta: Bank Persyarikatan Indonesia, 2003.

Beck, Herman. "The Borderline Between Muslim Fundamentalism and Muslim Modernism: An Indonesian Example". In *Religious Identity and the Invention of Tradition,* edited by Jan Willem van Henten and Anton Houtepen. Assen: Koninklijke Van Gorcum, 2001.

Boy, Pradana. "In Defence of Pure Islam: The Conservative-Progressive Debate within Muhammadiyah". M.A. thesis submitted to the Faculty of Asian Studies, Canberra, Australian National University, 2007.

Burhani, Ahmad Najib. "JIMM: Pemberontakan Generasi Muda Muhammadiyah Terhadap Puritanisme and Skripturalisme Persyarikatan" [JIMM: The Rebellion of the Young Generation of Muhammadiyah against Puritanism and Scripturalism of Muhammadiyah]. In *Reformasi Gerakan Keislaman Pasca Orde Baru: Upaya Merambah Dimensi Baru Islam.* Jakarta: Balitbang Depag RI, 2006.

————. *Pluralism, Liberalism, and Islamism: Religious Outlook of the Muhammadiyah Islamic Movement in Indonesia.* MSc thesis. Manchester, University of Manchester, 2007.

Desker, Barry. "Islam and Society in South-East Asia after 11 September". *Australian Journal of International Affairs* 56, no. 3 (2002): 383–94.

Diani, Hera. "Muhammadiyah Seen Leaning Toward More Conservative Bent". *Jakarta Post,* 3 February 2006.

Dwyer, Jim. *Two Seconds under the World: Terror Comes to America — The Conspiracy behind the World Trade Center Bombing.* New York: Crown Publishers, 1994.
El-Baroroh, Umdah. "Gus Dur: Saya Simpati pada Liberalisme Ulil" [Gus Dur: I Sympathize with Ulil's Model of Liberalism]. Islamlib.com, 16 December 2005. Online at <http://islamlib.com/id/index.php?page=article&id=943> (accessed 14 July 2007).
Eliade, Mircea. *Myth and Reality.* New York: Harper & Row, 1968.
————. *The Myth of the Eternal Return: Cosmos and History.* Bollingen series 46. Princeton, NJ: Princeton University Press, 2005.
Fathuri. "Masjid NU dan Muhammadiyah Direbut Organisasi Lain" [The NU and Muhammadiyah's Mosques taken over by Other Organizations]. *Syir'ah*, 12 February 2007. Online at <www.syirah.com> (accessed 14 July 2007).
Fuad, Muhammad. "Islam, Modernity and Muhammadiyah's Educational Programme". *Inter-Asia Cultural Studies* 5 (2004:) 400–14.
Gani, Radjab. *Goebahan Congress Moehammadijah ke 24 di Kalimantan (Bandjarmasin).* Soerabaja: M.S. Ibrohim, 1932.
Gillespie, Piers. "Current Issues in Indonesian Islam: Analysing the 2005 Council of Indonesian Ulama Fatwa No. 7 Opposing Pluralism, Liberalism and Secularism". *Journal of Islamic Studies* 18, no. 2 (2007): 202–40.
Hamka. *Moehammadijah Melaloei Tiga Zaman.* Soematera Barat: Markaz Idarah Moehammadijah, 1946.
————. *Tafsir Al-Azhar, Juzu' II.* 3rd ed. Jakarta: Pustaka Panjimas, 1994.
Hefner, Robert W. "Modernity and the Challenge of Pluralism: Some Indonesian Lessons". *Studia Islamika* 2, no. 4 (1995): 21–45.
————. *Civil Islam: Muslims and Democratization in Indonesia.* Princeton: Princeton University Press, 2000.
————. "Global Violence and Indonesian Muslim Politics". *American Anthropologist* 104, no. 3 (2002): 754–65.
Hidayatullah. "Syafii Maarif Larang 'Hukum' Anak Muda Muhammadiyah". Online at <http://www.hidayatullah.com/index.php?option=com_content&task=view&id=2046&Itemid=0> (accessed 13 November 2005).
al-Jabiri, Muhammad `Abid. *Naqd al-`Aql al-`Arabi (1): Takwin al-`Aql al-`Arabi* [A critique of Arabic reason (1): The Formation of Arabic Reason]. Beirut: Markaz Dirasat al-Wahda al-`Arabiyya, 2009.
Jones, Garth N. "Executing Priority National Development in Indonesia: Program Innovation of the Junior Minister". *International Journal of Public Administration* 6, no. 3 (1984): 345–66.
Latief, Hilman. "Post-puritanisme Muhammadiyah: Studi Pergulatan Wacana Keagamaan Kaum Muda Muhammadiyah 1995–2002" [the post-puritanism of Muhammadiyah: A Study of the Religious Discourse of Young Members of Muhammadiyah in 1995–2002]. *Jurnal Tanwir* 1, no. 2 (2003): 43–102.
Liddle, R. William. "Year One of the Yudhoyono-Kalla Duumvirate". *Bulletin of Indonesian Economic Studies* 41, no. 3 (2005): 325–40.

Lincoln, Bruce. *Discourse and the Construction of Society: Comparative Studies of Myth, Ritual, and Classification*. New York: Oxford University Press, 1989.

Lubis, Arbiyah. *Pemikiran Muhammadiyah dan Muhammad Abduh: Suatu Studi Perbandingan* [The Thought of Muhammadiyah and Muhammad Abduh: A Comparative Study]. Jakarta: Bulan Bintang, 1993.

Majelis Tarjih dan Pengembangan Pemikiran Islam (MTPPI). *Tafsir Tematik al-Qur'an Tentang Hubungan Sosial Antarumat Beragama* [Thematic Exegesis of the Qur'ann on Interfaith Social Interaction]. Yogyakarta: Pustaka SM, 2000.

Mansurnoor, Iik Arifin. "Response of Southeast Asian Muslims to the Increasingly Globalized World: Discourse and Action". *Historia Actual On-Line* 5 (2004): 103–11.

Margalit, Avishai. *The Ethics of Memory*. Cambridge, Mass: Harvard University Press, 2004.

Mazrui, Ali A. "Liberal Islam versus Moderate Islam: Elusive Moderation and the Siege Mentality". Online at <http://igcs.binghamton.edu/igcs_site/dirton27.htm> (accessed 25 June 2007).

Michel, Tom. "Implications of the Islamic Revival for Christian-Muslim Dialogue in Asia". *International Journal for the Study of the Christian Church* 3, no. 2 (2003): 58–76.

Muhammadiyah.or.id. "Yunahar: ini Muhammadiyah, bukan Dahlaniyah" [Yunahar: this is Muhammadiyah, not Dahlanism], 2 September 2008. Online at <http://www.muhammadiyah.or.id/index.php?option=com_content&task=view&id=893&Itemid=2> (accessed 30 April 2008).

Mulkhan, Abdul Munir. "Sendang Ayu: Pergulatan Muhammadiyah di Kaki Bukit Barisan". *Suara Muhammadiyah*, 2 January 2006.

Mulyadi, Sukidi. "Muhammadiyah Liberal dan Anti-liberal" [Liberal and Anti-liberal Muhammadiyah]. *Majalah Tempo*, vol. XXXIV, no. 20 (11–17 July 2005).

Nakamura, Mitsuo. *The Crescent Arises over the Banyan Tree: A Study of Muhammadiyah Movement in a Central Javanese Town*. Yogyakarta: Gadjah Mada University Press, 1983.

Nashir, Haedar. *Gerakan Islam Syariat: Reproduksi Salafiyah Ideologis di Indonesia* [Shari'a Movement: Reproduction of Salafy Ideology in Indonesia]. Jakarta: Pusat Studi Agama dan Peradaban Muhammadiyah, 2007.

Noer, Deliar. *The Modernist Muslim Movement in Indonesia, 1900–1942*. East Asian Historical Monographs. Singapore: Oxford University Press, 1973.

Nugroho, I.D. "Muhammadiyah Activist Held for Allegedly Harboring Terror Suspect". *Jakarta Post*, 11 June 2005.

Pasha, Musthafa Kamal. "Islam Liberal Meracuni Kalangan Muda" [Liberal Islam Poisons the Young Generation]. *Tabligh* 2, no. 8 (March 2004).

Peacock, James L. *Purifying the Faith: The Muhammadijah Movement in Indonesian Islam*. Menlo Park, Calif.: Benjamin/Cummings Pub. Co., 1978*a*.

———. *Muslim Puritans: Reformist Psychology in Southeast Asian Islam*. Berkeley: University of California Press, 1978*b*.

Qodir, Zuly. "Bangkitnya 'Second' Muhammadiyah" [Revival of the Second Muhammadiay]. *Kompas Daily*, 20 November 2003.

Rashid, Ahmed. *Taliban: Militant Islam, Oil, and Fundamentalism in Central Asia*. New Haven: Yale University Press, 2000.

——. *Jihad: The Rise of Militant Islam in Central Asia*. New Haven: Yale University Press, 2002.

Schwartz, Stephen. *The Two Faces of Islam: Saudi Fundamentalism and Its Role in Terrorism*. New York: Anchor Books, 2003.

——. "In the Shadow of a Fatwa: Religious Life Bustles in the World's Largest Muslim Nation: Pluralistic Indonesia". *Weekly Standard*, 9 July 2005.

Shiraishi, Takashi. "Indonesian Politics: Current Situation, Future Outlook". *Asia-Pacific Review* 6, no. 1 (1999): 57–75.

Sivan, Emmanuel. "Why Radical Muslims Aren't Taking Over Governments". *Middle East Review of International Affairs* 2, no. 2 (1998): 9–16.

——. "The Clash within Islam". *Survival* 45, no. 1 (2003): 25–44.

Smart, Ninian. *Dimensions of the Sacred: An Anatomy of the World's Beliefs*. Berkeley: University of California Press, 1996.

Smith, Anthony L. "The Politics of Negotiating the Terrorist Problem in Indonesia". *Studies in Conflict and Terrorism* 28, no. 1 (2005): 33–44.

Smith, Jonathan Z. *Imagining Religion: From Babylon to Jonestown*. Chicago Studies in the History of Judaism. Chicago: University of Chicago Press, 1982.

Sukidi [Mulyadi]. "Max Weber's Remarks on Islam: The Protestant Ethic among Muslim Puritans". *Islam and Christian-Muslim Relations* 17, no. 2 (2006): 195–205.

Sulistiyanto, Priyambudi. "Muhammadiyah, Local Politics and Local Identity in Kotagede". *Sojourn* 21, no. 2 (2006): 254–70.

Syamsuddin, Dien. "Pemikiran Islam Muhammadiyah dalam Pusaran Zaman" [Muhammadiyah Islamic Thought in the Pasage of Time]. In *Pemikiran Muhammadiyah: Respons Terhadap Liberalisasi Islam*. Surakarta: Muhammadiyah University Press, 2005.

Syariati, Ali. *On the Sociology of Islam: Lectures*. Translated from the Persian by Hamid Algar. Berkeley: Mizan Press, 1979.

Tabligh. "Laisa Minna: Liberalisme, Pluralisme, Inklusivisme" [These Do Not Belong to Us: Liberalism, Pluralism and Inclusivism]. *Tabligh* 2, no. 7 (February 2004*a*).

——. "Virus Liberal di Muhammadiyah" [The Virus of Liberalism in Muhammadiyah]. *Tabligh* 2, no. 8 (March 2004*b*).

——. "Talbis Iblis Fiqih Pluralis" [The Devil's Deception: Pluralist Islamic Law]. *Tabligh* 2, no. 9 (April 2004*c*).

Tuhuleley, Said, ed. *Reformasi Pendidikan Muhammadiyah: Suatu Keniscayaan* [Muhammadiyah Educational Reform, An Inescapable Project]. Yogyakarta: Pustaka Suara Muhammadiyah, 2003.

5

THE POLITICS OF SHARIAH: THE STRUGGLE OF THE KPPSI IN SOUTH SULAWESI

Mujiburrahman

Since the fall of Soeharto in 1998, Indonesia has been developing into a democratic polity. Indeed, it could be argued that Indonesia is the most democratic Muslim country in the world today. At the same time, the country has witnessed the emergence of various Islamic groups, particularly those with militant tendencies, in the public sphere. Although many of these groups have their roots in the long history of Indonesian Islam, their emergence today cannot simply be understood as the resurfacing of previously repressed movements. Local, national and transnational socio-political developments in past decades have helped to shape the current character, ideologies and strategies of these groups.

In many parts of Indonesia, Islam has played a significant role in politics. Between the fourteenth and the eighteenth centuries, several local kingdoms in the Archipelago adopted Islam as the official religion. During the colonial period and the revolutionary war following the declaration of independence in 1945, Islam was often used as a symbol of opposition to foreign enemies. However, the members of the Indonesian elite who wrote the 1945 Constitution disagreed with one another concerning the position of religion in the state. One group opted for the implementation of Shariah by the state, while another preferred a national secular state. After a series of debates and negotiations, they finally reached a compromise, stating that

Indonesia is based on *Ketuhanan Yang Maha Esa* (Belief in One Supreme Godhead), a principle which vaguely defines the state as neither secular nor Islamic, but more or less religious.

Looking at Indonesian history, we find that both secular nationalist and Islamic-oriented groups challenged this compromise, but none of them succeeded in imposing their views. The new political developments after the fall of Soeharto helped to reopen the debates on this ideological issue, but the same basic compromise was somehow maintained. During a session of the People's Consultative Assembly (MPR) in 2002, there were calls from some of the Islamic parties to insert a clause on Shariah implementation by the state into the Constitution, but they failed to gain sufficient political support in parliament, and the early compromise was ultimately reaffirmed.[1]

In the early years of the Soeharto period, after the failure to insert a clause on Shariah implementation in the Constitution during a session of the Provisional People's Consultative Assembly (MPRS) in 1968, certain regional governments took the initiative to introduce Shariah locally through regional regulations. The Soeharto regime, however, soon instructed the regional governments to withdraw the regulations (Mujiburrahman 2006, pp. 114–18). After the fall of Soeharto, regional demands for the implementation of Shariah re-emerged, particularly in some Muslim majority areas. Robin Bush observes that 52 of 470 districts and municipalities in Indonesia have issued "regional Shariah regulations" (Bush 2008, p. 176). Although post-Soeharto government policy on regional autonomy maintains that policies on religion are still controlled by the central government, local politicians have apparently found a way to issue religiously influenced regulations. Moreover, the special autonomous status given to Aceh province in 1999, allowing the implementation of Shariah, has made certain Muslim groups hopeful that the same status could also be granted to other regions.[2]

One of the regions where the political struggle to implement Shariah by the state has been strong is South Sulawesi, where the so-called "Preparatory Committee for the Implementation of Shariah" (KPPSI) was established. In this article, I will analyse the KPPSI's political struggle by exploring two main issues. First, I will look at the history of religion and politics in this region. This historical background will help us to better understand the present proponents and opponents of the KPPSI and their respective discourses. Second, the KPPSI's political successes and failures will be closely examined in the context of the many socio-political factors shaping the region.

RELIGION AND POLITICS IN SOUTH SULAWESI: A HISTORICAL OVERVIEW

According to statistics from 2000, Islam is the religion of 89.2 per cent of the total population of South Sulawesi, while with 9.4 per cent, Christians constitute the most significant religious minority. Other small religious minorities include followers of Hinduism (0.7 per cent), Buddhism (0.3 per cent), and other beliefs (0.4 per cent). The last category probably includes followers of Confucianism and local beliefs, but it is likely that some of the latter are officially registered as Hindus. In terms of ethnicity, the Buginese constitute the largest group (41.9 per cent), followed by the Makassarese (25.43 per cent), Toraja (9.02 per cent) and Mandarese (6.1 per cent) (Suryadinata, Arifin and Ananta 2003, pp. 27, 110, 116, 122, 127, 135). The majority of the Buginese, Makassarese and Mandarese are Muslim, while the majority of Torajan are Christian.

The first Christians of South Sulawesi were converted by Dutch missionaries during the first three decades of the twentieth century.[3] The majority of the province's Christians are ecumenical Protestants, followed by Catholics and Evangelicals. The province's Christians are centred in Toraja region, and the rest are dispersed throughout South Sulawesi. Being the capital city of the province, Makassar has also been home to many Christians over the years, at least since the Dutch colonial period. The city houses the Academy of Theology of Eastern Indonesia (STT Intim) and the Academy of Theology Jaffray (the former is ecumenical and the latter is evangelical). In addition, there is a small Catholic University in Makassar, known as Atma Jaya. The Christian missionaries also worked among the Buginese and Makassarese, which eventually resulted in the establishment of the South Sulawesi Church (GKSS). Over time, however, the GKSS became more heterogeneous, because Christian Javanese migrants also joined this church.

Islam was accepted in South Sulawesi much earlier than Christianity. Christian Pelras, a French scholar who has studied Bugis culture for many years, explains that the conversion of the Bugis, Makassar and Mandar people to Islam began in the period between 1605 and 1611. It was a top-down, formal conversion: the local rulers declared their conversion to Islam and instructed their subjects to follow them (Pelras 2001, pp. 211–66). The subsequent process of Islamization was not a smooth one. Although to a certain degree, the local rulers successfully implemented Shariah and local customs side by side, this policy was not really acceptable to some of the local Muslim scholars, who wanted stricter adherence to Islamic teachings. In the seventeenth century, Syekh Yusuf, who had returned home from studying in Mecca, attempted to introduce a more orthodox form of Islam, but this was rejected by the ruler. Yusuf's influence on the region, however, continued to develop, especially through the Khalwatiyah Sufi order.[4]

In general, those Muslims who studied Islam from orthodox sources, either with puritan or traditionalist orientations, would become reformers when they were confronted with local religious beliefs and practices. These efforts at reform apparently became more intensive and effective when Muslim leaders established Islamic organizations to spread Islam in the region. In 1923, a local reformist Muslim organization called al-Shirat al-Mustaqim was established by Abdullah Ibn Abdurrahman. Three years later, it united with the Muhammadiyah, the national Muslim reformist organization (Mattulada 1976, pp. 55–56). A Muslim traditionalist group was also organized under the leadership of Haji As'ad, who established a school called Madrasah Arabiyah Islamiyah (MAI) in Wajo in 1932. After his death in 1952, the school was renamed As'adiyah after him. In 1947, one of As'ad's disciples, 'Abdurrahman Ambo Dalle, established a traditionalist organization called Darud Da'wah wal Irsyad (DDI) (Ramli, Ahmad and Ch. 2006, pp. 77–95, 104–5). The national Muslim traditionalist organization, Nahdlatul Ulama (NU), had also established a branch in this region by the early 1950s. While the reformist al-Shirat al-Mustaqim decided to unite with the Muhammadiyah in 1926, however, the DDI and the NU remained separate organizations (Kabry 1983, pp. 4–12). The emergence of Muslim organizations with their respective social activities, particularly in the field of education, undeniably helped to further the spread of Islam, and at the same time, the leadership of aristocrats as formal Shariah officials had been gradually replaced by new Muslim leaders who had a significant following in society.[5]

THE SUKARNO PERIOD:
THE REBELLION OF KAHAR MUZAKKAR

The proclamation of independence on 17 August 1945 in Jakarta, followed by the revolutionary war (1945–49) against the returning Dutch, had a deep impact on the people of South Sulawesi. While the aristocrats were divided between those who supported the Republic and the pro-Dutch, the majority of them favoured the Dutch. There were a few nationalist movements in this region, but they were not strong. The opposition to the Dutch came from young people from rural areas, led by local aristocrats or Muslim leaders. Due to their lack of arms and skills, the Dutch were easily able to destroy the opposition. There were attempts by the republican army to send troops from Java to South Sulawesi, but these were also unsuccessful (Harvey 1989, pp. 106–52).

Nevertheless, the revolutionary war finally ended; at the Roundtable Conference in The Hague in November 1949, the Dutch handed over political authority to the Indonesian government. This political turn heralded a new period of political struggle in South Sulawesi. A particular problem at this time was that the army was beset by internal conflict. During the war, there had been many irregular armed groups consisting of young people with no formal military training. After the war was over, the Army Headquarters in Jakarta started a programme of reorganization and demobilization of these irregular units, by integrating some of them into the army and returning the rest to society. This programme did not work smoothly, and even helped to create regional rebellions by those who felt neglected and disappointed.

Abdul Kahar Muzakkar was probably the most important leader of the rebel movement in South Sulawesi.[6] After completing his elementary education in his hometown of Lanipa, near Palopo, in 1938 Kahar continued his studies at the Muhammadiyah teacher training school, Muallimin, in Solo, Central Java. He returned home in 1941 before finishing his studies.[7] In Palopo, besides teaching in a Muhammadiyah school, he was active in a Muhammadiyah boy scouts organization, Hizbul Wathan. Kahar denounced the existing feudal system, which brought him into conflict with local aristocrats. As a result, these aristocrats expelled Kahar from his hometown. In May 1943, Kahar once again left for Solo. Initially he established a small trading company there, but after the proclamation of independence, he became attracted to the independence movement. As a young, brave and energetic activist, he eventually became involved in the guerrilla war against the returning Dutch in Java.

In 1945, Kahar was assigned by Army Headquarters to free a large number of prisoners in Nusakambangan, most of whom had Bugis and Makassar ethnic backgrounds. These prisoners were then trained as troops under Kahar's leadership. After the revolutionary war, Kahar, now a lieutenant colonel, wanted to become the military commander of South Sulawesi, but the Army Headquarters denied him this position. Moreover, the government reorganization programme refused to include most of Kahar's troops in the national army, particularly due to their lack of formal military training. There were several attempts to negotiate between Kahar and the republican army, but they were ultimately unable to strike a compromise.

In 1952, Kahar and his followers went into hiding in the forest and started a rebellion against the Republic. Most observers think that this rebellion was simply a result of the abovementioned disappointments. The historian Anhar Gonggong, however, adds that Kahar's rebellion is also related to the Bugis cultural code of honour called *siri'*, meaning that personal honour should be defended at all costs (Gonggong 2004, pp. 413–31). As a man educated in a Muhammadiyah school and opposed to the aristocracy, it is perhaps not surprising that Kahar decided to ally with the Darul Islam movement, which had already been proclaimed in August 1949 by Kartosuwiryo in West Java. Kahar then became the commander of the Fourth Division of the Islamic Army of Indonesia (TII).

Over time, rather than following Kartosuwiryo, Kahar developed his own movement and theory of Islamic statehood. In certain areas under his control, Kahar tried to implement Shariah according to his own interpretation. Perhaps Kahar asked for advice from a few *ulama*, who either eagerly or reluctantly supported him. One of these was the leader of the DDI, Ambo Dalle, who was kidnapped by Kahar in 1955 and only released with the help of the Indonesian army in 1963 (Kabry 1983, pp. 112–13).[8] In general, Kahar's political ideology was a kind of Islamic socialism, which emphasized economic welfare and egalitarianism, in addition to the obligations of his followers to perform daily prayers, fasting and almsgiving (*zakat*). Kahar also implemented Shariah criminal law on killing, adultery and theft.

After years of war, Kahar was eventually killed by the Indonesian army in February 1965. The people of South Sulawesi have divergent memories and impressions of the Kahar rebellion. It seems that many of the movement's victims were Christians, but many Muslim families were also robbed by Kahar's troops. Contrary to Dijk's observation that Kahar treated Muslims and Christians equally well (Dijk 1981, p. 194), my informants said that Kahar used to force Christians to convert to Islam.[9] On the other hand, for his followers and sympathizers, Kahar is undoubtedly remembered as a heroic, pious Muslim leader.

In addition to Kahar's rebellion, another important development was the rise of Muslim political power. Although Kahar did not allow his followers to vote in the elections of 1955, many people in South Sulawesi did vote. Interestingly, religious parties received the most votes in South and Southeast Sulawesi in these elections. The largest party was the Muslim reformist party, Masyumi (40 per cent), followed by the traditionalist NU

(14.3 per cent) and Partai Sarekat Islam Indonesia (PSII) (10.3 per cent). The Christian party, Parkindo, also got a high vote (10.6 per cent) (Feith 1957, pp. 78–79). Perhaps religious parties did so well in the elections due to "anti-communist and anti-Javanese" feeling among the population. Another likely reason was that the elections had demanded the support of the masses, and Islamic leaders apparently had more contact with the people than the other elites. Whatever the reason, the result of the elections indicates that the leaders of Islamic groups gained political power in independent Indonesia.

Muslim politicians from the Masyumi party in this region suffered a setback in 1960 when Sukarno imposed a national ban on the party, partly because some of its leaders had been involved in a rebellion, and partly because the party had opposed Sukarno's idea of Guided Democracy, which had been introduced in 1959 following ideological deadlock in the Constitutional Assembly. Islam, however, continued to influence society, because Islamic private institutions, especially in the field of Islamic propagation, education and social work, continued to develop regardless of the political changes.[10] At least two Muslim private universities were founded in this period, namely the Indonesian Muslim University (UMI), established in 1958, and a Muhammadiyah University, established in Soppeng in the early 1960s. Moreover, in the 1960s, an important Muslim organization called the Ikatan Masjid dan Mushalla Muttahidah (IMMIM) was established (Mattulada 1976, pp. 88–99). IMMIM activists included traditionalist and reformist Muslims, and its programmes were mostly in the field of education, with a "modern" orientation.

It is also noteworthy that during this period, the NU took part in the government, representing the religious element of Sukarno's "synthetic" ideology of religion, nationalism and communism (Nasakom). Magenda notes that in South Sulawesi, the NU was unable to attract former Masyumi sympathizers, and by the end of the Guided Democracy period, the nationalist PNI had become the largest party in the region (Magenda 1989, p. 675). However, this does not mean that the NU made no contribution to the development of Islam at all. During this period, the NU became responsible for the Ministry of Religious Affairs, which was in turn responsible for administering Islamic education. At this time, a number of Islamic schools were founded in South Sulawesi with the support of the Ministry. The Ministry also appointed Islamic religious teachers to teach in public schools. In 1962, the Faculty of Shariah was founded in Makassar, as a branch of the State Institute of Islamic Studies (IAIN)

Sunan Kalijaga of Yogyakarta. Three years later, with the establishment of three other Islamic Faculties, on 10 November 1965, the Ministry established the IAIN Alauddin in the city (Mattulada 1976, pp. 74–75; 92–94).[11]

THE SOEHARTO PERIOD: THE GOLKAR POWER BASE

Given the fact that reformist Muslim groups were politically marginalized during the Guided Democracy period, it is understandable that in the months following the abortive coup of 30 November 1965, Muslim reformist organizations such as the Muslim Students Association (HMI) and the Indonesian Islamic Students (PII) were quite active in demonstrations criticizing the government and demanding the banning of the Indonesian Communist Party (PKI). Along with other student organizations, HMI activists were among the prominent figures in the army-backed United Students Action Front (KAMI).

Moreover, as a region in which Masyumi had been the strongest party in the elections of 1955, it is not surprising that HMI activists from Makassar joined the KAMI. The chairman of the HMI in Makassar, Jusuf Kalla, who was to become the Indonesian Vice-President in 2004, was elected the KAMI's most senior leader in the region. Jusuf Kalla was a student at the Faculty of Economics of Hasanuddin University.[12] In this period, the young Kalla was also the General Secretary of the IMMIM (Wawer 1974, p. 228). In addition to his organizational skills, the fact that Kalla's father was Hadji Kalla, well-known in the region as a pious Muslim businessman, probably helped to strengthen his position as the leader of the two organizations.

When the PKI and Sukarno had been defeated and the New Order regime of Soeharto consolidated itself, reformist Muslims once again felt politically marginalized. The army apparently considered reformist Muslims to be its most dangerous political rivals. When reformist Muslims demanded the rehabilitation of their party, Masyumi, Soeharto refused. Likewise, when a new party called Parmusi was established, Soeharto did not allow the former leader of Masyumi to be its chairman. Muslim leaders became more disappointed when Soeharto decided to ally with the Christians, especially Catholic activists.

This political frustration was also felt in South Sulawesi, as shown by one particular incident in 1967. The incident was related to the tensions between Muslim and Christian leaders in Jakarta. Christian politicians proposed a "Question on religious freedom" to the government, in response to the closing of a newly built Methodist Church in Meulaboh, Aceh. In response to this, Muslim politicians also proposed a "Question on foreign aid for religious institutions". The Muslims argued that the Christians were using foreign money to convert poor Muslims. This became a hotly debated issue in Muslim and Christian newspapers.

In Makassar, HMI and PII activists also became obsessed with this issue. The incident itself was triggered by a statement made by a Christian teacher, who told his students that Muhammad only married nine women and lived in adultery with other women, and that he was a stupid person because he was illiterate. The HMI's local radio stations and a few local newspapers took this statement as an indication that local Christians were hostile to Islam. On the evening of 1 October 1967, groups of people started to attack Christian buildings and facilities in the city. Some Christians were also physically attacked. A few days later, the Catholic Students Association (PMKRI) of Makassar declared its withdrawal from the KAMI. As explained above, in Makassar, the KAMI was dominated by HMI activists, and the activists of the PMKRI believed that they had been responsible for the attack. The incident soon became a national issue in Jakarta.[13]

Later on, when the new regime started marginalizing Islamic groups, some prominent Muslim figures in South Sulawesi took an accommodating stance. The career of Jusuf Kalla might be taken as an illustration of this. After finishing his undergraduate studies in 1968, Kalla decided to go into business rather than directly involve himself in politics. He became the CEO of his father's company, PT. Hadji Kalla. Kalla's success in business is said to have been due to his ability to build good relations with the governing party, Golkar. He became active in the Indonesian Chamber of Commerce and Industry (KADIN), known for its support for Golkar, and from 1985 to 1998 he was the chairman of KADIN of South Sulawesi. It was apparently through this link that he returned to politics in 1987 as a member of the MPR, and he was re-elected in 1992, 1997 and 1999.

A similar accommodating strategy was taken by the traditionalist Muslim leader of the DDI, Ambo Dalle, who decided to support Golkar from the elections of 1977 onward.[14] In the 1971 elections, Golkar won 78.36 per cent of the vote,[15] while in the 1977 elections, this figure increased to 85.18 per cent. Magenda notes that besides heavy-handed intervention by the military in the elections, the support from DDI *ulama* was another significant factor in increasing Golkar's share of the vote (Magenda 1989, p. 822). In return, the government gave financial support to the DDI's institutions. The large reformist Muslim organization, the Muhammadiyah, never formally encouraged its members to vote for any particular party, but since many of its members were civil servants, they probably also voted for Golkar. Likewise, when the NU withdrew from partisan politics in the mid-1980s and cut its formal ties with the Islamic party, the PPP, several prominent NU activists, including some in South Sulawesi, conveniently became Golkar politicians.

Thus, while the number of votes cast for the Islamic party, the PPP, decreased sharply from 14.0 per cent in 1977 to 7.3 per cent in 1997, votes for Golkar gradually increased from 85.2 per cent in 1977 to 91.6 per cent in 1997 (Biro Humas KPU 2000, pp. 90, 111, 134, 157, 179). In fact, South Sulawesi became Golkar's strongest regional power base. This was not only because of support from local Muslim leaders, but also because several national figures of South Sulawesi origin became important national Golkar leaders, especially after the 1990s. Aside from Jusuf Kalla, the most important figure was probably former President B.J. Habibie, who was born in Parepare, South Sulawesi. He gained renown as a genius with a Ph.D. degree in aerospace engineering from the University of Aachen in Germany, and he was Minister for Research and Technology in Soeharto's cabinets from 1974 to early 1998. There is no doubt that the Bugis people were very proud of him. Habibie's popularity increased when he became the chairman of the Indonesian Association of Muslim Intellectuals (ICMI) in 1990, and then Vice-President and President of Indonesia in 1998–99.

Political forces and alliances in South Sulawesi developed in parallel with the political ideas promoted by the state. During the Soeharto period, the Ministry of Religious Affairs was not generally controlled by the NU, as it had been under Sukarno, but by reformist Muslims promoting a non-ideological view of Islam. Therefore, all educational institutions under the Ministry, from elementary to university level, were influenced by a non-ideological conception of Islam. The IAINs, and especially the Postgraduate Programme that was established at the IAINs of Jakarta and Yogyakarta in the early 1980s, played key roles in the New Order's policy of promoting a modern, non-ideological conception of Islam. Many lecturers at the IAIN Alauddin of Makassar received grants to take this postgraduate programme.

On the other hand, the view of Islam as a political and economic ideology continued to exert strong appeal, in spite of state repression of dissent. It was especially influential among Muslim students, and the campus mosques of certain universities — more often than not secular universities — became centres of radical Muslim student activism. One of these mosques was the Sultan Alauddin Mosque, located in the housing complex of the UMI in

Makassar. Abdurrachman Basalamah, who was to become the leader of the KPPSI, played an important role here in the 1980s. Basalamah was a local cadre of the Indonesian Council for Islamic Propagation (DDII), which had been established in 1968 by the former Masyumi leader, Mohamad Natsir, to develop and propagate Islamic ideology. One of the DDII's programmes provided training in Islamic thought for Muslim lecturers employed at secular universities; these lecturers then became trainers for Muslim students in their universities. In 1974, the DDII launched a programme to develop mosques in secular universities as centres for Islamic propagation among students (one of these was the Sultan Alauddin Mosque in Makassar). The DDII's programmes in the South Sulawesi region were coordinated by Basalamah (Furkon 2004, pp. 126–27).

In the mid-1980s, the Soeharto government issued a regulation requiring all social and political organizations to adopt Pancasila as their basis, and for this to be written in their respective constitutions. Religious organizations that would have normally put religion as their basis had difficulties accepting this regulation. Under government pressure, however, most Muslim organizations decided to obey the regulation, with the exception of two reformist Muslim student organizations, the HMI and the PII. PII activists were united in disobeying the regulation. Unlike the PII, the HMI was divided on whether to disobey the government. Those who rejected the regulation later declared themselves the "HMI-MPO" (*Majelis Penyelamat Organisasi*, Council of Saviours of the Organization).[16] The group that accepted the regulation then became called "HMI Dipo", referring to its office in Jalan Diponegoro, Jakarta.

Following the policy of its central leadership, the PII's Makassar branch was united in rejecting the regulation. Aswar Hasan, who was to become the Secretary General of the KPPSI, was among the PII leaders in Makassar in this period (Juhanis 2006, p. 154). Because of its refusal to follow the government's policy, the PII was banned by the government. In Makassar, the PII did not engage in any public activities until the demise of the New Order, but it kept its office and leadership, and held regular informal meetings (*silaturrahmi*) for its activists.[17]

The split in the HMI central leadership also affected the HMI in Makassar. The chairman of the Makassar branch in 1987–88 was the son of Kahar Muzakkar, Abdul Aziz Kahar, who at that time was a student at the Fishery Faculty at Hasanuddin University. In response to the controversy over the Pancasila regulation, Aziz unsurprisingly took a position against the government. When the HMI-MPO separated itself from the main organization, he was appointed chairman of the HMI-MPO for the

Eastern Indonesia region in 1988–89.[18] It is also important to note that Tamsil Linrung, a man of South Sulawesi origin who was to become an important politician after the fall of Soeharto, was one of the central leaders of the HMI-MPO. Nurman Said, who was an HMI activist in Makassar in this period, notes that there was a "fight" between the HMI-MPO and HMI-Dipo activists to control the HMI office in the city, and the HMI-MPO won. Nurman also states that most of the HMI-MPO activists studied in secular universities, while most of the HMI-Dipo activists were students of the IAIN Alauddin.[19]

Moreover, remnants of Kahar Muzakkar's DI also still existed in South Sulawesi in various forms. A clandestine group around Sanusi Daris, who had been one of Kahar's Ministers, was perhaps the most significant of these. After Kahar was killed, Daris remained in hiding, living in a cave. When he came out of hiding in 1982, he was soon arrested and put on trial. He was eventually released due to the inter- vention of General M. Jusuf, a prominent army officer of Bugis origin. During his trial, Daris explained that he continued to promote Kahar's ideology, not through armed rebellion but by isolating himself and his followers from the life of the people of the Republic (Juhanis 2006, p. 117). According to a report by the International Crisis Group (ICG), after his release, Daris developed contacts with the secret "Ngruki network" that was, the report claimed, Al Qaeda in Southeast Asia. It is unclear, however, whether he ever developed a DI-like organization. Daris settled in Sabah in East Malaysia and died there in 1988 (ICG 2002, pp. 10–11).

Another important former DI figure was Ahmad Marzuki Hasan, who established an Islamic school called Pesantren Darul Istiqamah in 1970. There are branches of this school in various places in South Sulawesi, namely in Maros, Sinjai, Makassar, Gowa and Bulukumba. In his Ph.D. thesis, Hamdan Juhanis notes that Islamic ideology was not formally included in the curriculum of this pesantren, but that it was in the oral teaching of Marzuki Hasan, who romanticized the DI's ideals of an Islamic state. When the New Order government issued the regulation on Pancasila as the sole basis for organizations, the Foundation of the Pesantren Darul Istiqamah refused to compromise. Consequently, it was prevented from receiving any government funding (Juhanis 2006, p. 152). During the years 1983–2003, Darul Istiqamah was led by Arief Marzuki, the son of Marzuki Hasan. In 2003, Arief Marzuki handed the leadership over to his son, Mudzakkir M. Arief, who is a graduate of Imam Muhammad Ibn Sa'ud University,

Riyadh. Under Mudzakkir's leadership, Darul Istiqamah received financial support from Saudi Arabia and Kuwait.[20]

The last figure to be mentioned here is Fathul Muin Daeng Magading, a Muhammadiyah leader in Makassar who was in charge of the organization's cultural centre in that city, Ta'mirul Mu'minin. Fathul Muin was himself never directly involved in the DI movement, but he openly sympathized with it in his speeches in the late 1960s (Juhanis 2006, p. 153). One of his militant cadres was a certain Muhsin Kahar (no relation of Kahar Muzakkar). In 28 August 1969, there was a mass protest against the lottery in Makassar, in which the protesters ransacked and torched kiosks selling lottery tickets and other places of alleged gambling. The police suspected Muhsin Kahar of being the man behind the protests. To escape from the police, he migrated to Balikpapan, where he eventually established an Islamic school named Hidayatullah and changed his name to Abdullah Said.[21] Another important cadre of Fathul Muin was Agus Dwikarna, who was later to become the commander of the paramilitary wing of the KPPSI, Lasykar Jundullah (Juhanis 2006, p. 153). In 1988, several years after his death, Fathul Muin's followers established a foundation named after him. Ten years later, in 1998, its name was changed to the Islamic Unity Foundation, Yayasan Wahdah Islamiyah (YWI). In 2002, the YWI transformed itself into a membership-based association with the same name (Wahdah Islamiyah, or WI), concentrating on education and social work.[22] The WI is formally much more Salafi-oriented, being dominated by graduates of Madinah University in Saudi Arabia.

THE REFORMATION ERA: ISLAM AND THE RISE OF DEMOCRACY

At the time of writing, more than a decade has passed since the fall of Soeharto's government and the beginning of the Reformation Era. There have been significant changes in Indonesia, particularly in terms of socio-political development. References to Islam have become ubiquitous in Indonesian politics. As noted earlier, during the Soeharto period, the ideological view of Islam was suppressed; some of its proponents were killed, others languished in jail for many years, while those who remained at large had to be extremely circumspect and secretive in spreading their ideas and mobilizing their followers. Now, with the rise of democracy in the Reformation Era, these people have much more freedom to express their political ideologies and to develop their organizations.

Like other provinces, South Sulawesi witnessed the re-emergence of groups and movements promoting Islamic ideologies, and in news reporting, the province has often been mentioned as having one of the strongest movements in support of Shariah-based legislation. However, if we look at the results of the 1999 elections in the region, Golkar was still the most powerful party, obtaining 66.5 per cent of the total vote, while the Islamic parties, the PPP and the PBB, only received 8.4 per cent and 2.9 per cent respectively. Another Islamic party, the Justice Party (PK), obtained so few votes that it had no seats in parliament.[23] The fact that there was much more freedom in the elections of 1999 means that the strong support for Golkar was genuine. One important factor in the Golkar victory was probably the figure of B.J. Habibie, who was appointed President following Soeharto's resignation.[24] By supporting Golkar, many people in South Sulawesi probably hoped that this party could help Habibie to stay in office.

In the 2004 elections, however, Golkar's share of the vote decreased to 43.3 per cent, though it remained the largest party, holding 34 of 75 seats in the province's regional parliament. A number of Golkar voters apparently switched to a new party called the United Nationalist Democratic Party (PPDK), which had been established by Ryaas Rasyid, a well-known national figure of South Sulawesi origin. This party gained 6.7 per cent of the vote (eight seats). Former Golkar voters also appear to have switched to the PAN and the PKS. The PAN almost doubled its share of the vote, obtaining 6.5 per cent as opposed to 3.5 per cent in 1999; its association with the Muhammadiyah may have been a factor. The gains of the Islamist party the PKS, the successor of the PK, were more remarkable: from less than 1 per cent, it increased its share to 7 per cent of the vote in 2004, obtaining eight seats in the provincial parliament.[25]

These election results give an indication of the dynamics of Islam and politics in this region. Indeed, the public debates on the role of Islam in politics have become much more open since 2000. This was the year when the first *Kongres Ummat Islam* (Congress of the Islamic Community) was convened in Makassar, at which the KPPSI was established. Similar congresses were held in 2001, 2005 and 2010.

THE POLITICAL STRUGGLE OF THE KPPSI

In the preceding paragraphs, I presented an historical overview of the development of religion, particularly Islam, and politics in South Sulawesi up to the present day. In the light of this historical account, the following sections will cover the political struggle of the KPPSI from its inception in 2000 up to the general elections of 2009. In this regard, I will look at the successes and failures of the political struggle of the KPPSI and analyse the discourses developed by its proponents and opponents.[26]

The KPPSI rank and file

The rank and file of the KPPSI is diverse; it includes former student activists from the PII and the HMI-MPO, activists from Islamic organizations such as the DDII, the Muhammadiyah, the NU and the WI, and academics at secular and Islamic universities in Makassar. Only a few of them have direct links with Kahar Muzakkar's Darul Islam. Therefore, it is probably wrong to presume that all of these persons share the same political ideology and agenda. Nevertheless, they have at least one thing in common: they see that the current democratic system provides a good political opportunity for proponents of Shariah implementation.

The KPPSI originated from the Islamic Community Forum (FUI) established in 1999 by a number of activists, most of whom had graduated from Hasanuddin University and the UMI in Makassar (Ramli, Ahmad and Ch. 2006, pp. 138–39; Juhanis 2006, p. 161). The name of the organization indicates its exponents' dream to unite all Muslim forces. The FUI was led by the former rector of the UMI, Abdurrachman A. Basalamah. One of the FUI's activists, Agus Dwikarna, had studied at UMI (but did not graduate), and it is likely he came to know Basalamah there. Later on, Agus was also known as a DDII activist, while Basalamah, as noted earlier, was a DDII cadre who had become the Coordinator of Islamic Propagation in South Sulawesi during the New Order period. Perhaps it was also the DDII that linked other young FUI activists with Basalamah. The FUI then organized a few meetings with prominent local Muslim leaders from the Muhammadiyah and the NU to discuss the issue of the implementation of Shariah.

Perhaps it is important to note that Basalamah, along with other prominent FUI activists such as Agus Dwikarna and Aswar Hasan, also participated in the founding Congress of the Majelis Mujahidin Indonesia (MMI) in Yogyakarta in August 2000. At that Congress, Abu Bakar Ba'asyir was elected as the *amir* (commander) of the MMI, and Basalamah as the chairman of its economic council. Aswar Hasan was elected as a member of the council of the politics of Shariah, and Agus Dwikarna as the secretary of the executive council (Turmudi and Sihbudi 2005, pp. 204–05). It is unclear to me how close the relations between the leader of MMI, Abu Bakar Ba'asyir, and the FUI activists were. Irrespective of whether they had been in contact during the Soeharto period or not, they were united by two factors: first, they all had long track records as activists in reformist Muslim organizations (PII, HMI and DDII); and second, they adopted the implementation of Shariah as their main political objective.

Not long after the MMI Congress, in October 2000, the FUI activists organized the Congress of the Islamic Community in Makassar. Unsurprisingly, leaders of the MMI, such as Abu Bakar Ba'asyir and Irfan Suryadi Awwas, were among the participants. Nevertheless, Turmudhi and Sihbudi claim that there is no convincing evidence that this Congress had organizational links with the MMI Congress in Yogyakarta (Turmudi and Sihbudi 2005, p. 205). The Congress also invited Abdul Hadi Awang, the leader of a Malaysian Islamic party, the PAS, to talk about his party experiences in applying Shariah in his country. Another important figure was A.M. Fatwa, a member of the national parliament for the PAN. Fatwa is a well-known Bugis figure who spent many years in jail as a critic of the Soeharto regime. Other participants of the Congress included the Deputy Governor of South Sulawesi and various Muslim leaders and activists from the region (Pradadimara and Junedding 2002).

The Congress decided to establish the KPPSI and elected A. Basalamah as the chairman of its Consultative Council. Prominent local figures were listed as members of the Council, including Achmad Ali, Professor of Law at Hasanuddin University; Sanusi Baco, a prominent traditionalist Muslim leader (NU) and the chairman of the Indonesian Ulama Council (MUI) of South Sulawesi; and Djamaluddin Amin, the provincial Muhammadiyah leader. Although Baco did not renounce his membership of the Council, he complained that he had not been notified beforehand. A more serious complaint was heard from the leader of the DDI, Muis Kabry, who was also included in the Council without even being notified. In fact, he strongly opposed the KPPSI, because for him it was nothing less than a reincarnation of the DI that had kidnapped the founder of the DDI, Ambo Dalle, in the 1950s (Juhanis 2006, pp. 165–66).

The DI is strongly associated with the KPPSI due to the fact that a former DI figure, Marzuki Hasan, is one of the members of its Advisory Council. Moreover, Abdul Aziz Kahar was elected as the Chairman of the Executive Council. As noted above, Aziz was the Chairman of the HMI-MPO for Eastern Indonesia in 1988–89. Having completed his tenure in the

HMI, he joined the Pesantren Hidayatullah. As noted above, Hidayatullah was established by Abdullah Said (Muhsin Kahar) and has its centre in Balikpapan. Said is thought to be a strong sympathizer of Aziz's father, the legendary DI leader, Kahar Muzakkar. After some time, Said then authorized Aziz to establish and lead a Hidayatullah pesantren in Makassar.[27] After the fall of Soeharto, the political stage was open to Aziz, allowing him to play a central part in initiating the FUI and then the KPPSI.

Besides Aziz, other former FUI activists who had joined the HMI-MPO and the PII during their student days, like Aswar Hasan and Kalmudin, were elected as the Secretary General and Deputy Secretary of the Executive Council respectively. Several WI activists also became functionaries of the KPPSI.[28] As noted above, the WI is currently dominated by Salafi-oriented graduates of Madinah University, but the organization also has historical sympathies with Kahar Muzakkar's DI. One of the WI activists is Muhammad Ikhwan, who became the KPPSI's Secretary for Research and Development.

Overall, support for the KPPSI comes mostly from urban-based, university-educated males (Pradadimara and Junedding 2002). In the Consultative Council, we find Muslim academics with backgrounds in both secular formal education and Islamic education. Basalamah and Mansyur Ramli are among the former, while Jalaluddin Rahman and Muin Salim, who joined the KPPSI later, are among the latter.[29] It is perhaps also important to note that both Basalamah and Muin Salim are former rectors of the UMI and the IAIN respectively. By the time of the KPPSI's establishment, Basalamah was the chairman of the UMI Foundation, and Mansyur Ramli was the rector of the UMI. This was the reason why several UMI lecturers joined the KPPSI. Jalaluddin Rahman was a professor at the IAIN Alauddin, but later he became a politician for the PPP, an Islamic party that publicly demands Shariah implementation by the state.

As explained above, the most prominent leaders of the NU and the Muhammadiyah (Sanusi Baco and Djamaluddin Amin) were appointed to the KPPSI's Consultative Council. It should be noted, however, that their involvement in the KPPSI does not mean that the NU and Muhammadiyah formally supported the KPPSI. Another leader of the Muhammadiyah, Nasaruddin Razak, who was the executive chairman of the Muhammadiyah of South Sulawesi in 2000–05, did not support the KPPSI.[30] Likewise, neither did the late Harifuddin Cawidu, the executive chairman of the NU in the South Sulawesi region, support the KPPSI.[31] Both Nasaruddin and Harifuddin rejected the enforcement of Shariah by the state, preferring instead the so-called cultural approach, which implies that people are taught to understand and practise Islamic teachings without coercion by the state.

Ahmad Faisal observes that while most Islamic scholars in Indonesia are civil servants, the majority of KPPSI activists in the Executive Council are not.[32] They are mostly young, upwardly-mobile university graduates. When KPPSI branches were established in all of the districts of South Sulawesi, these were chaired by "university graduates with engineering, medical or social sciences degrees" (Pradadimara and Junedding 2002). Aswar Hasan has said that Muslim activists from secular universities played a central role in bridging conflicting opinions within the organization, especially between graduates of the IAIN and graduates of religious universities in the Middle East.[33] Aswar's statement presumably reflects the ideal role that these activists want to play, although the reality could be different.

In any case, the KPPSI's leaders and supporters are not a monolithic group. Besides the different backgrounds of the members of the Consultative Council and Executive Council, there is also another wing of the KPPSI called Lasykar Jundullah (Army of God Militia). Lasykar Jundullah is a paramilitary wing, which provided security at the Islamic Community Congress of the KPPSI. It was originally established in Solo in 1999, with Muhammad Agung Abdullah Hamid as its commander, a businessman of South Sulawesi origin. In 2002, Agus Dwikarna assumed leadership of Lasykar Jundullah (Turmudi and Sihbudi 2005, pp. 205–6). According to an ICG report, Lasykar Jundullah activists include former followers of Sanusi Daris and HMI-MPO activists (ICG 2002, p. 21). Hamdan Juhanis adds that members of Lasykar Jundullah include *remaja masjid*, members of mosque-based youth groups (Juhanis 2006, p. 180). In addition, the Lasykar Jundullah was reportedly sent to fight against the Christians in Maluku during the war in 2002. Moreover, the Lasykar has been involved in violent action against places and persons considered immoral according to Islamic codes.[34]

Shariah implementation: why and how?

Proponents of the implementation of Shariah in South Sulawesi have various arguments for justifying their cause. One of these is their ideological understanding of Islam. Muin Salim, who has been the chairman of the Consultative Council of the KPPSI since 2004, explained in an interview that Islam is almost identical to statecraft. He lamented that some Muslims understand Islam as a set of ritual prescriptions, sidelining its socio-political dimensions. In fact, he claimed, Islam is a comprehensive social and political system. This is indicated, argued Salim, not only by the fact that Prophet Muhammad was the head of state in Madinah, but also by the political positions held by other prophets before him, such as Yusuf (Joseph), Dawud (David) and Sulaiman (Solomon), mentioned in the Bible and the Qur'an. The role of the state, he explained, is to develop and maintain moral and spiritual guidance dictated by religion. In other words, Shariah should be implemented by the state. Yet, when I asked him about the state ideology, Pancasila, he said that Pancasila is not opposed to Islam, so he can accept the current Indonesian state.[35] Other KPPSI figures, such as Marzuki Hasan, Arif Liwa, Arsyad Lanu and Husein Hamzah, however, still maintain the necessity of an Islamic state (Faisal 2004, pp. 179–85).

Another reason adduced by KPPSI activists for their advocacy of Shariah implementation is grounded in a reading of local history. M. Sirajuddin, the Vice-Secretary of the Consultative Council, wrote that the rulers of the Makassarese kingdoms of Tallo and Goa, I Malingkang Daeng Manyonri (Sultan Abdullah Awwalul Islam) and I Mangerangi Daeng Manrabbia (Sultan Alauddin), converted to Islam in the early seventeenth century and declared Islam the official religion. For him, these two kings, followed by the rulers of the Bugis kingdom of Bone, should be considered the founding fathers of the implementation of Shariah in South Sulawesi. In their kingdoms, they successfully integrated Islam and customary law, known as *Pangngadereng* for Buginese and *Pangadakkang* for Makassarese. In 150 years, Islam became deeply embedded in the culture of the Bugis, Makassarese and Mandarese, the peoples of South Sulawesi. Thus, he said, the implementation of Shariah as promoted by the KPPSI is simply a continuation of local history (Siradjuddin 2004).

The socio-economic and political crisis since the late New Order has been also used by KPPSI supporters as a reason for adopting Shariah law. In this regard, they developed what can be called a "metaphysical" theory of crisis. They said that Indonesian Muslims have undergone an economic, social, political and moral crisis because they do not follow the teachings of Islam in their daily lives. Many Muslims, including the younger generation, are more attracted to Western culture, a culture that is often harmful to Islam. In short, as the revealed truth by God, Shariah is believed to be the panacea for the crisis, and the power of the state is needed to make Shariah work in society (Ramli, Ahmad and Ch. 2006, pp. 141–42, 162–63, 208–9).

If Shariah implementation is necessary, then how is it to be implemented? In an interview with the journal *Hidayatullah*, Aziz Kahar asserted that the KPPSI would not struggle for Shariah by force of arms as his father, Kahar

Muzakkar, had done. Instead, the KPPSI would attempt to implement Shariah by peaceful means within the existing Indonesian state. One of the important ways of implementing Shariah in South Sulawesi would be to seek constitutional recognition for a special autonomous status, like that granted to Aceh. Once this constitutional basis had been achieved, then it would be possible to introduce Shariah smoothly. Besides this political struggle, Aziz also emphasized the importance of educating Muslim people about Shariah. In short, the struggle for Shariah is both political and cultural.[36] Aziz has not made a clear statement on whether he agrees with the current democratic system or not, but the fact that he has been involved as a candidate in elections is evidence that he is willing to work within the existing system.

On the other hand, another KPPSI activist, Muhammad Ikhwan of the WI, explained to me that for him, the current democratic system in Indonesia is unacceptable because it considers the voice of the majority as the truth. In fact, he said, democracy would easily become "demo-crazy" (he was using the English expression), because of financial and political manipulation. Why then, I asked him, does the WI support the KPPSI? The support, he said, was based on the *situational* consideration of whether it was beneficial (*maslahah*) for the Islamic community or not.[37] The partial implementation of Shariah by the state within the current democratic system, he said, was not always good or bad, and the WI examined the issue on a case-by-case basis. The priority of the WI programme, therefore, was religious education, not politics.

Intellectual challenges to the KPPSI

Several influential Muslim intellectuals, most of whom work in the State Islamic University (UIN) Alauddin in Makassar, disagree with the KPPSI's agenda.[38] They owe their influence in society to their positions as regular preachers in the mosques of Makassar and to their positions in Islamic organizations. Qasim Mathar, Hamka Haq and the late Saleh Putuhena are probably the most prominent among them. Hamka and Qasim took their Ph.D. degrees at the IAIN Syarif Hidayatullah in Jakarta, while Putuhena received his Ph.D. at the IAIN (now upgraded to the UIN) Sunan Kalijaga in Yogyakarta. As noted earlier, the postgraduate programme in Jakarta and Yogyakarta promoted the critical study of Islamic theology, law and history. In 1994, a similar programme was established at the IAIN Alauddin in Makassar, and these three intellectuals are among the programme's lecturers. Saleh Putuhena is a former rector of the IAIN Alauddin, and in the early

years of this century, he played a significant role in the peace process in
Maluku after the war. When I visited Hamka Haq in 2002 and 2004, he
was the Secretary of the MUI of South Sulawesi. Qasim Mathar is now
the Assistant Director of the Postgraduate Programme at UIN Alauddin,
and he is a regular columnist for a local newspaper, *Fajar*.

These three Muslim intellectuals have repeatedly asked the KPPSI
the same question: "What do we mean by Shariah? What sort of Shariah
does the KPPSI want to implement?" For Qasim Mathar, there are two
understandings of the term Shariah: in the first, it refers exclusively to
Islamic law; in the second, it refers to the entire body of the teachings of
Islam. The KPPSI, argued Qasim, takes the first meaning of Shariah and
demands that the state implement it. Qasim, however, prefers the second
meaning, meaning that Shariah is not necessarily implemented through
state regulations. Muslims, he said, already practise Shariah in their daily
lives through activities such as praying, fasting, and helping the poor,
and none of these need state intervention. Qasim also disagreed with the
KPPSI's claim that the current Indonesian crisis was caused by the fact
that the state had not implemented Shariah. What is wrong, he said, is
not the law but the men behind the law. The use of religious issues by
the KPPSI, argued Qasim, made people ignorant of real problems, such
as poverty, social injustice and poor education. Qasim also criticized the
KPPSI for demanding that people follow its own understanding of Shariah.
When he was accused of Islamophobia, Qasim replied that what actually
exists is not Islamophobia, but a phobia of the existence of different views
within Islam.[39]

Hamka Haq posed another important question: "Which Shariah?"
In Indonesia, he argued, Muslim family law (including marriage and
inheritance law) is already applied by the state. The state has also issued
regulations on alms (*zakat*) and enabled banks to offer Shariah-compliant
services, besides continuing conventional banking. The state also funds
Islamic education and coordinates the logistical operations for numerous
Muslim citizens who wish to perform the *hajj*. The state is thus already
implementing the whole range of Shariah, except for Muslim criminal law.
With regard to the latter, Hamka argued, one has to critically rethink the
Islamic prescriptions in medieval books, such as amputating the hands of
thieves and stoning adulterers. According to him, these rules should be
reinterpreted for the present day. For him, in our time, cutting off a thief's
hands should be replaced by a prison sentence, as is in fact already the case
in Indonesian criminal law. Hamka was very critical of Muslim activists,
including those in the KPPSI, who claim to represent the Muslim majority.

In fact, he said, throughout Indonesian history, Islamic parties have never won more than 30 per cent of the vote in national elections. In other words, the majority of the Muslims never voted for the politicians who claimed to be their leaders.[40] With this idea in mind, Hamka decided to join the nationalist party, the PDIP, in the elections of 2004. He failed to get elected to the national parliament, but in 2007 he was appointed by the chairperson of the PDIP, Megawati, as the national leader of "Baitul Muslimin", the Islamic wing of the party.[41]

Saleh Putuhena is another Muslim intellectual who was openly critical of the KPPSI's agenda, though he was also briefly a member of its Consultative Council.[42] Like Hamka Haq, he argued that Shariah is already being implemented in Indonesia. Putuhena also emphasized that Islamic law can only be applied in Indonesia when it is integrated in the national legal system, and when it has been integrated, it should not be called Shariah or Islamic law, but simply national law. The problem with the KPPSI in particular and Muslims in general, Putuhena argued, is that they take religion as a symbol rather than search for its substance. The substance of religion, he said, is its function for the welfare of human beings. Religion is not for God, but for human beings.

Political and social challenges to the KPPSI

The KPPSI is not a formal political party, but its ambition to have the state implement Shariah is obviously political. As noted above, the KPPSI needs support from the political authorities in both South Sulawesi and Jakarta regarding its demand for a special autonomous status for the province. The provincial authorities apparently responded carefully to this demand. The responses of the central government and politicians were similar, if not indifferent. What I mean by "careful response" here is that politicians generally did not openly support or reject the KPPSI's agenda. They usually made vague statements or statements that were implicitly opposed to the idea of the implementation of Shariah by the state. Given the sensitivity of the Shariah issue in Muslim societies, this careful attitude is not unusual, for politicians always try to make political gains and avoid possible disadvantages arising from social issues.

The careful attitude could also be related to Golkar politicians, who have dominated the political scene in the region since the Soeharto period. Golkar's ideology is nationalist, and when it was established in early 1970s, it partly defined itself in opposition to Islamic ideologically oriented groups. Although in the 1990s, Golkar moved closer to the Islamic (reformist) side of the political spectrum, and in the Reformation Era its most senior leaders included former HMI activists (Akbar Tanjung and Jusuf Kalla), the party never changed its nationalist and secular principles. Ideologically, Golkar is therefore firmly opposed to the KPPSI, notwithstanding the latter's professed acceptance of the current Indonesian state.

However, it is probably wrong to assume that all Golkar politicians in South Sulawesi are opposed to the KPPSI. In fact, some important figures of the KPPSI were (former) Golkar supporters and, as we shall see, the regent of Bulukumba district, who issued Shariah-based regional regulations, was also affiliated with Golkar. How can this seeming ideological discrepancy be explained? As Robin Bush and others have observed, throughout Indonesia, it was predominantly politicians from "secular" parties who promulgated Shariah-based regulations — either playing the "Islamic card" to attract voters, or to divert attention from other issues, such as corruption cases (Bush 2008, pp. 186–87). However, it is not unlikely that some members of the Golkar elite in South Sulawesi share, at least in part, the political ideology of the KPPSI.

The former governors of South Sulawesi, H.Z.B. Palaguna (1997–2002) and M. Amin Syam (2002–07) were careful not to antagonize the KPPSI.[43] Invited to attend the Congress of the Islamic Community in 2000 and 2001, the governor reportedly did not come himself, but sent his deputy. In response to a request from the KPPSI to support its programme of Shariah implementation, Palaguna answered that it would be better to know first what the people of South Sulawesi thought of this issue. He then appointed a task force to study attitudes towards Shariah implementation, members of which included KPPSI activists, besides other Muslim intellectuals, including one known opponent of the KPPSI, Qasim Mathar.[44]

Between October 2001 and January 2002, the task force conducted an opinion poll among a select group of respondents: 24 district governors (*bupati*), 60 members of the regional parliament, 81 religious leaders, and 60 community leaders. The results of this poll were initially not published in full, and were couched in vague, apologetic terms: it was emphasized that Muslims have various understandings of Shariah, and that there was no unanimity on its formal implementation. After the KPPSI complained that this was not credible, the results of the poll were released. It appeared that 91 per cent of the respondents had declared themselves in favour of Shariah, and 59 per cent supported its implementation by the state, while only 32 per cent preferred to keep the state out of matters of Shariah. As Hamdan Juhanis observes, the hesitant way in which the results of the poll were released indicates that the provincial government was highly reluctant to endorse the drive for Shariah implementation (Juhanis 2006, pp. 277–82; Ramli, Ahmad and Ch. 2006, p. 219).

This careful attitude was also demonstrated by A.M. Fatwa, a national politician from the PAN of South Sulawesi origin. In a paper presented to the first Congress of Islamic Community in 2000, Fatwa did not clearly show his support for the formalization of Shariah by the state. He said that there are three understandings of Shariah implementation: (1) to establish an Islamic State; (2) to make Islamic law a supplement to the existing laws of a secular state; and (3) to make Islam an integral part of the national legal system. For him, implementation of Shariah means taking the third path. In this regard, he suggests that Islamic law should become the main inspiration for national law, while customary law and western law are taken as complementary elements. This seems to imply that national law should not be formally called Shariah law, even though the former is primarily inspired by the latter. There is also no clear statement in the paper supporting special autonomous status for South Sulawesi. In a footnote, Fatwa only said that because the majority of people in South Sulawesi are Muslim, it is *understandable* if they demand special autonomy similar to that granted to Aceh in 1999 (Fatwa 2000).

As the most significant religious minority, the Christians also responded to the KPPSI. A prominent Catholic intellectual, Ishak Ngeljaratan, said that the KPPSI's agenda is one of formalities and could increase tensions between religious communities in South Sulawesi. He asked: just as in Christianity, love is the highest value, why can we not start from the Qur'anic teaching that Islam was revealed as an act of mercy for the entire universe? Ngeljaratan suggested that instead of formalizing Islamic law, it might be more productive to stress universal values, on the basis of which different religious groups could work hand-in-hand to solve social problems.[45] Zakariya Ngelow, a former head of the Academy of Theology of Eastern Indonesia (STT Intim) in Makassar, said that if Shariah implementation means simply to uphold moral values in society, it could be good. However, in his perception, the KPPSI was aiming to turn Islam into the dominant political ideology, and that all Christians would strongly object to this.[46]

Another prominent Protestant minister, Daniel Sopamena, said that in the year 2000, he had made a modest survey of Christian responses to the Muslim ambition to implement Shariah in South Sulawesi. Of his respondents, 22 per cent said it was too early for the Christians to respond to the issue, and suggested that in order to have accurate information, Muslims should be invited to talk about it. Interestingly, 27 per cent said that if Shariah implementation were to bring a significant amelioration of social and political ills, then Christians should support it. Finally, the majority of Christians (53 per cent) said that they objected to Shariah implementation because Indonesia is not based on Islam but on Pancasila, and if the Muslims insisted on implementing Shariah, these Christians would prefer to secede, in "a good way" (read: not through armed rebellion).[47]

In a paper presented to a meeting of Christians, Sopamena suggests that (1) the Christians should support Muslims following Shariah in its generic meaning, namely as the divinely revealed path to salvation, but that Christians should reject Shariah if it is to become positive law in the country; (2) Christians, however, should consider those Muslims who want to make Shariah into positive law not as enemies but as brothers, with whom they should engage in dialogue; (3) instead of relying on secular nationalist groups, Christians should develop good relations with Muslim leaders and activists who cannot accept the implementation of Shariah by the state (Sopamena n.d.).

In addition to the challenges above, the KPPSI had to face another problem, namely its bad public image due to violent incidents in which its members were allegedly involved (Pradadimara and Junedding 2002; Juhanis 2006, pp. 197–98). One of those incidents was a bomb explosion in the arena of the KPPSI's second Islamic Community Congress. The organizers immediately blamed unnamed opponents who wanted to disturb the Congress, but the police suspected certain elements within the KPPSI of having set off the bomb in order to gain publicity. Moreover, because the Congress took place only a few months after the September 11 terrorist attacks in New York, the bomb reinforced the association between political Islam and violence. This association was further strengthened when, in March 2002, the leader of Lasykar Jundullah, Agus Dwikarna, along with Tamsil Linrung and Abdul Jamal Balfas, was arrested in the Philippines for possession of explosives. Linrung and Balfas were finally acquitted, but Agus Dwikarna was sentenced to ten years in prison. Yet another incident was a double bomb explosion in Makassar, on 5 December 2002, the last day of Ramadan. One bomb in a McDonald's killed two people besides the bomber; the second went off without reported casualties in an automobile showroom belonging to Jusuf Kalla. Again, several Lasykar Jundullah members were arrested after the incident and later found guilty.

BULUKUMBA: SHARIAH IN REGIONAL REGULATIONS

Despite the challenges, the KPPSI as an organization has continued to grow throughout South Sulawesi. The consolidation of Muslim activists with similar ideological orientations seems to have developed well since 2000. One important success was Aziz Kahar's election as one of four South Sulawesi delegates to the Regional Representative Council (DPD) in 2004. Aziz won 15 per cent of the vote, ending up in second place after the wealthy businessman, Aksa Mahmud, who obtained 19 per cent.[48] Likewise, Aswar Hasan, the General Secretary of the KPPSI, was appointed head of the Broadcasting Commission of South Sulawesi province. Several KPPSI activists were also successfully elected as members of regional parliaments at the provincial and district levels in the 2004 elections. Moreover, KPPSI activists found allies among the administrators of a number of districts. One of these districts is Bulukumba, where the KPPSI's third Islamic Community Congress was held in 2005.

Bulukumba is one of twenty-three districts in South Sulawesi province. It is located 150 km south-east of Makassar. In the second half of the 1950s, this district was one of the strongholds of Kahar Muzakkar's Darul Islam movement, and it is considered one of the province's most staunchly Islamic districts. According to statistics from 2003, the population of Bulukumba numbered 361,342 people, 99 per cent of whom were Muslims. In Bulukumba, there are about 800 Muslim prayer places (*masjid* and *mushalla*), 13 Islamic propagation centres, 143 Islamic study groups (*majelis taklim*) and 2 Islamic radio stations (Sila 2006, p. 95). The Muslims of Bulukumba, however, are not monolithic. There are different Islamic organizations active in this district, including not only the Muhammadiyah and the NU, but also a branch of Darul Istiqamah, and even the Ahmadiyah.[49] There are also Sufi orders such as the Khalwatiyah, Qadiriyah and Naqshbandiyah. Moreover, there are syncretistic communities such as *Haji Bawakaraeng*, *Ara* and *Tanah Toa Kajang*, which combine Islam and local religious culture. Finally there are small Christian, Buddhist, Hindu and Confucian minorities among the population (Ad'han and Umam 2006, pp. 58–60).

The perceived strength of Islam in Bulukumba, notwithstanding internal diversity, was probably the reason behind the effort to implement Shariah. Andi Patabai Pabokori, the regent (*bupati* or district governor) of Bulukumba for two terms (1995–2005), was the most important person behind this "project". Patabai is a Buginese from an aristocratic family, who studied at the State Academy for Government Administration

(APDN) and the Faculty of Political and Social Sciences of Hasanuddin University in Makassar. He did not have a formal Islamic education, but it is said that his father, who was active in the NU, gave him a good religious education at home (Sila 2006, p. 96). Like many other government officials in South Sulawesi, Patabai is affiliated with the Golkar party, not with an Islamic party.

In 2002–03, Patabai issued four regional regulations considered to be based on Shariah. It remains unclear to me, however, whether these regional regulations were issued in response to demands from KPPSI activists, or whether they were Patabai's personal initiative, which was then endorsed by local KPPSI activists. In any case, the KPPSI's activists were certainly not passive bystanders. It is also noteworthy that the leader of the KPPSI in Bulukumba is the leader of Darul Istiqamah in the region. As noted earlier, the founder of Darul Istiqamah, Marzuki Hasan, is a former leader of Kahar Muzakkar's Darul Islam movement (Juhanis 2006, p. 152).

Patabai's first regional regulation, issued in 2002, restricted the sale of alcoholic beverages, though it did not impose a total ban. Articles 2–5 of the regulation state that sale is only permitted in specific localities and with explicit permission from the regent; Article 8 adds that such localities have to be at least a kilometre away from places of worship, hospitals, schools, residential and office areas.[50]

In 2003, Patabai issued a regulation aiming to enforce the payment of *zakat*, the alms-giving that is a religious obligation for Muslims. The regulation authorizes the regent to establish procedures for the collection of *zakat* and its redistribution to be implemented by official bodies (Badan Amil Zakat or BAZ). Such bodies also exist elsewhere, but they do not have coercive powers; the regulation in Bulukumba represents an attempt to enforce the religious obligation. The most easily implemented form of *zakat* collection concerns civil servants' salaries; the regulation states that all Muslim civil servants are obliged to pay the so-called professional *zakat*, amounting to 2.5 per cent of their net income per year. Compared to other types of *zakat* in trading, farming, industries and private companies, this *zakat* is easier to collect because all civil servants' salaries are administered by the government, which directly deducts the sum from their monthly salaries.[51]

A third regulation, also issued in 2003, concerns the ability to read the Qur'an in the Arabic script. Article 3 of the regulation dictates that every Muslim student at elementary, junior and high school has to learn to read the Qur'an correctly. Article 4 states that every school must give extra classes for students to learn to read the Qur'an. Article 6 states that every Muslim couple who wish to get married have to show that they are able to read the Qur'an correctly.[52] The local government backed this up by making funds available for improving Qur'an literacy. It provided financial support to private Qur'an courses and appointed a number of Qur'an teachers who had been trained at the UIN Alauddin.[53] Patabai's ambitions in this area went even further than the letter of the regulation: he was reported to have said that government officials should set an example and be able to read the Qur'an fluently. In one case, the inauguration of a new government official in Bulukumba was allegedly postponed until the person concerned could demonstrate his ability to read the Qur'an.

Patabai's fourth regulation in 2004 concerned Muslim dress. In government and private offices, as well as in public and in private schools from secondary to university level, Muslims are required to wear Islamic dress, and Muslims working elsewhere are invited to follow their example. The regulation defines Islamic dress as a shirt and long trousers (or shorts covering the knees) for males, and for females, wide clothes covering the entire body, except the face, hands and feet. The implementation of this regulation is overseen by the regent, specially appointed officials and religious leaders. Failure to comply with the dress code is not a punishable offence, but the supervisors are expected to reprimand the person in question (Sila 2006, pp. 101–4).

Towards the end of his tenure, Patabai designated twelve villages in Bulukumba as "Islamic villages". In these villages, the above regulations are supposed to be followed strictly by the Muslim residents. Moreover, in one "Islamic village", named Padang, there was an initiative to implement parts of Islamic criminal law. In the year 2006, the village head of Padang issued a village regulation decreeing lashing as a punishment for the consumption and sale of alcohol or drugs, gambling, and fornication. Besides the punishment of lashing, however, national criminal law (KUHAP) remains applicable to offenders.[54] In November 2007, representatives of twenty villages in the Gatarang sub-district of Bulukumba had a meeting in which they agreed to go a step further and implement the Islamic punishment of amputation in cases of theft. The reason for this initiative was that there had been an increase of theft in Gatarang in recent months, but no thief had been apprehended. They hoped that the penalty of amputation would act as a deterrent. The district government of Bulukumba, however, prevented this proposal being put into practice, arguing that more discussion among the authorities was needed before such drastic measures were taken.[55]

The latter case appears to indicate that the drive for Shariah implementation in Bulukumba district has reached its limits. It also suggests that the new regent of Bulukumba who replaced Patabai in 2005, A.M. Sukri Sappewali, is less enthusiastic than his predecessor about the implementation of Shariah law.[56]

CRITICISM OF THE REGULATIONS

There has been a critical response to the regulations on the part of Muslim activists in South Sulawesi. Activists from a non-governmental organization (NGO) called Lembaga Advokasi dan Pendidikan Anak Rakyat (LAPAR) have been the most outspoken. LAPAR (the name literally means "hungry") was established in 1999 by former activists of the traditionalist Indonesian Muslim Student Movement (PMII), most of whom were graduates of the IAIN Alauddin. The activists were influenced by the critical Islamic discourse, leftist ideology and postmodernist philosophy that had developed among PMII activists in Yogyakarta since the mid-1980s, in the days when the NU was led by Abdurrahman Wahid. LAPAR has close relations with other traditionalist Muslim NGOs, such as the Institute of Social and Islamic Studies (LKiS) in Yogyakarta, and the Wahid Institute and Desantara in Jakarta.

Two of LAPAR's leading activists, Syamsurijal Ad'an and Zubair Umam, are from Bulukumba. Since the issuing of the regulations above, they have been active in organizing meetings and discussions with various groups in Bulukumba across the entire religious spectrum. Funded mostly by foreign (Western) sources, LAPAR also broadcasts its criticism of the regulations in printed bulletins and radio talk-shows on several stations in South Sulawesi. LAPAR's activities have been supported by traditionalist Muslim leaders of the NU and the DDI, liberal Muslim intellectuals, and Christian and other religious minorities in the region.

It is important to consider the criticisms of the regulations made by LAPAR activists and Muslim intellectuals.[57] In response to the regulation on the ability to read the Qur'an, they said that first of all, it is not entirely in line with Islamic teaching. The ability to read the Qur'an is not an obligation in Islam. It is true that in prayer, one has to recite the seven short verses of the Qur'an (al-Fatihah) in Arabic, but there is no obligation to learn it from Arabic script. Moreover, the requirement that a couple should be able to read the Qur'an before getting married is not line with Islamic law. This requirement has never been included as a condition for the validity of marriage in Islam. Finally, the requirement that a government official should be able to read the Qur'an is a strange policy because it generally has nothing to do with his or her job.[58]

The *zakat* regulation is also problematic. A number of civil servants, especially teachers, protested against the regulation, because their salaries are already low and subject to state taxation. According to Islamic law, *zakat* is only incumbent upon people whose annual income exceeds a certain minimum; the regulation, however, does not specify a minimum and simply takes a certain amount from each civil servant's salary. Moreover, *zakat* used to be collected and redistributed by private institutions in society. When *zakat* is managed by a state institution such as the BAZ, this can weaken civil society. Lastly, the regulation gives the regent the authority to determine how the collected *zakat* will be used. This means that *zakat* is susceptible to misuse by the government or, in other words, corruption.

The regulation on Muslim dress has been criticized on the basis that it undermines a woman's freedom to choose whether or not to cover her head. The critics argued that historically, Islam in South Sulawesi has always adapted to local culture, and this was notably the case among the Kajang, one of the traditional communities of Bulukumba where Muslim women do not consider it necessary to cover their heads. Moreover, in certain places in Bulukumba, women were not served by government officials if they did not dress properly in accordance with the regulation. According to the critics, this is discrimination and a violation of those women's civil rights.

The regulation on alcoholic beverages has also been criticized. First, the critics said that there is nothing new in the restriction of sales, because Presidential Decree No. 96 of 1997 already makes similar restrictions. However, the Bulukumba regulation allows for the sale of alcohol in hotels, restaurants and bars at Bira beach. The critics argued that this indicates that the government is willing to sacrifice principles in the interest of rich entrepreneurs who earn money from tourism. On the other hand, the government never even considered the fact that certain rituals in traditional communities in the district require the consumption of alcoholic beverages, and the regulation represents an infringement of these communities' rights.

Last but not least, the LAPAR activists, and *ulama* supporting them, were very critical of the regent's unilateral decision to declare certain villages "Islamic" without even consulting their inhabitants. They decried this as a violation of citizens' rights and probably unconstitutional, because the regulation appears to overrule existing legislation and judicial procedures. Moreover, the partial implementation of Islamic criminal law in Padang village ignored the wisdom of traditional *ulama* that Islamic teaching should be applied in accordance with local culture. The *ulama*, therefore, suggested that one should look at the main purpose of Islamic law, namely to achieve the common good for human beings, rather than the formal codes, such as amputating the hands of thieves.

In short, for the opponents, the regulations were not in line with Islam, and did not benefit the Muslim community. They even suspected that the regulations were simply pretexts used by government elites to cover corrupt practices. Several cases of corruption in Bulukumba, which were reported in the media, seemed to be forgotten after the local government adopted its formal Islamic image, while real social problems, such as poor education and healthcare services, were not taken seriously.

This criticism of the regulations did not persuade the proponents of Shariah implementation to withdraw their support. However, it appears to have led to a debate within the KPPSI as to whether the regulations were a pure expression of Shariah. Most members concluded that it would be better not to speak of "Shariah regulations" but seek another term that would not compromise the concept of Shariah. They continued to support the regulations, but came up with a proposal to call them "regional regulations on commanding right and forbidding wrong" (*Perda Amar Ma'ruf Nahi Munkar*). As one insider told me, there is no agreement among KPPSI activists on what should be the model for Shariah implementation.[59]

In general, however, the KPPSI strongly supported Patabai's pioneering efforts. It was claimed that the rate of crime sharply decreased after the regulations were applied. Moreover, the government regulation on *zakat* was said to have increased government revenue from 2 billion rupiah per year to 40 billion rupiah. It was also claimed that Qur'an reading ability among the Muslims of Bulukumba improved by up to 100 per cent in 2005.[60] The critics, however, argued that in fact, if one checks the records of the Bulukumba Police Office, there was no decrease, but in fact an increase, in the crime rate.[61] With regard to *zakat* revenue, the critics suspected that this had evaporated due to government corruption. One indication of this is a project for an Islamic Centre in Bulukumba, for which it was claimed 10 billion rupiah had been spent, but there was no evidence of this.[62]

AZIZ KAHAR AND THE GUBERNATORIAL ELECTIONS OF 2007

The most recent political contest in South Sulawesi involving prominent KPPSI activists was the gubernatorial election, held in November 2007.

Aziz Kahar, who was successfully elected as one of the four delegates from South Sulawesi to the Regional Representative Council (DPD) in 2004, decided to compete for the position of governor. The participation of Aziz as one of the candidates in this election sheds light on the dynamics of Islam and politics in the region, especially in relation to the role of the KPPSI. As we shall see, the negotiations among the political parties to promote a certain candidate, the issues raised by the candidates during the campaign, the responses of intellectuals to the candidates and, finally, the results of the elections, all indicate that Aziz Kahar lacks political clout as the "icon" of the KPPSI.

Three teams of candidates contested the elections, namely: (1) M. Amin Syam — Mansyur Ramli; (2) Syahrul Yasin Limpo — Agus Arifin Nu'mang; and (3) Aziz Kahar Muzakkar — Mubyl Handaling. The first team was promoted by the biggest party, Golkar. M. Amin Syam was the incumbent governor of South Sulawesi, while Mansyur Ramli was the former rector of UMI, a member of the KPPSI Consultative Council, and the brother-in-law of Jusuf Kalla. People said that Kalla strongly backed this team, hoping that the two men would support him in the next presidential election.

The second team was also a strong one. Syahrul Yasin was the incumbent vice-governor of South Sulawesi, while Agus Arifin was a former provincial Secretary General of Golkar. Syahrul was known as an intelligent and experienced man who had climbed up from the bottom; that is, from being a head of village (lurah), through head of sub-district (camat), regent (bupati) to vice governor. The team was supported by the PAN, the PDIP and the PDK. Most Christians probably voted for this team.

Most importantly, with a view to our discussion, the last team consisted of Aziz Kahar and Mubyl. In the beginning, Aziz was invited by Syahrul to be the latter's partner as a candidate for vice-governor, but Aziz refused. Aziz apparently wanted to become the governor, not the vice-governor. Aziz then took Mubyl as his partner, the former chairman of the Union of HMI alumni (KAHMI) in South Sulawesi. This team was initially supported by three Islamic parties: the PPP, the PBB and the PKS, but at the last moment, the PKS left the coalition and decided to throw its weight behind M. Amin Syam. There were rumours about money and politics being behind this, but one can also imagine that the PKS simply preferred a stronger candidate. The PKS's withdrawal was a problem, because with support from the PPP and the PBB alone, Aziz could not obtain the mini- mum 15 per cent of support in parliament. However, Aziz was eventually able to stand for election because some of the tiny parties (which do not have any seats in the parliament) decided to join a coalition with the PPP and the PBB to promote Aziz-Mubyl. In short, only small parties supported this team.

Islamic organizations in South Sulawesi, such as the Muhammadiyah, the NU, the WI, the IMMIM and the DDI did not want to risk formally supporting one of the teams. KPPSI activists, however, generally became Aziz supporters. The Vice-Secretary of the KPPSI Consultative Council, Siradjuddin, was apparently the most enthusiast and active member of the Aziz team for the election.[63] The former Secretary General of the KPPSI, Aswar Hasan, however, realized that it would be very difficult for Aziz to win the election. "I put my hope on him [Aziz], but I am not optimistic", he said.[64] As noted earlier, Mansyur Ramli is also a KPPSI man, but in public he was seen more as an NU activist whose father was one of the founders of the NU in South Sulawesi. Likewise, Amin Syam was a member of the Advisory Council of the NU of South Sulawesi. Syahrul Yasin is close to the Muhammadiyah because his father and mother were functionaries in this organization, while his partner, Agus Arifin, is close to the NU.[65] Thus, in general it is difficult to ascertain where the votes of members of Islamic organizations would go, and Aziz was clearly not the only choice for them.

When I asked Muslim intellectuals and activists who were known opponents of the KPPSI about the Aziz-Mubyl team, they confidently said that no one should be worried because the team would not win. Among them, it seemed that only Qasim actively engaged in public discourse against the Aziz team. When the media reported that Aziz was mobilizing Islamic preachers to become his campaigners, Qasim made a sharp statement in the local paper, *Fajar*: "I warn them, do not sell religion for political interests!" A good Muslim preacher, he said, should be neutral in the election because as a preacher, he or she should welcome everybody to the religion of Islam. Qasim also reminded Muslims that they should not forget the lessons of history; the DI/TII rebellion under Kahar Muzakkar had caused much trouble in South Sulawesi, and this was because religion had been used to achieve political ends.[66] After the publication of his statement, Qasim was immediately summoned by a PPP politician who asked him to control himself.[67]

Some Christian intellectuals whom I met were worried about the possibility that Aziz would win the election. The Christian intellectual, Daniel Sopamena, said: "Do not underestimate Aziz because it is possible that the Aceh case [when the former leader of the Aceh Freedom Movement, Irwandi, won the gubernatorial election] would happen here".[68] Another Christian minister, Lidya K. Tandirerung, said that if Aziz won and proceeded to apply Shariah, Christians would feel uneasy living in such an environment. "But we could perhaps comfort ourselves that Shariah would only be applied to Muslims, not us", she added.[69] These responses indicate that most Christians, if not all, did not support Aziz-Mubyl team.

Surprisingly, Ishak Ngeljaratan, a well-known Catholic intellectual in the city, supported Aziz's candidacy. He even gave a speech during the inauguration of Aziz-Mubyl as electoral candidates. Ngeljaratan said that Aziz-Mubyl would be elected by people "who have a conscience and healthy minds" (*punya hati nurani dan akal sehat*). Why did Ngeljataran support Aziz while he opposed the idea of the formalization of Shariah, as promoted by the KPPSI? He explained: "They know that I oppose the formalization of Shariah, but they also know the reason why I support Aziz. I said to him, I support you because you have not been tainted by corruption yet."[70] Perhaps Ngeljaratan had already calculated that Aziz would not win the elections, but that it would be important for a moral voice to sound in the midst of a dirty political game.[71]

During the campaign, the Aziz team promised clean government rather than Shariah implementation as their main agenda. In his religious programme, Aziz proposed: "the religious condition of South Sulawesi society in which people live their lives according to the values of their respective religions" [*Kondisi masyarakat Sulsel yang agamis dengan menjalankan kehidupannya berdasarkan nilai agama yang dianutnya masing-masing dan saling menghormati*].[72] Thus there is no explicit statement on Shariah, even though the statement can be interpreted as a basis for Shariah implementation. The Aziz team apparently realized that politically, Shariah was not very marketable.

By contrast, in October 2007, Syahrul Yasin Limpo made an important political promise in his campaign: if he won, he would make education and health services free. He also said that if he could not realize his promise after two years in his office, he would resign. In a public meeting, Syahrul asserted that his promise was a political contract with the people. Among the intellectuals, Qasim Mathar openly welcomed Syahrul's offer, saying that the idea was very good because it could be properly established whether it had been achieved.[73] Amin Syam apparently realized that Syahrul's manoeuvre was a strong challenge, to which he responded by saying that he would make schools, not all education, free, and this was more realistic than Syahrul's promise.[74] By contrast, as far as I know, Aziz did not offer another alternative challenge on this particular issue.

When the results of the elections were announced, Syahrul Yasin Limpo-Agus Arifin Nu'man won the elections with 39.53 per cent of the votes, while Amin Syam-Mansyur Ramli were in second position with 38.80 per cent of the votes. As many observers had predicted, Aziz-Mubyl came last with 21.69 per cent of the votes.[75] Given the fact that the numbers of votes for Amin and Syahrul were very close, the former could not accept the results and argued that voting in some districts had been unfair. The case was then brought to the Supreme Court. The Court supported Amin, demanding re-elections in some districts. The Regional Election Committee of South Sulawesi, however, opposed the verdict and proposed a review of the Supreme Court. Syahrul's supporters also took part in huge demonstrations in Makassar in January 2007. South Sulawesi was then led temporarily by Tanribali Lamo, a caretaker appointed by the central government. [76] On 19 March 2008, the Supreme Court finally announced its verdict, approving the Syahrul Yasin-Agus Arifin team as the winner of the election.[77]

THE KPPSI AFTER THE ELECTIONS OF 2009

The regional elections of 2007 suggest that while the KPPSI under Aziz Kahar's leadership was not very strong politically, the organization should not be ignored. Aziz clearly has a significant social power base, particularly in his region of origin, Luwu, where his father previously had significant political influence. On the other hand, Aziz and the KPPSI activists still have to overcome serious obstacles to win the political struggle, especially if they consistently make Shariah implementation their main political agenda.

The general elections of 2009 and the Fourth Congress of the Islamic Community in 2010 reaffirmed this observation. In the 2009 elections, Aziz Kahar was successfully re-elected to the Regional Representative Council (DPD) as the candidate with the highest number of votes (948,151 votes), almost double the number gained by his chief competitor, Aksa Mahmud (who was also re-elected, with 507,411 votes).[78] With this amazing result, Aziz clearly demonstrated that he enjoys significant support in society. It is not surprising, therefore, that several politicians in South Sulawesi wish to establish a political coalition with Aziz and the KPPSI, particularly to contest the next gubernatorial elections in 2012.

Between 6 and 8 February 2010, the KPPSI held its Fourth Congress of the Islamic Community in Pangkep (Pangkajene dan Kepulauan) District.[79] Pangkep was chosen as the location of the Congress because the district head, Syafrudin Nur, was praised by the KPPSI for his recent attempts to implement Shariah-based regulations in his region. Syafrudin was to have been honoured as the most senior leader of the local organizing committee of the Congress, but he passed away before the event took place. Another rising star is Bahar Ngitung, a rich businessman who, like Aziz Kahar, successfully won the DPD seat in the elections of 2009. Bahar Ngitung became the head of the central organizing committee of the Congress. As the leader of the Association of Goods and Services Suppliers in Indonesia (Asosiasi Pengadaan Barang dan Jasa Indonesia, or ASPANJI) of South Sulawesi, it is likely that Bahar Ngitung provided financial support to the Congress.

A few days before the Congress took place, Bahar Ngitung announced to the press that the Congress would be attended and officially opened by the Minister of Religious Affairs, Suryadharma Ali. The Minister of Justice, Patrialis Akbar, was also expected to come. However, neither minister came in the end, and they were represented by the first echelon officials of their respective ministries. The Congress was then officially opened by Nasaruddin Umar, a Muslim intellectual with a Bugis background and the first echelon official of the Ministry of Religious Affairs. The Governor, Syahrul Yasin Limpo, did not come either, because he was hospitalized in Singapore. However, the Vice-governor, Agus A. Nu'mang, and the Mayor of Makassar City, Ilham Arief Sirajuddin, attended the opening ceremony. Likewise, it was reported that important religious leaders from the NU and the Muhammadiyah attended the Congress.

During the Congress, it was discussed whether Aziz Kahar should be given the new position of "Amir" (perhaps as the highest spiritual leader of the organization), while the executive council would be led by another person. In this regard, the press reported that Ilham Arief Sirajuddin and Bahar Ngitung were among the candidates to take Aziz's previous position as the chairman of the executive council. Other names, including Patabai Pobokari and Aswar Hasan, were also mentioned.[80] However, it was also said that these candidates would not persist if Aziz Kahar still wanted the position. On the final day, Aziz was re-elected by acclamation, and he was given sole authority by the Congress to choose the personnel of the KPPSI. The KPPSI activists apparently realized that Aziz remained a very important figure, especially to attract people who had romanticized memories of his father, Kahar Muzakkar.

Although Aziz was re-elected, it is important to note the appearance of the name of the Mayor of Makassar City, Ilham Arief Sirajuddin, as one of the candidates. Presently, he is the most prominent challenger to Syahrul Yasin Limpo in the upcoming election for a new governor. Ilham has joined the newly established mass organization, Nasional Demokrat (ND), which recently has been transformed into a political party. The ND is established and sponsored by Surya Paloh, a rich Jakarta-based businessman and a former national Golkar leader. Whether Aziz and Arief become a team in the next gubernatorial election remains, of course, a big question. The most crucial issue for this coalition is probably who will contest the position of governor.

There were some important decisions and recommendations made in the Congress. One of them was that the word "*persiapan*" (preparation) in the acronym of the KPPSI would be changed into "*perjuangan*" (struggle).[81] It seems that "*persiapan*" was no longer considered appropriate because of the KPPSI had already existed for about ten years. The Congress also demanded that the media not broadcast programmes violating Islamic values.[82] With regard to the elections, the Congress appealed to the Islamic community to vote for candidates supporting Shariah implementation, with track records free from corruption. The Congress also demanded that the central government free Agus Dwikarna from jail in the Philippines. Finally, the Congress recommended that the KPPSI give a "Shariah award" to those leaders who supported Shariah implementation.[83]

In general, however, the Congress attracted little attention from the public. The Muslim intellectuals and activists who had previously challenged the idea of Shariah implementation decided to keep silent during the Congress. Having looked at the political achievements of the KPPSI, many of the KPPSI's opponents now have come to believe that Shariah is in fact not a very marketable political commodity in South Sulawesi. Partly due to the absence of controversy on Shariah implementation, the media coverage of the Congress was also limited. One informant even said that there was more media coverage of the PORDA (Regional Sporting Competition), which was held during the same period, than the Congress. Moreover, since the Congress, the KPPSI has hardly engaged in any public activities.[84]

CONCLUSION

The emergence of the KPPSI and its political struggle can only be understood in the context of the history of religion and politics in South Sulawesi. If we look at developments in the region in the seventeenth century, we see that there was an attempt to implement Shariah and local customs side by side. However, it seems that the use of Shariah as a political ideology only started in independent Indonesia. During the Sukarno period, the Darul Islam (DI) movement undertook an armed struggle, and in South Sulawesi, this movement was led by Kahar Muzakkar. After several years, Sukarno finally succeeded in containing the movement. The next president, Soeharto, followed a policy of suppressing proponents of Islamic ideology and supporting a non-ideological view of Islam. Thus the failure of Kahar Muzakkar's rebellion and Soeharto's policy of suppression apparently weakened proponents of the ideological view of Islam.

The rise of democracy after the fall of Soeharto has created opportunities for Islamic-oriented groups to participate in politics. In South Sulawesi, these groups are organized under the banner of the KPPSI. In fact, the activists of the KPPSI come from diverse backgrounds, and only a few of them have direct historical links with Kahar Muzakkar's DI. Nevertheless, they all share the same political discourse, namely Shariah implementation by the state. Ideally the KPPSI would want an Islamic state, but for the time being, this ideal is obviously very difficult to achieve. Being given special autonomous status like Aceh province was apparently considered the best way to achieve a "semi-Islamic state", but such demands were not met with success. The scale was then narrowed again, namely, to apply Shariah at the district government level by adopting Shariah-based regulations.

The process of narrowing the scale is clearly a compromise in the face of political realities. It is true that the free public sphere in the currently democratic Indonesia has opened up opportunities for KPPSI activists to be involved on the political stage, but a condition for this should be that they follow the rules of the game, and do not attempt to force others to agree with their demands. The success of Aziz Kahar in the 2004 and 2009 elections for the Regional Representative Council (DPD), and his failure in the gubernatorial elections of 2007, also shed light on the political strengths and weaknesses of the KPPSI.

In this context, what is to be done about the future of Islam and democracy in this region in particular, and in Indonesia in general? In my view, as long as the current democratic political system is properly maintained, one should not worry about this phenomenon. The debates and discussions should remain open, so that a healthy process of consensus can be achieved. The following comment from a local Christian intellectual, Daniel Sopamena, also illustrates this point:

Of course as a religious minority, the Christians feel afraid of those people who want to implement the Shariah formally. However, in a way, this phenomenon is actually positive. In the past (during the New Order), this kind of movement could not show itself openly in public, so we did not know who they were and what they really wanted. But now, it is more transparent. We know who they are, and we can invite them to talk about what they really want, and also we can tell them about our own opinions.[85]

Notes

[1] See "Perubahan Keempat UUD 1945 Disahkan", *Kompas*, 11 August 2002.

[2] For a critical study of the implementation of Shariah in Aceh, see Avonius (2007).

[3] For the history of Christianity in South Sulawesi, see Steenbrink and Aritonang (2008), pp. 455–91.

[4] On this Sufi Order, see Bruinessen (1991).

[5] The complexities of political contest between aristocrats and commoners, including Muslim leaders, are discussed in Chapter 4 of Magenda (1989).

[6] The earliest study of Kahar Muzakkar is Harvey (1989), originally a Ph.D. thesis at Cornell University in 1974. Other studies include van Dijk (1981) and Gonggong (2004).

[7] The original name of Kahar Muzakkar was La Domeng. He took the former name when he studied in the Muhammadiyah school, in imitation of the name of his beloved teacher, Abdul Kahar Muzakkir (Harvey 1989, p. 145).

[8] According to Gonggong, however, the kidnapping was just a charade agreed to by both sides (Gongong 2004, pp. 232–33).

[9] Confidential interview in June 2007.

[10] Interview with Saleh Putuhena, Makasar, 15 December 2002. He was a PII activist in those days.

[11] See also <http://pmu-alauddin.org/index1.php?id=uin>.

[12] For the biography of Jusuf Kalla, see <http://en.wikipedia.org/wiki/Jusuf_ Kalla>.

[13] For a detailed account, see Mujiburrahman (2006), pp. 38–40. On the withdrawal of the PMKRI from the KAMI, see *Kompas*, 16 October 1967.

[14] It is noteworthy that an important figure in the DDI, Ali Yafie, became a PPP national politician (Kabry 1983, pp. 4–12).

[15] The total vote for the Islamic parties in the 1971 elections was 18.45 per cent, namely NU: 9.15 per cent, Parmusi: 5.05 per cent and PSII: 4.25 per cent (Biro Humas KPU 2000, p. 67).

[16] On HMI-MPO, see Karim (1997).

[17] E-mail communication with Nurman Said, a lecturer at UIN Alauddin, 27 February 2008.

18   See "Abdul Aziz Qahhar Mudzakkar Angkat Bicara", *Suara Hidayatullah*, vol. XIV, no. 2 (June 2003): 22–23.

19   E-mail communication with Nurman Said, 27 February 2008.

20   See the interview with Mudzakkir M. Arief, "Kampanyekan Islam itu Damai, Indah dan Mandiri", *Fajar*, 20 November 2007.

21   On Hidayatullah and Abdullah Said, see Subhan (2006) and Bruinessen (2008).

22   See <www.wahdah.or.id> and the WI's pamphlet (Anonymous 2007). Now the WI has twenty-two branches, to be found in Sulawesi, Kalimantan, Java, Maluku, West Nusa Tenggara and Papua.

23   The PK shared 1.12 per cent of the vote with thirty-nine other parties! The PAN and the PKB, which are not formally based on Islam but commonly associated with the Muhammadiyah and the NU respectively, also obtained a very low share of the vote: the PAN got 3.84 per cent, and the PKB got 1.58 per cent (Biro Humas KPU 2000, p. 233).

24   See "Prediksi Pemilu Sulsel: Mengepung Lumbung Golkar", *Kompas*, 26 February 2004.

25   This percentage is calculated from Lembaga Informasi Nasional (2004), pp. 54–55. See also <www.dprdsulsel.go.id/anggota.php>.

26   Besides my own interviews and observations, the following sections owe a debt to existing studies of the KPPSI, particularly Ramli, Ahmad and Ch. (2006), Juhanis (2006), Faisal (2004) and Pradidimara and Junedding (2002).

27   Later in 2002, Aziz was elected as a member of the Consultative Council of Hidayatullah, which led him to stay in Jakarta.

28   Interview with Muhammad Ikhwan, Makassar, 21 June 2007.

29   Muin Salim took the position that had been held by Abdurrachman Basalamah, after the latter passed away in 2004. Interview with Muin Salim, Makassar, 22 January 2004.

30   Interview with Nasaruddin Razak, Makassar, 23 December 2002.

31   Interview with Harifuddin Cawidu, Makassar, 24 December 2002.

32   See the table in Faisal (2004), p. 148.

33   Interview with Aswar Hasan, Makassar, 24 June 2007.

34   Interview with Saleh Putuhena, 21 June 2007.

35   Interview with Muin Salim, Makassar, 22 January 2004.

36   *Suara Hidayatullah*, vol. XIV, no. 2 (June 2003): 21–22.

37   Interview with Muhammad Ikhwan, Makassar, 21 June 2007. In the interview, he gave an interesting example of how Shariah norms can be problematic if applied by the state. For the WI, he said, having a beard is mandatory or even obligatory for every male Muslim, but he disagreed with the notion that the state should oblige every male Muslim to keep his beard, because enforcing this kind of rule in the present situation would create animosity towards Islam.

38 The IAIN Alauddin was upgraded to a university (UIN, State Islamic University) in 2006.
39 Interview with Qasim Mathar, 17 December 2002. See also his columns in *Fajar* on 11 November 2001, 11 July 2006, 4 July 2006 and 1 August 2006.
40 Interviews with Hamka Haq, Makassar, 18 December 2002 and 20 January 2004. See also Hamka Haq (2001).
41 See "Syafi'i Maarif, Said Agil dan Sobary Merapat ke PDIP", *Rakyat Merdeka*, 6 August 2007.
42 Interviews with Saleh Putuhena, Makassar, 24 January 2004 and 21 June 2007.
43 Interviews in Makassar with Saleh Putuhena, 21 June 2007; Qasim Mathar, 17 December 2002.
44 In the first meeting of the task force, according to Qasim, the KPPSI activists demanded that he withdraw or they themselves would withdraw from the team. But Qasim still came to the next meeting. He then said, "I decided to stay in the team, and I hoped that some of the others would themselves withdraw today." The KPPSI activists, however, remained. Interview with Qasim Mathar, 17 December 2002.
45 Interview with Ishak Ngeljaratan, Makassar, 21 December 2002.
46 Interview with Zakariya J. Ngelow, Makassar, 23 December 2002.
47 Interview with Daniel Sopamena, Makassar, 20 June 2007. See also Ramli, Ahmad and Ch. (2006), pp. 219–20.
48 The two other elected DPD members are Ishak Pamumbu Lambe (5.04 per cent) and Benyamin Bura (4.20 per cent), both of whom are Christian. For the votes, see <www.kpu.go.id/suara/hasilsuara_dpd_sah.php>.
49 Interview with an Ahmadiyah activist, M. Syaeful 'Uyun, Makassar, 20 June 2007.
50 For the full text of the regulation, see Ramli, Ahmad and Masroer (2006), pp. 645–57.
51 For the full text of the regulation, see Ramli, Ahmad and Masroer (2006), pp. 659–75.
52 For the full text of the regulation, see Ramli, Ahmad and Marroer (2006), pp. 680–85.
53 Muh. Adlin Sila notes that in 2004, there were 605 Qur'an reading schools in Bulukumba (Sila 2006, p. 100).
54 For the full text of the regulation, see *Halaqah*, no. 05 (April 2006): 7–10.
55 See "Hukuman Potong Tangan di Bulukumba", *Fajar*, 21 November 2007; "Muspida Segera Bahas Hukuman Potong Tangan", *Fajar*, 22 November 2007.
56 A.M. Sappewali was elected as the regent of Bulukumba in 2005. Patabai Pobokari was then appointed as the head of the National Education Office of South Sulawesi provincial government.

57 The following account of criticisms of the regulations is drawn from Ad'han and Umam (2006), pp. 56–77; *Halaqah* bulletin no. 01 (2005) and nos. 02, 03, 04 and 05 (2006); and conversation with Syamsurijal Ad'han, Mubarak and Aswan Achsa in LAPAR office in June 2007.

58 A Christian minister and lecturer at the Academy of Theology in Makassar said that this policy also discriminates against Muslim officials, because it is not applied to non-Muslim officials. Interview with Rampalodji, Makassar, 20 June 2007.

59 Interview with Aswar Hasan, former Secretary General of the KPPSI (2000–05), Makassar, 24 June 2007.

60 Juhanis (2006), p. 206 quoting *Tribun Timur*, 8 September 2005.

61 On the crime figures, see Syamsurijal Ad'han (2007).

62 See *Fajar* and *Tribun Timur*, 30 June 2007.

63 Interview with Siradjuddin, Makassar, 19 June 2007.

64 Interview with Aswar Hasan, Makassar, 24 June 2007.

65 See "Calon Gubernur Berebut Simpati Ormas" and "Muhammadiyah dan NU Netral", *Fajar*, 18 June 2007.

66 See "Para Da'i Bertobatlah, Akui Kesalahan Kepada Tuhan", *Fajar*, 22 June 2007.

67 Interview with Qasim Mathar, Makassar, 22 June 2007.

68 Interview with Daniel Sopamena, Makassar, 20 June 2007.

69 Interview with Lidya K. Tandirerung, Makassar, 20 June 2007.

70 Interview with Ishak Ngeljaratan, Makassar, 22 June 2007.

71 See also Ngeljaratan's column in *Fajar*, 23 June 2007.

72 This is directly recorded from the Secretary of the KPPSI, Siradjuddin, in Makassar, 19 June 2007.

73 See his column in *Fajar*, 23 October 2007.

74 See "Syahrul Teken Kontrak Politik", *Fajar*, 31 October 2007 and "Jika Gagal Syahrul Siap Mundur", *Fajar*, 16 November 2007.

75 See "Syahrul Gubernur Sulsel", *Fajar*, 12 November 2007.

76 See "Juru Damai Turun Temurun", *Tempo*, 28 January–3 February 2008.

77 See "Pendidikan Gratis, Itu Komitemen Kami", *Fajar*, 20 March 2008.

78 See "Aziz Kahar Muzakkar dan Aksa Mahmud Terpilih Jadi DPD", *Tempo Interaktif*, 1 May 2009, <http://www.tempointeraktif.com/hg/Pemilu2009_berita_mutakhir/2009/05/01/brk,20090501-173872,id.html>.

79 My account of the KPPSI Congress relies heavily on the following media reports: "Komite Persiapan Penegakan Syariat Islam Sulsel Pertegas Urgensi", *Tempo Interaktif*, 2 February 2010, <http://www.tempointeraktif.com/hg/nusa/2010/02/02/brk,20100202-222968,id.html>; "Struktur KPPSI Berubah", *Tribun Timur*, 8 February 2010; "KPPSI: Pilih Kepala Daerah Pro Syariat Islam", *Tribun Timur*, 9 February 2010; "KPPSI Desak Pembebasan Agus Dwikarna", *Metro News*, 8 February 2010.

80 See "Ilham AS Masuk Bursa Ketua KPPSI", *Tribun Timur*, 7 February 2010; and "Ilham Fokus di ND dan Bahar Siap", *Tribun Timur*, 8 February 2010.

81 It is also noteworthy that in the media coverage, we can see that KPPSI activists now seem to prefer to use the term "amar ma'ruf nahi munkar" [commanding good and forbidding wrong] rather than the term "perda syariah" [religious Shariah-based regulations]. This is probably the result of the internal discussion among the KPPSI activists mentioned by Aswar Hasan above.

82 This point was probably related to Aswar Hasan's position as the Head of the Regional Broadcasting Commission (KPID) of South Sulawesi.

83 These leaders are Sanusi Baco (Chairman of the Indonesian Ulama Council of South Sulawesi), Djamaluddin Amien (former leader of the Muhammadiyah of South Sulawesi), the late Abdurrahman A. Basalamah (former rector of the Indonesian Muslim University (UMI), M. Amin Syam (former governor of South Sulawesi), Patabai Pobokari (former head of Bulukumba district) and the late Syafrudin Nur (former head of Pangkep district).

84 Telephone conversations with Hamdan Juhanis and Mubarak, 29 January 2011.

85 Interview with Daniel Sopamena, Makassar, 20 June 2007.

References

Ad'han, Syamsurijal. "Wajah Islam Yang Paradoks di Bumi Panrita Lopi". Unpublished paper. Makassar, 2007.

Ad'han, Syamsurijal and Zubair Umam. "Politik Kekuasaan dibalik Perda Syariat Islam di Bulukumba". *Tashwirul Afkar* 20 (2006): 58–60.

Anonymous. *Selayang Pandang Wahdah Islamiyah*. Makassar: Wahdah Islamiyah, 2007.

Avonius, Leena. "Morality and Islam in Post-Conflict Aceh". *Suomen Antropologi: Journal of the Finnish Anthropological Society* 23, no. 3 (2007): 75–89.

Biro Humas KPU. *Pemilu Indonesia Dalam Angka dan Fakta Tahun 1955–1999*. Jakarta: Biro Humas KPU, 2000.

Bruinessen, Martin van. "The Tariqa Khalwatiyya in South Celebes". In *Excursies in Celebes. Een Bundel Bijdragen bij het Afscheid van J. Noordyun*, edited by Harry A. Poeze and Pim Schoorl. Leiden: KITLV Uitgeverij, 1991.

———. "Traditionalist and Islamist Pesantrens in Contemporary Indonesia". In *The Madrasa in Asia: Political Activism and Transnational Linkages*, edited by Farish A. Noor, Yoginder Sikand and Martin van Bruinessen. Amsterdam: Amsterdam University Press, 2008.

Bush, Robin. "Regional Shariah Regulations in Indonesia: Anomaly or Symptom?". In *Expressing Islam: Religious Life and Politics in Indonesia*, edited by Greg Fealy and Sally White. Singapore: Institute of Southeast Asian Studies, 2008.

Dijk, C. van. *Rebellion under the Banner of Islam: The Darul Islam in Indonesia.* The Hague: Martinus Nijhoff, 1981.

Faisal, Ahmad. *Rekonstruksi Syariat Islam: Kajian Tentang Pandangan Ulama Terhadap Syariat Islam oleh KPPSI di Sulawesi Selatan.* Ph.D. thesis. Yogyakarta: UIN Sunan Kalijaga, 2004.

Fatwa, A.M. "Syariat Islam, Otonomi Khusus dan Masa Depan Masyarakat Sulawesi Selatan". Paper presented to the Islamic Community Congress, Makassar, 19–21 October 2000.

Feith, Herbert. *The Indonesian Elections of 1955.* Ithaca, NY: Cornell Modern Indonesia Project, 1957.

Furkon, Aay Muhammad. *Partai Keadilan Sejahtera, Ideologi dan Praksis Politik Kaum Muda Muslim Indonesia Kontemporer.* Bandung: Teraju, 2004.

Gonggong, Anhar. *Abdul Kahar Mudzakkar, Dari Patriot Hingga Pemberontak.* Yogyakarta: Ombak, 2004.

Haq, Hamka. *Syariat Islam, Wacana dan Penerapannya.* Ujung Pandang: Yayasan Al-Ahkam, 2001.

Harvey, Barbara S. *Pemberontakan Kahar Muzakkar: Dari Tradisi ke DI/TII.* Jakarta: Grafiti Pers, 1989.

International Crisis Group. (ICG). "Al-Qaeda in Southeast Asia: The Case of the 'Ngruki Network' in Indonesia". ICG Indonesia Briefing, 8 August 2002.

Juhanis, Hamdan. *The Struggle for Formalist Islam in South Sulawesi: From Darul Islam (DI) to Komite Persiapan Penegakan Syariat Islam (KPPSI).* Ph.D. thesis. Canberra: Faculty of Asian Studies, Australian National University, 2006.

Kabry, Abdul Muiz. *Sejarah Kebangkitan dan Perkembangan Darud Da'wah Wal Irsyad.* Pare-Pare: Pondok Pesantren Putri DDI, 1983.

Karim, M. Rusli. *HMI-MPO dalam Kemelut Modernisasi Politik di Indonesia.* Bandung: Mizan, 1997.

Lembaga Informasi Nasional. *Hasil Pemilu DPR, DPD dan DPRD Tahun 2004.* Jakarta: Lembaga Informasi Nasional, 2004.

Magenda, Burhan Djabier. *The Surviving Aristocracy in Indonesia: Politics in Three Provinces of the Outer Islands.* Ph.D. thesis. Ithaca: Cornell University, 1989.

Mathar, Qasim. "Saya Takut pada Kelompok Penegak Syariat Islam". *Fajar,* 11 November 2001.

———. "Dua Jenis Syariat Islam". *Fajar,* 11 July 2006a.

———. "Islam Phobia?". *Fajar,* 1 August 2006b.

———. "Perda Agama dan Wacana Politik". *Fajar,* 4 July 2006c.

Mattulada. *Islam di Sulawesi Selatan.* Jakarta: LEKNAS, LIPI and DEPAG, 1976.

Mujiburrahman. *Feeling Threatened: Muslim-Christian Relations in Indonesia's New Order.* Amsterdam: Amsterdam University Press/ISIM, 2006.

Ngeljaratan, Ishak. "Agama Niscaya Memihak". *Fajar,* 23 June 2007.

Pelras, Christian. "Religion, Tradition and the Dynamics of Islamisation in South Sulawesi". In *The Propagation of Islam in the Indonesian-Malay Archipelago*, edited by Alijah Gordon. Kuala Lumpur: Malaysian Sociological Research Institute, 2001.

Pradadimara, Dias and Burhaman Junedding. "Who is Calling for Islamic Law?". *Inside Indonesia* (October–December 2002): 25–26.

Ramli, Andi Muawiyah, Abdul Kadir Ahmad and Masroer Ch. *Demi Ayat Tuhan: Upaya KPPSI Menegakkan Syariat Islam*. Jakarta: OPSI, 2006.

Sila, Muh. Adlin. "Perda Syariat Islam di Bulukumba, Sulawesi Selatan". *Harmoni: Jurnal Multikultural & Multireligius* 5, no. 17 (2006): 93–110.

Siradjuddin, M. "Penerapan SI dalam Masyarakat Plural". *Fajar*, 9 November 2004.

Sopamena, Daniel. "Sikap Kristen Terhadap Gagasan Pemberlakuan Syariat Islam di Indonesia". Unpublished paper. Makassar.

Steenbrink, Karel A. and Jan Aritonang, eds. *History of Christianity in Indonesia*. Leiden: Brill, 2008.

Subhan, Arief. "Pesantren Hidayatullah: Madrasah-Pesantren Independen Bercorak Salafi". In *Mencetak Muslim Modern: Peta Pendidikan Islam Indonesia*, edited by Jajat Burhanuddin and Dina Afrianty. Jakarta: Rajawali Pers, 2006.

Suryadinata, Leo, Evi Nurvidya Arifin, and Aris Ananta. *Indonesia's Population: Ethnicity and Religion in a Changing Political Landscape*. Singapore: Institute of Southeast Asian Studies, 2003.

Turmudi, Endang and Riza Sihbudi, eds. *Islam dan Radikalisme di Indonesia*. Jakarta: LIPI Press, 2005.

Wawer, Wendelin. *Muslime und Christen in der Republik Indonesia*. Wiesbaden: Franz Steiner Verlag, 1974.

6

MAPPING RADICAL ISLAM: A STUDY OF THE PROLIFERATION OF RADICAL ISLAM IN SOLO, CENTRAL JAVA

Muhammad Wildan

INTRODUCTION

Solo is a unique city.[1] Previously known as the centre of the great Islamic Mataram Kingdom, Solo is also well known as the heartland of Javanese culture, a culture into which Islam has been mixed. The people of Solo are famous for their distinctive behaviour, graciousness and refined manners, besides their gorgeous *batiks*.[2] These characteristics also permeate their language, which is the most highly evolved Javanese in Java.[3] On the other hand, since the late twentieth and early twenty-first centuries, Solo has become a place where various Islamic radicals have flourished. In the middle of the New Order period, some of the leaders of the Pondok Pesantren Al-Mukmin in Ngruki opposed the government and openly expressed their desire to establish an Islamic state. Their involvement in the *Usrah* movement in the 1980s forced Abdullah Sungkar and Abu Bakar Ba'asyir to flee to Malaysia. Abu Bakar Ba'asyir's involvement in the establishment of *Majelis Mujahidin Indonesia* (MMI) in 2000 signified the re-emergence of *Darul Islam's* power in Indonesia in general, and in Yogyakarta and Solo in particular. More recently, the issue of Pondok

Ngruki resurfaced with the school's alleged connections to radical Islamic violence, including the Bali bombings. The International Crisis Group (ICG) first introduced the term the "Ngruki Network" as the "group" most responsible for acts of radical violence since the beginning of the twenty-first century. In its further development, the network has become notorious as Jama'ah Islamiyah (JI), one of the factions of S.M. Kartosuwiryo's Darul Islam, which allegedly acts as the link to Al-Qaeda in Southeast Asia.[4]

Solo became notorious for the "sweeping" of hotels and bars by vigilante groups targeting Americans and other Western aliens. Although the *Front Pemuda Islam Surakarta* (FPIS) has been at the forefront of such activities, it is not the only vigilante group in Solo. The decline of the Soeharto regime in 1998 was marked by the emergence of vigilante groups who tried to participate in social and political issues, either locally or nationally. All of the above suggests that Solo is rife with radical Islamic groups. Although not all Islamic vigilante groups are "radical", to a certain extent, they are all similarly involved in violent activities.

Despite the proliferation of Islamic radical groups in the city, there have been no significant efforts to adopt *shariah*-based local regulations (*peraturan daerah shariah*). Although some radical groups are concerned with *shariah*, their demand for *shariah*-based regulations has not found widespread support among the Solonese. In other words, only a fraction of society supports the Islamic radical groups in the city. As far as Solo is concerned, the reason for this is simple: Solo and its surrounding regions are overwhelmingly *abangan* in character. *Santri*, or pious Islam, is only an ideal for a minority in the region; radical Islam meets with even less public approval. Thus, minimal support for radical Islam at the grassroots level means that it is impossible for *shariah* legislation to be accepted in the city. The minority position of devout Muslims may explain why this group tends towards radicalism. The fact that they have only recently "converted" to *santri* Islam could be another reason for their radical disposition. To understand the full implications of Islam in the city, we need to start at the beginning.

SOCIAL AND HISTORICAL BACKGROUND OF SOLO

Understanding Islam in Solo requires that we start by analysing the origins of the religion's development in the city. The role played by the region's kings was significant for the later development of Islam in Solo. It was the kings who had, during the colonial period, established the first major educational institutions of Solo, the Pondok Jamsaren and the Madrasah Manba' al-'Ulum. In addition, several villages that played a significant role in the early development of Islam in the city deserve mention, such as Kauman, Pasar Kliwon, and Laweyan. These villages (now wards of the city) have long been strongholds of orthodox Islam, but in order to understand the dynamics of Islamic activism in Solo, it is important to understand that in most other parts of the city and regency, there is a strong *abangan* (nominal Muslim, syncretistic) majority. Finally, I will briefly sketch the role played by the Communist Party in Solo after the coup of 1 October 1965.

Well known today as a major centre of Javanese culture, Solo was founded 265 years ago. The history of the city can be traced back to the history of the Islamic kingdom of Mataram in Kartasura, which was established in 1680 by Susuhunan Amangkurat II (1677–1703). Following a rebellion that destroyed the kingdom, the Mataram Kingdom moved to the eastern region known as Sala (Solo) in 1746. After being divided into two kingdoms under the Treaty of Giyanti (Kasunanan in Surakarta and Kasultanan in Yogyakarta), in 1757, under the Treaty of Salatiga, the Kasunanan kingdom was further divided into two parts: Kasunanan and Mangkunegaran. Initially, Solo was just a small village at the edge of the Bengawan Solo River in the Kingdom of Kartasura. Bengawan Solo, the longest river in Java, played a significant role in supporting the life of the Solonese and in connecting Solo with other districts in Central and East Java, as well as to the ocean. The geographical position of Solo in the middle of four other districts — Yogyakarta (West), Semarang (North), Madiun (East) and Wonogiri (South) — gave a significant push to the later socio-economic development of Kasunanan Surakarta. In the 1800s, to control both kingdoms in Surakarta, the Dutch government established an overarching governmental institution, the Residency of Surakarta, which was headed by a European Resident.

Since the mid-eighteenth century, Islam has been a significant phenomenon in the Kingdom of Surakarta. Historical accounts relate that Islam in Solo was well established by the reign of Susuhunan Pakubuwono II (1726–49). Succeeding to the throne at the age of sixteen, under the strong guidance of his grandmother Ratu Pakubuwono, he was deeply concerned about religious issues. For example, Pakubuwono II interacted with Kyai Kasan Besari, the leader of the pesantren Gebangtinatar at Tegalsari Ponorogo in East Java, when he was fleeing the rebellion. Since then, a number of the royal families of Kasunanan Surakarta have sent their sons to pesantren Tegalsari, Ponorogo. Several other royal families also studied Islam with Kyai Hanggamaya at the pesantren in Kedu Bagelen. As a consequence, a number of prominent Javanese royal poets graduated from these pesantrens: Bagus Banjar (Yasadipura I, 1729–1803), Bagus Wasista (Yasadipura II, 1760–1845), and Bagus Burham (Raden Ngabehi Ranggawarsita, 1802–73).[5] Raden Ngabehi Ranggawarsita, however, is more famous as a visionary than as a royal poet, since his predictions on *Serat Kalatidha* have come to pass in modern times. The Islamic content of some of the above works proves that the development of Islam in Solo in particular cannot be separated from the authority of the Kingdom of Kasunanan; Islam in Solo was mostly developed by the kingdom and tended to be mixed with Javanese values (syncretism). This is one of the reasons why an *abangan* Muslim majority exists in Surakarta in the modern era. However, as the leading historian Ricklefs has observed (1997), the strength of Javanism (*kejawen*) does not prevent the Javanese from being radical or fundamentalist Muslims.

The development of Islam in Solo was encouraged by Susuhunan Pakubuwana IV (1788–1820). Initially, he invited *ulama* from many different places to stay and develop Islam in the city. One of the most famous and prolific of these *ulama* was Kyai Jamsari, from the Banyumas region. He lived and built a mosque and pesantren or pondok (boarding school) on the south-western side of the Kingdom of Surakarta, in what later became known as Jamsaren village (and Pondok Jamsaren). Kyai Jamsari not only taught Islam to the people who lived in the village's surroundings, but also to the kingdom's aristocrats and bureaucrats. The pesantren, however, was destroyed by Dutch colonial troops during the Diponegoro War of 1825–30. In 1878, Kyai Muhammad Idris from Klaten rebuilt and revived the pesantren, which finally reached its peak at the end of the nineteenth and beginning of the twentieth centuries. This development was marked by hundreds of students coming from many parts of Java and its outer islands. Although the pesantren was established by the kingdom, however, it was not fully under the kingdom's control. The involvement of its *santri* during the Diponegoro War reflected the resistance of the pesantren to the kingdom, as well as to the government of the Dutch East Indies.

The success of Pondok Jamsaren inspired the court officials R. Hadipati Sosrodiningrat and Penghulu Tafsir Anom to establish a formal educational institution to encourage more *ulama* to become *penghulu*.[6] In 1905, with the support of Susuhunan Pakubuwana X, they established a modern Islamic school called Madrasah Mamba' al-'Ulum (the source of knowledge), and appointed Kyai Muhammad Idris as its leader. Unlike other indigenous educational institutions in the form of traditional pesantren, the *madrasah* was the first indigenous educational institution to establish a modern system of education. At that time, the *madrasah* had 11 levels of classes: 1–4 for elementary education, 4–8 for secondary education, and 9–11 for higher-level education.[7] The last level to be developed was that of higher education at Mamba' al-Ulum. Although the *madrasah* was initially for royal and aristocratic families, after the demise of the Dutch East Indies government and the consequent decline of the Kasunanan Kingdom, the *madrasah* was opened to the common people (Ardani 1983).

To understand the development of Islam in Solo, we should take account of the role played by a number of pious Muslim majority villages, such as Kauman, Pasar Kliwon and Laweyan. They were deliberately established by the Dutch government and the Kasunanan Kingdom to help them control the various communities. The division of the communities into enclaves was also designed to accommodate the roles they would have to play: Kauman for the religious employees of the kingdom (*priyayis*), Pasar Kliwon for Arabs, Laweyan for Javanese-Muslim businessmen (*santri*), Jebres for Chinese businesspeople, and the other regions for Javanese *abangan*. The enclaves were also arranged to indicate social status; all of the above-mentioned enclaves were high on the social ladder compared to the common people. In the end, given the social and historical factors described above, the *abangan* comprised a majority of the Solonese. Not only were there *abangan* in all suburban areas of Solo, but also in the city's urban areas. Of the existing sub-districts, Pasar Kliwon, Banjarsari, and Jebres have the region's largest *abangan* majorities.

Another key social phenomenon is that of the existence of ethnic Chinese in the city. The presence of Chinese in Indonesia, and in Solo in particular, is not a new phenomenon. According to Cribb, the Chinese only became a "problem" for Indonesians in the nineteenth century, when the Dutch government introduced and maintained a system of racial classification that distinguished between Westerners, other Eastern foreigners, and native people (*inlanders*). Chinese descendants, having initially been classified as *inlanders*, were later separated from the category of "Indonesians" (Cribb 2006). Despite discrimination against this ethnic group, the Dutch government and local kingdoms offered the Chinese privileges during the colonial period, in large part due to their talent in business. To this day, the Chinese are more successful than other ethnic groups in business, not only in Solo, but also in Indonesia as a whole. Although the majority of Arabs in Solo are also traders, even they have not been able to surpass the Chinese in business. Since the early development of the Javanese middle classes, most Javanese traders have benefited from the presence of Chinese or Arab businesses.

From the early period of the Dutch East Indies government onwards, the success of the Chinese in business gave them a higher social status than the Arabs, let alone the Javanese.

The phenomenon of the *abangan* majority in Solo may also explain the mass adherence to Communism during the Old Order. Several months before the Communist Revolt in Madiun in 1948, Solo was one of the power bases of the *Front Demokrasi Rakyat* (FDR), Amir Syarifuddin's Socialist party, which opposed the presidential cabinet of Mohammad Hatta. About 17,000 followers of Syarifuddin went on strike during the Indonesian National Revolution (Onghokham 1978). After the coup d'état of 1 October 1965, unrest spread rapidly to Central Java, where Communists rose in support. On the same day, a *Dewan Revolusi* (Revolutionary Council) was formed in Central Java. A number of government officials in Central Java were involved in Communist Party activities, including the mayor of Surakarta, Utomo Ramelan, and the *bupati*s of Boyolali, Sragen, Wonogiri, and Karanganyar. In fact, the above districts, including Klaten, were the regions that were most heavily influenced by Communism. The special forces of the *Resimen Para Komando Angkatan Darat* (Army Para-Commando Regiment, or RPKAD), led by Sarwo Edi, that were sent to subdue the Communist uprising, finally seized and secured the city. In November 1965, about 3,000 Communists in Surakarta surrendered, and the Communist Party's secretary general, D.N. Aidit, was reportedly captured and shot dead in the region. Mass killings continued in the countryside, especially in Klaten, where being *abangan* was sufficient reason for being killed.

DAKWAH IN SOLO DURING THE NEW ORDER: PONDOK NGRUKI AND THE *USRAH* MOVEMENT

The New Order period was highly conducive to the emergence of Islamic radicalism. Government pressure on Muslims during the first phase of this era provoked the rise of Muslim resistance movements. Local conditions in Solo also accelerated the emergence of local Islamic radical groups. Two men in particular, and a pesantren that was founded by them, gained nationwide notoriety as embodying the radical tendencies of Solo. The pesantren Al-Mukmin, better known as Pondok Ngruki after the village where it is located, was founded by Abdullah Sungkar and Abu Bakar Ba'asyir in order to teach a more rigorous version of Islam than was taught in other schools. Sungkar and Ba'asyir became increasingly disaffected with the New Order regime, and in the course of the 1970s became involved in the underground movement, *Negara Islam Indonesia* (NII), which believed in the armed struggle for an Islamic state. They were arrested and jailed in connection with the *Komando Jihad* affair, a series of terrorist acts carried out by NII activists, and their names surfaced again in a subsequent wave of arrests concerning the *Usrah* affair, a network of clandestine Islamic study groups. In 1985 they fled to Malaysia to escape arrest, thereby losing influence in Pondok Ngruki, but as was reported later, they were the first to send young militants to Pakistan and Afghanistan for *jihad* training.

These two radical preachers were only the most visible Muslim activists in Solo. Their activities were, however, part of a much broader spectrum of *dakwah* activities, in Solo as well as nationwide. The early New Order period saw a shift from Muslim party politics to *dakwah*, at least partly in response to the fact that the main reformist Muslim party Masyumi remained banned. A number of the most prominent ex-Masyumi leaders established an association for *dakwah*, the Dewan Dakwah Islamiyah Indonesia (Indonesian Council for Islamic Propagation, DDII) in 1967. This organization established close connections with the Muslim World League (Rabitah al-'Alam al-Islami) and supported the government's programme to eradicate latent remnants of Communism. Explaining the shift in paradigm of Muslim activism, Mohamad Natsir (1908–93), the founder and leader of the DDII, asserted that "previously we carried out *dakwah* through politics but now we run politics through *dakwah*" (Hakiem and Linrung 1997, p. 8). Natsir urged his ex-Masyumi colleagues to establish DDII branches in many parts of Indonesia, including Solo, Central Java. During a speech in Solo in the late 1960s, he asked his ex-Masyumi counterparts to establish more pesantrens and Islamic hospitals to counter attempts to Christianize the local population, which were quite significant in the region at the time. According to Ahmad Chusnan, former leader of the Solo DDII branch, the establishment of Pondok Ngruki, as well as the hospitals Kustati and Yarsi (Yayasan Rumah Sakit Islam) was in direct response to Natsir's suggestion. Along with its general efforts to help Islamic institutions gain access to financial support from Middle Eastern donors, the Solo DDII also helped Pondok Ngruki in various ways. With assistance from the Solo DDII, about ninety new mosques were built across Central Java, including three by Pondok Ngruki. After the death of Natsir in 1993, the Solo DDII declined significantly, and it is no longer an active organization.

Pondok Ngruki was established as an attempt by *ulama* to develop Islam in Solo. Initially, some *ulama* in Solo conducted Islamic teaching (*taklim*) after holding *dluhur* (the noon prayer) in the Masjid Agung. In 1969, they expanded their activities to include more intensive Islamic teaching, and founded a *madrasah diniyah* (Islamic school), which was located in the southern part of Kasunanan palace, Gading Kidul. Besides establishing Radio Dakwah Islam Surakarta (RADIS) to extend the scope of their *dakwah*, they also developed the Islamic school into a boarding school in 1972. Several years later, the boarding school moved to the village of Ngruki. Finally, the boarding school joined *Yayasan Pendidikan Islam Al-Mukmin* (the Islamic Education Foundation of Al-Mukmin, or YPIA), which had been established earlier as an umbrella organization.

Although Pondok Ngruki had many founders, Abdullah Sungkar and Abu Bakar Ba'asyir became the figureheads of the boarding school. Many teachers from various educational backgrounds assisted with the development of Pondok Ngruki, but Sungkar and Ba'asyir occupied key positions in shaping the boarding school. However, we should not neglect the roles played by graduates from the reformist pesantren of Persis in Bangil, East Java and especially by graduates from the Middle East. Suwardi Effendi, Ahmad Chusnan, Muhammad Ilyas, M. Ya'kub Basya, and Jazri Mu'alim were among the young men who had been chosen by the DDII to pursue Islamic studies in the Middle East, and upon return they not only taught in Ngruki but also helped the school find financial support from Middle Eastern Islamic foundations. In its later development, however, most of the Pondok Ngruki *ustadz* (religious teachers) were recruited from among its own graduates, who held on to the spirit of Sungkar and Ba'asyir. For this reason, it is interesting to examine the backgrounds of these two figures in more detail.

Abdullah (Ahmad) Sungkar was born into a family of Yemeni descent in the Pasar Kliwon sub-district of Solo in 1937. Although his formal education was only up to junior high school level and he never attended a pesantren, he acquired considerable knowledge of Islam through self-study. Having been an active member of Masyumi's youth wing, Gerakan Pemuda Islam Indonesia (Indonesian Muslim Youth Movement, or GPII), he moved on to the parent organization, the Masyumi, until this was banned in 1960 (Nursalim 2001). His involvement in Masyumi led to his close relationship with M. Natsir, was strengthened further when Natsir established the DDII during the New Order period. Thus the spirit of Masyumi undeniably played an important role in shaping his Islamic thought. His spirit of Islam guided him as a good and tough *da'i* (Islamic preacher) in Solo, and his concern with politics directed his opposition to the government of the New Order era. Sungkar's character became clearer when he co-founded RADIS and Pondok Ngruki.

Abu Bakar Ba'asyir, who was also of Yemeni descent, was born in Jombang, East Java, in 1938. He spent his youth in Jombang until the second grade of senior high school, when he continued his study in the modern pesantren of Gontor. Finishing his study there, he continued at Al-Irsyad University in Solo and the State Institute for Islamic Studies (IAIN), Sunan Kalijaga Yogyakarta, in 1964. The political polarization of those years caused Ba'asyir to discontinue his studies and become vigorously involved in the GPII and Al-Irsyad until the late 1960s. As a means of further study, he taught himself by employing the basis of Islamic knowledge that he had already acquired. Being active in the GPII and Al-Irsyad greatly influenced his thought. Through these organizations, he met Abdullah Sungkar, which later shaped his attitude towards politics. Compared to his counterpart Sungkar, Ba'asyir was initially less concerned about politics. However, due to his involvement in Sungkar's activities, he was tried in the courts, detained, and jailed together with his colleague.[8]

After this, both Sungkar and Ba'asyir continuously criticized and opposed the government's regulatory stance towards Muslims. A key focus of their criticism was the imposition of the state ideology of Pancasila (which they perceived as directed against political Islam) and the Pancasila indoctrination course P-4, which was obligatory for all civil servants and students.[9] They were detained in late 1978 for involvement in the NII, the underground Darul Islam network that H. Ismail Pranoto (Hispran) was trying to resuscitate. Finally, on trial in 1982 after having been held in detention without trial for three years and ten months, they were sentenced to exactly the same amount of time for distributing Abdul Qadir Baraja's book, *Jihad dan Hijrah*, and for refusing to fly the Indonesian flag. Objecting to the light sentence, the prosecutors took the case to the Supreme Court. In 1985, Sungkar and Ba'asyir were summoned by the district court to hear the Supreme Court verdict on their case.[10] To avoid further detention, they fled to Malaysia, and were joined by some of their devout disciples in the following years. In their view, it was not an escape from justice, but a form of *hijrah* (emigration) to escape from the enemies of Islam, similar to the Prophet Muhammad's *hijrah* from Mecca to Medina. Although they fled to exile, they left a number of key issues related to the NII behind them: the possible involvement in *Komando Jihad*, the *Usrah* case, and the clandestine Islamic activism within Pondok Ngruki.

Komando Jihad was the name given to the shady network behind a string of violent incidents — armed robberies and bombings of cinemas, night clubs and churches — in various parts of Sumatra and Java in the late 1970s. The perpetrators appeared to belong to the underground NII network that connected remnants of the Darul Islam rebellion and was reviving the struggle for an Islamic state (and which Sungkar and Ba'asyir had recently joined). Key figures of this network were known to be monitored by the State Intelligence Coordinating Agency (Badan Koordinasi Inteligen Negara, BAKIN), and the degree of involvement of this agency in the affair never became clear. The authorities referred to some of the actions, raids to collect funds and weapons as the "*Warman terror*", after the suggestive name of the leader of the group, Asep Warman. The first *Komando Jihad* actions in the Solo and Yogyakarta region took place after the arrest of Sungkar and Ba'asyir. The vice rector of the Universitas Negeri Sebelas Maret (UNS), Parmanto, M.A., was assassinated by the Warman group on January 1979, allegedly because he was suspected of informing the police of Sungkar and Ba'asyir's joining NII. In the same month, a student of IAIN Sunan Kalijga in Yogyakarta, Hassan Bauw, was murdered by Warman fighters because he was suspected of giving information on Purwanto's escaped assassins to the police. After this, Warman disappeared for a long time and was finally shot dead in Bandung in July 1981.[11]

Although the *Usrah* affair was not as spectacular as *Komando Jihad*, it played a quite significant role in the regions of Central Java, Yogyakarta, and Jakarta. Initially, *usrah* was a kind of *tarbiyah* (intensive Islamic education) method used by university students, adopted from the method used by the Muslim Brotherhood (al-Ikhwan al-Muslimin) in Egypt to educate its members. Developed extensively at the Salman mosque of the Institut Teknologi Bandung (ITB) by Imaduddin Abdurahim, *usrah* later became widespread in a number of big universities in Java, such as at the Universitas Indonesia (UI) in Jakarta and the Universitas Gadjah Mada (UGM) in Yogyakarta.[12] Almost at the same time, Sungkar adopted this cell system to broaden his networks. To support the new *tarbiyah* method, Ba'asyir composed an *usrah* manual (Santosa 1996). Sungkar's *usrah* system developed rapidly in Central Java, Yogyakarta, and Jakarta, largely due to the networks of the NII branch he came to lead. This mechanism was very effective in attracting new members, especially youths. Among the networks of the *usrah* were the activists of the Sudirman mosque in Yogyakarta, which published the tabloid *al-Risalah*.[13] This tabloid was circulated in many regions using the *usrah* networks. Nevertheless, only two years after its establishment, in 1985, the government cracked down on the *usrah* activities, arresting and imprisoning of about twenty-nine of the activists, including Irfan Suryahardi (currently better known as Irfan S. Awwas) and Shobarin Syakur. Irfan, the editor of *al-Risalah*, was sentenced to thirteen years in jail, a very heavy sentence even during the Soeharto regime.

In the wake of Sungkar and Ba'asyir's departure for Malaysia, the NII network within Pondok Ngruki continued to function well. Although some of their devout disciples had joined them in Malaysia, other top leaders were still at Pondok Ngruki. The changing political attitude under the New Order in the late 1980s encouraged underground Islamic activists at Pondok Ngruki to expand their networks. Unlike before, during this period, they tried to acquire more followers by establishing further closed Islamic study circles in the pesantren. The numbers of Ngruki students eager to join these closed study circles kept increasing, especially from the Kulliyah al-Mu'allimin (KMI) and Kulliyah al-Mu'allimat (KMA), the schools with an exclusively religious curriculum for male and female students, respectively.[14] However, the "virus" of *harakah* (the clandestine Islamic movement) also reached the other schools in Ngruki, such as the Madrasah Aliyah of Al-Mukmin (MAAM). Whereas in the early 1980s it had been only a few students, who appeared to be exceptionally pious and dedicated, who would be regularly taken aside for special instruction by some of the militant *ustadz*, by the end of the decade, almost all of its pre-graduates swore an oath of loyalty to the leaders of the clandestine Islamic movement, although most of them did not really understand what this entailed, nor did they care about it. The underground network within Pondok Ngruki grew rapidly in the early 1990s. It was clear, therefore, that although Sungkar and Ba'asyir were not physically present, they still controlled the underground elements of the pesantren.

The progress of Islamic activism within Pondok Ngruki was halted by an incident known as the "case of 1995". For a long time, Pondok Ngruki, especially at the schools of the KMI and KMA, had been a breeding ground for Islamic activists. The YPIA foundation that managed the school (and that cared more about good relations with the authorities) thought that this contradicted the guidelines of the foundation. The foundation then issued a regulation to limit *harakah* activity within the pesantren, which eventually brought about a dispute between the foundation and a number of senior *ustadz*. The fierce dispute finally led to the dismissal of three senior *ustadz* — Abdul Manaf, Abdurrahim, and Djamaluddin — from the pesantren, later followed by the resignation of about 50 junior *ustadz* and 400 *santri*, who believed that Pondok Ngruki had lost its Islamic spirit. This enormous loss of staff and students was a great shock for the foundation and the pesantren. The three fired *ustadz*, followed by their devout followers, eventually established a new higher educational level boarding school at

Gading, Ma'had 'Ali An-Nur. A number of other junior *ustadz* and *santri* joined another pesantren in outer Surakarta, Boyolali, the pesantren of Dar al-Syahadah. The new boarding schools proved to be quite similar to Pondok Ngruki in many respects, particularly ideologically.

The "case of 1995" in Pondok Ngruki was also the result of a number of other problems facing the Islamic clandestine organization. Around 1993, Abdullah Sungkar, the leader of the NII in the Central Java and Yogyakarta region, ran into difficulties with the top leader of the NII, Ajengan Masduki, concerning his request to establish an autonomous branch of the NII in Malaysia. Ajengan Masduki rejected the request and Sungkar was dismissed from the NII, leading Sungkar to establish a new faction of the NII, which later became known as Jama'ah Islamiyah (JI). The establishment of the new faction brought about enormous changes within the NII, especially in its membership. Another explanation for the founding of this faction is that Sungkar was gradually shifting towards a more Salafi position. Since Sungkar and Ba'asyir had been in touch with radical Arab ulama in Afghanistan, they had been strongly influenced by Middle Eastern thought, especially Salafism. Eventually, many members of the clandestine organization had to choose between the leadership of Sungkar or Masduki.

Meanwhile, Sungkar and Ba'asyir used their presence in Malaysia to broaden their network. During their fourteen years in Malaysia, besides being involved in many religious activities, they had the good fortune to build an international network. Although they were in exile, their network in Indonesia functioned well, including their spiritual roles in Pondok Ngruki. In Malaysia, besides preaching in some districts, they also co-founded an Islamic school called Madrasah Luqman al-Hakim in the sub-district of Kuala Pilah, Johor Malaysia. Through the Luqman al-Hakim, Sungkar and his disciples taught Islam as they had done in Pondok Ngruki. Therefore, Luqman al-Hakim graduates were very similar to the graduates of Pondok Ngruki in terms of their militancy and opposition to the government. Noordin M. Top and Azahari Husin, the key figures in the JI, who were to become notorious in Indonesia as the masterminds behind numerous bombings, were among the activists of this madrasah. In late 1999, when the political situation in Indonesia changed dramatically, Sungkar and Ba'asyir went home. Sungkar suffered a heart attack and died in Bogor in November 1999, before he had had a chance to reorganize Pondok Ngruki. His death left many questions concerning the existence of JI, the organization that would be suspected of organizing a series of violent and devastating bombings in Indonesia in 2000 and later.

OTHER *DAKWAH* ACTIVITIES IN SOLO:
MAJELIS TAFSIR ALQUR'AN AND JAMA'AH GUMUK

As *abangan* are still the majority in Solo, Islamic organizations conduct many *dakwah* efforts in the region. Although one could not claim that Muhammadiyah and Nahdatul Ulama (NU) have failed altogether to conduct *dakwah* in Solo, they are less prominent in Solo than some other organizations. A number of "home-grown" Islamic organizations, such as Majelis Tafsir al-Qur'an (MTA) and the Jama'ah Gumuk, appear to be widely accepted by the Solonese. But in the end, not one of the above Islamic organizations could be considered as the mainstream in this *abangan* majority region.

Although Muhammadiyah and the NU have exceeded other moderate Muslim organizations in terms of establishing educational institutions, they have failed to re-Islamize and modernize the Solonese. The *abangan* are still in the majority and there are some radical groups in the city. Therefore, it is difficult for board members of Muhammadiyah and the NU in the region to give a clear answer when asked where the main base of each of organization is. Even among the people of Solo's Kauman district, who tend to be the most "modernist" Muslims, Muhammadiyah has no strong presence, unlike the Kauman of Yogyakarta.[15] As far as Muhammadiyah in Solo is concerned, only a small number of the organization's Muslim figures are from the Kauman. The success of Sarekat Islam in Solo in the early twentieth century may be the reason why the NU and Muhammadiyah never became very influential there.

The district of Kauman has lost its position as the centre of Islamic life in Solo; at present, Laweyan, with its industrious Muslim middle class, is seen as the heart of the Muslim community. Amien Rais, the former leader of Muhammadiyah and the chairman of the People's Consultative Council, the MPR, is from Laweyan. Even so, one could hardly call Laweyan a major base for Muhammadiyah. No organization from outside ever became very influential there, perhaps because the peculiarities of the Solonese are not fully understood by "alien" Islamic organizations. The successful organizations are all local ones.

Majelis Tafsir Alqur'an

The Majelis Tafsir Alqur'an (the Council of Qur'anic Exegesis, or MTA) is the most successful Islamic organization in Solo in terms of its membership. Abdullah Thufail Saputra's (d. 1992) desire to purify Muslims' Islamic beliefs in Surakarta drove him to become involved in Islamic activities. Initially, together with other ulama in Solo, he was involved in the radio station for Islamic *dakwah*, RADIS, in the late 1960s. Several years later, in 1972, by which time Sungkar and Ba'asyir had established a boarding school in Ngruki, Thufail established a forum for Islamic teaching, which later became the MTA, in Pasar Kliwon sub-district. At the same time he worked with Abdullah Marzuki to develop a boarding school: Pondok Pesantren Modern Islam (PPMI) Assalaam, the most modern Islamic boarding school in the region. Thufail was eventually inspired to develop his own activities.

There are no significant doctrinal differences between the MTA and Muhammadiyah; indeed, Thufail initially also participated actively in Muhammadiyah. Thufail is said to have established a separate organization, MTA, because he was disappointed with Muhammadiyah's less rigorous attitude towards dubious local beliefs and practices. Like Muhammadiyah, MTA's stated purpose is to purify Muslims' Islamic beliefs. Therefore, Thufail invited Muslims to study, comprehend, and apply the Qur'an purely and consistently, in the way that the first generation of Muslims or companions had done. This implied dissuading Muslims from any *bid'ah*, *khurafat* or *takhayyul*, the practices reformists condemn as deviating from the genuine Shariah.[16] In this respect, the MTA and Muhammadiyah shared the same purpose. However, as Abdullah Thufail's successor Ahmad Sukino asserts, Muhammadiyah did not exert sufficient effort to ensure that its members follow proper Islamic teachings, and especially to avoid *takhayul*, *bid'ah* and *khurafat*. He claims that there is no significant difference between the MTA and Muhammadiyah, except that the MTA compels its members to actually stick to the pure teachings of Islam. Another significant difference is that the MTA does not have periodical congresses at which a new leadership is elected, as Muhammadiyah does. It is clear that Ahmad Sukino will run the organization as long as he remains alive, as did Abdullah Thufail before him.

Currently, the MTA is a large Islamic organization, no longer only locally in Surakarta, but also nationally. In 2007 the MTA claimed to have about 25 provincial branches (*perwakilan*), more than 128 district branches (*cabang*), and no fewer than 100,000 members all over Indonesia.[17] By 2011, the MTA had spread to almost all provinces of Indonesia, and is now present in almost all districts in Java, with the exception of the West Java and Banten provinces. In the city of Solo itself, the MTA has a large following, especially in sub-districts with *abangan* majorities, such as Pasar Kliwon and Banjarsari. However, in other regions of the former Surakarta residency, the MTA has more than 50 sub-district branches. One interesting aspect of this organization is that most of its members are lower-level *abangan* people on the periphery and in rural areas. Clearly, the MTA's simple approach to Islam does not attract much attention among educated people, let alone university students. Currently, to support its *dakwah* activities, the MTA runs several junior and senior high schools and broadcasts a radio station from its headquarters, and also broadcasts live on the Internet.[18]

The high level of social solidarity among members of the MTA is one of the most interesting aspects of the organization. The organization collects money in the form of *infaq*, *zakat*, *sadaqah*, and other charity funds, so as to finance the organization and help its members. This commitment to social solidarity led the organization's leader to stipulate that all animals offered at rites celebrating 'Id al-Adha (the Feast of Sacrifice) should be collected and distributed equally among the members. On the occasion of the 2006 'Id al-Adha celebration for instance, the MTA collected around 110 cows and 300 goats. In the same way, the MTA collected charity funds to help its members during the earthquake in Yogyakarta and Central Java in 2006, and also the Merapi eruption in 2010. This attitude has attracted many people from low-level social groups to the organization; religious issues, initially, are not the main reason for *abangan* to become involved in the community.

Like other Islamic organizations, the MTA does not actively campaign for the adoption of Shariah-based local regulations. Although the organization holds that ultimately all legislation should be based on the *Shariah*, it has not put the issue on its main agenda. For the MTA, according to Sukino, the demand for Shariah implementation will emerge automatically from society when people know more about Islam. Therefore, the MTA's main task is to educate Muslims about their religion. Furthermore, the organization does not hold that the state should necessarily be an Islamic state. For the MTA, in its current form as Negara Kesatuan Republik Indonesia (Unitary State of the Republic of Indonesia, NKRI), Indonesia makes it possible for Muslims to live in accordance with the Shariah. Hence, the notion of *jihad* is not a concern of this organization, except in the general sense of making an effort for improvement. The enormous MTA membership and network has led many politicians to attempt to recruit the MTA as a mass constituent. Sukino turned down invitations by some politicians to join their parties. The MTA tells its followers that any Muslim political party is acceptable as long as it strives to promote Islam. So far, therefore, the MTA has not become attached to any particular Islamic political parties.

From the above we can clearly conclude that the MTA is not a radical movement. Although the MTA does have about 4,000 uniformed and trained vigilantes, this force is deployed for general purposes and not for any violent activities. Sukino maintains that radical activities, such as the "sweepings" (i.e. raids on night clubs and hotels) conducted by vigilante forces in Solo, are unnecessary. Such radicalism, he adds, could even damage the image of Islam. Indeed, the MTA's vigilante force has joined demonstrations in Solo, but only in support of certain issues that were debated in the national parliament, such as the draft law on national education (*Sistem Pendidikan Nasional* or *Sisdiknas*),[19] the draft law on pornography,[20] and the demand to ban the Ahmadiyah in Indonesia. Moderate and non-violent, MTA's ability to mobilize large numbers suggests that it will remain a significant Islamic social movement in the near future.

Jama'ah Gumuk

Another influential Islamic organization in Solo is the Muslim community known as Jama'ah Gumuk. Founded by H. Mudzakir in 1976, this community is located at a mosque in the ward of Gumuk, Mangkubumen, in the city of Solo. Initially, it only offered informal religious teaching for local residents. But over time, Mudzakir's activities attracted increasing numbers of people to study Islam with him. Although the Islamic teaching of this group differs little from that of other modern Islamic organizations, it tends to be quite an exclusive organization. However, Chalid Hasan, one of the leaders of the community, asserts that his solid community has a broad network covering the Surakarta region. The community's cell system has enabled it to become widespread, not only in Solo but also in some other regions in the ex-residency of Surakarta.

Many people consider the Gumuk mosque community to be fairly exclusive, since the organization and its activities are closed to the surrounding society. It was not surprising, therefore, that in the 1980s, other groups suspected the Gumuk mosque community of being Shi'ites. In fact, there are many reasons why other groups made this assumption. The leader of the community, Mudzakir, once studied Islam at Yayasan Pendidikan Islam (YAPI) in Bangil, which is one of the major centres of Shi'ite learning in Indonesia. Moreover, Mudzakir also spent some time in Iran studying Islam. However, judged by their actual teachings and their daily activities, the Jama'ah Gumuk cannot be considered Shi'ite. In my observations, the way in which this community prays is like that of other Muslim groups, though they are clearly not mainstream. They also distinguish themselves from the politically radical Islamist groups in rejecting the Qur'anic exegesis by Sayyid Qutb, the chief ideologue of the Muslim Brotherhood, which provides a revolutionary, political reading of the holy text. Instead, this community uses the modern Qur'anic exegesis by Ahmad Mustafa al-Maraghi, popular among reformists, and the classical one by Imam Ibn Katsir. The way they dress is reminiscent of Salafis: the men grow beards and wear trousers that do not cover the ankles;[21] the women of this group, however, do not wear head-to-toe coverage as Salafis do, but only regular *hijab*. Unlike other Salafis, however, who do not usually question the legitimacy of existing governments as long as the head of state is a Muslim, the Jama'ah Gumuk regards the Indonesian government as well as the Indonesian state as basically illegitimate. Even to merely acknowledge the legitimacy of the Indonesian government is *haram* for followers of the movement, and so is participation in any project or organ of the state. There is no explicit instruction to members not to join any political party, but most members make it quite clear that they consider Islamic political parties as useless. In the vocabulary of other Salafis, the Gumuk congregation is Salafi in terms of its ideology (`aqidatan*) but not in its overall approach (*manhaj*).

Like the MTA, the Jama'ah Gumuk was originally a local (Solo-based) Islamic organization. This may have made it easier for the Solonese to accept it. In terms of its followers, most of the members of the community are lower-class Javanese from the periphery or suburbs of Solo; that is, people of *abangan* background. It is probably true that this conservative group, like the MTA, exerted a strong attraction precisely to *abangan* who were turning to a more explicitly Islamic identity. Another interesting aspect of the *Jama'ah Gumuk* is that during the New Order era, the community tended to concentrate on basic Islamic teaching (*taklim*), and was not interested in social and political issues. However, in the Reformation era, the community began to engage in social and political issues, and it even developed vigilante forces known as the Front Pemuda Islam Surakarta (Islamic Youth Front of Surakarta, FPIS) and the Hawariyyun (Disciples). We will discuss the FPIS in more detail in the next section.

Oppositional mobilization in the late New Order period

A further interesting aspect of Islam in Solo during the New Order era was the phenomenon of *Mega-Bintang*. Prior to the general election in 1997, many people demanded that Soeharto resign from the presidency, even before the monetary crisis at the end of 1997. As was common during New Order elections, the government party of Golongan Karya (Functional Groups, Golkar) was set to win a vast majority. Solo had, however, long been a mass base for the oppositional Partai Demokrasi Indonesia (PDI) and, after a government-engineered conflict in this party, of the Partai Demokrasi Indonesia Perjuangan (PDI-P), led by Sukarno's daughter Megawati. Dissatisfaction with the regime was widespread in Solo, especially among the poorer segments of the population, mostly *abangan*, and the demand for Soeharto's resignation galvanized them. In this situation a unique coalition of forces emerged. Mudrick M. Sangidoe, a popular leader of the Solo branch of the Muslim Partai Persatuan Pembangunan (PPP), saw an opportunity to defeat the "unbeatable" party, Golkar, and concluded an alliance between the two opposition parties. This unlikely coalition, which soon became known by the name of Mega-Bintang,[22] aroused much enthusiasm locally and mobilized much support. The alliance between an Islamic party and a secular nationalist party against the domination of Soeharto and Golkar had not earlier happened during the New Order, and it was popular in both parties at the grassroots level, not only in Solo but also in other major Indonesian cities. The national leaders of both parties, however, did not see this as their chance to defeat Golkar, and therefore refused to conclude a formal coalition. Although both parties were defeated in the 1997 election, Mega-Bintang can be regarded as a genuine grassroots phenomenon.

The Mega-Bintang movement reflected the general social situation in Solo. That is to say, Mega-Bintang was not a balanced coalition between the followers of the PPP and the PDI-P, since the PPP could draw on significantly less support in Solo. The lower-class *abangan* people are a politically volatile group that can be swayed by other groups. In the early twentieth century, when the first political movements emerged, lower-class *abangan* people had been attracted to *Sarekat Islam* and the fascinating mix of Islamic and Communist ideas of local Sarekat Islam leader, Haji Misbach. In general, I would say that what attracted people to Sarekat Islam then and to Mega-Bintang more recently was not any specific Islamic teaching but the prospect of overcoming their powerlessness, or at least showing defiance of hegemonic powers. In the future, these lower-class people may be drawn in other directions that promise an improvement in their current social status.

Although organizations such as the MTA, Jama'ah Gumuk and Muhammadiyah have been successfully conducting campaigns of Islamization (sometimes called *santrinisasi*, i.e. turning *abangan* into *santri*), the vast majority in Solo continue to be *abangan*. On the other hand, the Islamization process will not automatically make people moderate Muslims. In fact, most radical movements draw a large part of the following from former *abangan*. In the end, it will depend on which organization can successfully attract and lead them in a particular direction.

RADICAL ISLAM IN SOLO IN THE
POST-SOEHARTO ERA

The dramatic political changes in Indonesia were signalled in part by the emergence and re-emergence of radical Islamic groups. These groups emerged in various forms, either formally as the Majelis Mujahidin Indonesia (Council of Indonesian Islamic Warriors, MMI), clandestinely as the *Jama'ah Islamiyah* (JI), or in the form of vigilante forces (*laskar*) such as the Front Pembela Islam (Islamic Defenders Front, or FPI). The new era has also been marked by the increasing demand for Shariah implementation in many parts of Indonesia. Along with the demand for Shariah, vigilante forces have emerged throughout the country that took control of the streets and attempted to impose public morality (i.e., ban alcohol, gambling and prostitution). In the context of Solo, there has not been a significant demand for Shariah, but vigilante forces emerged during the early years of the post-Soeharto era. The Pondok Ngruki phenomenon re-emerged after it was revealed that some of the bombers behind the Bali blast in 2002 were from Ngruki networks. This section will explore several vigilante forces in Solo; Pondok Ngruki networks will be addressed in a separate section.

Unlike other cities in Indonesia, vigilante forces in Solo are significant in terms of their numbers and activities. Over time, there have been at least nine vigilante forces of local (Solonese) origin, as well as a few local chapters of national level paramilitary movements. These forces are the Front Pemuda Islam Surakarta (Islamic Youth Front of Surakarta, FPIS), Laskar Jundullah (Soldiers of God Militia), Laskar Umat Islam Surakarta (Militia of Surakarta Muslims), Tim Hisbah (Team for Upholding God's Law),[23] Laskar Hizbullah Sunan Bonang (Sunan Bonang's Party of God militia),[24] Hawariyyun (the Disciples), Brigade Hizbullah (the Party of God Brigade), Barisan Bismillah (Bismillah Forces), and Al-Ishlah (Reform). Local branches of Jakarta-based movements include the Gerakan Pemuda Ka'bah (the Ka'bah Youth Movement, or GPK), which is affiliated with the PPP, and the Front Pembela Islam (Islamic Defenders Front, FPI). Each of these forces reflects the diversity of the Muslim community in Solo. In many cases, the organizations act together to respond to issues they are concerned about. However, since most of them emerged in political circumstances, only a few are still active as vigilante forces. For this reason, I will only explore the FPIS as representative of the other vigilante forces in Solo.[25]

Front Pemuda Islam Surakarta

The FPIS emerged in response to the inter-religious conflict in Ambon in the early 1999, as did some other paramilitary groups in Indonesia, such as Laskar Jihad. Although the organization was not as involved in the Ambon battlefield as Laskar Jihad, it has a significant presence in Solo and in Indonesia in general. As a local Islamic group, however, the FPIS is not only concerned with local issues in Solo, but also national and even international issues affecting Muslims. The organization's activities have included flocks of people taking to the streets to protest against government policies or U.S. policies in the Muslim world. Warsito Adnan, the most prominent leader of the FPIS, acknowledges that the emergence of a number of radical Islamic groups in Indonesia, including Solo, has mostly been in response to U.S. hegemony and the perceived war on Islam, notably the invasions of Afghanistan and Iraq and U.S. support for Israeli policies in Palestine. Although the FPIS was initially an inclusive organization that was intended as an umbrella organization for all Islamic groups, in its later development it became exclusively affiliated with the Jama'ah Gumuk. The "acquisition" of the FPIS by the Jama'ah Gumuk is among the more interesting aspects of the FPIS.

Similar to other vigilante forces in Indonesia, most of the actions carried out by the FPIS are what are called anti-*maksiat* (anti-immorality) actions: heavy-handed operations against gambling, alcohol consumption and illicit sex. Although the FPIS recognizes that Indonesia is not an Islamic state, it nevertheless demands that the existing regulations concerning moral issues should be reinforced. Therefore, the FPIS periodically sweeps such places as brothels, gambling centres, cafes, and hotels, which it regards as immoral and in violation of God's law. During the fasting month of Ramadan, the FPIS usually intensifies its activities, not only with regard to the above places, but also *vis-à-vis* regular restaurants. The FPIS demands that restaurants be closed during daytime, out of respect for Muslims who are fasting, or at least that there should be no visible eating. The group's most controversial action has been the "sweeping" of international hotels in Solo and the expulsion of foreigners, especially American nationals, in response to the U.S. policies such as the invasion of Iraq.

The religious ideology of FPIS and the Jama'ah Gumuk remains elusive. Unlike some other vigilante groups, the FPIS has not shown much interest in demanding local Shariah regulations. On this issue, one of the leaders of the Jama'ah Gumuk, Chalid Hasan, asserts that it only makes sense to adopt such regulations when society is ready to accept the *Shariah*. He holds up the experience of Aceh as an example from which Muslims should learn: Aceh was given Shariah legislation from above, well before society was ready for it, and that caused a backlash. In his view, therefore, it is the task of Islamic organizations to strengthen Islamic awareness at the grassroots so that the entire Shariah will be accepted as part of the body of Islam. Once society is ready for it, it will be possible for Muslims to not only propose regional Shariah regulations, but also to coerce observance by society.[26] Therefore, the Gumuk people have not responded positively to the escalating demands by Muslims in many parts of Indonesia for the regional regulation of Shariah. Mudzakir asserts that regional Shariah regulations are good politically, but not ideologically, since they do not change the non-Islamic character of the state. Rather, Mudzakir asserts that Shariah should be implemented from the smallest systems of society upwards: the family or the school.[27]

Unlike in Pondok Ngruki, *jihad* is not widely discussed in the Gumuk community. While the Ngruki people tend to say that *jihad* should be interpreted more in terms of actual physical struggle, the Gumuk community, as asserted by Chalid, believe that this term has much a broader interpretation than just fighting and wars, although these latter activities should not be neglected. In the same way, some radical Islamists' interpretations of *jihad* in terms of violence are not readily accepted by this community. Chalid believes that the Prophet Muhammad himself did not require the existence of an Islamic state for the implementation of *Shariah*. For him, therefore, *jihad* in terms of violent actions should be the last resort for the implementation of the Shariah. Nor is a coup d'état the best road towards the implementation of the Shariah.[28]

Chalid resolutely rejects such actions as the Bali bombings, although he can understand why some people become involved in such violent activism. He recognizes that there may be situations in which violence might be necessary to protect Muslim interests. On the other hand, the Gumuk group believes that regional violent conflicts such as those in Ambon and Poso are completely different from the Bali bombings, and cannot be seen as terrorism. On one occasion, Mudzakir asserted that the Ambon and Poso wars had happened primarily as a result of the government's inability to deal with the social problems in those regions. Similarly, the Gumuk group believes that the economic problems faced by Indonesians since the downfall of the Soeharto regime have been due to the government's ignorance of Islamic social and political teachings, as well as simple incompetence. The Gumuk community rejects the labelling of some radical Islamists in Indonesia as terrorists.

Much like many other radical Islamists, the Gumuk group considers the West to be part of the current problems faced by Muslims. The hegemony of the West, as represented by the globalization and modernization of many aspects of life, is regarded as a threat. The West, especially the U.S., is considered to be hostile to Islam, on the grounds that U.S. actions are seen as being driven by Jewish interests (the Jews being the arch-enemies of Islam). Democracy and pluralism, as part of Western culture and civilization, are considered by the community to be *haram,* since they violate God's law. In their view, democracy as a state system mixes truth (Islam) with falsehood (democracy).[29] The Gumuk group argues that introducing democracy will not lead to a reduction in any immoral practices (*maksiat*) in society, as these are widespread in Western countries.[30] Rather than democracy, Islam has a much more perfect political system, namely *shura,* consultation.[31] For them, Islam is more than just a religion; it is a way of life, which organizes the relationship not only between human beings and God, but also between human beings.

As a result, the unity of the *ummah* is the main and ultimate agenda of the Gumuk group. The group's discourse, as outlined above, is constructed to draw support from society in such a way as to unite all Muslims. Mudzakir also asserts that one of the weaknesses of Muslims is that they are split into many different Islamic organizations, each of which has its own individual purposes. To achieve unity among Muslims, therefore, he argues that the Gumuk community should not consider itself an Islamic organization. He believes that Islamic organizations and parties do not unite Muslims, but divide them.[32] Based on the same reasoning, the Gumuk group believes that Islam does not recognize the existence of *madzhabs* (schools of Islamic jurisprudence). Mudzakir argues that the existence of *madzhabs* such as the Shafi'i or Hanafi schools only divides Muslims. He believes that the only proper *madzhab* in Islam is that of the *salaf,* that is, the generation of the Prophet, his companions, and the two generations after them. Other Islamic schools of thought, such as the Hanbali *madzhab*, do not represent an authentic interpretation of Islam. Therefore, Muslims should not only study Islam as practised by the first generations of Muslims, but they also should imitate their outlook and behaviour.

Komite Aksi Penanggulangan Akibat Krisis (Kompak)

Another significant radical organization in Solo is Kompak (Komite Aksi Penanggulangan Akibat Krisis, the Action Committee for Crisis Response). Although it remains unclear where and when the first *Kompak* was established, the *Kompak* branch in Solo was established in August 1998 by members of the Solo branch of DDII. Since historically, the Solo branch of DDII has had a relationship with the former leader of Pondok Ngruki, Abdullah Sungkar, the *Kompak* was supported by a number of Pondok Ngruki associates, especially Aris Munandar, a Ngruki graduate. Abu Bakar Ba'asyir reportedly served as advisor to the DDII's Kompak, besides a number of other prominent figures in Solo. The outbreak of religious conflict in Ambon inspired some JI members to use the Kompak as a means to act in Ambon and Poso. In addition, the Kompak also has branches in Ambon and Makassar. In many ways, then, the Kompak and JI have become intertwined, making it difficult to distinguish between the two. The Kompak, however, has also been involved in many social causes, such as helping Muslim victims of floods or earthquakes. For this reason, Kompak is now widely known as a prominent agent in the provision of emergency aid to victims. The cooperation between Kompak and the MER-C (Medical Emergency Rescue-Centre), an Indonesian Muslim humanitarian organization, in helping Muslims in Afghanistan after the U.S. bombing campaign in late 2001, was one of the reasons why some international Muslim organizations sent financial aid to Kompak.

THE NGRUKI NETWORK IN THE POST-SOEHARTO PERIOD

After having been mostly involved with mainstream educational issues since the mid-1980s, Pondok Ngruki resurfaced at both the national and international levels in the post-Soeharto era. During the fourteen-year period of absence of Sungkar and Ba'asyir, Ngruki had developed into the centre of close-knit network of like-minded people, as graduates settled all over the country, and several of them established similar boarding schools elsewhere. Some of these schools — Al-Islam in Lamongan, Ma'had 'Ali Al-Nur in Sukoharjo, Muttaqien in Rembang, and Dar al-Syahadah in Boyolali — were to draw attention because former students were involved in terrorist actions, but most of the schools stayed aloof from radical activism.[33] Tensions between radicals and more moderate elements in this network were inevitable, as Ba'asyir's return to Ngruki appeared to strengthen the hand of the radicals.

After his return from Malaysia in 1999, Ba'asyir took up his previous activities as a teacher at Pondok Ngruki. The foundation could not forbid him doing so because he is one of the founders of the pesantren. To limit Ba'asyir's influence, the foundation did not give him a strategic position in the boarding school. Rather, it gave him a non-structural position as a spiritual leader (*sesepuh*), which lacked any real power within the pesantren. In Ngruki, besides Ba'asyir, there is yet another successor to Sungkar: Ustadz Wahyuddin, the son-in-law of Sungkar, who now acts as the director of the pesantren. However, since it is clear that Wahyuddin has a tendency to see Ba'asyir as his mentor, there appears to be no possibility of disagreement between the two as to who should be heir to the Sungkar legacy.[34] Wahyuddin apparently defers to Ba'asyir but he tends to have more moderate views than him. According to one of my respondents in Ngruki, Wahyuddin sees the pesantren as an educational institution only and not as the base for any Islamic movement (*harakah*).

Ba'asyir's presence in Indonesia brought new life to his old networks of Islamic radicals, notably the *Usrah* network. He allowed or instructed two of his previous disciples in the *Usrah*, Irfan S. Awwas and Sobarin Syakur, to establish a formal, legal association that would bring together various groups and individuals who shared the ideal of an Islamic state, the Majelis Mujahidin Indonesia (MMI). At the founding congress in Yogyakarta in August 2000, Ba'asyir himself was chosen as the *amir* (top leader) of the decision-making body, *ahl al-halli wa al-'aqdi*. Several well-known activists of the former *Komando Jihad*, such as Abdul Qadir Baraja and Timsar Zubil, also attended this congress. The MMI operates within the frame of Indonesian law, although it makes no secret of its desire to change the legal system and replace it by the systematic application of the Shariah. It rejects the parliamentary system and boycotts the general elections.

Ba'asyir is also accused of leading the underground Jama'ah Islamiyah, which he had founded with Sungkar during their Malaysian exile. Much of the violent radicalism during the post-Soeharto era has been attributed directly or indirectly to Ba'asyir. The detention of some members of Al-Qaeda in Southeast Asia in Singapore, the ICG publication on the Ngruki networks, the involvement of some Ngruki graduates in the Bali bombings, and the revelation that the JI had been responsible for devastating bombings convinced the authorities that Ba'asyir was the spiritual leader of the JI, and that this was the branch of Al-Qaeda in Southeast Asia. After an exhaustive search, the authorities arrested him in October 2002 and brought him to trial. The case against him was strengthened when it was found that two Ngruki graduates were involved in the Bali bombing in 2002, six in the J.W. Marriot bombing in 2003, five in the Kuningan bombing in 2004, and finally, two Ngruki graduates were involved in the second Bali bombing in 2005. Based on all of the above evidence, it was widely taken for granted that Pondok Ngruki was a major centre for violent Islamic radicalism in Indonesia. However, the above facts were insufficient to prove that Ba'asyir was the spiritual leader of the JI and directly involved in any of the said violent incidents. After having been incarcerated for about four years, Ba'asyir was released in June 2006.

A few years later, Ba'asyir resigned from the MMI over a conflict concerning the organization's internal democratic procedures (more precisely, on the rule that the periodical congress elects the *amir* and that therefore theoretically he might lose that position). In July 2008, he established a new organization, named Jama'ah Ansar al-Tauhid (JAT). While he was engaged in broadening his new organization in many regions in Indonesia, Ba'asyir was detained again by the authorities in August 2010 on the charge of having established a guerrilla training camp in Aceh, and at the time of writing he remains incarcerated.

The stigma of terrorism put Pondok Ngruki in a difficult position. Although only some Ngruki graduates have been involved in violent actions in the name of Islam in Indonesia, the belief that it is a nest of terrorism has not been expunged. In other words, even though violent Islamic radicalism is not mainstream at Pondok Ngruki, the fact that the school has been the centre of a clandestine Islamic movement is undisputable. Indeed, there are many Ngruki graduates who know nothing about the clandestine Islamic organization and cannot give clear answers as to why their counterparts were involved in such violent actions. Whatever the reason, the fact of its graduates' radical involvement cannot be denied. At the very least, Pondok Ngruki planted the seeds of radical ideology in its pupils, which eventually grew and developed.

In Ngruki itself, not much remains of the radical spirit that characterized it in the days of Abdullah Sungkar's leadership. Ba'asyir remains respected as one of the founding fathers and the successor to Sungkar, but his influence in the pesantren is limited. Pondok Ngruki appears to be at a crossroads, as there are many interests and different groups within the pesantren. Ba'asyir's new organization, the JAT, and its ideology have not found much support in Ngruki. While some of the senior teachers want to push Ngruki more towards Salafism, the foundation to which Pondok Ngruki is attached wants it to be a moderate educational institution. It is likely that radical groups (underground organizations) will be increasingly marginal in Pondok Ngruki, although they may retain stronger support in some of the other pesantren of the Ngruki network.

As mentioned before, many of the most radical *ustadz* and *santri* left Ngruki in 1995, and joined or established pesantren that were more open to radical ideas. Thus the centre of radicalism shifted to such pesantren as Dar al-Syahadah in Boyolali, Al-Islam in Lamongan, Muttaqien in Rembang, and the Ma'had Ali Al-Nur in Sukoharjo.[35] These are mostly small educational institutions, but they remain significant, if only because they have gravitated towards, and receive support from, Salafi groups in the Middle East. In the following paragraphs, I examine two of these schools, both located in the larger Surakarta region: the pesantren Dar al-Syahadah in Boyolali and the Ma'had Ali Al-Nur.

Dar al-Syahadah was founded in 1994 and is currently led by Mustaqim, who graduated from Ngruki in 1989 and who continued his study at the Ma'had 'Ali of Pondok Ngruki while at the same time serving as a teacher in the pesantren. Not only does Dar al-Syahadah imitate Pondok Ngruki's educational system, but Mustaqim also considers Abu Bakar Ba'asyir to be his spiritual leader, especially in managing the pesantren. Located in the western part of Surakarta, this pesantren has about 40 *ustadz* and some 850 *santri*. Mustaqim acknowledges that for building his school he received financial assistance from various institutions in the Middle East as well as from Indonesia, thanks to his connections in the Salafi/Wahhabi network. He also claims to have good relations with the local authorities in Boyolali. Local police officers, however, have admitted that they know little about this pesantren, although they meet Mustaqim quite often. Furthermore, they add that the pesantren is often closed.[36] Judging by Mustaqim's network and his attachment to Ba'asyir's ideology, I believe that this pesantren is currently more conservative and more strictly Salafi than Pondok Ngruki. The involvement of some of its graduates — Gempur Budi Angkoro (a.k.a. Jabir), Lufti Haidaroh (a.k.a. Ubeid), and Salik Firdaus — in violent activities in Indonesia reveals its connections with the clandestine Islamic movement, the JI.[37]

Ma'had Ali Al-Nur was established by loyal followers of Abdullah Sungkar, who had left Ngruki following the internal conflict in 1995 and Sungkar's split from the NII in 1993. The founders, Abdurrahiem and Abdul Manaf, supported by devout followers, initially established the new school at Gading village, near Ngruki. This institution proved to be quite successful, which encouraged the managing foundation, Al-Nur, to acquire a better location in Waru, in the district of Sukoharjo. Unlike Pondok Ngruki and Dar al-Syahadah, this institution only offers college-level (*Ma'had Ali*) education. Therefore, all the students of this institution are graduates of other pesantren in the Ngruki network. Some former students of the Ma'had Ali Al-Nur have also been involved in violent activities in Indonesia.[38] However, the school itself appears to be drifting towards a

Saudi-style variety of Salafism, which is politically quietist. Bahruddin, who led the Ma'had Ali Al-Nur until recently, is a Ngruki graduate who continued his studies at the Saudi-sponsored Lembaga Ilmu Pengetahuan Islam dan Bahasa Arab (the Institute Islamic and Arabic Studies, or LIPIA) in Jakarta. Unlike Pondok Ngruki, which has no formal relations with any specific Middle Eastern movement or institution, Bahruddin claims that the *Ma'had Ali* has affiliated itself with a Salafi university in Saudi Arabia. Bahruddin's ambition was to produce, in cooperation with this institution, well-trained graduates who are steeped in knowledge of the original sources of Islam and capable of challenging those Indonesian Muslim scholars who have been influenced by Western values.

NII, JI AND SALAFISM

Since Abdullah Sungkar broke with Ajengan Masduki's NII and established his own organization JI, the Ngruki network, or at least the underground activism within it, has been split along ideological lines. The massive exodus of *ustadz* and *santri* from the pesantren in 1995 was due to a conflict between the cautious governing board and Sungkar loyalists, who followed the latter's trajectory of religious and political radicalization. At the time of foundation, the new pesantrens Dar al-Syahadah and Ma'had 'Ali an-Nur were therefore dominated by JI supporters. Masduki's NII had, however, been well entrenched in the entire Ngruki network and it maintained a presence in some parts of the network even after the formation of JI. After Sungkar's death, the NII (currently led by Dadang Hafidz) appears to have regained strength. This strengthening appears not to have been due to defections from JI; there was also an ideological shift in JI after Sungkar's death, but this took it closer towards Saudi-style Salafism. NII and JI are distinct and to some extent competitors, but from outside it is often difficult or impossible to distinguish between these two streams in the Ngruki network.

There are thus, in the Solo region, a number of different groups that we have described as Salafi, but there are obvious differences between them. In the academic literature (e.g., Wiktorowicz 2006; Meijer 2009), it is usual to distinguish between "purist" or "quietist" Salafism, political or *haraki* ("activist") Salafism and *jihadi* Salafism. All share the principle of taking the Prophet and his first followers as the models to be emulated and rejecting rationalist and modernist interpretations. "Purists' focus exclusively on personal piety and reject all forms of political activism, including the democratic process. *Haraki* Salafism emerged from the encounter of the political ideology of the Muslim Brotherhood and purist Salafi doctrine. *Harakis* establish formal organizations and engage in various forms of political activism, although they too reject democracy as an un-Islamic institution. *Jihadi* Salafism finally proclaims *jihad*, conceived as actual warfare, to be a central religious duty.

Jihadi Salafism is an elusive category, and its relation to the other styles of Salafism is not obvious. The Laskar Jihad, with its headquarters in Yogyakarta, that took part in the regional conflicts in the Moluccas and elsewhere in the early 2000s, emerged from a "purist" Salafi network, and it was disbanded on the instruction of a Salafi sheikh in Saudi Arabia (Hasan 2006). Other jihad warriors involved in regional conflicts were affiliated with the Jama'ah Islamiyah network, and others yet were not Salafi at all. There are a number of institutions in the Solo region that are evidently "purist" Salafi, such as the Dar al-Salaf foundation, the Ittiba' al-Sunnah foundation, and the pesantrens Imam Bukhori, Al-Ukhuwwah, and Ibnu Taymiyah. As befits "purists", they have not been involved in any form of political or societal activism. The most significant Salafi groups in the region, however, are the activist or *haraki* ones; I am inclined to place both the Ngruki network and the Jama'ah Gumuk in this category.

More important than the classification of types of Salafism is perhaps the increasing orientation towards religious authorities based in the Middle East. Among the purist Salafis, some are recognized as more learned than others, but in all important matters they consult sheikhs in Saudi Arabia or Yemen. In the Ngruki network, Abdullah Sungkar used to be the highest authority in religious as well as political matters, but even during his lifetime, followers who took jihad training in Pakistan came under the influence of Saudi sheikhs they met there. After Sungkar's death, some followed Ba'asyir as the supreme leader, but there has been a general shift of authority towards Saudi Arabia. Some individuals who fought in Afghanistan have retained relations with Saudi veterans of the Afghan jihad. Others have established new relations with Saudi persons and institutions that provide both funding and religious guidance. Both the pondok Dar al-Syahadah and the Ma'had Ali An-Nur have established their own connections with Saudi Islamic foundations for funding — the latter through the good services of Ba'asyir's eldest son, Abdul Rasyid, who graduated from a Saudi university.

The Jama'ah Gumuk also tends to Salafism (as shown by the literature that is being used), but does not appear to have direct connections with the Middle East. Because of its vigilante activism and its rejection of Indonesia's political system on religious grounds, I consider it a *haraki* Salafi movement, like the Ngruki network. Both aim for a change of the political order, but believe this should be accomplished by first educating and shaping individuals and society. They may allow for the possibility of violent action in the future, when conditions are ripe, and individual members of both networks may be drawn to jihadist action, as we have seen. The leaders of both networks, however, are quite emphatic in proclaiming that in the present situation, they consider violence inappropriate.

CONCLUSION

Solo is rife with radical Islamic groups, as has been highlighted in this chapter. It is not just a matter of the pesantren of Ngruki and its network, the only group that has received ample international attention. As I have shown, there is a much wider range of radical movements in this city and the surrounding districts. This is perhaps surprising, because Solo also has the reputation of being the centre of Java's syncretistic court tradition as well as lower class *abangan* culture. Orthodox Muslims remain a minority among the Solonese. But it is probably precisely this minority position that has given Islam in Solo its radical edge.

Another factor of significance is the weakness of the mainstream organizations that channel Muslim activism elsewhere. Although Muhammadiyah and Nahdlatul Ulama are not entirely absent, they are definitely not the dominant organizations that they are elsewhere and therefore cannot have the same moderating influence. Solo lacks a traditional leadership that could take care of social cohesion. Unlike Yogyakarta, the royal houses of Solo (Kasunanan and Mangkunegaran) do not play a significant role in society and do not command much respect among the population. Religious authority is highly fragmented; social relations are loose and polarized. The city is dominated by organizations of local provenance, but these have not played an integrating role but rather contributed to further polarization.

Muslim organizations in Solo have not expressed demands for *shari`a*-based regional regulations, which were foremost on the agenda of Muslim groups in many other regions (notably in West Java and South Sulawesi). This is probably because they were aware of their minority position here. Islamic radicalism has been expressed in two distinct ways: the struggle for an Islamic state, as in the NII and JI networks, and vigilantism. The perception that orthodox Muslims remain a minority and that Solonese society is still, to a large extent, *abangan,* has persuaded activists that the first objective in the Islamic struggle should be not to fight the *abangan* but to bring them over to a stricter version of Islam. Both the Majelis Tafsir Alqur'an and the Jama'ah Gumuk have specifically been targeting *abangan* and have been reasonably successful in recruiting them. The process of conversion of *abangan* to *santri* religious belief and practice has been taking place all over Java, and the Muhammadiyah and the NU have been major actors in this process. In Solo, with its large *abangan* majority and deeply rooted *abangan* traditions, the modalities of this process will be of crucial importance to the public expressions of Islam.

Notes

[1]   Solo and Surakarta are alternative names for the same city. The official name of the city is Kotamadya Surakarta (the municipality of Surakarta). The word Solo, however, is commonly used nowadays.

[2]   *Batik* refers to a generic wax-resistant dyeing technique used on textiles.

[3]   On traditional language in Solo, see Siegel (1986).

[4]   International Crisis Group (2002). Although the accusations of connections with Al Qaeda were never proven, many still believe that Ba'asyir was involved in this clandestine organization and hold him responsible for a string of violent incidents including the bombing of churches at Christmas 2000 and the 2002 Bali bombing.

[5]   Famous books written by the above poets include *Serat Ambiya, Serat Centhini, Serat Cabolek, Serat Kalatidha, Serat Sabdajati, Serat Sabdatama*, and *Pustaka Radja*. For further accounts see Sukri (2004), Florida (1996).

[6]   Both R. Hadipati Sosrodiningrat and Penghulu Tafsir Anom served as royal employees (*abdi dalem*) of the Kasunanan Kingdom. Since the school was a royal school, the kingdom covered all of the *madrasah's* expenses. In traditional Java, *penghulu* is a religious authority in districts or sub-districts.

[7]   At its peak in 1925, the students of the *madrasah* numbered as many as 700. Moh. Ardani (1983) asserts that Madrasah Mamba' al-'Ulum was the oldest Islamic modern school in Indonesia after that which had been founded by *Jami'at al-Khair* in Jakarta. However, since the influence of this *madrasah* did not reach as far as West Java and Batavia, the Indonesian government does not regard this *madrasah* as having played a significant role in the development of Islamic education in Indonesia. For further remarks on this issue, see Ardani (1983).

[8]   For a further account of Ba'asyir's life, see *Sabili* IX, no. 16, 8 February 2002, p. 38; *Republika*, 20 October 2002, available at <www.republika.co.id> (accessed 18 December 2006); Sudarjat (2006).

[9]   P-4 stands for Pedoman Penghayatan dan Pengamalan Pancasila, "Guide for the Understanding and Practising of Pancasila".

[10] For more on these events, see Suryahardi (1982), pp. 300–5; Ba'asyir (2006).

[11] On this, see "Akhir Perburuan di Soreang", *Tempo*, 1 August 1981, Jakarta, pp. 12–13.

[12] In fact there is no clear and definitive information about who initially used *usrah* as a *tarbiyah* method. However, Imaduddin was among the first to employ and adopt *usrah* for university students in Bandung. Imaduddin was a lecturer at the ITB and was well known as a leading figure of Islamic activism in Indonesia. For more information on *usrah*, see Syukur (2003).

[13] The tabloid was initially published in 1981. After being banned by the government in 1984, the tabloid resurfaced under the name of *Al-Ikhwan*, until it was banned for good in 1985. Some Gajah Mada University lecturers were involved as the tabloid's board members: Dr Amien Rais, Dr Kuntowijoyo, and Dr Sahirul Alim.

[14] Pondok Ngruki is a large boarding school, within which there are a number of distinct educational streams, some offering a partly general curriculum (called *madrasah* in Indonesia), others exclusively religious (the said two *kulliyah*).

[15] The Kauman is the district adjoining the central mosque, where religious functionaries live. The historical centre of Muhammadiyah is in the Kauman of Yogyakarta.

[16] *Bid'ah* ("innovation") includes all religious beliefs and practices that did not exist in the time of the Prophet and the first Muslim community and that are presumably borrowings from other cultural traditions; *khurafat* are superstitions and fairy tales; *takhayyul* are (beliefs based on) fantasies and hallucinations. These three are commonly announced as the chief targets in campaigns for the purification of Islam.

[17] Interview with Ahmad Sukino, the most senior leader of the MTA, in Solo on 7 February 2007.

[18] See further the MTA homepage, available at <http://mta-online.com>.

[19] The most controversial issue surrounding the 2003 education law concerns a school's obligation to provide all students with religious education in their own religion, which would oblige Christian schools to offer Islamic education. (Many Muslim parents send their children to Christian schools because of their reputation for better quality education; very few Christian parents send their children to Muslim schools.)

[20] The *Rencana Undang-undang Anti Pornografi dan Pornoaksi* (RUU APP) has not been issued yet, as it lacks widespread public support, especially among the local government in Bali, although it has been enthusiastically supported by many Islamic organizations, such as the MTA.

[21] Salafis consider *isbal*, the wearing of garments that hang below the ankles, as prohibited (haram),

[22] *Mega-Bintang* literally means "big star". *Mega* was a short name for Megawati Sukarnoputri, who represented the PDI-P, while the *Bintang* or star was part of the symbol of the Islamic party, the PPP.

23 *Hisbah* is the principle of commanding right and forbidding wrong, i.e., controlling public morality. The Tim Hisbah is a relatively new organization (established in 2008), that gained some notoriety when its leader, Sigit Hermawan Wijayanto alias Sigit Qordhowi, was shot dead by an anti-terror police unit on 14 May 2011. Sigit was suspected of being responsible for several terrorist bombings. See International Crisis Group (2012), p. 2.

24 Sunan Bonang is one of the nine saints who reputedly brought Islam to Java; his grave on the north coast is a place of pilgrimage.

25 The FPIS is not to be confused with the Jakarta-based *Front Pembela Islam* (Islamic Defender Front, FPI) led by Habieb Rizieq. The FPIS has nothing to do with the FPI, although the FPI also has its branch in Solo. Journalists have frequently wrongly described the FPIS as the *Front Pembela Islam Surakarta*.

26 Interview with Chalid Hasan in Solo on 9 November 2006.

27 Conversations with Mudzakir, Solo, 17 November 2006 and Yogyakarta, 21 February 2007. See also *Suara Front*, no. 01/II/29 June 2001, p. 3.

28 Interview with Chalid Hasan in Solo on 9 November 2006.

29 Their conviction is based on verse 42 of the Quranic sura Al-Baqarah saying *"wa la talbisu al-haqq bi al-batil wa taktumu al-haqq wa antum ta'lamun"* (and cover not Truth with falsehood, nor conceal the Truth when ye know). Interview with Mudzakir, Solo, 17 November 2006.

30 *Suara Front*, no. 31, I, 15–21 December 2000.

31 The notion of *shura* (consultation) differs from that of (liberal) democracy. However, many people see in *shura* an Islamic variety of democracy. Unlike liberal democracy, in which supreme authority lies in the hands of people or their representatives, *shura* is a concept in which supreme authority lies in the hands of God, disseminated through humans as rational beings. In other words, the notion of *shura* is a kind of guided democracy in which the authority of the people does not conflict with the sovereignty of Allah.

32 Mudzakir's conviction regarding the necessity of the unity of *ummah* is based on Muhammad's famous saying that "Muslims would split into 72 or 73 factions and all of them would go to the hell except one, i.e., *'ahlu al-sunnah wa al-jama'ah*".

33 Other schools in the Ngruki network include: Pondok Abidin and Mujahidin in Solo, Pondok Syuhodo and Ulil Albab in Sukoharjo, Pondok Ibnu al-Qayyim in Yogyakarta, and Pondok Tarbiyah al-Mukmin in Magelang. And there are other such *pesantren* outside Java in Sumatera and Nusa Tenggara Timur. These *pesantren* may be radical in terms of their ideology, but not in action.

34 When Ba'asyir established the MMI in Yogyakarta, for instance, Wahyuddin took part, and he even acted as one of the board members of MMI in Surakarta. However, when Ba'asyir broke with the MMI and established a new organization, the Jama'ah Ansar al- Tauhid, or JAT, Wahyuddin did not

follow him.

[35] *Ma'had 'Ali* is a generic term for a tertiary religious school open to graduates of Islamic high schools or *Madrasah Aliyah*.

[36] The *Jakarta Post*, 16 October 2003, available at <www.thejakartapost.com> (accessed 17 January 2007).

[37] Jabir, who was recruited (but not deployed) as a suicide bomber for the 2004 Kuningan bombing, is the cousin of well-known JI activist Fathurrahman Al-Ghozi. He was finally shot dead in his hiding place in Wonosobo in April 2006. Ubeid was involved in the preparation for the Kuningan bombing in 2004, while Salik was one of the suicide backpack bombers in the Bali II bombing in 2005.

[38] These include Sardona Siliwangi, Suramto (a.k.a. Deni), Bagus Budi Prawoto (a.k.a. Urwah), Lutfi Haedaroh (a.k.a. Ubeid), and Heri (a.k.a. Umar). It is significant here that some of the above men also graduated from or attended either Pondok Ngruki or *Dar al-Syahadah*.

References

Ardani, Moh. *Agama dan Perubahan Sosial di Indonesia: Mamba'ul Ulum Kasunanan Surakarta 1905–1942, Studi Kasus*. Jakarta: Proyek Penelitian Keagamaan Departemen Agama RI, 1983.

Awwas, Irfan S. *Mengenal Majelis Mujahidin: Untuk Penegakan Syariah Islam*. Yogyakarta: Markaz Pusat Majelis Mujahidin, 2001.

Ba'asyir, Abu Bakar. *Catatan dari Penjara: Untuk Mengamalkan dan Menegakkan Dinul Islam*. Depok: Penerbit Mushaf, 2006.

Berg, L.W.C. van den. *Hadramaut dan Koloni Arab di Nusantara* (originally published in French in 1887). Jakarta: INIS, 1989.

Cribb, Robert. "Criminality, Violence and the Chinese in the Decolonization of Indonesia, 1930–1960". Paper presented for International Conference on "Dekolonisasi dan Posisi Etnis Tionghoa Indonesia 1930–1960". Padang, 18–21 February 2006.

Florida, Nancy K. "Pada tembok keraton ada pintu: unsur santri dalam dunia kepujangaan 'klasik' di Keraton Surakarta". Paper presented at the symposium on *Tradisi Tulis Indonesia* at Universitas Indonesia (UI), Jakarta, 1996.

Hakiem, Lukman and Tamsil Linrung. *Menunaikan Panggilan Risalah: Dokumentasi Perjalanan 30 Tahun Dewan Dakwah Islamiyah Indonesia*. Jakarta: DDII, 1997.

Hasan, Noorhaidi. *Laskar Jihad: Islam, Militancy and the Quest for Identity in Post-New Order Indonesia*. Ithaca, NY: Cornell Southeast Asia Program, 2006.

International Crisis Group. "Al-Qaeda in Southeast Asia: The Case of the 'Ngruki Network' in Indonesia". Jakarta/Brussels: ICG, 2002.

———. "Indonesia Backgrounder: Why Salafism and Terrorism Mostly Don't

Mix". Southeast Asia/Brussels: ICG, 2004.

———. "Indonesia: From Vigilantism to Terrorism in Cirebon". Jakarta/Brussels: ICG, 2012.

Kuntowijoyo. *Raja, Priyayi & Kawulo: Surakarta 1900–1915*. Yogyakarta: Penerbit Ombak, 2004.

Mandal, Sumit K. *Finding Their Place: A History of Arabs in Java under Dutch Rule, 1800–1924*. Ph.D. thesis. New York: Columbia University, 1994.

Meijer, Roel, ed. *Global Salafism: Islam's New Religious Movement*. London: Hurst & Company, 2009.

Nursalim, Muh. "Faksi Abdullah Sungkar dalam gerakan NII era Orde Baru (Studi Terhadap Pemikiran dan Harakah Politik Abdullah Sungkar)". Tesis Magister. Surakarta: Universitas Muhammadiyah Surakarta, 2001.

Onghokham. "Pemberontakan Madiun 1948: Drama Manusia dalam Revolusi". *Prisma 7*, August 1978.

Ricklefs, M.C. "Islam and the Reign of Pakubuwono II, 1726–1749". In *Islam: Essays on Scripture, Thought and Society: A Festschrift in Honour of Anthony H. Johns*, edited by Peter G. Riddell and Tony Street. Leiden: Brill, 1997.

Santosa, June Chandra. *Modernization, Utopia and the Rise of Islamic Radicalism in Indonesia*. Ph.D. thesis. Boston: Boston University, 1996.

Siegel, James T. *Solo in the New Order: Language and Hierarchy in an Indonesian City*. New Jersey: Princeton University Press, 1986.

Soedarmono and Muh. Amin. *Solusi Konflik Pribumi dan Non-Pribumi di Kota Solo*. Laporan Penelitian Dosen Muda at UNS, 2002.

Sudarjat, Edi. "Abu Bakar Ba'asyir: Sebuah Biografi Ringkas". In *Catatan dari Penjara: Untuk Mengamalkan dan Menegakkan Dinul Islam*, edited by Abu Bakar Ba'asyir. Depok: Penerbit Mushaf, 2006.

Sukri, Sri Suhandjati. *Ijtihad Progresif Yasadipura II dalam Akulturasi Islam dengan Budaya Jawa*. Yogyakarta: Gama Media, 2004.

Suryahardi, Irfan. *Perjalanan Hukum di Indonesia*. Yogyakarta: Ar-Risalah, 1982.

Syukur, Abdul. *Gerakan Usroh di Indonesia: Peristiwa Lampung 1989*. Yogyakarta: Penerbit Ombak, 2003.

Wiktorowicz, Quintan. "Anatomy of the Salafi Movement". *Studies in Conflict and Terrorism* 29, no. 3 (2006): 207–39.

7

POSTSCRIPT:
THE SURVIVAL OF LIBERAL AND
PROGRESSIVE MUSLIM THOUGHT
IN INDONESIA

Martin van Bruinessen

The developments discussed in this volume appear to have marginalized liberal and progressive Muslim discourses, which in the 1980s and 1990s had been favoured by the regime and had received much sympathetic coverage in the press. The New Order's Ministers of Religious Affairs, notably Munawir Syadzali (1982–92), strongly endorsed liberal religious thought and made efforts to develop the State Institutes of Islamic Studies (IAIN) into centres of Muslim intellectualism. The Muhammadiyah, and especially the NU in the Abdurrahman Wahid years (1984–99) provided young thinkers and activists to some extent with a protective umbrella (although there has always much criticism of unconventional thinkers in these organizations). That degree of institutional support for liberal and progressive thought and action no longer exists, whereas other Muslim discourses, including some that were suppressed under the New Order, have gained greater prominence and official endorsement.

The same is also true of the audience leading Muslim intellectuals have. During the final decade and a half of the New Order, a significant segment of the educated and increasingly affluent Muslim middle class felt attracted to the liberal Muslim intellectualism of Nurcholish Madjid and his friends, as an alternative to the puritan or politicized and Shariah-oriented discourse of mainstream reformist preachers. Other alternatives emerged, however, that appeared to be even more attractive to an upwardly mobile middle class public, such as the hugely popular preacher Aa Gym with his message of tolerance and self-help through pop psychology (Watson 2005). The upheavals and inter-religious violence of the years of transition further increased the demand for such messages and cures for the soul. Many of those who were dismayed with the upsurge of Islamism flocked to gurus offering Sufi teachings and spiritual therapy. Courses on mysticism, collective meditation sessions (*dzikir berjama'ah*) and mental training courses, rather than seminars on Muslim intellectualism, are currently the middle class' preferred alternative to political Islam (Howell 2001 and 2007; Rudnyckyj 2009).

However, the extent to which progressive and liberal thought remained entrenched in certain niches and continued to flourish and develop is easily overlooked. The IAINs had produced numerous graduates with an interest in philosophy and social science, many of whom went on to postgraduate studies abroad before returning to take up positions in the religious bureaucracy or as lecturers at IAINs. Especially the faculties of Ushuluddin (Religious Studies) of the IAINs in Jakarta and Yogyakarta remained bulwarks of intellectual freedom and tolerance.[1] As is shown by Mujiburrahman in his contribution to this volume, in South Sulawesi the main Muslim critics of the programme of enforcing the Shariah were IAIN lecturers and graduates, and the continuing influence of the IAIN contributed to a situation of trust, in which the Christian minority did not feel seriously threatened. It is by no means the case that the IAINs are dominated by liberal Muslims — in fact, many well-known liberals have lost previously influential positions there — but at least they continue providing a vitally important space for intellectual independence.[2]

Although overshadowed by assertive Islamist voices, the various strains of progressive and liberal Muslim thought that had developed in the course of the 1980s and 1990s, in fact continued to flourish and even became more assertive in defence of religious freedom and pluralism in the post-Soeharto years. A range of Muslim NGOs, including some that were primarily concerned with the critical study of religious discourse, also profited from the international funding for the development of civil society that flowed to the country. This included such NGOs as LKiS (Institute for Islamic and Social Studies) in Yogyakarta, which had previously introduced critical social thought and hermeneutics into the *pesantren* environment and continued to disseminate religious ideas focusing on liberation and empowerment of subaltern groups, Rahima, which focused on women's

rights and carried out programmes of gender awareness training, and
Syarikat, which strove for reconciliation between the social groups that had
been perpetrators and victims of the mass killings of 1965–66, i.e. for the
highly controversial accommodation of Muslims with (alleged) communists.

The most controversial of the NGOs, and the most immediate target
of the notorious MUI *fatwa* of 2005 as well as the purges in NU and
Muhammadiyah was the Liberal Islam Network, JIL, which had most
explicitly and most provocatively challenged the increasingly vocal Islamist
discourses. One of the first public clashes between Islamists and JIL occurred
in response to a short film clip titled "Islam has many colours" (*Islam
warna-warni*), for which JIL had bought air time on several commercial
television channels in mid-2002. The clip showed colourful images of
Muslim rituals and festivities, including music and dance, a variety of local
styles of mosque architecture and of dress styles that differed from the
new Islamic covering style favoured by the Islamists. It was a celebration
of the distinctly Indonesian forms of expression of Islam, and of the rich
cultural variety of these expressions. At least one group of Islamists took
offense at this film. The Majelis Mujahidin Indonesia, one of the more
militant organizations striving for an Islamic state, wrote a letter to the
television channels calling the film an insult to Islam and threatening court
action if they would not stop airing the film. The MMI's argument was
simple: Muslims could have many colours, but there is only one Islam and
God's commands are unequivocal. By suggesting that the divine message
could be adapted to local circumstances, the liberals were blasphemously
misrepresenting Islam. Although many prominent lawyers and intellectuals
came out in support of the film, the letter proved effective and the channels
stopped broadcasting it.[3]

Besides their defence of local varieties of Islamic belief and practice,
another theme on which the JIL members insisted much concerned the
need to understand Qur'anic verses and *hadith* in their proper context
rather than believing them immediately applicable. (JIL contributors often
contrasted "liberal Islam" and "literal Islam".) A third major theme in its
discourse is respect for other religious traditions and recognition of their
validity. The group's concerns were presented eloquently in a programmatic
statement by its main thinker, Ulil Abshar-Abdalla:

> I consider Islam as a living organism (…) and not as a dead monument
> erected in the seventh century (…) There is a strong tendency these
> days to treat Islam as a monument, petrified and immutable, and
> it is time to challenge that attitude. We need interpretations that are

non-literal, substantive, contextual, and consonant with the heartbeat of a human civilization that is ever-changing. The substance of Islam should be separated from the culture of the Arabian peninsula, and it is that universal substance that has to be interpreted in accordance with the local cultural context. Whipping, stoning and the cutting of hands, the *jilbab* (full female covering) and beard are Arab cultural peculiarities and there is no reason why other Muslims should follow them. There is not really a detailed divine law, as most Muslims believe, but only the general principles known as *maqasid al-shari`a*, the objectives of Islamic law, and these basic values have to be given concrete content in accordance with the social and historical context. We have to learn to understand and accept that there cannot be a single interpretation of Islam that is the only or the most correct and final one. We must open ourselves to what is true and good, even if it comes from outside Islam. Islamic values can also be found in Christianity and the other major religions, and even in minor local religious traditions. Islam should be seen as a *process*, never completed and closed; new interpretations may emerge, and the major criterion to judge interpretations by is *maslaha*, i.e., what is beneficial to mankind.[4]

Though there are quite significant differences between the various groups of progressives and liberals in Indonesia, this statement sums up nicely the major concerns they have in common (as well as bringing out clearly what are the areas of conflict with Islamists as well as ordinary orthodox believers). Intellectually, JIL is heir to two distinct currents of religious thought of the New Order period, which had Nurcholish Madjid and Abdurrahman Wahid as their most prominent spokespersons (echoes of both of whom can be detected in the statement quoted above). Numerous personal and intellectual connections link JIL to the other movements and institutions that are tributary to these predecessors. This includes not only the NGOs mentioned above but also the Paramadina Foundation, the institution most closely associated with the thought of Nurcholish Madjid, and a number of related institutions, largely staffed by graduates of Jakarta's IAIN.

Paramadina, which had since the mid-1980s catered to Jakarta's upwardly mobile middle class, offering seminar-like discussions on modern religious thought, became one of the staunchest defenders of religious pluralism in response to the violent inter-religious conflicts of the transition years, organizing various joint activities with representatives of other religions. It provoked the anger of many orthodox believers (including members of its own board) when it published a book on inter-religious relations in which the authors, against the virtual consensus of Indonesia's ulama, provided arguments allowing inter-religious marriage (including that between Muslim women and non-Muslim men).[5]

Nurcholish Madjid and Abdurrahman Wahid had been confronted with fierce criticism in their day (see e.g. Hassan 1980 for responses to Nurcholish), but they enjoyed powerful protection, which their successors did to a far lesser extent. Soon after the emergence of JIL, a fierce polemic started, in public debates, printed publications and internet discussions. Just like the liberals and progressive are a heterogeneous group, their critics had different backgrounds and represented different interest. The first and loudest critics, unsurprisingly, belonged to the more radical Islamist fringes, such as the Majelis Mujahidin Indonesia (MMI) and the radicalized younger generation of DDII activists.[6] They pointed to some real issues, such as the liberals' emphasis on context and rational interpretation in understanding sacred scripture, but also hinted at conspiracies and foreign interests lurking behind the liberal façade. They succeeded in alarming a broad section of the mainstream Muslim public, ulama and religious functionaries. JIL's public utterances were moreover often quite confrontational and challenging authority, which did not help to make its message more palatable. By the middle of the decade, the term "liberal" had become a stigma that all Muslim NGOs did their utmost to avoid. It was no longer only radicals who opposed JIL and Islamic liberalism, but many who belonged to the moderate mainstream did so as well (e.g., Buchori 2006).

NGOs working at the grassroots level found their activities greatly impeded when people associated them with "liberal Islam". Most Muslim NGOs therefore distanced themselves from JIL in order to avoid blame by association. The NU and Muhammadiyah congresses of 2004 represented at first sight a setback for liberal and progressive thought, as only very few persons known to be associated with liberal ideas retained formal positions in these organizations. However, as shown by Burhani (in this volume) for the Muhammadiyah and by myself for the NU (Bruinessen 2010), liberal and progressive voices remain present in both organizations, though perhaps less prominently than in the past. JIL's best-known member, Ulil Abshar-Abdalla, made a valiant attempt to be elected into the NU's leadership and obtained a significant number of votes.

JIL always retained the support of liberal and progressive intellectuals of the older generation, most notably of Abdurrahman Wahid who, until his death in December 2009, appeared regularly in the weekly radio talk show "Kongkow bareng Gus Dur" ("Hanging out with Gus Dur") that was broadcast by JIL. Since 2005, however, JIL's news value has decreased; there have been no major new controversies. The JIL website, <http://islamlib.com>, is still active and is regularly updated with interesting essays, but the Network organizes far fewer public activities than in the first years of its existence. The same may be said of most of the Muslim NGOs that represented liberal and progressive Islamic thought. There is less external funding for their activities since the economic and political crises have been overcome, and the audiences reached by their intellectual contributions have become distinctly smaller. Most members have moreover moved on with their lives and now have their main activities elsewhere. Two small think-tanks close to, but formally independent of, the Muhammadiyah and NU, The Maarif Institute and The Wahid Institute, constitute safe havens for young critical intellectuals of these large associations. The IAINs and UINs, and such institutions as the Paramadina Foundation also provide niches where liberal and progressive thinkers continue working.

It appears likely that liberal and progressive Muslim intellectuals will remain tolerated within mainstream institutions and organizations, as long as they do not openly challenge established authority. Some of them may even rise to positions of influence again and have an impact on public debate. In their modest formulation, after all, the ideas of rational interpretation of the sacred texts, adaptation of the message of Islam to local conditions, and respect for other religions continue to be shared by numerous Indonesian mainstream Muslims.

Notes

[1]   The liberal atmosphere in these institutions was the reason for a particularly virulent attack by an Islamist critic, who accused them of being places where Muslims are made into apostates (Jaiz 2005). This book has been very influential in bringing about a broad suspicion of the IAINs, especially of the Ushuluddin faculties.

[2]   In the early 2000s, several of the IAINs, including those of Jakarta and Yogyakarta, were transformed into universities (UIN, State Islamic Universities), by the addition of several non-religious faculties such as economics, medicine, social and political sciences. In these new faculties, Islamist movements gained influence among the students, leading to a considerable change in atmosphere on campus.

[3]   The letter to the television stations and various reactions to the issue, along with a range of other criticisms of JIL are reproduced in Al-Anshori 2003. Al-Anshori was at the time one of the two spokespersons of the Majelis

Mujahidin. JIL's view of pluralism was defended by one of its leading thinkers, Luthfi Assyaukani, in an op-ed article in the daily *Koran Tempo* (Assyaukanie 2002).

⁴   This is a summarizing translation of the first part of Abshar-Abdalla (2002). Much of the second part of the text consists of a fierce critique of the Islamists' project of implementing the Shariah as a ready-made solution for all problems and of their Manichaean worldview that places "Islam" and "the West" in mutual opposition.

⁵   Kamal (2004). Paramadina later withdrew this book from circulation because of the strong responses, notably from board member Quraish Shihab. The Majelis Mujahidin organized a public debate with the authors of the book, which rather resembled a public trial, proceedings of which it published under a title that showed they considered Paramadina no longer to be Muslim (Majelis Mujahidin Indonesia 2004).

⁶   Jaiz (2002); Adiani and Hidayat (2002); Al-Anshori (2003); Armas (2003). Al-Anshori was at the time one of the MMI's spokespersons; Jaiz is former journalist and DDII activist, who since 1998 is "head of research" in the small institute LPPI, which is dedicated to the struggle against all deviations from pure Islam. Husaini is one of DDII's brightest and most vocal and radical young activists, obsessed with Christian efforts to subvert Islam; he was one of the radicals invited to join the Majelis Ulama Indonesia. Armas and Husaini both studied at the Institute for the Study of Islamic Thought and Civilization (ISTAC) in Malaysia and work together in a small NGO called INSISTS that reflects the views of ISTAC in Indonesia.

References

Abshar-Abdalla, Ulil. "Menyegarkan Kembali Pemikiran Islam" [Refreshing Islamic Thought]. *Kompas*, 18 November 2002. Reprinted in Abshar-Abdallah 2005.

———. *Menjadi Muslim Liberal* [Becoming a Liberal Muslim]. Jakarta: Nalar, 2005.

Al-Anshori, Fauzan. *Melawan Konspirasi JIL "Jaringan Islam Liberal"* [Against the Conspiracy of the Liberal Islam Network]. Jakarta: Pustaka Al-Furqan, 2003.

Armas, Adnin. *Pengaruh Kristen-Orientalis terhadap Islam Liberal* [The Influence of Christian and Orientalist Thought on Liberal Islam]. Jakarta: Gema Insani Press, 2003.

Assyaukanie, Luthfi. "Islam Warna-warni" [Islam Has Many Colours]. *Koran Tempo*, 13 August 2002. Online at <http://islamlib.com/id/artikel/islam-warna-warni>.

———. *Wajah Liberal Islam Indonesia* [The Liberal Face of Indonesian Islam]. Jakarta: Jaringan Islam Liberal, 2002.

Bruinessen, Martin van. "New Leadership, New Policies? The Nahdlatul Ulama Congress in Makassar". *Inside Indonesia*, no. 101 (2010). Online at <http://www.insideindonesia.org/weekly-articles-100-apr-june-2010/new-leadership-new-policies-16061866>.

————. "What Happened to the Smiling Face of Indonesian Islam? Muslim Intellectualism and the Conservative Turn in Post-Suharto Indonesia". Working paper. Singapore: S. Rajaratnam School of International Studies, 2011.

————. "*Ghazwul Fikri* or Arabization? Indonesian Muslim Responses to Globalisation". In *Muslim Responses to Globalization in Southeast Asia*, edited by Ken Miichi and Omar Farouk Bajunid. Forthcoming.

Buchori, KH. Abdusshomad. *Santri Menggugat JIL & Sekte Pluralisme Agama.* [A Santri Accuses JIL and the Sect of Religious Pluralism]. Surabaya: MUI Propinsi Jatim, 2006.

Hassan, Kamal. *Muslim Intellectual Response to New Order Modernization in Indonesia.* Kuala Lumpur: Dewan Bahasa, 1980.

Howell, Julia Day. "Sufism and the Indonesian Islamic Revival". *Journal of Asian Studies* 60 (2001): 701–29.

————. "Modernity and Islamic spirituality in Indonesia's New Sufi networks". In *Sufism and the "Modern" in Islam*, edited by Martin van Bruinessen and Julia Day Howell. London: I.B. Tauris, 2007.

Husaini, Adian. *Islam Liberal, Pluralisme Agama & Diabolisme Intelektual* [Liberal Islam, Religious Pluralism, and the Diabolical Mind]. Surabaya: Risalah Gusti, 2005.

————. *Liberalisasi Islam di Indonesia: Fakta & Data* [The Liberalization of Islam in Indonesia: Facts and Figures]. Jakarta: Dewan Dakwah Islamiyah Indonesia, 2006.

Husaini, Adian and Nuim Hidayat. *Islam Liberal: Sejarah, Konsepsi, Penyimpangan dan Jawabannya* [Liberal Islam: Its History, Concepts, Deviance, and the Response to These]. Jakarta: Gema Insani Press, 2002.

Jaiz, Hartono Ahmad. *Bahaya Islam Liberal* [The Danger of Liberal Islam]. Jakarta: Pustaka Al-Kautsar, 2002.

————. *Ada Pemurtadan di IAIN* [There is Apostasy at the IAIN]. Jakarta: Pustaka Al-Kautsar, 2005.

Kamal, Zainun, et al. *Fiqih Lintas Agama: Membangun Masyarakat Inklusif-Pluralis* [Inter-Religious Fiqh: Building an Inclusive, Plural Society]. Jakarta: Yayasan Wakaf Paramadina, 2004.

Majelis Mujahidin Indonesia. *Kekafiran Berfikir Sekte Paramadina* [The Heathen Thought of the Paramadina Sect]. Yogyakarta: Wihdah Press, 2004.

Rudnyckyj, Daromir. "Spiritual Economies: Islam and Neoliberalism in Contemporary Indonesia". *Cultural Anthropology* 24, no. 1 (2009): 104–41.

Watson, C.W. "A Popular Indonesian Preacher: The Significance of AA Gymnastiar". *Journal of the Royal Anthropological Institute* 11 (2005): 773–92.

INDEX

A

Aa Gym 225
abangan 12–15, 42, 191, 192, 193,
   195, 203–4, 207, 218–19
'Abduh, Muhammad 128, 135
Abdullah Said 157, 161
Abdurrahman al-Baghdadi 18
Abdurrahman Wahid xxi, xxiii, 2,
   4, 16, 27, 29, 33, 44, 45, 47,
   61, 66, 67, 71, 82, 93, 94,
   224, 227, 228–29
Abu Deedat 70
Abu Nida 51–52
Aceh 3, 10, 28, 35, 38, 42, 69, 91,
   146, 153, 164, 168, 178, 210,
   214
Adi Sasono 45, 46
Adian Husaini 45, 63, 83, 92, 93,
   114, 230
Afghanistan, veterans of jihad in
   37, 48, 196, 201, 217
Agus Dwikarna 157, 159, 162,
   169, 181
Ahmad Dahlan 23, 107, 131–33
Ahmadiyah xi, xiii, 4, 6, 7, 10, 18,
   39, 49, 70, 84–88, 98, 99,
   124–25, 170

Aisyiah vii, 108, 114–15, 126
Ajinomoto affair 67, 71, 96
Akbar Tanjung 167
Al Irsyad vii, 13, 24, 198
Ambo Dalle, Abdurrahman 148,
   150, 153
Ambon *see* Moluccas
Amidhan 98
Amien Rais, M. xx, 34, 93, 94,
   109, 140, 220
Amin Abdullah 109, 112, 113,
   117, 139
Amin Djamaluddin xvii, 38, 64,
   70, 85, 86, 92
*al-amr bi-l-ma'ruf wa-l-nahy
   'an al-munkar* 68, 175,
   187
Ansharut Tauhid *see* Jama'ah
   Ansharut Tauhid
Arabization 5, 18
Arabs vii, xxii, 5, 12, 13, 18, 24,
   50, 194
As'ad, Haji (Wajo) 148
Aswar Hasan 155, 159, 161, 170,
   180
Athian Ali M. Da'i xi, 81
azas tunggal 39, 94–5, 155, 198

Aziz Kahar (Abdul Aziz Kahar)
    11–12, 155–56, 160–61,
    163–64, 170, 175–81
Azyumardi Azra 66, 82, 137

B
Ba'asyir, Abu Bakar xiv, xix, 13, 15,
    18, 36–38, 136, 159–60, 190,
    195–201, 212–15, 221
Baitul Muslimin Indonesia viii, 42,
    166
Bakom-PKB vii, 28
Bali bombings 2, 52, 106, 135,
    136, 191, 208, 210, 213, 219,
    222
Bambang Sudibyo 113
Bank Bali affair 67, 94
Bank Muamalat Indonesia viii, 65,
    73, 96, 97
Baraja, Abdul Qadir 198, 213
Basalamah, Abdurrachman 155,
    159, 161, 187
BAZ (Badan Amil Zakat) viii, 171,
    174
bid'ah, khurafat and takhayul 25,
    134, 138, 203, 220
BKPRMI (Badan Kontak Pemuda
    dan Remaja Masjid Indonesia)
    viii, 40–41
BKSPP (Badan Kerjasama Pondok
    Pesantren) viii, 41
Brigade Hizbullah viii, xx, 208
Bulukumba 11, 99, 156, 167, 170–73

C
Chamamah Suratno, Siti 115
charity 21, 48, 204, 212; see also
    zakat
Chinese xxi, 12, 28, 194
Cholil Ridwan, KH. 64, 70, 92

Christianization 62, 70, 77–78,
    153, 230
Christian minorities 147, 168–69,
    173, 182–83
communism 12, 23, 25, 54, 67,
    151, 152, 192, 195, 207, 226

D
Dahlan Rais 113
dakwah 13–14, 32, 41–42, 195–206
Darul Arqam (religious movement)
    viii, 51
Darul Islam (see also NII / TII)
    ix, xii, xiv, xvi, xviii, 10–11,
    13–14, 31, 42, 150, 156, 159,
    161, 170, 182, 191
Darul Istiqamah, Pesantren 156–57,
    170, 171
Dawam Rahardjo, M. xviii, 43, 45,
    66, 82–83, 86, 109, 139
DDI (Darud Dakwah wal Irsyad)
    ix, 148, 153, 173, 183
DDII (Dewan Dakwah Islamiyah
    Indonesia) ix, xv, 6, 11, 13,
    32, 41, 48, 63, 68, 78, 155,
    159–60, 196–97, 212, 228
Depag (Departemen Agama) see
    Ministry of Religious Affairs
Desantara 48, 173
"deviant sects" (aliran sesat) 70, 84,
    85, 86, 92, 99
Din Syamsuddin 8, 42, 78, 79, 81,
    93, 98, 113–14, 126, 140
Djohan Effendi 82
Djohantini, Siti Noordjannah 126
Dompet Dhuafa 48, 55

E
èLSAD (Lembaga Studi Agama dan
    Demokrasi) ix, 40, 47

F
Fahmina Institute x, 46
Fatayat x, 47
Fathul Muin Daeng Magading 157
fatwa xi, xxviii, 3–4, 6, 7, 10,
    17–18, 60, 62, 63, 67, 69, 71,
    73, 75, 79, 81, 82–83, 84–88,
    90, 98, 99, 226
Fatwa, A.M. 160, 168
Fazlur Rahman 109, 127
feminism, Muslim 46–47, 92–93,
    130–31
FKAWJ (Forum Komunikasi
    Ahlussunnah Wal Jama'ah) x,
    52, 69–70
FPI (Front Pembela Islam) x, 38,
    69, 84, 208, 221
FPIS (Front Pemuda Islam
    Surakarta) x, 14–15, 191, 208,
    209–11, 221
FUI (Forum Ukhuwah Islamiyah)
    x, 62, 69, 77, 95
FUI (Front Umat Islam) x, 11, 64,
    95
FUUI (Forum Ulama Umat Islam)
    xi, 81

G
Golkar 10, 12, 28, 32, 49, 53, 153–54,
    158, 166–67, 171, 176, 206–7
Gontor, pesantren of 13, 36, 198
Goodwill Zubir 113
GPII (Gerakan Pemuda Islam
    Indonesia) xi, 197, 198
GPK (Gerakan Pemuda Ka'bah) xi,
    208

H
Habibie, B.J. xiii, 6, 10, 44, 60–61,
    65, 67, 71, 93, 94, 154, 158

Haedar Nashir 118, 122, 126, 140
al-Hafidy, Usman 42
halal certification 71–73, 96
Hamka Haq 164, 165–66
Hartono Ahmad Jaiz 229, 230
Hasyim Muzadi 42
Hawariyyun 206, 208,
hermeneutics 8, 16, 17, 111, 112,
    225
Hidayatullah xii, 11, 83, 157, 161,
    184
Hizbut Tahrir see HTI
HMI (Himpunan Mahasiswa
    Indonesia) xii, 11, 39–40,
    152–52, 155, 167
HTI (Hizbut Tahrir wilayah
    Indonesia) xii, 3, 6, 9, 38, 63,
    70, 78, 95, 106, 120, 121
Husein Muhammad, KH. 46

I
IAIN (Institut Agama Islam Negeri)
    xii, 151–52, 154, 164, 173,
    224, 225, 229
ICIP (International Center for
    Islam and Pluralism) xii, 48,
    98
ICMI (Ikatan Cendekiawan
    Muslim Indonesia) xiii, 44,
    65, 94, 96
IJABI (Ikatan Jama'ah Ahlul Bait
    Indonesia) xiii, 50
IMM (Ikatan Mahasiswa
    Muhammadiyah) xiii, 40, 108
IMMIM (Ikatan Masjid dan
    Mushalla Muttahidah) xiii,
    151, 152
INSISTS (Institute for the Study
    of Islamic Thought and
    Civilization) xiii, 45, 230

inter-faith relations 64, 82, 83, 112,
    129, 131, 133, 150, 227–28
inter-religious conflict xv, 2, 48, 52,
    67, 94, 209, 225
inter-religious marriage 4, 63, 70,
    228
inter-religious prayer 4, 63
Irfan Suryahardi Awwas xix, 160,
    199, 213
Islam Jama'ah xiii, xvi, xvii, 49
Islamic banking 65, 73–74
Islamization 147, 207, 218–19

J
Ja'far Umar Thalib 15, 18, 51–52
Jakarta Charter 2, 31, 54, 146
Jalaluddin Rachmat 50
Jama'ah Ansharut Tauhid xiv, 38,
    52, 92, 214, 221
Jama'ah Gumuk 15, 52, 202,
    205–6, 209, 217, 219
Jama'ah Islamiyah xiv, 14, 37, 52,
    191, 201, 212, 213–14, 215,
    217
Jama'ah Tabligh *see* Tablighi Jama'at
Jamsaren, Pondok 192, 193
Jaringan Islam Liberal *see* JIL
JATMI (Jam'iyah Ahlith Thoriqah
    al-Mu'tabarah Indonesia) xiv,
    53
JATMN (Jam'iyah Ahlith Thoriqah
    al-Mu'tabarah Nahdliyyin) xiv,
    53
jihad 38, 79–80, 141, 204, 210,
    217
jihadism, jihadi Salafism 2, 14, 38,
    51, 52, 216, 217, 218
JIL (Jaringan Islam Liberal) xi, xiv,
    4, 16, 44, 64, 81, 98, 117,
    124, 226–29

JIMM (Jaringan Intelektual Muda
    Muhammadiyah) xv, 44, 98,
    113, 116–17, 134, 136
Jundullah, Lasykar 11, 157, 162,
    169, 208
Jusuf Kalla 10, 152–53, 167, 169,
    176

K
Kahar Muzakkar 10, 11, 149–50,
    156, 161, 182
KAMI (Kesatuan Aksi Mahasiswa
    Indonesia) xv, 39, 152, 153
KAMMI (Kesatuan Aksi Mahasiswa
    Muslim Indonesia) xv, xxiii, 40
Kartosuwiryo, S.M. 37, 150, 191
al-Khatthath, Muhammad 76, 95
KISDI (Komite Indonesia untuk
    Solidaritas Dunia Islam) xv,
    41–42
Komando Jihad 36, 196, 198–99,
    213
KOMPAK (Komite Aksi
    Penanggulangan Akibat Krisis)
    xv, 48, 211–12
Kongres Umat Islam Indonesia
    (KUUI) xvi, 62, 65–66, 75,
    81, 85–86
KPPSI (Komite Persiapan
    Penegakan Syari'ah Islam) xvi,
    10–12, 146, 155, 157, 159–69,
    170, 171, 175, 179–82
Kuwaiti funding 5, 51, 157
KW IX (Komando Wilayah IX) xvi,
    36

L
Lakpesdam (Lembaga Kajian dan
    Pengembangan Sumber Daya
    Manusia) xvi, 47, 98

LAPAR (Lembaga Advokasi dan
    Pendidikan Anak Rakyat) xvi,
    40, 173–74
Laskar Jihad x, 15, 52, 69–70, 136,
    209, 217
LDII (Lembaga Dakwah Islam
    Indonesia) see Islam
    Jama'ah
LDK (Lembaga Dakwah Kampus)
    xvii, 40
Lemkari (Lembaga Karyawan Islam)
    see Islam Jama'ah
Liberal Islam 4, 8, 16, 17–18, 64,
    80–83, 108–12, 116–17,
    127–29, 130–34, 224–29
LIPIA (Lembaga Ilmu Pengetahuan
    Islam dan Arab) xvii, 216
LKiS (Lembaga Kajian Islam dan
    Sosial) xvii, 40, 44, 47, 173,
    225
LPPI (Lembaga Penelitian dan
    Pengkajian Islam) xvii, 38–39,
    84, 85, 230
LPPOM-MUI (Lembaga Pengkajian
    Pangan, Obat-Obatan dan
    Kosmetika Majelis Ulama
    Indonesia) xvii, 71–3
LP3ES (Lembaga Penelitian,
    Pendidikan dan Penerangen
    Ekonomi dan Sosial) xvii, 43,
    45–46
LSAF (Lembaga Studi Agama dan
    Filsafat) xviii, 43
LSP (Lembaga Studi Pembangunan)
    45
Luqman al-Hakim, Madrasah 201
Luthfi Assyaukani 117, 230

M
Maarif Institute xviii, 44, 229

Majelis Mujahidin Indonesia
    (MMI) xviii–xix, 11, 37–38,
    63, 70, 93, 159, 208, 213,
    221, 226, 228, 230
Majelis Tabligh 110, 114
Majelis Tafsir al-Qur'an see MTA
Majelis Tarjih 109, 114, 117, 123
Malik Fadjar 77
Maluku see Moluccas
"market Islam" 74, 90
Ma'ruf Amin, KH. 61, 73, 76, 87,
    97
Marzuki Hasan, Ahmad 156, 160,
    163, 171
Masdar F. Mas'udi 46, 64
Masduki, Ajengan 14, 15, 37, 201
Masyumi xvi, xviii, xxi, 25, 31–32,
    41, 150–51, 152, 197
Megawati Sukarnoputri 6, 33, 42,
    67, 93, 207
MER-C xviii, 48, 212
Ministry of Education 69, 76–77
Ministry of Religious Affairs ix, 2,
    32, 68–69, 72, 75, 83, 88, 96,
    151–52, 224
Misbach, Haji 12, 207
Moeslim Abdurrahman 82–83
Moluccas, interreligious conflict 14,
    48, 52, 67, 70, 94, 162, 210,
    212, 217
mosque conflicts 118–19, 123–25
MTA (Majelis Tafsir Alqur'an) xix,
    14, 202–5, 219
Muhammadiyah xviii, xix, xxi, 3–5,
    7–10, 21, 23–24, 77, 105–44,
    148, 154, 170, 202, 203, 224
MUI (Majelis Ulama Indonesia)
    xvi, xix. 3–4, 6–7, 10, 30,
    60–100, 230
Muin Salim 161, 162–63, 184

Mulkhan, Abdul Munir 109, 113,
    117, 119, 132, 139
Munawir Syadzali 224
munkarat 75, 81, 91, 100
Musdah Mulia, Siti 64, 92–93
Muslimat NU xix
Muslim Brotherhood (al-Ikhwan
    al-Muslimun) xxi, xxxi, 3, 13,
    15, 30, 36, 37, 118, 139, 199,
    205, 217
Muslim World League (Rabitat
    al-'Alam al-Islami) 42, 87, 196

N
Nahdlatul Ulama *see* NU
Naqshbandiyya 52
Natsir, Mohamad 25, 32, 41, 155,
    196, 197
Ngruki, Pondok 13–14, 36, 41,
    190–91, 195–201, 212–16
NII/TII (Negara Islam Indonesia/
    Tentara Islam Indonesia) xix,
    13–14, 31, 35–37, 195–96,
    198, 199–201, 216
NU (Nahdlatul Ulama) xvi, xix,
    xxi, xxii, xxiii, 3–5, 9, 21,
    25–27, 32–33, 47–48, 53, 78,
    107, 148, 150–51, 154, 170,
    173, 202, 224
Nurcholish Madjid xii, 2, 16, 29,
    39, 43, 66, 224, 227

P
Pam Swakarsa xix–xx, 6
PAN (Partai Amanah Nasional) xx,
    17, 34, 66, 121–22, 125, 158,
    168
Pancasila 1, 39, 42, 63, 68, 69,
    94–95, 155, 156, 163, 169,
    198

Paramadina xx, 43, 227
Parmusi (Partai Muslimin
    Indonesia) xx, xxii, 32, 152
PBB (Partai Bulan Bintang) xx, 32,
    158
PDII (Pusat Dakwah Islam
    Indonesia) xx, 42
pembaruan pemikiran Islam
    movement 29, 43, 44, 224,
    227
Persis (Persatuan Islam) xx, 24–25,
    68
Perti (Persatuan Tarbiyah Islamiyah)
    xx–xxi, 28, 31
PII (Pelajar Islam Indonesia) xxi,
    11, 39, 152–53, 155
PITI (Persatuan Islam Tionghoa
    Indonesia) xxi, 28
PK (Partai Keadilan) xxi, xxiii,
    34–35, 158
PKB (Partai Kebangkitan Bangsa)
    xxi, 17, 27, 33, 94
PKS (Partai Keadilan Sejahtera) xxi,
    xxiii, 3, 9, 34–35, 78, 118–25,
    158, 176
pluralism, religious 7–8, 43, 110,
    111–12, 138, 211, 225
pluralism, liberalism and secularism,
    condemnations of 3, 7, 17–18,
    61, 63, 65, 70, 80–83, 90, 91,
    126, 134, 139
PMB (Partai Matahari Bangsa) xxi,
    9, 34, 121–22
PMI *see* Parmusi
PMII (Pergerakan Mahasiswa Islam
    Indonesia) xvi, xxi, 40, 47, 173
polygamy 129, 137
pornography and "porno-action" 7,
    10, 61, 75–76, 90, 97, 205,
    220

PPP (Partai Persatuan
Pembangunan) xxii, 25, 27,
28, 32–33, 154, 158, 207
P3M (Perhimpunan Pengembangan
Pesantren dan Masyarakat)
xxii, 46, 98
PPTI (Partai Politik Tharikat Islam)
xxii, 52–53
PSI (Partai Sosialis Indonesia) 31,
43, 45
PSII (Partai Syarikat Islam
Indonesia) xxii, 25, 31, 151
PTDI (Pendidikan Tinggi Dakwah
Islam) xxii, 42
Puan Amal Hayati 46
PUSA (Persatuan Ulama Seluruh
Aceh) 28, 35
Putuhena, Saleh 164, 166

Q
Qasim Mathar 164, 165, 167, 177,
178, 185
al-Qiyadah al-Islamiyah 70, 99
Qur'an and *hadith*/Sunnah, return
to 7, 17, 22, 23, 25, 26, 82,
111, 124, 127–29, 131–33,
138, 226
al-Qur'an Suci 99
Qutb, Sayyid 127, 205–6

R
Rabitat al-'Alam al-Islami *see*
Muslim World League
Rahima xxii, 46, 225–26
Rizieq Syihab, Habib x, 18, 38
Rumah Zakat 48

S
Sahal Mahfudh, KH. M.A. 97
Salafi movements xxiii, 3, 11, 14,

15, 29, 51–52, 69, 105, 157,
201, 206, 211, 215–16, 217
Sanusi Baco 160, 161, 187
Sanusi Daris 156, 162
Sarekat Islam xxiii, 25, 202, 207
Saudi Arabia, funding xvii, 5, 87,
157, 216, 217
Saudi Arabia, influence 42, 120,
157, 216, 217
Saudi universities, graduates 5, 15,
38, 51, 157, 161, 197, 217
Saudi version of Islam 24, 26,
51, 87, 105, 216; *see also*
Wahhabism
*sayyid*s xxii, 24, 50
Shariah banking *see* Islamic banking
Shariah, implementation of 129,
145–46, 150, 162–64,
173–75, 181–83, 209–10
Shariah regulations, regional 3, 10,
11–12, 17, 89–90, 146, 167,
170–73, 210
Shi'a xiii, xxiii, 6, 50
Shobarin Syakur 93, 199, 213
Solo 11, 12–15, 25, 36, 41, 52,
149, 162, 190–223
Sudibyo Markus 113
Sukidi Mulyadi 132
Sukino, Ahmad 203–5
Sulawesi, South 77, 145–189
Sungkar, Abdullah xiv, 13–14, 15,
18, 36–37, 190, 195–201, 212
Suryadharma Ali 33, 69, 88
Syafi'i Anwar 66, 82
Syafi'i Maarif, Ahmad xviii, 4, 44,
109, 113
Syarikat xxiii, 40, 47–48, 226

T
Tablighi Jama'at xiv, 3, 50–51

Tafsir Tematik Al-Qur'an 112, 117, 129, 131
Tamsil Linrung 156, 169
Tarbiyah movement xv, xxiii, 9, 29, 40, 111, 118–25, 139, 140
tausiyah xxxi, 60–64, 65, 91
terrorism 2, 79–80, 106, 135, 198–99, 210, 212, 213–14
Thufail, Abdullah 202–3

U
Ulil Abshar-Abdalla xi, 81, 82, 117, 226–27, 228
usrah movement 13–14, 36, 196, 198, 199, 220

V
vigilante action 7, 14, 18, 38, 68, 69, 191, 205, 206, 208–12

W
Wahdah Islamiyah xxiii, 11, 52, 157, 161, 164, 184
Wahhabism 105, 135, 138

Wahid Institute xxiii, 173, 229
Wahyuddin 213, 221
Warman group 199
women's emancipation 115–16, 117, 126, 130–31
women's rights 16, 46, 174, 225–26

Y
YAPI (Yayasan Pesantren Islam) xxiii, 50, 205
Yogyakarta 8, 23, 24, 37–38, 44, 47, 77, 78, 107, 164, 173, 190, 192, 199, 201, 202, 204, 213, 217, 221, 225
Yudhoyono, Susilo Bambang 72, 140
Yunahar Ilyas 113, 116, 118, 124, 132

Z
zakat xxxi, 12, 48, 150, 165, 171, 174–75, 204
Zamroni 113